333.7616
A281
Agrodiversity: learning from
Agrodiversit   farmers across the world

P9-CCL-785

DATE DUE

GAYLORD   PRINTED IN U.S.A.

JOLIET JUNIOR COLLEGE LIBRARY
JOLIET, ILLINOIS

This book presents part of the findings of the international project "People, Land Management, and Environmental Change", which was initiated in 1992 by the United Nations University. From 1998 to 2002, the project was supported by the Global Environment Facility with the United Nations Environment Programme as implementing agency and the United Nations University as executing agency.

The views expressed in this book are entirely those of the respective authors, and do not necessarily reflect the views of the Global Environment Facility, the United Nations Environment Programme, and the United Nations University.

Agrodiversity: Learning from farmers across the world

Edited by Harold Brookfield, Helen Parsons, and Muriel Brookfield

United Nations University Press

TOKYO · NEW YORK · PARIS

UNEP   GEF

© The United Nations University, 2003

The views expressed in this publication are those of the authors and do not necessarily reflect the views of the United Nations University.

United Nations University Press
The United Nations University, 53-70, Jingumae 5-chome,
Shibuya-ku, Tokyo, 150-8925, Japan
Tel: +81-3-3499-2811　Fax: +81-3-3406-7345
E-mail: sales@hq.unu.edu (general enquiries): press@hq.unu.edu
www.unu.edu

United Nations University Office in North America
2 United Nations Plaza, Room DC2-2062, New York, NY 10017, USA
Tel: +1-212-963-6387　Fax: +1-212-371-9454
E-mail: unuona@ony.unu.edu

United Nations University Press is the publishing division of the United Nations University.

Cover design by Rebecca S. Neimark, Twenty-Six Letters

Printed in the Hong Kong

UNUP-1087
ISBN 92-808-1087-1

Library of Congress Cataloging-in-Publication Data

Agrodiversity : learning from farmers across the world / edited by Harold Brookfield, Helen Parsons, and Muriel Brookfield.—1st American pbk. ed.
　　p.　cm.
Includes bibliographical references and index.
ISBN 92-808-1087-1
1. Agrobiodiversity. I. Brookfield, H. C. II. Parsons, Helen. III. Brookfield, Muriel.
S494.5.A43 A48 2003
333.76′16—dc21　　　　　　　　　　　　　　　　　　　　2003010734

333.7616
A281

Contents

v

JOLIET JUNIOR COLLEGE LIBRARY
JOLIET, ILLINOIS

List of tables and figures

Tables

List of acronyms

AEZ	agro-ecological zone
AGRIFEX	International Food and Agriculture Trade Fair (Ghana)
AMEXTRA	Asociación Mexicana para la Transformación Rural y Urbana
AVODEP	Association des Volontaires pour le Développement et Protection de l'Environnement (Guinée)
BAG	biodiversity advisory group
BECO	Banana Export Company (Jamaica)
CAMP	Collaborative Agroecosystems Management Project
CARE	An international humanitarian aid organization
CHACRA	Centro del Hombre, Ambiente y Conocimiento de Recursos Amazonicos (Peru)
CICA	Centro de Investigación en Ciencias Agropecuarias (Mexico)
DAT	demonstration advisory team
DBH	diameter (of trees) at breast height
ESD	Environment and Sustainable Development programme
FAO	Food and Agriculture Organization of the United Nations
FMBC	Forest Management and Biodiversity Conservation Programme in Gaoligongshan (China)
FT	field type
GEF	Global Environment Facility
GIRA	Grupo Interdisciplinario de Tecnologia Rural Apropriada (Mexico)
GPS	geographic position system
IIAP	Research Institute of Peruvian Amazonia
IPAM	Instituto de Pesquisa Ambiental da Amazonia (Brazil)

IUCN/UNESCO	International Union for the Conservation of Nature/United Nations Educational, Scientific and Cultural Organization
IVI	importance value index
KARI	Kenya Agricultural Research Institute
LER	land equivalent ratio
LUS	land-use stage
MESMIS	Metodología de Evaluación de Sistemas de Manejo Incorporando Indicadores de Sustentabilidad
NAFTA	North American Free Trade Agreement
NGO	non-governmental organization
NRI	National Research Institute, Papua New Guinea
PLEC	People, Land Management, and Environmental Change project
PNG	Papua New Guinea
PRA	participatory rural appraisal
SAM	sustainability assessment map
STAT	scientific and technical advisory team
UNAP	Universidad Nacional de la Amazonia Peruana
UNEP	United Nations Environment Programme
UNU	United Nations University
UWI	University of the West Indies
YAF	Yunnan Agroforestry Systems Research Project and Indigenous Land Resources Management Programme (China)

List of colour plates

1. Brazil. Farmers of the floodplain locate their houses on the levee banks of the river. Perennials are grown around the house and planting boxes above the flood level are used for herbs and medicinal plants. (Photo: C. Padoch)
2. Brazil. Innovative Amazonian farmers in the floodplain have developed diverse agroforestry systems to minimize the impact of the Moko disease in bananas. PLEC-Amazonia has been demonstrating and disseminating this technology. (Photo: C. Padoch)
3. Guinée, Fouta Djallon. Expert farmer demonstrating his method of aboveground compost making to PLEC students. (Photo: H. Brookfield)
4. Guinée, Fouta Djallon. Women farmers' group with a display of cloth they have dyed using local plants. (Photo: H. Brookfield)
5. Guinée, Moussaya. A group of women weeding rice. (Photo: H. Brookfield)
6. Southern Ghana. A village display of yam diversity (PLEC scientist at the right). (Photo: H. Brookfield)
7. Southern Ghana, Jachie. Expert farmer and demonstration site leader, Cecelia Osei, discussing a group of cultivated plants. (Photo: H. Brookfield)
8. Southern Ghana, Gyamfiase. A PLEC play. The 'scientist' is seeking to persuade a dubious farmer to plant trees on his land. (Photo: H. Brookfield)

Preface

The United Nations University is an international community of scholars engaged in research, postgraduate training, and dissemination of knowledge in furtherance of the purposes and principles of the Charter of the United Nations. The University's academic activities are coordinated and carried out by the UNU Centre at Tokyo and the research and training centres/programmes located in 17 different places in the world, as well as through a global network of associated and cooperating institutions and scholars. The UNU groups its work within two major thematic areas – Peace and Governance and Environment and Sustainable Development. The Environment and Sustainable Development (ESD) programme area focuses on the interactions between human activities and the natural environment, in particular the challenges facing developing countries. This book results from one of the ESD projects – the UNU project on People, Land Management, and Environmental Change (PLEC), which involves a collaborative effort between scientists and smallholder farmers across the developing world.

Founded in 1992, with Global Environment Facility (GEF) support from 1998 to 2002, and with the United Nations Environment Programme as implementing agency and UNU as executing agency, PLEC brought together the best of scientists and smallholder farmers for identification, evaluation, and promotion of small-scale farmers' resource management systems and practices that conserve ecological processes and embrace biodiversity for generating income and coping with changes in social and natural conditions. PLEC empowered expert farmers and their expertise in agriculture and resource use by linking them to their fellow farmers, young generations, extension workers, and officials as well as about 150 scientists. PLEC operated through a global network of locally based multidisciplinary clusters that have been established in all the countries discussed in this book. Demonstration sites are located in a wide range of agro-ecosystems in formerly forested regions, semi-arid regions, mountains, and wetlands of globally significant biodiversity.

This book reports rich and successful experiences of PLEC project findings and results, mainly over the four-year period of GEF support. Apart from an overview of PLEC history and methods, a foreword, and a concluding chapter, this book contains 12 country chapters. The content of each covers an introduction to the national team and demonstration sites, and a review of project methods, activities, and outcomes at the demonstration sites and beyond. Here one can only highlight some successful PLEC experiences.

PLEC clusters work in substantially different environments in 12 developing countries. Not only the biophysical environments but also economic, social, and cultural contexts are quite different among clusters. These clusters had developed their own research and working methods suitable to their local situations and individual projects before GEF support started in 1998. Since GEF-funded work focused on demonstration activities and demonstration sites, there was a need to promote best methods suitable to demonstration site work as well as to ensure that all assessment methods meet accepted scientific standards. As a result, a variety of these best methods developed in the clusters were brought together through working guidelines, including assessment and promotion of best practices in the communities.

Over the past few years, national clusters have established 27 demonstration sites and tested and demonstrated many good practices of biodiversity management with over 300 expert farmers in their fields, fallows, and forests. The demonstration is an expert farmer-led sharing of knowledge, techniques, and planting materials between farmers, and between farmers, scientists, and other local stakeholders. For example, PLEC-Brazil identified a total of 136 good production and management systems; 19 of them were selected for demonstration because they provide important sources of income for families and help them to maintain high levels of biodiversity in their landholdings. There is ample evidence that the resource base, including biodiversity and soil fertility, could actually be enhanced by management, rather than necessarily be reduced under human use.

Through training and participation in PLEC, many researchers, technicians, and local officials have replaced their former view, looking down upon farmers' practices, with a view that respects farmers' knowledge and innovations. This behavioural change has also raised collaborating farmers' self-esteem and enabled farmers to feel confident and responsible for resource conservation. The demonstrations of best practices enhanced capacities of farmers and communities in coping with new problems and opportunities for their livelihoods. Farmers' associations empowered farmers in negotiation for support from various sources. Community conservation rules were built up or strengthened for regulating access to and use of resources, especially common and overexploited resources. PLEC has been a pioneer in developing new forms of collaborative research and action between scientists and farmers in developing countries, and its work has achieved a lot of favourable notice. Through all these activities, PLEC has succeeded in formulating its unique culture of research and development. This book sets out to bring it together.

I would like to express my gratitude to all PLEC members, including collaborating farmers, for their contribution to the project success. Most have worked with only minimal reward, or no reward, in pursuit of the project objectives. The editorial team led by Professor Harold Brookfield deserve special thanks for their painstaking work in making this book. I would also like to acknowledge the financial support from GEF/UNEP over the last few years.

Building upon the successful PLEC experiences, UNU will continue to play its part to the best of its ability in supporting research, training, and dissemination that contribute to rural poverty reduction through integrated management of biodiversity, soil, and water in agricultural landscapes.

Motoyuki Suzuki
Vice Rector
Environment and Sustainable Development

Foreword: Mainstreaming PLEC's vision and upscaling PLEC's goals

Miguel Pinedo-Vasquez

This book summarizes much of what PLEC has accomplished over the last four years. As such, it looks backward. But each chapter also outlines a continuing and clear future for the PLEC approach and activities; thus it is also a forward-looking work. The PLEC demonstration approach has empowered dozens of expert farmers, and identified and evaluated scores of biodiversity-friendly and economically rewarding production technologies and conservation practices developed by farmers with local knowledge, tools, and organization. It attempted to disseminate such practices to a broader group of stakeholders, including other farmers as well as those who influence them. It doubtless achieved much, as is reported here by cluster leaders and discussed in broader perspective by Harold Brookfield and his co-editors. These chapters provide a summary of a job very well done but also of a job not yet finished, a vision not yet realized.

The PLEC coordinators did not start thinking about the future of PLEC only at the end of the four years of the GEF-funded phase. Since the beginning of this global programme, farmers and other stakeholders have asked about the future again and again. Most members of PLEC teams gave an honest answer: "It will depend on the results, on how effectively this approach has met the expectations of farmers and people working in rural communities." Farmers reminded PLEC teams that as members of poor rural communities they had participated in many similar projects and had enjoyed the short-term economic benefits brought by such projects. But, PLEC farmers warned, the interest and prosperity brought by projects was impossible to sustain after the projects were done. Although PLEC was a demonstration initiative rather than a development or conservation project, PLEC activities – as is mentioned in the country chapters – also brought some short-term economic benefits to almost all of the sites in the 12 countries. And GEF-funded PLEC was also a project restricted to a mere four years.

The cycle of short-lived initiatives that characterizes rural development and conservation programmes in most poor countries is as persistent and chronic a feature of the conservation and development landscape as are the problems of poverty, environmental degradation, and biodiversity loss that the projects are supposed to resolve. Multiple and intractable political and economic factors that underpin development and conservation programmes are responsible. Even the best projects seem unable to escape these limitations to achieve long-term effects and sustain the benefits achieved by short-term efforts. In many of the rural regions where PLEC demonstration activities were implemented, the teams found little positive evidence of the achievements of past development or conservation programmes. Most of PLEC's sites were at some time host to a number of conservation, development, and other projects. Several of these we knew had achieved very impressive and valuable results; but they have since vanished. Can we break these cycles and achieve lasting change and benefits that incorporate the experiences and results of our short-term projects? This is a most important challenge that, as PLEC participants, we are ready to confront. We are committed to working in innovative ways to translate the hard-won achievements of our teams, and especially of the expert farmers, into long-term programmes with durable benefits. As is discussed in the chapters of the book, PLEC members have already begun paving the way for the transition of PLEC from a rather small and short-term project into a programme with broader and lasting impacts.

Our next steps will be to build upon the accumulated experiences of PLEC to both upscale PLEC activities and mainstream PLEC approaches. We plan to achieve these goals through a series of focused and linked activities. These activities are aimed at altering the behaviour of those groups that directly affect the conservation, use, or erosion of globally important resources of biodiversity, soils, and water. The most important of these target groups are smallholder farmers themselves and their advisers, including agricultural technicians, researchers, and extension agents.

By upscaling and mainstreaming the results of demonstration activities, the scope of the long-term PLEC programme will be extended to new regions and countries and it will reach out to other conservation and rural development projects. The future "long-term" PLEC will continue building functional networks that promote the movement of knowledge among stakeholders. These new networks will help to disseminate the production systems, conservation practices, expert farmers, and successful demonstration activities on regional, national, and international scales. We envision that current PLEC teams will reach out to identify, contact, and invite members of projects working on similar issues in other localities or countries of the region to join in PLEC activities. The participants of the networks will be encouraged to extend efforts to identify, test, promote, and monitor environmentally sustainable and economically rewarding production and management systems using PLEC demonstration approaches. Networks will base their work on sound knowledge of the area and its resources, environmental, social and political trends, and economic opportunities.

But to mainstream PLEC's vision, ideas, and approaches effectively we must go beyond creating and strengthening networks. Working together with stakeholders, PLEC must seek multiple effective modalities for shifting the way scientists, policy-makers, extensionists, and other opinion-formers view and promote development and environmental conservation. We must learn how to promote the new conservation and development paradigms that PLEC embodies. In the future PLEC must more effectively use its many members and friends who are renowned academics, highly placed government functionaries, and skilled communicators to help place the PLEC approach solidly in the mainstream of agricultural, forestry, fisheries, and conservation activities throughout the developing world.

PLEC needs to invest its talents and work more intensively in innovative regional training programmes using the existing facilities of academic and research centres. These programmes can help rethink and rewrite academic and training curricula for those who will be policy-makers and opinion-formers in the future. We can help make possible the incorporation of PLEC's central ideas, such as valuing and working with locally developed successful farming practices, employing local innovative "expert farmers" as teachers, and carrying out training in farmers' fields, into the everyday *modus operandi* of governmental and non-governmental agencies.

In the future, PLEC will strive to provide ever better and more relevant field-based information to national and international private and public agencies that are engaged in rural conservation and development programmes through a diversity of channels. We will continue using the usual print media, but we will also continue to build upon some teams' experience using video approaches, and PLEC will continue to add to and expand its web-based information and news service to broadcast the activities of the new programme and its constituent networks.

A broad set of activities and focus on capacity development on multiple levels will improve – if it cannot guarantee – the likelihood of long-term sustainability for PLEC's efforts. The success of the future PLEC programme will make the most of the diversity and expertise of its existing and new members, from expert farmers to renowned academics. The training of the next generation of farmers, extension agents, politicians, journalists, and members of other groups that influence rural development and conservation is critical for making PLEC a long-term global programme. Our vision is that by mainstreaming the lessons learned during the last five years, and upscaling our activities to other regions and countries, we will help to bring solutions to chronic rural poverty, environmental degradation, and erosion of biological diversity to more people in more communities around the world.

Introduction

Harold Brookfield, Helen Parsons, and Muriel Brookfield

Through generations of innovation and experiment, smallholder farmers have nurtured a great diversity of plants and animals, both wild and domesticated, and accumulated rich knowledge of their local biodiversity. The process of learning, experiment, and innovation continues throughout the developing world, even in the modern context of globalization. Much has been written on the loss of biodiversity under threat from commercial and intensified production, but only a few individual researchers publishing through academic channels have worked on how farmers manage their resources to sustain and enhance them. Whereas most biodiversity projects relate to protected areas or to crop plants alone, large numbers of farmers conserve biodiversity in the entire landscape of their farmland and its surrounds. This book describes the work in the field of the United Nations University project on People, Land Management, and Environmental Change (PLEC), which has been seeking to learn from farmers how they use their knowledge and skills to manage diversity and their resources conservatively and profitably.

PLEC is a global network of country clusters, set up by the United Nations University in 1992. From 1998 until 2002 it was funded by the Global Environment Facility (GEF) via the United Nations Environment Programme (UNEP); the United Nations University has provided modest funds throughout. In August 2002, a meeting concerned largely with planning future PLEC work decided to replace the final term in the name by "Ecosystem Conservation", thus retaining a popular acronym while better

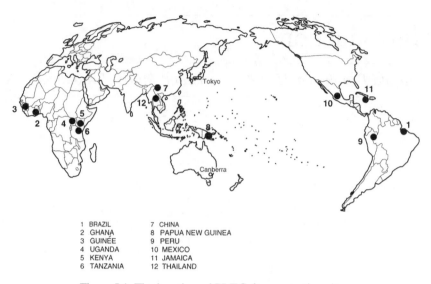

1 BRAZIL	7 CHINA
2 GHANA	8 PAPUA NEW GUINEA
3 GUINÉE	9 PERU
4 UGANDA	10 MEXICO
5 KENYA	11 JAMAICA
6 TANZANIA	12 THAILAND

Figure I.1 The location of PLEC demonstration sites

describing PLEC's central concerns. Throughout the period described in this book, however, the original title was current.

By 2002 the project had brought together more than 200 professionals, almost all in developing countries, and including over 130 scientists and researchers, over 100 skilled or expert farmers, and several thousand other farmers. It has trained about 180 students, undergraduate and graduate. PLEC members, coordinators, and advisers work out of over 60 institutions in Brazil, China, Ghana, Guinée, Jamaica, Kenya, Mexico, Papua New Guinea, Peru, Thailand, Tanzania, Uganda, Britain, the USA, Japan, and Australia. From the beginning until 2002, scientific coordination of the project was based in the Department of Anthropology in the Research School of Pacific and Asian Studies at the Australian National University, the workplace of the editors of this volume. Associate scientific coordinators, Christine Padoch and Michael Stocking, respectively of the New York Botanical Garden and the University of East Anglia in Norwich, UK, contributed very substantially to the project.

The work of the clusters is the main subject matter of this book. Only a necessary minimum about the general work and philosophy of the project is presented. These aspects and the methodology are discussed in depth in a previous book and the project periodical (Brookfield *et al.* 2002; *PLEC News and Views*). Here the editors devote two initial chapters and a short concluding chapter to general issues and methodology. The other chapters about the work of the clusters are built on edited versions of the final reports to UNEP and the GEF from the GEF-supported clusters, or to the

United Nations University from the four clusters not supported by GEF funds.

Because of the nature of its work, PLEC has focused on particular small areas in each country where scientists are able to develop close relations with the farmers, learn about their management methods, and assist them in many technical ways. In these areas, PLEC looks for the exceptional, or expert, farmers who manage resources better than others, and encourages these farmers to demonstrate their successful methods to other farmers and stakeholders. Since 1998 the research sites selected by project scientists in collaboration with farmers in the 12 developing countries have been termed "demonstration sites". About 25 demonstration sites are fully developed, and more limited work has been done in a number of others.

PLEC has acquired an enviable reputation for working with farmers in their fields using farmers' own ideas and evaluation criteria. Farmer-to-farmer training has been particularly successful at several of the demonstration sites, as described in subsequent chapters of this book. For instance, in Tanzania (Chapter 8), "the farm becomes a chalkboard, the expert farmer a teacher, the scientists and technicians become facilitators, and participating farmers the adopters, modifiers, or improvers of the technology". PLEC deliberately dwells on positive experiences in order to draw lessons to support "agrodiversity" as a developmental approach with policy relevance towards reversing loss of biodiversity and controlling land degradation, while at the same time improving small farmers' livelihoods.

The farmer-to-farmer training promoted by PLEC, in contrast to top-down intervention, has been more comprehensively adopted in some countries and sites than in others. Reasons for this variation are discussed in general terms in Chapters 1 and 2, and are discussed in a national context in several of the country chapters. They are perhaps best put by Elizabeth Thomas-Hope and Balfour Spence of Jamaica, in Chapter 13. They write:

The knowledge flow occurred between farmer and scientist in a two-way direction, but it has also occurred between farmers ... The specifics of the relationships and the process are unique to each group and are different from one community to another. There is no template or fixed model for the successful transfer of knowledge at a demonstration site, except that both agricultural practices and social relations must be considered in facilitating the process of agrodiversity knowledge transfer. The way in which the process unfolds is always tentative. The researchers must therefore be led by the specific dynamics of each demonstration site in which they may work.

Most country chapters, while mainly based on the cluster final reports, are enriched by information derived from other reports and publications by the cluster members. Additional sources used in the editorial process are included in the Bibliography for each country chapter. The names of the original authors appear on each chapter, but most texts have been significantly modified and reduced in the course of editing. The editorial work has been done in Canberra by Harold Brookfield, Helen Parsons, and Muriel Brookfield. Formatting assistance was given by Ann Howarth, and final preparation of the maps was by Ian Heyward in the Australian National University's Cartography Unit.

The order of country presentation is approximately geographical from west to east in the case of the GEF-supported clusters. The final four chapters concern the countries in which work was not supported by GEF finance, but only by the UNU and other sources. Thailand is placed last because in this cluster successful steps had already been taken before the end of the project to secure the continuity of PLEC work.

PLEC has been a learning experience for all its members. Almost none of them had undertaken work of this nature before, nor had entered into close partnerships bonding farmers with scientists. Few of the farmers had encountered scientists or technicians in any similar role. In practice, almost all PLEC scientists agreed that learning from farmers has been a valuable and important experience, with a great deal of potential application to other situations. It is, perhaps, the most important lesson the PLEC project has to offer to the wider scientific and professional community in the development and conservation fields. Hence the title of this book, discussed and unanimously agreed by a meeting of the PLEC scientists who are its authors in Paris in August 2002.

The editors are grateful to two anonymous referees for their comments on an earlier draft of the manuscript, and have endeavoured to take account of their suggestions. The editors also appreciate the kindness of Professor Motoyuki Suzuki in contributing a preface, and of Dr Miguel Pinedo-Vasquez, now the scientific coordinator of PLEC, for writing a foreword which links the work described in this book to the programme's future plans.

REFERENCES

Brookfield, H., C. Padoch, H. Parsons, and M. Stocking (eds). 2002. *Cultivating Biodiversity. Understanding, Analysing and Using Agricultural Diversity*. London: ITDG Publications.
PLEC News and Views, available at www.unu.edu/env/plec.

1

The evolution of PLEC's work, 1992–2002

Harold Brookfield[1]

Origins and early evolution, 1992–1997

PLEC began life in 1992 as a United Nations University project of collaborative research, with the objective of studying the management of land resources and biodiversity in the context of environmental and socio-economic conditions. "Population", rather than "people", was then the first word in its title, because the original UNU proposal reflected a then-active international concern with the so-called "nexus" between population growth, unrewarding farming, and land degradation (United Nations Population Fund 1991; Cleaver and Schreiber 1992; Myers 1993). The aim was a set of scientific findings with potential input to policy; the intended scale was regional, and initial methods proposed were for work at this scale. The purpose was to establish whether developing-country farmers were conserving or degrading their natural resources and especially their biodiversity. Expressed in this way, the original aim has, in fact, been sustained, but its context has changed greatly.

Mainly using their professional contacts, Brookfield, Padoch,[2] and Stocking,[3] as the foundation scientific coordinators, found lead scientists of the enquiring type they were seeking in, ultimately, 12 countries. The lead scientists each recruited small multidisciplinary working teams ("clusters"), and by 1994, when PLEC attracted the attention of the United Nations Environment Programme, some had already achieved useful results (Gyasi *et al.* 1995; Rerkasem and Rerkasem 1995). The teams included a number of agricultural and soil scientists and ecologists, but also members of several other disciplines, principally botany, geography, anthropology, and economics.[4] Almost all were based in national developing-country institutions.

The population-degradation link on which PLEC had initially been invited to work was already severely dented by research findings from Africa, especially those of Tiffen, Mortimore, and Gichuki (1994) in Kenya. This encouraged the small core team in modifying the original objective in ways closer to the interests of many participants. By 1995 PLEC still saw its principal concern as research, but into farmers' methods for the maintenance and enhancement of biological diversity and sustainable intensification (PLEC 1995). This meant moving down from regional to ecosystem and landscape levels, and to the farm. In fact, certain PLEC clusters had never adopted a regional approach and concentrated from the beginning on what they called "pilot sites", "focus sites", or "focus areas". In these places, stress was increasingly laid on discovering sustainable methods either evolved or adapted by the farmers themselves, supplemented by scientific work to validate or improve these methods. It was at this point that it was decided to put "people" into the title, while Brookfield published a paper seeking to detach PLEC from the barren discussion of the supposed "population-environment nexus" (Brookfield 1995).

By August 1996 PLEC's first objective had become "to develop methodologies for collaborative linkages between professionals and local people in the design and implementation of conservationist management" (PLEC 1996). Later in 1996 came the GEF-inspired retitling of the "pilot sites" as "demonstration sites", so that by January 1997, when a final version of the project proposal went to the GEF, the principal goal became:

To develop sustainable and participatory approaches to biodiversity conservation within agricultural systems, by setting up over 20 demonstration sites where sustainable and conservationist resource-use practices can be developed in participation with farmers and other stakeholders. (PLEC 1997)

Thus it has remained in the subsequent project document (PLEC 1998).

Final approval by the GEF Council in April 1997 involved only the clusters in Brazil, Ghana, Guinée, Uganda, Kenya, Tanzania, China, and Papua New Guinea. For different reasons in each case, the GEF secretariat was unable to forward to Council the proposals from Peru, Mexico, Jamaica, and Thailand. The four latter clusters continued to be funded by the UNU, but at a much lower level of support than was available to the GEF-funded clusters during the four years (1998–2002) of GEF project life.

The wider background

Between 1992 and 1997, PLEC evolved from a rather top-down research project into a farmer-oriented demonstration project in which research was a subsidiary objective, concerned especially with agrodiversity and biodiversity. This was, in one sense, merely a logical development from views expressed in the early days by two of the project principals. Brookfield and Padoch (1994: 43) wrote that: "effective [resource] management systems do not have to be invented only by modern science. They exist, and have been continuously developed by the world's farmers." But while this is true, it is also true that the transition reflected important changes in the intellectual and political environment in which the initiative has evolved.

Before PLEC began, new "farmer-first" approaches to the evaluation of farmers' methods and experiments had already taken root internationally (Richards 1985; Chambers, Pacey, and Thrupp 1989). Also, new recognition had emerged of farmers' contribution in nurturing a wide range of species useful to people, and varieties or "landraces" of these species (Keystone Center 1991). At a 1992 African conference, Hardon and de Boef (1994: 120) had already argued the need for work on the management of natural resources by resource-poor farmers in the search for sustainable production systems that would conserve plant genetic resources. At the same meeting, Okigbo (1994), one of PLEC's early advisers, linked the different land-use stages of African farming systems to crop biodiversity. As the movement for *in situ* conservation of crop genetic diversity gathered pace, the limited recognition given to farmers' contribution in several Agenda 21 chapters (UNCED 1992) advanced to the much stronger statements made by the Third Conference of Parties to the Convention on Biological Diversity in 1996 (Conference of the Parties 1996).

There were other important consequences of the new thinking. Until the 1990s, all agriculture was believed to be the enemy of biodiversity. Conservation of biodiversity meant keeping farmers out of the conserved areas. Quite a few scientists and decision-makers still adhere to these views. Yet modern non-equilibrium ecology was already downgrading the value of trying to preserve areas of the wild intact so that they could advance to a climax state. Scientific support was growing for the view that biodiversity could be sustained in agricultural areas. It was realized, at first only by a minority, that certain areas managed by smallholders contain almost as much biodiversity as the unmanaged wild.

By proposing to involve farmers directly in biodiversity conservation at landscape level, PLEC had moved ahead of the times by 1997, when its formal documentation within the GEF was finally completed. The project was in parallel with what was simultaneously taking place in the area of indigenous soil and water conservation in Africa (Reij, Scoones, and Toulmin 1996). The common aim, which went beyond that set out in the "farmer-first" literature of the late 1980s and early 1990s, was to add the fields and fallows of the best or most "expert" farmers to the experimental farms as recognized foci of innovation.

Change within PLEC, 1996–1999

Except for the fact that research was at that time discouraged by the GEF, these approaches were not imposed on PLEC from above. Already in the initial draft documentation (PLEC 1995), the clusters in the Brazilian Amazon, West Africa, and China had embraced the practical objectives of encouraging conservationist methods and aiding farmers in concrete ways. Some of these ways were not unlike the standard procedures of agricultural extension, but they also included development of systems in which scientific understanding of the farmers' ways contributed to improvements in the latter. They evolved in PLEC's unique context of agrodiversity, rather than only agricultural biodiversity, and thus concerned the diversity of the fallow and managed wild, not only the farm crops. There followed the further and distinctive objective of assisting the best farmers in promoting their methods among their neighbours and other farmers to improve the sustainability of production for a larger population.

PLEC was proud of the diversity of approaches within the project in the mid-1990s, and saw them as a source of strength. In the GEF system, however, many quickly picked them up from differences in presentation between the clusters, and saw them instead as a source of weakness. After the project had overcome reluctance to believe that farmers could cultivate biodiversity, there still remained, even through 1997, a critical view that it would be impossible to bring such a diverse project together. Although clusters had common goals, they lacked an agreed common methodology. An early attempt by a member of the Brazilian Amazon cluster to propose a standard and randomized method for landscape-level biodiversity assessment (Zarin 1995) had not attracted wide support; it was seen as very difficult to make operational. The China cluster quickly proposed a variant, introducing the "land management type" as a sampling unit (Guo, Dao, and Brookfield 1996). Still following original research intentions, some groups continued to use the transect methods with which they were familiar and which had, in fact, been encouraged in the early stages (PLEC 1995). Although all talked about agrodiversity, there was still no clear methodology for its analysis in the critical areas of resource management and farm organization. While a few demonstration sites were already in existence, with evolving farmer cooperation, in other parts of PLEC their development was still only being investigated in a cautious manner.

The emergence of internal advisory groups

All this had quickly to be faced once PLEC became a single GEF project in 1998. There were three imperatives. First was to produce guidelines for the analysis of diversity in management and organization; second was the development of more readily applicable guidelines for the assessment of biodiversity and agrobiodiversity; third was to make more general within PLEC the development of farmer-centred demonstration site work. In its first two meetings, the management group made solution of these needs its first priority.[5]

A first set of guidelines for the recording of diversity in the natural environment, its management, and in the organization of that management were developed by mid-1998 and made available to clusters. A summary statement was published (Brookfield and Stocking 1999). A specialist biodiversity advisory group was formed from within the project membership with representatives from the clusters in Brazil (Daniel Zarin), Ghana (Lewis Enu-Kwesi), and China (Huijun Guo) in the second half of 1998. It met in China in January 1999 and its proposals were made available electronically in February. Because the new biodiversity guidelines involved creation of a sampling scheme which could equally serve the study of management, the "agrodiversity" guidelines were then quickly revised to harmonize with the biodiversity guidelines and published together with them in April (Zarin, Guo, and Enu-Kwesi 1999; Brookfield, Stocking, and Brookfield 1999). Because both sets of guidelines involved working downward from the land-use stage or type to the field types developed by farmers, and working in them with farmers' participation, the use of these guidelines promptly led in all cases to concentration on particular small areas.

This was a critical moment in time. It created a common sampling scheme for all survey work, and for the detailed study of farmers' practices. This scheme, which has been varied to suit the field conditions in different project areas, is more fully set out in Chapter 2. Publication of the guidelines led to the end of reconnaissance work along transects, some of which had, by 1998, extended over many kilometres. Work in Ghana, Brazil, Peru, and Tanzania was in 1998 already focusing on differences between individual farmers. In China, where the individual farmer as decision-maker is, in the modern context, only a post-1982 phenomenon, biodiversity assessment itself was further restructured in 1999 to survey separately the land of individual households (Guo *et al.* 2000). Members of the biodiversity advisory group visited clusters in East and West Africa, Mexico, Thailand, and Papua New Guinea.

Development of demonstration sites was not as simple as changing survey and assessment methods. The first initiatives were taken in Brazil, Peru, and Ghana, and in China under the auspices of the MacArthur Foundation, all in rather different ways (Amazonian Brazil 1994; Pinedo-Vasquez 1996a, 1996b; Gyasi and Enu-Kwesi 1996; Brookfield 1996; Quong 1996). From Brazil and Peru, Pinedo-Vasquez (1996b) stressed the centrality of finding the right "expert farmer" leadership. In the more hierarchical social environment of Ghana, Gyasi and Enu-Kwesi (1996) put emphasis on forming associations under the patronage of chiefs, which is essential in most parts of the country. Later Ghanaian associations have been built, with chiefly support, around prominent or outstanding farmers having particular forms of expertise, whether or not the farmers had chiefly social roles (Gyasi 2001). In China, the one association set up concentrated specifically on bringing the more conservationist farmers together. PLEC in China has continued to use this approach.

The first general statements on demonstration site work appeared only when the enlarged project was already funded (Gyasi 1998; Padoch and Pinedo-Vasquez 1998). The project documentation (PLEC 1998) had specified that work done on the demonstration sites was the farmers' own, and had indicated that it was hoped to harness expert farmers as teachers. But it was only in the Padoch and Pinedo-Vasquez (1998) paper that a model for doing this was first presented to the membership. Although the model, from work in the Brazilian Amazon, was given only as example, the use of expert farmers as teachers of other farmers was already adopted in more than half of PLEC by late 1999. It later became almost universal, except in some areas where there are social difficulties in the way of its implementation, for example in Papua New Guinea. However, Thomas-Hope and Spence (2002) have described how severe difficulties have, at least partly, been overcome in Jamaica.

The role of expert farmers is not the same everywhere. In all cases they are the farmers with whom PLEC scientists principally interact, and who also interact with external specialists brought on to the site by PLEC to advise on specific activities or innovations. The ways of farming that they demonstrate are sometimes their own inventions, but also methods they have learned, tested, and improved. Everywhere, they are the bridge between the project and the ordinary farmers, reaching the latter by a wide range of means that are specific to the social conditions of each country and region. In a few instances they have become the true leaders of demonstration site activity, initiating work on their own.

To facilitate harmonization of method, and help overcome the reluctance of some scientists to adopt farmer-to-farmer methods, the management group formed a second internal advisory group on demonstration activities in 1999. It comprised Miguel Pinedo-Vasquez (Brazil and Peru) and Edwin

Gyasi (Ghana). They provided an initial set of guidelines (Pinedo-Vasquez 1999). Together or separately they visited a large part of PLEC between 1999 and 2001, and eventually, together with Kevin Coffey, produced a definitive statement on demonstration site method for use within and beyond PLEC (Pinedo-Vasquez, Gyasi, and Coffey 2001).

Harmonization is far removed from standardization. Given the hugely varied physical, social, and political conditions of the PLEC countries, it was never imagined that all demonstration sites could follow the same methods, and this was made explicit by Padoch and Pinedo-Vasquez (1998). PLEC has thrived on diversity, and every group has adapted the general approaches in its own way. This is where networking has been of major importance, using the rather rare meetings, visits by scientific coordinators and members of the internal advisory groups, correspondence and comment on reports, and, perhaps especially, the twice-yearly periodical, *PLEC News and Views*. Information has been diffused throughout the network in these ways and, notwithstanding the difficulties, the degree to which common approaches have been adopted is rather remarkable.

The changing role of PLEC scientists since 1997

PLEC's evolution has therefore been uneven, with successful initiatives from one region then encouraged for adoption in others, but always adapted rather than copied. A lot was asked of some of the participants. They were urged to become more rigorous in their inventory work, and at the same time to give up some cherished research notions and preconceptions so as to learn from farmers and work with them as equal partners. It helped that almost all PLEC's collaborators came from research backgrounds, rather than from more constraining experience in project management. Even so, after first being encouraged in the use of the farming-systems-research style approaches, such as participatory rapid rural appraisal, focus group discussions, and the like, they were later asked to go beyond the search for community generalizations. They were asked instead to deal with collaborating farmers as individuals, and to recognize the very considerable differences in methods, skills, and knowledge between them.

For many PLEC scientists, this also required a change in the habits of a professional lifetime. To regard farmers as knowing what they were doing and why they did it was an approach hitherto confined mainly to a few anthropologists and ethnobotanists. When it was more generally employed by PLEC scientists it led to a great increase in farmers' self-confidence, and greater willingness to cooperate in the project. The search for best practices was also the search for the best farmers, and for those among them who could most readily relate to other farmers. These became the "expert farmers" – those who innovated, quickly adapted their practices, and could be encouraged to instruct others. The farmers who were initially pointed out as the best, by officials and other recognized "key informants", were often the ones who had done what they had been told to do by the extension services. They were only sometimes those who made up their own minds and experimented in their own ways, and it was often among the experimenters that the real experts were to be found (Kaihura 2002). Recognition of the true experts came quickly in some areas, more slowly in others, and was itself a major development of skills among PLEC's scientists. None of this was easy, but the majority did succeed in making these multiple transitions.

Assisting the farmers

The idea of assisting farmers materially in improving their livelihoods, as well as of encouraging them in biodiversity conservation, goes back in PLEC to 1995. Few farmers would make efforts in conservation if they saw no actual or potential benefit in doing so, although some, with or without prompting, could see such benefits for themselves. It was never possible, or wise, for PLEC to offer more than token financial incentives – although some of PLEC's expert farmer demonstrators and teachers have more recently received subsidies from other organizations. Some support had to be given, but the preference was to offer expertise, and some material aid, which farmers themselves could convert into improved livelihoods. This approach had appeal. Kaihura (2002) recounts the words of one Tanzanian farmer: "A person who gives you knowledge is a thousand times better than the one giving you money because one can do a lot with the knowledge." In all areas, PLEC concentrated mainly on support for activities that would create value out of biodiversity. Gyasi (2001) has listed the whole range employed in Ghana.

The work of PLEC scientists in helping farmers in this way has differed quite widely from country to country. Often it has meant setting up nurseries to assist the expansion of forms of agroforestry suitable for local conditions. It has included assistance in the exchange and importation of germplasm, and the encouragement of conservation through fairs and open days. Very specifically, it has involved the encouragement of biodiverse farming, the introduction of fruiting trees to diversify income sources, and support for other activities that create value out of biodiversity. In one striking case in the Republic of Guinée, scientists offered practical support to a group of women who were spontaneously seeking to revive an ancient practice of dyeing cloth for sale in the local area (Boiro et al. 2002). In the same country, and in line with the PLEC preference to encourage ways that "hybridize" traditional and modern practices (Padoch 2002), an improved form of compost-making was proposed by specialists to the expert farmers in 1998. It combines old and new, and has been developed by the farmers and widely used to enlarge the area of intensively cultivated land used for commercial production.

The first step was discovery of what the farmers were doing themselves and what they knew. Innovators occur in small numbers in most rural societies. Some of the innovations are potentially viable and widely usable, others are not. Some farmers are already very knowledgeable, and also learn quickly. Many are keen experimenters who will try out any new germplasm or get ideas from other areas, and nowadays even from the media. Some have picked up ideas promoted by PLEC scientists or others, taken them away, and applied or improved them. As is described in the country chapters that follow, the methods demonstrated by the expert farmers have commonly been varied by other farmers, sometimes with real success. Important occasions were visits between the farmers from different demonstration sites, facilitating interchange of ideas as well as germplasm and experience. For the PLEC scientists, the skill has been to find out what will work. Although from very different intellectual backgrounds, farmers and scientists have in common that they learn from observation and experiment. The key to success in PLEC demonstration work has been to develop this mutual bond, best done where scientists spent a long time learning what the farmers were doing by seeing their land and talking with them before beginning any demonstration activities.

The last two years of GEF-PLEC, 2000–2002

By the third GEF project year, 2000, PLEC had achieved its programmed goal of developing more than 20 active and productive demonstration sites. Because of the demanding nature of the work in relation to resources, some of the more than 40 sites initiated earlier had to be downgraded to data-collection sites or even abandoned. Nonetheless, the most successful had achieved considerable regional impact, and the work of some is described in a group of recent papers in *PLEC News and Views* (Pinedo-Vasquez and Pinedo-Panduro 2001; Gyasi 2001; Tumuhairwe, Nkwiine, and Nsubuga 2001; Dao *et al.* 2001; Thong-Ngam *et al.* 2002; Thomas-Hope and Spence 2002; Kaihura 2002).

In 2000 the project was reviewed at mid-term (Brush 2000). Among a number of other proposals, the reviewer argued that the research element should to some degree be restored around the analysis of the large body of descriptive data collected, especially on biodiversity. He wanted PLEC to focus on threats to biodiversity, and their management. The participants were glad to accept this challenge, because an underlying hypothesis of PLEC had from the beginning been that it is possible not only to conserve biodiversity within small-scale agricultural systems, but positively to enhance it. A clear example of such a result achieved by farmers had already been demonstrated at one of the sites in Brazil (Pinedo-Vasquez *et al.* 2000).

To test the underlying hypothesis more widely demanded quantitative analysis, but, while PLEC's leading members included a large number of excellent field scientists, few had strong training in quantitative and analytical methods. Most of those who had such training were younger members, and they were identified as the persons responsible for database and analysis work in each cluster. There had been delay even in assembling the necessary databases; the original biodiversity advisory group had provided only very brief guidelines on how to do this (Zarin, Guo, and Enu-Kwesi 1999). Soon after the mid-term review, the management group fused the old biodiversity and demonstration activities advisory groups into a single scientific and technical advisory team (STAT), and Kevin Coffey of this new team prepared and distributed a database manual (Coffey 2000). He went on in 2001 to prepare clear guidelines on the analysis of data, presenting discussion of the main diversity measures and of principal components analysis. This was made available electronically to all parts of the project, and is published in a project book that appeared during 2002 (Coffey 2002). Several PLEC clusters plan to use the post-project year very largely on analysis of the enormous amount of data that they have acquired.

Incomplete and ongoing work

PLEC has achieved a lot, but its work is not finished. Nor should it be, because there are wider objectives that can only be achieved over a longer time. Recommendations made in late 2001 have only begun to have an impact. The widest purpose of PLEC is to give support to new approaches in research, conservation, and development in the marginal lands and resource-poor communities of rural areas in the developing countries. The demonstration site work has shown a way, but it can be developed further. A more specific aim is to demonstrate that biodiversity can be managed successfully, and even enhanced, in agricultural contexts. Here, data analysis work, although advancing, is incomplete. Except where management extends into the fallow, it seems likely that the original hypothesis will be qualified to stress particular forms such as agroforestry and home gardens.

A central objective has been capacity-building, beginning at the local level and extending to the national level. It must also have outreach to a wider audience in the international conservation and development field. Capacity-building starts with the farmers, empowering the best and encouraging others. It then extends to local and regional officials, and to the technical and extension workers. It includes both graduate and undergraduate students in national universities. A significant number are being trained in the PLEC approach and in its scientific methods of monitoring change in farm practices and biodiversity. Progress in these areas has been substantial, but the job is unfinished. It needs only modest financial resources, but it will be hard to make advances in the absence of continued support.

The first stage in reaching a wider international audience has been through six-monthly progress reports to the United Nations Environment Programme and the Global Environment Facility, and especially through wide distribution of the project periodical, *PLEC News and Views*, of which 20 issues have appeared since 1993. All issues are now available through the PLEC website (www.unu.edu/env/plec). There has also been a flow of articles in journals. Two PLEC-related books have been written and published, one about agricultural diversity (agrodiversity) as a whole and one about a farmer-centred approach to work on land degradation (Brookfield 2001; Stocking and Murnaghan 2001).

During the last GEF-supported year, PLEC published a book setting out its ideas and methodology, and including more than a dozen case studies of work done using this methodology (Brookfield *et al.* 2002). Regional publication has taken place mainly in Brazilian and Peruvian Amazonia, West Africa, and China. The Amazonian material has appeared mainly in papers written for international journals, as well as in *PLEC News and Views*.[6] A book has appeared about West Africa and another is now offered for publication (Gyasi and Uitto 1997; Gyasi forthcoming). The East African cluster also has a book under consideration. In China, use has been made of the journal *Acta Botanica Yunnanica* (2000; 2001) for two special issues. A third is in progress at the time of writing.

Conclusion

PLEC is about biodiversity, food security, and income enhancement. So are many other projects. But there are five central aspects of PLEC that distinguish it from most others.

- First, it recognizes that the means to conserve biodiversity, and especially agrobiodiversity, is a place-specific knowledge system held variably by different people, and that it includes understanding of a myriad of interactions between people and environment. Conservation is not so much a matter of protecting specific biota, but of sustaining the habitat in which biodiversity thrives. The people who understand and manage this best are the core of PLEC's group of expert farmers.
- Second, the use of expert farmers to demonstrate to and teach other farmers has been particularly strongly developed in PLEC, and it has widened as additional expert farmers have emerged. This aspect is praised as particularly "innovative" by the Global Environment Facility (2001), and its wider adoption is strongly encouraged.[7] However, the

recognition of expert farmers is not simple, and the use made of them among their fellows is constrained by local institutions and social organization, which also need to be understood. Moving with success into the truly participatory method of farmer-to-farmer teaching requires that a series of barriers have to be overcome, calling for patience and sensitivity on the part of the promoters, be they scientists, technicians, or officials. This is abundantly shown in the country chapters that follow.

• Third, conservation and development are not seen as trade-offs, but as twin aims that can be combined into a single set of activities among the farmers. This is made possible by the fact that cultivating biodiversity can, in many areas, be a profitable activity for farmers, and PLEC has shown this to be feasible.

• The fourth aspect is that while farmers' practices may well be capable of improvement, PLEC sees the improvement as something that can be built on what the best of them do, not as something that should be promoted only from outside.

• Fifth, PLEC has been a project mainly at landscape level, and in this way it offers a distinctive contribution to the field of agricultural biodiversity, setting work on genetic variation, crop plant conservation, and systems of seed supply into an ecosystem-level context. The role of whole farming systems, including livestock, tree crops, and utility trees, and extending into managed fallow land, is also incorporated at this level. Work has extended beyond the fields and home gardens into the managed fallow lands and adjacent forest. By repeatedly studying the same small areas over periods of from four to seven years, and for longer in cases where PLEC scientists have chosen areas in which they had previously worked, a temporal dimension has been added to the spatial perspective. Land-use stages have been seen for what they really are, as stages in transition. The wider view thus gained offers lessons that should contribute importantly to the further development of the fields of agricultural biodiversity and integrated ecosystem management.

Notes

1. This chapter draws on a paper entitled "The conservation and promotion of biodiversity on-farm: The evolution of PLEC's mission, 1992–2002", delivered at the New York meeting on 23 April 2002, and published in *PLEC News and Views*, No. 20, pp. 7–18 (2002). Grateful acknowledgement is made to Helen Parsons and Muriel Brookfield for valuable comment and assistance.
2. Dr Christine Padoch, Institute of Economic Botany, New York Botanical Garden.
3. Professor Michael Stocking, School of Development Studies, University of East Anglia, Norwich, UK.
4. Few economists were attracted to the project, since the majority among them were disinclined to work at village level, or to accept farmers as being themselves knowledgeable.

5. The PLEC management group, consisting of the heads of each of the GEF-funded clusters, the scientific coordinators, and the responsible officers in UNU and UNEP, was proposed in 1996 and set up in 1998. After a preliminary meeting in Uganda, it has met in Tokyo, Mexico, Brazil, and Tanzania during each of the four years of GEF-PLEC project life. Together with leaders of the non-GEF clusters, it held a final meeting in Paris in 2002.
6. An important book on work in the Amazon floodplain of Brazil and Peru (Padoch *et al.* 1999) was published in 1999. However, this book was based on a conference held in 1994, at a time when the PLEC programme in Amazonia had scarcely begun. The book contains no reference to PLEC.
7. The GEF (2001: 75) writes

PLEC introduced on-farm "expert farmers"-led demonstrations i.e. local expert farmers teach others on conservation farming. As PLEC demonstration models are being further improved, they are now also being replicated by other projects or organizations. In Brazil and Tanzania, several rural extension and conservation programmes are adopting PLEC's demonstration approaches. Even international attention is being paid to this innovative approach.

REFERENCES

Acta Botanica Yunnanica. Suppl. XII. 2000. "Agrobiodiversity assessment and conservation."
Acta Botanica Yunnanica. Suppl. XIII. 2001. "Agrobiodiversity assessment and conservation."
Amazonian Brazil. 1994. "Reports from the clusters: Amazonian Brazil", *PLEC News and Views*, No. 2, p. 18.
Boiro, I. A., K. Barry, A. Diallo, S. Fofana, F. Mara, A. Baldé, M. A. Kane, and O. Barry. 2002. "Improvement of production and livelihood in the Fouta Djallon, République de Guinée", in H. Brookfield, C. Padoch, H. Parsons, and M. Stocking (eds) *Cultivating Biodiversity: Understanding, Analysing and Using Agricultural Diversity.* London: ITDG Publications.
Brookfield, H. 1995. "Postscript: The 'population-environment nexus' and PLEC", *Global Environmental Change: Human and Policy Dimensions*, Vol. 5, No. 4, pp. 381–393.
Brookfield, H. 1996. "A journey to Baoshan and Gaoligong Mountain (Gaoligongshan), western Yunnan", *PLEC News and Views*, No. 6, pp. 6–8.
Brookfield, H. 2001. *Exploring Agrodiversity.* New York: Columbia University Press.
Brookfield, H. and C. Padoch. 1994. "Appreciating agrodiversity: A look at the dynamism and diversity of indigenous farming practices", *Environment*, Vol. 36, No. 5, pp. 6–11, 37–45.
Brookfield, H., C. Padoch, H. Parsons, and M. Stocking (eds). 2002. *Cultivating Biodiversity Understanding, Analysing and Using Agricultural Diversity.* London: ITDG Publications.
Brookfield, H. and M. Stocking. 1999. "Agrodiversity: Definition, description and design", *Global Environmental Change: Human and Policy Dimensions*, Vol. 9, No. 2, pp. 77–80.

Brookfield, H., M. Stocking, and M. Brookfield. 1999. "Guidelines on agrodiversity assessment in the demonstration site areas (revised to form a companion paper to the BAG guidelines)", *PLEC News and Views*, No. 13, pp. 17–31.

Brush, S. B. 2000. "Midterm review: The review report", *PLEC News and Views*, No. 16, pp. 3–7.

Chambers, R., A. Pacey, and L. A. Thrupp (eds). 1989. *Farmer First: Farmer Innovation and Agricultural Research*. London: Intermediate Technology Publications.

Cleaver, K. M. and G. A. Schreiber. 1992. *The Population, Agriculture and Environment Nexus in Sub-Saharan Africa*. Washington, DC: Agriculture Division, Technical Department and Agriculture Operations Division, Western Africa Department, Africa Region, World Bank.

Coffey, K. 2000. *PLEC Agrodiversity Database Manual*. New York: United Nations University.

Coffey, K. 2002. "Quantitative methods for the analysis of agrodiversity", in H. Brookfield, C. Padoch, H. Parsons, and M. Stocking (eds) *Cultivating Biodiversity: Understanding, Analysing and Using Agricultural Diversity*. London: ITDG Publications, pp. 78–95.

Conference of the Parties to the Convention on Biological Diversity. 1996. *Report of the Third Meeting of the Conference of the Parties to the Convention on Biological Diversity, Buenos Aires, Argentina, 3–14 November 1996*. Secretariat of the Convention on Biological Diversity, www.biodiv.org.cop3/docs.html.

Dao, Z., X. H. Du, H. Guo, L. Liang, and Y. Li. 2001. "Promoting sustainable agriculture: The case of Baihualing, Yunnan, China", *PLEC News and Views*, No. 18, pp. 34–40.

Global Environment Facility. 2001. *Project Performance Report 2001*. Washington, DC: Global Environment Facility.

Guo, H., Z. Dao, and H. Brookfield. 1996. "Agrodiversity and biodiversity on the ground and among the people: Methodology from Yunnan", *PLEC News and Views*, No. 6, pp. 14–22.

Guo, H., C. Padoch, Y. Fu, Z. Dao, and K. Coffey. 2000. "Household agrobiodiversity assessment (HH-ABA)", *PLEC News and Views*, No. 16, pp. 28–33.

Gyasi, E. A. 1998. "PLEC experiences with participatory approach to biophysical resources management in Ghana", *PLEC News and Views*, No. 10, pp. 27–31.

Gyasi, E. A. 2001. "Development of demonstration sites in Ghana", *PLEC News and Views*, No. 18, pp. 20–28.

Gyasi, E. A. (ed.). Forthcoming. *Managing Biodiversity: The Traditional Way in Ghana and Guinea*. Tokyo: United Nations University Press.

Gyasi, E. A., G. T. Agyepong, E. Ardayfio-Schandorf, L. Enu-Kwesi, J. S. Nabilia, and E. Owusu-Bennoah. 1995. "Production pressure and environmental change in the forest-savanna zone of southern Ghana", *Global Environmental Change: Human and Policy Dimensions*, Vol. 5, No. 4, pp. 355–366.

Gyasi, E. A. and L. Enu-Kwesi. 1996. "Collaborative Agroecosystems Management Project (CAMP): A proposed community-based initiative in Ghana, by WAPLEC in collaboration with the chief and the people of Gyamfiase", *PLEC News and Views*, No. 6, pp. 11–13.

Gyasi, E. A. and J. I. Uitto (eds). 1997. *Environment, Biodiversity and Agricultural Change in West Africa*. Tokyo: United Nations University Press.

Hardon, J. J. and W. S. de Boef. 1994. "Local management and use of plant genetic resources", in A. Putter (ed.) *Safeguarding the Genetic Basis of Africa's Traditional Crops*. Wageningen and Rome: Technical Centre for Agricultural and Rural Cooperation and International Plant Genetic Resources Institute, pp. 115–126.

Kaihura, F. B. S. 2002. "Working with farmers is not simple: The case of PLEC-Tanzania", in H. Brookfield, C. Padoch, H. Parsons, and M. Stocking (eds) *Cultivating Biodiversity: Understanding, Analysing and Using Agricultural Diversity*. London: ITDG Publications, pp. 132–144.

Keystone Center. 1991. *Keystone International Dialogue Series on Plant Genetic Resources. Oslo Plenary Session. Final Consensus Report: Global Initiative for the Security and Sustainable Use of Plant Genetic Resources*. Washington, DC: Genetic Resources Communication Systems.

Myers, N. 1993. "Population, environment and development", *Environmental Conservation*, No. 20, pp. 205–216.

Okigbo, B. N. 1994. "Keynote address: Conservation and use of plant germplasm in African traditional agriculture and land-use systems", in A. Putter (ed.) *Safeguarding the Genetic Basis of Africa's Traditional Crops*. Wageningen and Rome: Technical Centre for Agricultural and Rural Cooperation and International Plant Genetic Resources Institute, pp. 15–38.

Padoch, C. 2002. "Spotting expertise in a diverse and dynamic landscape", in H. Brookfield, C. Padoch, H. Parsons, and M. Stocking (eds) *Cultivating Biodiversity: Understanding, Analysing and Using Agricultural Diversity*. London: ITDG Publications, pp. 96–104.

Padoch, C., J. M. Ayres, M. Pinedo-Vasquez, and A. Henderson (eds). 1999. *Várzea: Diversity, Development, and Conservation of Amazonia's Whitewater Floodplains*. Advances in Economic Botany 13. New York: New York Botanical Garden Press.

Padoch, C. and M. Pinedo-Vasquez. 1998. "Demonstrating PLEC: A diversity of approaches", *PLEC News and Views*, No. 11, pp. 7–9.

Pinedo-Vasquez, M. 1996a. "The Upper Amazon Várzea (Iquitos, Peru) team in the Amazonian cluster", *PLEC News and Views*, No. 6, pp. 4–5.

Pinedo-Vasquez, M. 1996b. "Local experts and local leaders", *PLEC News and Views*, No. 6, pp. 30–32.

Pinedo-Vasquez, M. 1999. "DAT: Facilitating the exchange of experiences on demonstration activities", *PLEC News and Views*, No. 14, pp. 11–16.

Pinedo-Vasquez, M., E. Gyasi, and K. Coffey. 2001. "PLEC demonstration activities: A review of procedures and experiences", *PLEC News and Views*, No. 17, pp. 12–30.

Pinedo-Vasquez, M., C. Padoch, D. McGrath, and T. Ximenes. 2000. "Biodiversity as a product of smallholders' strategies for overcoming changes in their natural and social landscapes: A report prepared by the Amazonia cluster", *PLEC News and Views*, No. 15, pp. 9–19.

Pinedo-Vasquez, M. and M. Pinedo-Panduro. 2001. "PLEC's demonstration and training activities in a dynamic political landscape", *PLEC News and Views*, No. 18, pp. 15–19.

PLEC. 1995. "Draft GEF project document, February 1995." Canberra: PLEC, unpublished report.

PLEC. 1996. "Project brief for the GEF operational panel, August 1996." Canberra: PLEC and Tokyo: United Nations University, unpublished report.

PLEC. 1997. "GEF project proposal for review, January 1997." Tokyo: United Nations University, Nairobi: United Nations Environment Programme, and Washington: Global Environment Facility, unpublished report.

PLEC. 1998. "Project document and annexes as submitted to the secretariat of the Global Environment Facility (GEF) for final approval, January 1998." Canberra: PLEC and Tokyo: United Nations University, unpublished report.

Quong, A. 1996. "ABA conundrums", *PLEC News and Views*, No. 7, pp. 26–32.

Reij, C., I. Scoones, and C. Toulmin (eds). 1996. *Sustaining the Soil: Indigenous Soil and Water Conservation in Africa*. London: Earthscan.

Rerkasem, K. and B. Rerkasem. 1995. "Montane mainland Southeast Asia: Agroecosystems in transition", *Global Environmental Change: Human and Policy Dimensions*, Vol. 5, No. 4, pp. 313–322.

Richards, P. 1985. *Indigenous Agricultural Revolution*. London and Boulder, CO: Hutchinson and Westview.

Stocking, M. and N. Murnaghan. 2001. *Handbook for the Field Assessment of Land Degradation*. London: Earthscan.

Thomas-Hope, E. and B. Spence. 2002. "Promoting agrobiodiversity under difficulties: The Jamaica-PLEC experience", *PLEC News and Views*, No. 19, pp. 17–24.

Thong-Ngam, C., T. Areethamm, P. Kaewpha, S. Thepsarn, N. Yimyam, C. Korsamphan, and K. Rerkasem. 2002. "Scaling-up a PLEC demonstration site for the National Pilot Programme: A case example of a Hmong Njua village in northern Thailand", *PLEC News and Views*, No. 19, pp. 7–16.

Tiffen, M., M. Mortimore, and F. Gichuki. 1994. *More People, Less Erosion: Environmental Recovery in Kenya*. Chichester: John Wiley.

Tumuhairwe, J., C. Nkwiine, and E. Nsubuga. 2001. "Using farmer-led exhibitions of agrobiodiversity to reach policy makers and other farmers: Experience of PLEC-Uganda", *PLEC News and Views*, No. 18, pp. 29–33.

UNCED (United Nations Conference on Environment and Development). 1992. *Agenda 21: The United Nations Programme of Action from Rio*. New York: United Nations Department of Public Information.

United Nations Population Fund. 1991. *Population, Resources and the Environment: The Critical Challenges*. London: Banson.

Zarin, D. J. 1995. "Diversity measurement methods for the PLEC clusters", *PLEC News and Views*, No. 4, pp. 11–21.

Zarin, D. J., H. Guo, and L. Enu-Kwesi. 1999. "Methods for the assessment of plant species diversity in complex agricultural landscapes: Guidelines for data collection and analysis from the PLEC biodiversity advisory group (BAG)", *PLEC News and Views*, No. 13, pp. 3–16.

2

How PLEC worked towards its objectives

Harold Brookfield, Helen Parsons, and Muriel Brookfield

Introduction

PLEC firmed up its data-collection methodology in 1999, as described in Chapter 1. Demonstration site methodology took more time to evolve. PLEC's methods have three main elements: an emphasis on agrodiversity and its value in sustaining biodiversity; a common system for the recording of agrodiversity and biodiversity in agricultural landscapes; and the value of farmer-to-farmer exchanges based on expert farmers and supported by scientists. The guidance to clusters, described in this chapter, came in part from the scientific coordinators, and principally from the internal advisory bodies. These were the biodiversity advisory group (BAG), the demonstration advisory team (DAT), and finally the scientific and technical advisory team (STAT), which combined the first two (Chapter 1). Below, these methodologies are summarized in the context of the first two of the project's four main stated objectives, which were:

- to establish historical and baseline comparative information on agrodiversity and biodiversity at the landscape level in representative diverse regions
- to develop participatory and sustainable models of biodiversity management based on farmers' technologies and knowledge within agricultural systems at the community and landscape levels.

Discussion in this chapter is focused on the means developed to achieve these objectives. It is made clear that the uptake of advised methodology was uneven between different clusters, especially in the period before 2000, and this unevenness is briefly discussed in a concluding section of the chapter. For most of its participants PLEC has been a voluntary activity, and uptake has had to rely on persuasion and example; no means of enforcement were available, even had they been desired.

Two aspects are omitted from this chapter and from this book. One is the formation of a meta-database from the detailed biodiversity databases provided by clusters. What can be made available publicly in this case is importantly restricted by considerations of intellectual property rights. The members of the project's scientific and technical advisory team provide more detail in a separate report, published in part in the new electronic *PLEC News and Views* (No. 1, 2003: 3–8). The other aspect dealt with only in passing is capacity-building, on which Luohui Liang and Wakako Ichikawa of the UNU have provided a largely statistical summary in a report to UNEP.

Analysing agrodiversity

The concept of agricultural diversity was adopted in PLEC from the outset. For thousands of years farmers have applied adaptive management in their utilization and cultivation of biodiversity for food and livelihoods. Generations of learning, experiment, and innovation on the use and management of biodiversity have nurtured diversity of plants and animals, both wild and domesticated, and built up what one can call "agrodiversity" – "the many ways in which farmers use the natural diversity of the environment for production, including not only their choice of crops but also their management of land, water and biota as a whole" (Brookfield and Padoch 1994: 43). Despite the modern trend towards uniformity in agricultural landscapes, a great number of farmers and communities continue to use and evolve agrodiverse practices, creating a dynamic landscape of different land uses.

Agrodiversity has been discussed and exemplified in two books (Brookfield 2001; Brookfield *et al.* 2002). Broadly, its management activities can be viewed in two major overlapping categories (Brookfield and Padoch 1994). One category is composed of environment-adaptive technologies that emphasize skilful but non-overriding adaptation to local diversity. For example, management of successional fallows widely practised in the humid tropics is often an effective use of natural processes. Another category is environment-formative technologies, which stress creation of substantial and enduring physical changes, creating landesque capital with a life expectation well beyond a single crop or crop cycle. Building and maintenance of wet rice terraces on slopes is only the most striking of such long-term investments for cultivation.[1]

There is more to agrodiversity than land management: agrodiversity emphasizes farmers' resource management as a whole. From 1999, the PLEC project scientific coordinators proposed to members that, for purposes of description and analysis, agricultural diversity be classified into four interrelated elements: biophysical diversity, management diversity, agrobiodiversity, and organizational diversity (Table 2.1), and their interactions.

The methods used to categorize and record diversity are summarized below. Discussion is based on Brookfield, Stocking, and Brookfield (1999) and Zarin, Guo, and Enu-Kwesi (1999). Modified versions also appear in Brookfield *et al.* (2002). This approach was not fully taken up in all clusters. The large sample category of "land-use stages" was not determined by the recommended means in Guinée, Kenya, or Papua New Guinea, although work was carried down to field level in these countries. In several clusters, scientists felt they had their own established ways of inventory which were more appropriate to an especially distinctive agriculture; Guinée is an example.

Table 2.1 Four elements of agrodiversity

Agrodiversity categories	Description
Biophysical diversity	The diversity of the natural environment, including the intrinsic quality of the natural resource base that is used for production. It includes the natural resilience of the biophysical environment, soil characteristics, plant life, and other biota. It takes in physical and chemical aspects of the soil, hydrology, and climate, and the variability and variation in all these elements.
Management diversity	All methods of managing the land, water, and biota for crop and livestock production, and the maintenance of soil fertility and structure. Included are biological, chemical, and physical methods of management.
Agrobiodiversity	This is all species and varieties used by or useful to people, with a particular emphasis on crop, plant, and animal combinations. It may include biota that are indirectly useful, and emphasizes the manner in which they are used to sustain or increase production, reduce risk, and enhance conservation.
Organizational diversity	This is the diversity in the manner in which farms are operated, owned, and managed, and the use of resource endowments from different sources. Explanatory elements include labour, household size, capital assets, reliance on off-farm employment, and so on.

Source: Stocking (2002)

Land-use stages and field types

The advocated first stage in description and sampling is the determination of land-use stages and field types, and this applies to the recording of both agricultural diversity and biodiversity (including agrobiodiversity).

Land-use stages

Land-use stages are areas of broadly common ecology, land use (or its absence), and especially recent land-use history. Without detailed inventory, they look like one class of land use, with one class of land cover. They may occupy several square kilometres in extensive systems, or much smaller and fragmented areas in more intensive, highly managed systems. An assemblage of related land-use stages makes up a landscape. The ecologists' term "land-use stage" is used, rather than the commoner "land-use type", because they are transient rather than permanent, changing to other stages both by processes of natural succession and by farmers' management.[2] Over the years of PLEC, stage transitions have been observed in most study areas.

Even where a land-use map is available, or could be generated from remote-sensing imagery or photographs, transects in the company of farmers are an essential early step in the identification of land-use stages. This was the "participatory rural appraisal" task, as it is described by most clusters; several did this before 1999. Whether large or small, land-use stages have to be recognizable at a landscape scale, broadly at a map scale of about 1:20,000–50,000, depending on the amount of detail present. Examples are groups of fields under annual (or semi-annual or longer-than-annual) crops, agroforests, fallows, orchards (including fuelwood plots and cash crop plantations), native forests, house gardens, and the edges between different types. Land-use stages are the basic sampling categories for more detailed survey.

Field types

The distinction between land-use stages and the usually smaller field types is that the latter are specifically defined by farmers' practices, and not just by observation. This is the level of detail that farmers themselves recognize. It is the level where farmers assign vernacular names to soil types, and where microclimates are employed as specific production opportunities. Field types are categories of individual fields, managed sections of fallow or forest, agroforests, and orchards in which a similar characteristic set of useful plants is encountered, and in which resource management methods have strong similarity.

Field types often arise in response to ecological conditions, but while specific ecological niches may be used in specialized ways, these ways tend to be repeated over a large area. Although each individual field is different, there is often considerable similarity between fields over quite a large area. Commonly, farmers develop specific sets of field types, in each of which they recognize similar biophysical attributes, use similar management methods, and grow similar sets or combinations of crops. There may be only one field type or a large number of field types within each land-use stage. In some systems, the field types shift across the landscape from year to year. In some regions in which there are two growing seasons in a year, different field types may arise on the same plot of land every few months.

Field types are also the means by which farmers most effectively mobilize their labour and allocate their resources. In many areas of the world, the basic reason why repeated patterns of field types come into existence would seem to be that they simplify work routines and the problems of daily decision-making. PLEC recording followed the farmers' own categories for management of diversity.

Where land rotation is practised, formerly cropped fields leave behind them successional (fallow) management types from which crop plants may continue to be taken, and in which the successional vegetation may be planted or managed. They can be conceptualized as a further set of field types. The 1999 progress report from the PLEC Amazonia cluster in Brazil contains a classification of managed and unmanaged fallows at Amapá, where they are of major importance as production spaces. Five distinct fallow field types are identified (Chapter 3).

Even where fallows are not specifically managed, the different phases are usually recognized by farmers. At Tumam in Papua New Guinea (Chapter 10), five fallow phases are recognized by name and, as the fallow passes from phase to phase, the species richness as well as its composition changes. As in other regions, farmers get produce of different kinds from different phases of the fallow. The farm does not end where the field meets the forest, and temporal diversity in the fallow is important to the farmers.

In many systems, field types change in response to processes such as land degradation or external pressures such as market forces.[3] At the demonstration site in Bushwere, Uganda (Chapter 6), bananas and coffee dominated the lower slopes of the landscape. As urban demand for bananas has increased and coffee has become increasingly susceptible to berry diseases, field types have shifted, but only after a time lag occasioned by farmers' reappraisal of what was in their own best interests with these perennial crops. Meanwhile, the upper slopes have been exploited for their soil fertility through crops such as sweet potatoes. As soil quality declines, land use changes to cassava cropping and increasingly lengthy fallows. So, field types change over time and space. However, any assessment at this level also needs to recognize that field types in different land-use stages are linked. In the Uganda case, sediment eroded from the upper slopes was providing the opportunity for increasing the area devoted to the down-slope banana-based field type.

In systems where land-use stage transitions take place infrequently, the field types are more permanent. An example is the intensively cultivated and manured infield, versus the more extensively used outfield, common in the savanna regions of Africa and most clearly represented within PLEC by the Fouta Djallon of Guinée (Chapter 5). Another example is the division of land between irrigated terraced or ponded rice fields, wet rice fields fed only by rainfall, dry fields which are alternately cropped and fallowed, planted and managed agroforests, and very mixed home gardens. This repeated pattern of just five main types is commonly found in Yunnan (Chapter 9), and occurs widely across south-eastern Asia.

Fields also have edges, whether separating fields of different types or of the same type. At the field level, the edges may have a specific management role and a distinctive plant ecology. A particular case in Thailand is discussed in some detail in Chapter 14. Live hedgerows and the risers separating terraces are edges. They may have a role in soil and water management as well as being used to provide or grow distinctive useful plants. At the most micro-level, edges also include trash lines, small stone walls, or small wooden fences. While not all these smaller features are significant from the point of view of plant biodiversity, they are significant from the point of view of resource management.

Notwithstanding the enormous internal diversity of cropping patterns, it is quite common to find the land used under only a small number of basic management systems, even across significantly different ecological zones. To recognize them necessitates not only repeated observation, but also the cooperation of the best and most alert farmers. It is easy for observers not trained to look for micro-features in the managed landscape to miss a great deal of relevant detail.

Sampling and recording methods

Once the sampling or selection frame, in the form of identification of land-use stages and especially of field types, has been done sufficiently for detailed work to begin, observers need to seek a range of information. Discussion of the information needed can best be classified within the four elements of agrodiversity. Brookfield, Stocking, and Brookfield (1999) provided a lengthy checklist, especially for management diversity. This was very widely used. As the country chapters demonstrate, there was considerable variation between clusters and sites within countries in the detail with which management was recorded. An edited compilation of the resulting information on management systems and resource access was distributed within the project, and sent to UNEP, at the end of 2001 (Brookfield and

Parsons 2001). It was not published, but much of it is now included in the country chapters below.

Biodiversity

In the guidelines for assessment of biodiversity, random sampling is advocated only in natural forest (Zarin, Guo, and Enu-Kwesi 1999). In all other land-use stages a biased sample is advocated, although not insisted upon, with preferred bias toward those fields seeming to exhibit the highest species richness on inspection. Sample quadrats of a size appropriate to the field type are used for biodiversity assessment, including agrobiodiversity.[4] A sufficient degree of replication is advised, although this could not always be fully obtained in some areas with difficult access. It is also advised that all sample plots be marked to facilitate resurvey. Here too there was some difficulty, as farmers sometimes objected to the marking of their plots, fearing that they might lose land. A number of sample plots in community forests, for example in China, were found to have been cleared for conversion to agriculture a year later, and the marks removed.

One particular field type calls for special treatment. This is the home garden, sometimes very clearly demarcated but elsewhere only a more intensively managed variant of multistorey agroforest (Nair 2001). Always sites of great diversity, multi-layered home gardens can only effectively be subsampled if they are large, and Zarin, Guo, and Enu-Kwesi (1999) recommend that biodiversity inventory within them covers the whole area of selected home gardens. This advice was followed in most clusters, but in some a stratified sampling design was adopted.

The choice of database system for recording was changed during the project for easier computation of statistical measures. Detail on the methods advised for database recording were provided to all clusters (Coffey 2000), and subsequent advice was given on methods of analysis, initially by electronic distribution and later in published form (Coffey 2002). A paucity of expertise in quantitative analysis among the members of some clusters, together with the sheer size of the job, including all the necessary checking of redundancy due to duplicate recording and misspelling, retarded progress. Some parts of the whole database were not fully supplied for creation of the metadatabase until after the formal end of the project.

Management diversity

For the assessment of management diversity within agrodiversity, the whole field becomes the sample, together with its edges. The detailed checklist of management practices, supplied by Brookfield, Stocking, and Brookfield (1999), is mentioned above. A matrix can be prepared in which different sampled fields within the field types are treated as units within each of which particular methods, and crops, can be simply recorded by their presence or absence. In practice this was not done, but the Tanzania cluster, which completed work quickly, developed a descriptive matrix of practices within each field type. Published in abbreviated form in the project periodical (Kaihura, Ndondi, and Kemikimba 2000), this system of presentation was then used by other clusters in their reports during the last two project years, and is employed in several chapters of this book. An extract from the original Tanzanian presentation appears in Table 2.2.

One problem was not really solved. Tabulated data can readily oversimplify complexity. Data tabulated or presented on maps have to be divided into classes, creating a false impression of uniformity over tracts of land sharply distinguished from other tracts of land. The sample quadrats used for biodiversity inventory are free from these problems, but they are not appropriate for analysis of management practices, where the unit had to be the field. This is because data obtained only from within or close to quadrats may omit important features that lie outside their limits but have a role in relation to what is observed within them.

Household-based agrobiodiversity assessment

In China, the progressive individualization of farm management decision-making since the break-up of the communes in 1983 and institution of the "household contract responsibility system" has dramatically transformed the conditions of agrobiodiversity (Chapter 9). Under this system, households established on land leased from the collective still had to provide mandatory deliveries of crops required by the local or regional authorities, but all other decisions were left to the individual, who could also sell pri-

Table 2.2 Extract from the description of land-use stages and field types in Olgilai/ Ng'iresi, Tanzania

Land-use stage	Field types	Field type description
Agroforest	Crops and trees	Complex mixes of crops and trees depending on farm size, season, and farmer preference; coffee, banana, and trees with maize and beans most typical. Varying slopes.
	Maize and beans with trees	Maize and beans as intercrops with trees as hedges on contours and boundaries; the most economic crop(s) occupy the largest area.
	Potatoes in rotation with vegetables	Commercial potatoes in the first season, followed by cabbage and fallow in the third season of the year.
	Maize	Maize planted as monocrop.

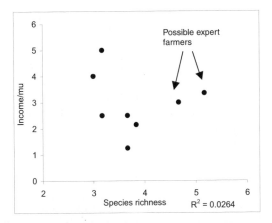

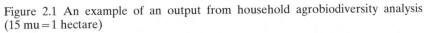

Figure 2.1 An example of an output from household agrobiodiversity analysis (15 mu = 1 hectare)

vately all produce not required for the government quota. The system has been progressively further liberalized. Biodiversity assessment sampling at the level of the whole community or a wider landscape risked totally missing the important variation in production methods and content that quickly began to emerge, so that in 1999 it was decided to survey separately the fields and private woods of individuals selected partly at random, partly through purposive selection. The sampled households were also selected for more detailed socio-economic investigation. The result, in one Chinese village, is summarized in Figure 2.1, drawn from Guo *et al.* (2000). Other results are discussed in Chapter 9.

While the Chinese method did not become general, several other clusters also inventoried biodiversity within the farms and private agroforests and woods of individual farmers, although on a selective basis. Often some fields of the collaborating expert farmers were inventoried in this way. The means of linking household-level to landscape-level inventory in an analytic manner are still being explored.

Recording biophysical diversity

Most of the project's scientists are natural scientists, but only some are earth scientists. While most felt they could adequately record biophysical diversity, there were large differences between clusters in available expertise. In order to compensate, the checklist included considerable detail on what was needed in terms of site characteristics, soils and their qualities, and on the simple observation of soil erosion and transportation.

Information was sought in one of the interim reports on the causes of land degradation in the project areas. Clusters were visited by two specialists, but local scientists who could follow up their advice were often not available. Comprehensive guidance on land degradation work was not available until the project was close to its end (Stocking and Murnaghan 2001).[5] The information on "causes of land degradation" provided by the clusters sometimes listed explanations standard in the literature, whether or not these were locally valid. Such worthwhile information as was obtained is included in the compilation on management methods and resource access distributed, and submitted to UNEP, towards the end of the project (Brookfield and Parsons 2001).

Recording organizational diversity

By "organizational diversity" PLEC means what are commonly called the "socio-economic aspects" in the farming systems literature. Because the latter term tends to marginalize these issues, PLEC proposed a term that would more effectively indicate their centrality. Most clusters used it, but some continued to refer to the "socio-economic" aspects.[6] It includes diversity in the manner in which farms are owned and operated, and in the use of resource endowments and the farm workforce. Elements include labour, household size, the differing resource endowments of households, and reliance on off-farm employment or business. Also included are age group and gender relations in farm work, dependence on the farm as against other sources of support, the spatial distribution of the farm, and differentials between farmers in access to land and other resources.

Organizational diversity embraces all management of resources, including land, crops, labour, capital, and all other inputs. It underpins and helps explain "management diversity" and its variation between particular farms, communities, and societies. The relationship of the farm household and community to the larger society, local, regional, national, and global, are important elements that shape the relationship of organizational diversity to the larger world. Changes in these external relationships can have a major impact on all agrodiversity at the level of the farm and community. Investigations of the variable resource endowments among farm households needed to begin at community level, and were an important preliminary to the selection of expert farmers. Although all PLEC's farmers are smallholders, not all are equal. Where there are large differences between richer and poorer farmers, some ranking was essential before work among farmers could begin.[7]

Organizational diversity differs from the other elements in that it cannot be recorded except at the level of whole farms compared with one another. Farm layout is an element capable of being mapped, but recording of other aspects called for repeated discussion with farmers. Although some clusters used formal methods of enquiry, others did not. Land tenure can be a particularly important variable, as it can have important consequences for land management and agrobiodiversity. This emerges at many points in this book, first and most clearly in Chapter 4 (Ghana). Data needed to be complemented by information on the population of the landscape area, including its demography, migration history, form of social organization, and arrangements for marketing of produce. In turn, this nested into wider-area information on the regional and national economies, policies, and political forces. This wider social, political, and demographic context was, as the country chapters demonstrate, more unevenly covered than the physical aspects of the land and the farming systems.

Demonstration site method

The evolution of PLEC demonstration sites and the method of work within them has been described in general terms in Chapter 1. Here, some specific aspects are developed further.

Demonstration site selection

The basic criterion for demonstration site selection was that they be in agricultural areas with significant biodiversity, but not in any way necessarily in proximity to areas reserved by government for biodiversity conservation. They were to be in agricultural landscapes, with emphasis on mountains, semi-arid regions, wetlands, and formerly forested areas under apparent pressure from population growth, broadly in accordance with the GEF priorities of the mid-1990s. Two of the three sites in China were, in fact, developed in immediate proximity to state nature reserves, because one was first developed under a preceding MacArthur Foundation project which had that criterion, and one of the others was fortuitously adjacent to a nature reserve that had been enlarged at its expense (Chapter 9). Several others were found to be close to small natural areas reserved by custom rather than law. The first site developed in Ghana was set up at the invitation of a chief who sought help in protecting such an area.

Although coordinators offered advice, the selection of demonstration sites was principally the responsibility of the clusters themselves. Not surprisingly, many of the cluster principals selected areas with which they were already familiar through earlier research. This had advantages, because it offered some time depth in available data and simplified the initial stages of site characterization. There were also disadvantages, in that sites chosen were sometimes inconveniently located for access, and remoter sites had later to be downgraded, or even abandoned and replaced by others that were easier for the scientists to reach.

The Ghanaian group was the first to propose a working definition:

PLEC demonstration sites can be described as places or areas in which PLEC scientists, farmers and other environmental stakeholders carry out work in a participatory manner to conserve and even enhance agricultural and biological diversity and the biophysical resources underpinning it. These sites are areas where the scientists work with farmers in the creation of projects that are the farmers' own, and where, together, the scientists and farmers demonstrate the value of locally-developed techniques and technologies. (Abdulai, Gyasi, and Kufogbe 1999)

Pinedo-Vasquez, Gyasi, and Coffey (2002) presented a people-centred view:

The PLEC demonstration activity is ideally a farmer-driven group with the conservation of agrodiversity and the improvement of farmer livelihoods as outputs. The optimum activity achieves both conservation and development objectives. This is clearly no easy task. A particular activity may require the participation of government agents, NGOs, scientists, researchers, technicians, extensionists and farmers. Bringing together such an eclectic group of participants often results in complex, sometimes contentious interactions. The complexity is heightened because the various actors assume unfamiliar roles during demonstration activities. Expert farmers, rather than scientists or extension agents, supply and transfer the technical knowledge. PLEC members facilitate, monitor, observe and record this process.

This definition emphasizes the fact that the sites are not so much physical places as people-centred processes, and the locale of coalition and partnership between scientists, real farmers, local communities, and other stakeholders searching for sustainability on the ground.

Both the definitions cited above have been used in defining sites and the work done in them, and this becomes evident in the country chapters that follow. Even within Brazil, there is greater relative emphasis on place at Santarém than at Macapá, and in West Africa there is less emphasis on place in Guinée than in Ghana. However, in all sites both place and people are involved, so that all are people-centred processes taking place in specific areas. It was never possible, and never expected, that only one model would be followed.

The stages of demonstration site work[8]

Assembling an assessment team

The simultaneity of both conservation and development is central to the PLEC demonstration concept. To achieve this harmonization, PLEC clusters began their work with rigorous, multidisciplinary assessments of the variation among households of the communities at their demonstration sites. Each cluster brought together an assessment team. The make-up of the teams has varied considerably. They varied in the number of individuals involved, the time they could spend in the field, their backgrounds, and the specialized knowledge they brought to the task. All included experienced researchers and exceptional farmers. In some cases the teams also included respected extension agents, local authorities, and religious leaders. The inclusion of external individuals had to be done without compromising the basic goals of the assessment.

An important issue was the different types and degrees of outside intervention in the form of conservation or development efforts that had been, or were currently, taking place in the community. To include persons closely identified with those that use an incompatible approach risked prejudicing the assessment teams' outputs. Care taken in assembling teams was always important, and was rewarded not only in good research results, but also later when the demonstration activities took over as the central element of the work.

Local farmers played a special role as members of the assessment teams. Their knowledge of the community, local production technologies, resources, and landscapes was invaluable to a perceptive and reliable inventory process. The ties that the PLEC team could forge with selected farmers while doing assessments were also important for the success of later work.

Farmer-based site assessment

Farmers, especially expert farmers, are at the core of all PLEC demonstration activities (Padoch and Pinedo-Vasquez 1998). To identify those farmers and technologies that might contribute most towards the improvement of the community's development and biodiversity conservation, and to identify the needs, trends, and priorities of communities, the clusters carried out detailed and multi-focused site assessments, as described above.

Many of the outputs of the assessments supply the data and create the foundations necessary for the successful planning and implementation of demonstration activities. Agrobiodiversity inventories, for instance, provide a picture of the existing variation in the level and type of biodiversity in different landholdings. Identifying those that maintain large numbers of rare and unusual species and varieties is a major step in choosing an appropriate demonstration activity or farmer demonstrator. Striking examples are presented in some country chapters, especially Chapters 3, 8, 9, and 14.

Biodiversity data are complemented with information on the performance of households as social and economic units. The household is the primary unit of measurement and analysis because in most rural areas decisions on how, where, when, and what to produce are usually made at this level. These household surveys reveal differences between households in a large number of crucial economic and social variables. Knowledge of both the means and ranges in income, labour availability, ownership of capital goods, and other variables helps demonstration teams identify particularly successful, flexible, and resilient farmer households. Research on variations in the types of fields managed, the crops produced, and the technologies employed by the households is necessary to ascertain the technologies that are good candidates for inclusion as demonstration activities.

Site assessments take into account a broad range of information that can also help demonstration teams understand processes of change and the actors who participate in these changes. A variety of ethnoscientific methods is employed, including the reconstruction of landscape histories and interviewing of knowledgeable villagers. The results of this research help scientists understand trends in local biodiversity management and identify particularly dynamic, resourceful, and resilient components of the community. These inventories provide an understanding of the innovative technologies developed by farmers that might be especially important in helping their neighbours overcome production constraints, cope with looming problems, or take advantage of likely opportunities.

Some problems

In reviewing PLEC's experiences in carrying out household and field assessments that readily feed into successful demonstration planning, a few common difficulties are worth mentioning. One is the difference in what members of different disciplines see in the field. Soil scientists tend to see soils, botanical scientists plants. A well-balanced interdisciplinary team with clearly defined goals was necessary to ensure that assessments provided insights from agrobiodiversity and agrodiversity, as well as landscape and household surveys. In some small clusters it was not possible to achieve sufficient interdisciplinary participation, although most attempted to recruit short-term inputs from others.

Another common limitation in the identification, documentation, and selection of farmer-developed technologies stems from a mechanical or perfunctory use of categories and concepts. Some of the terms commonly used to define how farmers organize their crops, such as monocropping, polycropping, or intercropping, actually reveal little that is useful about the diversity of the farming system, nor how it adapts to change. Greater insights into responses to change can be achieved by dismantling the general categories and recording the technical diversity used at several stages: clearing, hoeing, ploughing, planting, weeding, protecting, harvesting, or fallowing fields. An undiscriminating reliance on common terms and definitions of cropping systems sometimes leads to misinterpretation of both existing diversity and directions of change.

Integrating outputs

Conclusions drawn from agrobiodiversity inventories, socio-economic surveys, and agrodiversity studies supply the framework upon which activities can be planned. Among the important variables that need to be determined are:

- the crucial economic, political, and environmental changes affecting land-use practices and household incomes of smallholders
- how local smallholders deal with the problems that arise with change
- the farmers who are most innovative and successful in dealing with these problems
- the technological diversity and specific management technologies developed by successful farmers
- the levels of agrobiodiversity and other forms of biological diversity resulting from the application of these technologies.

From among these individuals or groups, expert farmers are selected who can then be invited to show and teach promising technologies to their neighbours in the course of demonstration activities.

Translating the results of field assessments into a successful programme of demonstration activities is not an easy task. Information collected by many clusters has, however, identified many cases that readily show how concentrating on variation and change among villagers can yield a rich store of expert individuals and expert practices that were appropriate for dissemination. There is considerable room for variation in demonstration activities, as well as a need for such variation. Each cluster developed distinct and evolving interpretations of what constitutes an appropriate demonstration activity for a particular situation (Padoch and Pinedo-Vasquez 1998; Guo *et al.* 2000; Allen and Sowei 2001; Pinedo-Vasquez and Pinedo-Panduro 2001; Gyasi 2001; Tumuhairwe, Nkwiine, and Nsubuga 2001; Dao *et al.* 2001; Thong-Ngam *et al.* 2002; Thomas-Hope and Spence 2002).

Perhaps the greatest challenge has been to resist the tendency for demonstration activities to become standard development and conservation initiatives. There was still a penchant for demonstrating "modern" or "improved" techniques developed by agronomists and other scientifically trained experts, and to instruct farmers, thus threatening the core concepts of PLEC demonstration. Concerted and constant efforts had to be made to ensure that activities did not merely copy conventional extension and training models. Some clusters followed such approaches for a considerable time. There are often good reasons for seeking to assist farmers in this more direct way, but much is lost by not fully using the skills and abilities of the farmers. The most effective way to confront and overcome these biases was for researchers and technicians to increase the time they spent in the field learning from farmers before demonstration began.

Identification of expert farmers

Expert farmers cannot be identified without scientists having a great deal of field experience interacting with members of the smallholder societies at local community level. Other authors, including Fairhead (1993), have also pointed out that exchange of production technologies should begin by identifying who knows what. Among the several characteristics that make demonstration activities different from standard extension programmes is that this first step is emphasized. Most PLEC scientists take much care in identifying expert farmers by first asking who knows what.

The process of identification of expert farmers has proven to be a long and complex one. In many cases expert farmers with successful and biodiversity-rich systems of management have had unfortunate past experiences with scientists, extensionists, and development projects, and sometimes are not eager to cooperate again. Farmers who in the past may have been singled out and praised as progressive farmers and therefore recruited for multiple projects are not often the ones called upon to teach. The new mode of working proved confusing to some farmers. Experience in several countries shows that true expert farmers are often hesitant to share their knowledge with any or all of their farmer neighbours. PLEC has been careful to consult closely with farmers and allow them to choose which technologies and which part of their technologies they want to impart to all or some of their neighbours. The demonstration teams suggest which technologies might be of interest, and the expert farmer decides which of those she or he would like to demonstrate.

Conducting demonstration activities

Although the success of demonstration activities depends largely on identifying and selecting appropriate expert farmers, the composition of the entire team and the attitude of each member towards farmers are also important determinants of success. A demonstration team can integrate field researchers, extension agents, technicians, and, more importantly, expert farmers. Where the members developed strong relationships with farmers the teams have been especially successful.

The main role of expert farmers is to explain and demonstrate their production and management techniques. It becomes the job of researchers, technicians, and other members of the team to facilitate meetings and activities, make appropriate suggestions, encourage farmer demonstrators when difficulties are encountered, and monitor how farmers are adapting or rejecting the techniques learned in demonstration activities. This is one of the reasons why members of most demonstration teams attend every demonstration activity.

The focus on demonstration is based on the principle that farmers are always teaching and learning from other farmers, and one of the most important products of this mutual exchange of knowledge is the agrodiversity and agrobiodiversity that are found in landholdings. The modes of dissemination of information are varied, but mostly farmers learn from and exchange experiences with farmer demonstrators by working together in the fields managed by the expert farmers. Only rarely do they learn by sitting in classrooms. Farmers who participate in demonstration activities are always free to try, change, or reject the technologies. Many forms of local gatherings have been very successful in demonstrating particular production systems and conservation practices. They are discussed further in several of the following chapters, especially Chapters 3, 8, 9, 11, and 13.

Special circumstances and special considerations

One of the key achievements of the research components of PLEC has been a strengthened realization that many of the biodiversity-conserving practices of smallholders are essentially different from "modern" systems embraced by agronomists and promoted by agricultural planners throughout the world. Many of the demonstrated smallholder technologies are long-term multi-stage management systems where fields tend not to go through distinct stages of cropping and fallow, but where management changes year by year. The exact forms of management tend to be spatially and temporally variable and highly contingent.

Examples of such systems include the very diverse swidden agroforestry production types central to demonstrations at the Macapá sites in Amazonia (Chapter 3), as well as many of the agroforestry systems in the Tanzanian and Chinese sites (Chapters 8 and 9). Demonstrating such production systems is a complex undertaking since at different stages of these multiphase systems the variation in management intensity, management techniques, and the resulting production is extreme. Giving a demonstration of only one stage in the production of, for instance, fast-growing timbers in the Amazon floodplain may not adequately characterize the system. Taking all participants to view examples of all stages may be impractical. This problem tends to arise only when technicians, scientists, or policy-makers are included in the demonstration groups, since local farmers already largely understand the multi-stage processes. Expert farmers did, however, need to be reminded that not all members of their audiences were equally conversant with some of the long-term complexities of the systems.

Another aspect of smallholder management is the importance of peripheral or edge production and the need to include these areas in demonstration activities. Although spatially insignificant, locally they can be the richest in biodiversity, including agriculturally, culturally, and nutritionally important plants and animals. Edge systems may include edges of swidden fields or banks between crop fields, as in northern Thailand (Chapter 14), and the "fences" between upland fields in Mexico or China. Other variants were noted in Tanzania and Kenya. The economic and ecological importance of these systems makes them prime candidates for demonstration activities. In most cases edge-cropping systems have been overlooked because they are small in area and have rarely been significant sources of income. Most of their production is for household consumption, and generally they are ignored by development projects and extension services with their emphasis on cash production. Featuring them in demonstration activities was difficult; their composition is usually highly variable and the management looks haphazard to many an observer. Nonetheless, perception of subtleties is a key element in the success of PLEC work.

Monitoring the results of demonstration activities

Careful monitoring of demonstration activities and the responses of participants is necessary, along with follow-up monitoring after demonstration sessions and site visits. Visits to the participants' landholdings are included as part of the monitoring process. Monitoring is most critical for understanding how farmers and other participants are adapting or rejecting the technologies demonstrated by the expert farmers. The number of people participating cannot be taken as a measure of the success of the demonstration activity. Superficial notions of "participation" do not reveal the socio-political complexity of settings where expert farmers interact with other farmers, technicians, and other rural agents. Information on the number of farmers adapting, rejecting, or assimilating the technologies, immediately after and much later, is required. There are many examples that show how farmers experiment with and modify the management systems and techniques they learned.

PLEC monitoring teams are composed of researchers, field assistants, union and religious farmer leaders, and extensionists. Expert farmers are rarely part of the monitoring team, because experience shows that some of them do not appreciate the variations made by the participant farmers. Some PLEC clusters recruit young farmers or the sons or daughters of farmers as field assistants for the monitoring team. Some rely on students as field assistants for monitoring.

Demonstration activities are continuously evolving. The diversity of approaches and strategies being employed for conducting demonstration activities, while following the "farmers-teaching-farmers" approach, is indicative of the developing process. In the short period that PLEC participants have been engaged in demonstration activities, the experience has produced valuable information supporting the tenet that poor and marginalized farmers are holders of great knowledge, as well as developers of efficient, effective, and ingenious ways of managing the world's biodiversity.

The uptake of PLEC methodology

PLEC had to develop its methodology "on the fly", and advice to clusters sometimes came after they were already some way down their own paths. Had the GEF-funded project endured for five years instead of four, there would have been more time for corrective action to be taken with the assistance of the internal advisory groups. Recommended survey and assessment methods for biodiversity and agrodiversity were in use in most parts of PLEC by the end of 1999, but there was resistance from a few scientists who felt their familiar methods were better. Some cluster groups never adopted the advised methodology in all its aspects. The project did make heavy demands. However, both biodiversity and agrodiversity were from adequately to excellently characterized in almost all areas.

Demonstration methods, for valid reasons, were never adopted exactly as in the model, but were enthusiastically adapted rather than adopted. Despite the speed and enthusiasm with which demonstration work was taken up in areas where it was quite unfamiliar, such as Tanzania, some groups were slower. Chapter 7 contains a candid discussion of the reasons for delay in Kenya. An informative account of the difficulties that had to be faced, and in part overcome, is presented for Jamaica in Chapter 13. Even a core area such as the Xishuangbanna area of China, where PLEC work has a continuous history since 1993, the expert farmer-to-farmer demonstration model had still been adopted only in embryonic form as late as 2001 (Chapter 9). In the end, by 2002 only Papua New Guinea – where it was felt that strong social reasons prevented uptake of this method – remained without farmer-to-farmer demonstration activities (Chapter 10).

The farmer-to-farmer approach, employing carefully selected expert farmers and greatly changing the role of scientists, was a major innovation to almost everyone in the project. As with any innovation of this magnitude, uptake has been irregular. While some clusters report great success with the farmer-to-farmer approach, others have been more cautious in moving away from familiar ground. It will only be in successor projects, now being planned, that full adoption and adaptation of this key element of PLEC's innovation is likely to become general.

Notes

1. Evidence is accumulating that not only is there a wealth of good practice in many previously overlooked local techniques for biodiversity conservation, but also that such techniques can reduce land degradation risks, support local livelihoods, and give tangible evidence of sustainability. PLEC specifically concentrates attention on those "sustainable adaptations by small farmers to varied environments under growing population pressure

and all other forms of stress ... [and on its value for biodiversity conservation and enhance-ment], principally through the high degree of structural, spatial and trophic, as well as species diversity that is involved" (Brookfield 1995: 389).

2. In other ways they are broadly comparable with the land-utilization types discussed in the FAO land evaluation literature (FAO 1976). FAO (1983: 26) sets out a useful table of head-ings for describing land-utilization types, plus some suggestions for descriptive and semi-analytical quantification.

3. This paragraph extracts from unpublished writing by Michael Stocking.

4. Three plot sizes were selected as standard frames for the collection of core species diversity data: 1×1 m, 5×5 m, and 20×20 m. The 1×1 m frame may be appropriate for sampling some Field Types within the annual cropping stage and as a nested sub-plot for sampling the herbaceous layer of Field Types within the agroforest, fallow, orchard, native forest and house garden stages. As appropriate, the 5×5 m frame may substitute for or be used in con-junction with the 1×1 m frame; the 5×5 m frame may also be sufficient as the basic unit for sampling some Field Types within the agroforest stage. The 20×20 m frame is appro-priate for use in agroforest Field Types characterized by wider spacing, and as the basic frame for sampling Field Types within fallow, orchard and native forest stages. Within the grass and shrub-dominated fallow sub-stages, we recommend establishment of the 20×20 m frame even if only nested 1×1 m and 5×5 m plots are sampled. Marking the corners of the 20×20 m frame, and sampling nested 1×1 m and 5×5 m plots within it, establishes the basis for representative repeated measurement of the same fallow plots even if they make a sub-stage transition as they age. (Zarin, Guo, and Enu-Kwesi 1999: 10)

5. The preparation of this handbook was funded by UNEP, not by PLEC.

6. Especially in the early period, there was sometimes a dual marginalization. The task of being the "socio-economist" was often given to female members of the teams, whatever the speciality in which they had been trained. While this genderization of work never vanished, it later became less marked.

7. Because of very wide differences in social conditions between clusters, no general guidance on ranking was given, although copies of useful articles were made available to those who sought advice. In general, clusters followed common-sense methods in collaboration with the farmers, using such indicators as house style, ownership of livestock and implements, and farmers' own comparative ranking of their neighbours.

8. This whole section of the chapter draws heavily on Pinedo-Vasquez, Gyasi, and Coffey (2002: 110–123).

REFERENCES

Abdulai, A. S., E. A. Gyasi, and S. K. Kufogbe. 1999. "Mapping of settlements in an evolving PLEC demonstration site in northern Ghana: An example in collabora-tive and participatory work", *PLEC News and Views*, No. 14, pp. 19–24.

Allen, B. J. and J. Sowei. 2001. "Activities at the PLEC site at Tumam village, East Sepik Province, Papua New Guinea, August 1999 to October 2000", *PLEC News and Views*, No. 17, pp. 34–39.

Brookfield, H. 1995. "Postscript: The 'population-environment nexus' and PLEC", *Global Environmental Change: Human and Policy Dimensions*, Vol. 5, No. 4, pp. 381–393.

Brookfield, H. 2001. *Exploring Agrodiversity*. New York: Columbia University Press.

Brookfield, H. and C. Padoch. 1994. "Appreciating agrodiversity: A look at the dynamism and diversity of indigenous farming practices", *Environment*, Vol. 36, No. 5, pp. 6–11, 37–45.

Brookfield, H., C. Padoch, H. Parsons, and M. Stocking (eds). 2002. *Cultivating Biodiversity: Understanding, Analysing and Using Agricultural Diversity*. London: ITDG Publications.

Brookfield, H. and H. Parsons. 2001. "Agrodiversity in the GEF-PLEC countries: A summary from cluster material." Canberra: Department of Anthropology, unpublished PLEC project report electronically distributed.

Brookfield, H., M. Stocking, and M. Brookfield. 1999. "Guidelines on agrodiversity in demonstration site areas", *PLEC News and Views*, No. 13, pp. 17–31.

Coffey, K. 2000. *PLEC Agrodiversity Database Manual*. New York: United Nations University.

Coffey, K. 2002. "Quantitative methods for the analysis of agrodiversity", in H. Brookfield, C. Padoch, H. Parsons, and M. Stocking (eds) *Cultivating Biodiversity: Understanding, Analysing and Using Agricultural Diversity*. London: ITDG Publications, pp. 78–95.

Dao, Z., X. H. Du, H. Guo, L. Liang, and Y. Li. 2001. "Promoting sustainable agriculture: The case of Baihualing, Yunnan, China", *PLEC News and Views*, No. 18, pp. 34–40.

Fairhead, J. 1993. "Representing knowledge: The 'new farmer' in research fashions", in J. Pottier (ed.) *Practising Development: Social Science Perspectives*. London: Routledge, pp. 187–204.

FAO. 1976. "A framework for land evaluation", *Soils Bulletin*, No. 32.

FAO. 1983. "Guidelines: Land evaluation for rainfed agriculture", *Soils Bulletin*, No. 52.

Guo, H., C. Padoch, Y. Fu, Z. Dao, and K. Coffey. 2000. "Household agrobiodiversity assessment (HH-ABA)", *PLEC News and Views*, No. 16, pp. 28–33.

Gyasi, E. A. 2001. "Development of demonstration sites in Ghana", *PLEC News and Views*, No. 18, pp. 20–28.

Kaihura, F. B. S., P. Ndondi, and E. Kemikimba. 2000. "Agrodiversity assessment in diverse and dynamic small-scale farms in Arameru, Arusha (Tanzania)", *PLEC News and Views*, No. 16, pp. 14–27.

Nair, P. K. R. 2001. "Do tropical homegardens elude science, or is it the other way around?", *Agroforestry Systems*, Vol. 53, No. 2, pp. 239–245.

Padoch, C. and M. Pinedo-Vasquez. 1998. "Demonstrating PLEC: A diversity of approaches", *PLEC News and Views*, No. 11, pp. 7–9.

Pinedo-Vasquez, M., E. A. Gyasi, and K. Coffey. 2002. "PLEC demonstration activities: A review of procedures and experiences", in H. Brookfield, C. Padoch, H. Parsons, and M. Stocking (eds) *Cultivating Biodiversity: Understanding, Analysing and Using Agricultural Diversity*. London: ITDG Publications, pp. 105–125.

Pinedo-Vasquez, M. and M. Pinedo-Panduro. 2001. "PLEC's demonstration and training activities in a dynamic political landscape", *PLEC News and Views*, No. 18, pp. 15–19.

Stocking, M. 2002. "Diversity: A new strategic direction for soil conservation", in *Sustainable Utilization of Global Soil and Water Resources. Proceedings of the 12th International Soil Conservation Conference, May 26–31, 2002, Beijing*, Volume 1. Beijing: Tsinghua University Press, pp. 53–58.

Stocking, M. and N. Murnaghan. 2001. *Handbook for the Field Assessment of Land Degradation.* London: Earthscan.

Thomas-Hope, E. and B. Spence. 2002. "Promoting agrobiodiversity under difficulties: The Jamaica-PLEC experience", *PLEC News and Views*, No. 19, pp. 17–24.

Thong-Ngam, C., T. Areethamm, P. Kaewpha, S. Thepsarn, N. Yimyam, C. Korsamphan, and K. Rerkasem. 2002. "Scaling-up a PLEC demonstration site for the National Pilot Programme: A case example of a Hmong Njua village in northern Thailand", *PLEC News and Views*, No. 19, pp. 7–16.

Tumuhairwe, J. K., C. Nkwiine, and E. Nsubuga. 2001. "Using farmer-led exhibitions of agrobiodiversity to reach policy makers and other farmers: Experience of PLEC-Uganda", *PLEC News and Views*, No. 18, pp. 29–33.

Zarin, D. J., H. Guo, and L. Enu-Kwesi. 1999. "Methods for the assessment of plant species diversity in complex agricultural landscapes: Guidelines for data collection and analysis from the PLEC biodiversity advisory group (BAG)", *PLEC News and Views*, No. 13, pp. 3–16.

3

Brazil (Amazonia)

Miguel Pinedo-Vasquez, David G. McGrath, and Tereza Ximenes

Para conservar no precisa poner cerca, precisa mudar a mentalidade da gente principalmente dos politicos. [To conserve you don't need to build a fence, you need to change people's thinking, principally that of politicians.]

These were the recommendations made by the expert farmer from the Brazilian Amazon who became the main adviser in rural development and conservation to the governor of the state of Amapá in Brazil. The expert is also one of only two women of a total of 19 members of the advisory team to the governor.

Introduction

The várzea *environment*

The *várzea* is the floodplain of the whitewater tributaries of the Amazon and the combined lower river. Including the portion in Peru, it occupies up to 180,000 square kilometres, over a length of 4,000 km. The whitewater rivers derive most of their sediment content from the Peruvian Andes, which provide 80 per cent of all the alluvium along the river. There is a common group of landscape elements in the *várzea*: the high levees along the rivers and their major distributaries, the backslopes of these levees, and lakes or swamps behind them and between the rivers and the firm ground. The combinations of these elements, and their dynamics, differ greatly

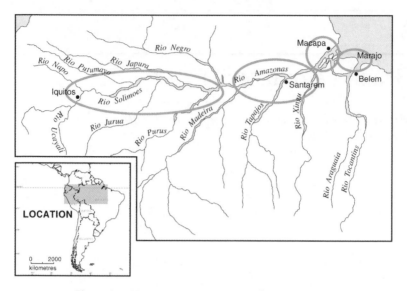

Figure 3.1 The Amazon Valley, showing PLEC sites

between different sections of the river. The pulse of the annual flood is the main variable for most of the length of the river. Its mean amplitude is about 9–10 m in the upper sections of the river, falling to about 8 m at Santarém. Below this, in the delta and estuary sections, the twice-daily tidal pulse becomes dominant, with a normal amplitude of 2.4 m at spring tides and 1.7 m at neaps near Macapá, rising to higher levels when the river flood is added and/or is amplified by exceptional high tides.

The PLEC Amazon cluster has been organized to capture the regional diversity in ecological characteristics, settlement, and resource management. The cluster works at three main sites on the floodplain of the lower reach of the Amazon River and at a fourth site at Iquitos in the Peruvian Amazon (Figure 3.1). These sites are located to sample the major regional environments of the floodplain: the seasonal and tidal grasslands of Marajó Island in the estuary, the tidally flooded forests of the delta, the seasonally inundated savannas of the lower Amazon, and the seasonally flooded forests of Iquitos on the upper Amazon. The Peruvian site, which had no GEF funding, is separately described in Chapter 11.

Evolution of the cluster

An initial PLEC cluster in Brazilian Amazonia was formed in 1992–1993, linking together what were then four separately funded research and extension projects. One of these came to an end in 1995 and another was withdrawn from PLEC, leaving two main groups – one working near the mouth of the river on either side of Macapá, and one in the lower-middle Amazon near the city of Santarém. A third, smaller, group was later added on the island of Marajó in the delta region. From 1995 onward funds for work in Brazil were administered through an NGO (Instituto de Pesquisa Ambiental da Amazonia – IPAM) at the Nucleo de Altos Estudios Amazonicos, Universidade Federal de Pará, at Belém. Although GEF-PLEC support has funded all core project activities, approximately 75 per cent of the funds used for implementing demonstration activities in Brazil have come from other sources, in Brazil and abroad. The availability of money from the other sources greatly helped team members devote time to PLEC activities without encountering undue difficulties in their home institutions.

Many PLEC-Amazonia team members have spent most of their lives looking for ways to promote the enhanced well-being of rural Amazonians while also ensuring that biodiversity and environmental services are conserved for future generations. An important characteristic of the team is its composition: Amazonians, non-Amazonian Brazilians, and other nationalities, specialists in anthropology, ecology, agronomy, geography, forestry, and sociology from three non-Brazilian and seven Brazilian institutions. Several members (including the head of the cluster) are the sons and daughters of rural Amazonians, and all members have previously worked in other related projects in several floodplain regions. Included as integral members of the team are a large number of floodplain farmers, or *ribeirinhos*, and leaders of *ribeirinho* organizations from 12 different communities in the three sites. The diversity of the team has helped it to implement PLEC's complex agenda, including its demonstration activities over the five years of the project.

While the number of researchers and field assistants in the team changed little over the period of GEF funding, the numbers of expert farmers, students, and technicians involved increased substantially. The third year of the project saw an especially large expansion of the expert farmer and student members of the team, from nine to 24 and eight to 36 respectively. This increase reflected and made possible a significant expansion of the number of demonstration activities at the three sites.

Since the beginning of the project, PLEC-Amazonia has been working with selected expert farmers, individuals from NGOs, rural extension agencies, local universities, rural unions, and environmental agencies. A combination of household surveys following farmers in their daily activities and other in-field activities have helped the team to identify a group of exceptional expert farmers who use biodiversity-enhancing and economically rewarding production and management technologies. Team members identified, selected, and built partnerships with 44 expert farmers in the three *várzea* sites. Expert farmers work closely with the team, which is composed of eight field assistants, seven researchers, and 29 students. A total of 136 agricultural, agroforestry, and forest management systems and 36 conservation practices that are economically rewarding and ecologically friendly were identified. Of these, 19 systems and 13 conservation practices were demonstrated by expert farmers. Results of more than five years of work showed that PLEC's demonstration method of "farmers learning from expert farmers" is an effective and realistic approach to furthering the conservation of biodiversity while enhancing the livelihoods of rural Amazonians.

PLEC-Amazonia emerged at a time when Brazilian society was taking important measures toward implementing the Convention on Biological Diversity. It is one of the many projects implemented by governmental and non-governmental agencies that aim to find solutions to the complex problem of biodiversity erosion. While most GEF projects are working in protected areas, PLEC-Amazonia is entirely working outside conventional protected areas and has tested its demonstration methods for more than five years.

The processes of exchange of knowledge between expert farmers and participant farmers have been thoroughly documented by members of the team. Agroforestry systems, such as "banana *emcapoeirada*" that allows farmers to produce bananas despite the ravages of moko disease, are among several production systems that help farmers not only to increase biodiversity in their fields but also to solve problems of disease and pests.[1] Forest management systems that enrich fallows with timbers, fruits, and other valuable species have also been demonstrated by expert farmers. Conservation practices, such as the restoration of riparian forests by farm families in Amapá sites, have greatly increased local populations of shrimp and fish and increased household incomes. Similarly, the establishment of lake reserves near the city of Santarém has improved environments and livelihoods. The conversion of degraded pastures and agricultural lands into palm forests on Marajó Island has led to increased production of açaí fruits and other important economic products. These in turn have boosted household incomes. PLEC-Amazonia has also made major advances in quantifying agrobiodiversity, fish diversity, and other forms of biological diversity found in the landholdings of farmers as well as in village lake and forest reserves. Technological diversity is an important and valuable resource for rural Brazilian society in its quest to achieve sustainable development and successfully implement the Rio Convention on Biological Diversity signed in 1992.

Várzea *environment and site selection*

PLEC-Amazonia works among 234 *ribeirinho* communities. Approximately 55,000 farmers have been directly or indirectly affected by PLEC-Amazonia work in the three *várzea* sites. It was decided to focus work on *várzea* environments because historically most of the rural population live on or near the whitewater floodplains and the *várzea* provides fish and other critical biological resources. Unfortunately, the expansion of buffalo ranching, uncontrolled and destructive timber extraction, and other modern unsustainable practices are accelerating the depletion of *várzea* resources and producing massive migration of *ribeirinhos* to shanty towns on the periphery of Amazonian cities. The steady loss of population is allowing large-scale cattle ranchers to expand their operations and convert biodiversity-rich *várzea* habitats to pastures. As a direct impact of changes in land use several important habitats for plant and animal species have been destroyed, and species such as the giant pirarucu fish have been over-fished.

Várzea environments are the most dynamic in Amazonia; their natural and social landscapes are constantly changing. The three PLEC sites are located in areas with very different patterns. Differences in the kind, frequency, and duration of floods produce clearly differentiated landscapes, ecosystems, and biological diversity in the Santarém, Amapá, and Marajó sites. The landscape of Santarém is characterized by wide and shallow lakes. Most of these lakes are totally connected to the main river during flood season and totally disconnected during the dry season. In contrast, the Marajó landscape features no lakes but small streams and swamp areas during the dry season, while during the rainy season the entire site is flooded. In the estuarine *várzea* areas of Amapá there are very few and very small lakes, but the landscape is composed of several different kinds of riverine environments and ecosystems. Some of the most common ecosystems are permanently flooded savannas known locally as *campos alagados*. Swamp savannas are very critical environments in the Amapá estuarine *várzea* because they serve as reproduction and resting grounds for fish, birds, turtles, and other wildlife, but they are threatened by the expansion of buffalo ranches.

Seasonal variation on the *várzea* is driven by the twin rhythms of the flood and precipitation regimes. The combination of these patterns results in two distinct seasons, referred to locally as *verão* (summer), or the dry season when water levels are falling, and *inverno* (winter), the rainy season, when water levels are rising. The relatively slow rise and fall have contributed to the evolution of a floodplain flora and fauna adapted to take advantage of both terrestrial and aquatic phases. Many plant species produce fruits and nuts during the flood season, and many species of fish, birds, and wildlife have adapted to take advantage of these resources. Despite the similarity in flood and rain regimes among the three sites, each has unique and important environmental conditions and ecological processes.

The interaction between the annual flood and precipitation regimes is critical to *ribeirinhos* in selecting and scheduling their activities. Farmers in all three sites cultivate most crops during the period when river levels are low and rains are relatively light. Production of annual crops is limited largely to the six months between June and December.

While *ribeirinhos* cope remarkably well with the complexities of floods – even Santarém's eight-metre changes in water level – it is variation in the timing and intensity of floods and rains that make farming in *várzea* environments a very risky activity. In Santarém, in years when unexpected rises in the river level (locally known as *repiquetes*) occur during low-river-level season, agricultural fields can be severely affected. *Repiquetes* can last only three days or a week, but they destroy all annual crops planted on silt and sand bars and the production of beans and other crops falls to very low levels. But in years with *repiquetes*, *ribeirinhos* expect not a very high annual flood, and therefore bananas and cassava fields are usually not damaged and production is higher than in years when floods are very high.

Farmers in the Amapá site are affected by periodic but unpredictable high tides known locally as *lançantes*. These produce floods that cover even the high levees, with the result that farmers can lose their annual crops and the production of fruits is greatly reduced. During such years shrimp and fish tend to be abundant, and constitute the main source of household income. In addition, farmers usually extract more timber from their landholdings. Farmers in Ilha Marajó also expect to lose their annual crops in years when rains are too early or too late, but to improve the production of palm fruits and other agroforestry crops.

These "trade-offs" show how important biodiversity and agrodiversity are in the household economies. In all three sites, the diversity of resource use and conservation practices helps *ribeirinhos* cope with economic uncertainty and extreme changes in flood and rain patterns. *Ribeirinhos* not only have a large and complex tool-box of management technologies, but they keep developing new technologies and using new production strategies. Management systems and conservation practices are directed towards both short-term economic production and maintenance of a wide resource base. Agrodiversity helps *ribeirinhos* to "produce to conserve and conserve to produce". The existing agrobiodiversity and other forms of biodiversity found in local landholdings cannot be appreciated without understanding the diversity and sophisticated knowledge and practice of the local farmers. PLEC's demonstration activities have used and built upon this wealth of knowledge and experience.

PLEC activities

Identifying, understanding, and evaluating local production and conservation patterns

PLEC-Amazonia has built its demonstration activities on a solid base of knowledge obtained through surveys and inventories. Initial characterization of sites was done through household surveys, inventories of biodiversity, and land surveys. Standard landscape ecology methods were used for understanding patterns of land-cover change and variation of biodiversity in space and time. In addition, PLEC members collected historical and geographic information from local archives. Long interviews and field observations were conducted to understand how *ribeirinhos* respond to changes and how such changes influence existing biological, cultural, and technological diversity. Participant observation methods were employed to record, understand, and evaluate biodiversity-rich production and conservation practices.

Through household surveys and extensive interviews and observation, the team identified and recorded in the database a number of agricultural, agroforestry, and forest management technologies developed and used by *ribeirinhos* in the three sites.[2] Of the 325 surveyed households, a total of 136 production and management systems that are biodiversity-friendly and economically attractive were identified. The team also identified 36 conservation practices that were employed effectively.

After evaluation, the team selected 19 practices to promote through demonstration activities (Table 3.1). They were selected because they provide important sources of income for families and help maintain high levels of agrobiodiversity in their landholdings. In the first year the team focused on four systems to test ways of knowledge exchange among farmers. They were also testing the "farmers learning from expert farmers" dissemination method that later was used within most of the PLEC project. The positive response from farmers allowed them to select other management systems as part of demonstration activities. Over the five years PLEC-Amazonia more than quadrupled the number of systems and techniques demonstrated.

While it is difficult to differentiate production from conservation activities in *ribeirinho* societies, PLEC-Amazonia identified some specific conservation practices that concentrated more on resource protection than use. Conservation practices were defined as:

- strategies and management operations used by *ribeirinhos* for the establishment of household, village, or inter-village protected areas
- rules regulating access to and use of resources, particularly resources that are overexploited or endangered.

During the last five years PLEC-Amazonia has demonstrated only 13 of the 36 documented conservation practices (Table 3.2), four of which were integrated into demonstration activities at the beginning of the project. The difficulty of monitoring the adoption of conservation practices and the suspicions that were created among farmers when specific practices were promoted are some of the reasons why the team decided to include only a few of them as demonstration activities.

Table 3.1 Systems and techniques demonstrated and promoted by expert farmers

Production technologies and practices demonstrated	1998	1999	2000	2001–2002
Banana *emcapoeirada* – agroforestry system	×	×	×	×
Madeira em capoeiras – forest management system	×	×	×	×
Afastamento-cedo – forest management by thinning young fallow	×	×	×	×
Crescimento de solos – agriculture system	×	×	×	×
Mudas em paxubas – agriculture system		×	×	×
Jogo de semente na mata – a system of managing natural regeneration in forests and fallows		×	×	×
Guarda sementes em chimbo – a system for storing seeds		×	×	×
Mandioca na várzea – an agriculture system for the production of less flood-tolerant crops		×	×	×
Afastamento – a forest management technique			×	×
Sameamento de semente – an agroforestry technique			×	×
Producao de mudas em roças – a technique for the production of seedlings in fields			×	×
Legumens em hortas – a multicropping system for the production of vegetables			×	×
Coleta da flor de açai – an agroforestry technique			×	×
Transplante de mudas da mata no quintal – enrichment agroforestry and forest systems			×	×
Como usar tucupi para controlar formigas de fogo – a technique for controlling pests using cassava juices			×	×
Enraicemento de buriti para formacao de solos – a system for building soils				×
Copas para producao de melancias – an agriculture system for the production of water-melon				×
Inga com cipo – an agroforestry system for the production of maracuja and other fruits				×
Limpa arvore – a forest management technique for managing individual trees				×

Expert farmers and demonstrations

A predominant philosophy guiding past and current extension programmes is that farmers must be taught how to farm properly. PLEC-Amazonia began with a different premise, by questioning *ribeirinhos* on how they

Table 3.2 Number of conservation practices demonstrated

Conservation practices demonstrated	1998	1999	2000	2001–2002
Toma conta de ninhais – a conservation practice for the conservation of habitat for resident and migratory birds	×	×	×	×
Moradia de bichos – a conservation practice for the establishment of household reserves	×	×	×	×
Restoração de capims nos lagos – a conservation practice for the restoration of meadows in lakes when the lakes fully drain away	×	×	×	×
Proteção de tabluleiros – a conservation practice for the conservation of beaches as nesting grounds of turtles	×	×	×	×
Acordos de pesca – a conservation practice for regulating fishing rights in the communities		×	×	×
Proteção de fruteiras nos lagos – a conservation practice for the enrichment of lake vegetation with fruit species		×	×	×
Proteção dos corpos d'água na seca – a conservation practice for protecting vegetation in streams and lakes during the dry season			×	×
Recuperação da mata ciliar – a conservation practice for the conservation and management of riparian forests for the production of shrimp and fish			×	×
Control de timbó – a conservation practice that prohibits the uses of toxic resins for fishing			×	×
Proteção de filhos de tatarugas – a conservation practice for the reintroduction of the endangered giant river turtles in lakes			×	×
Proteção de buritizal – a conservation practice for the conservation of palm forests			×	×
Deixa arvores mães – a conservation practice for protecting seed trees of endangered species in the landholdings and forest			×	×
Proteção dos campos alagados – a conservation practice for protecting permanently flooded savannas from the expansion of buffalo ranches				×

learn and adapt production and management techniques to their own environments and needs. The great majority replied that they learn by interacting among themselves. PLEC-Amazonia built upon these existing patterns and facilitated a "farmers learning from expert farmers" approach to dissemination of conservationist production practices.

Table 3.3 Number of expert farmers, demonstration sites, and production systems and conservation practices demonstrated

Components methodology	1998	1999	2000	2001–2002
Expert farmers	12	16	36	44
Demonstration subsites	18	36	78	85
Production systems	4	9	16	19
Conservation practices	4	6	12	13

All demonstration activities are conducted following the model of selecting expert farmers to act as instructors and using their fields, fallows, house gardens, and forests as demonstration sites. There was a steady increase in the numbers of selected expert farmers, demonstration sites, and the techniques and conservation practices demonstrated (Table 3.3).

Expert farmer selection was an extended process. Both men and women were included, and not only experts in agricultural production, but also agroforesters, forest managers, fish and shrimp producers, and especially those who integrate many production types and products in diverse and complex systems. Many production practices integrate both terrestrial and aquatic systems – some expert farmers manage forest stands in order to produce fish.

Most expert farmers were integrated as members of the team and were gradually included by governmental and non-governmental agencies as advisers in their conservation and development projects. Seven expert farmers are advising the governor of Amapá on "how to produce to conserve and how to conserve to produce" resources. Several of the production and management systems as well as conservation practices demonstrated by expert farmers have been included as part of rural extension programmes by government and non-government agencies in the three sites. In the Santarém site expert farmers are also advising members of NGOs and government institutions on how to establish community-based protected areas. Expert farmers from the village of São Miguel have been consulted by government officials on how to conserve lake resources and how to enforce community rules that regulate access to and uses of lake resources.

The nature and composition of the PLEC-Amazonia team have played a key role in the successful implementation and monitoring of demonstration activities. Local communities have appreciated the inclusion of expert farmers in the team and have interacted more favourably with other members of the team when expert farmers have accompanied them. The selection of field assistants from villages has also played a key role in advancing the exchange of technologies and germplasm during and after demonstration activities. Negotiations and the establishment of partnerships with the selected expert farmers have been aided by the participation of local researchers who have roots in rural communities.

Methods of demonstration

The integration of expert farmers into all phases of demonstration activities made possible identification of several specific approaches. Initially, the team planned to conduct demonstration activities as part of *encontros*, which are community or inter-community meetings where village-related problems, including those affecting production and conservation of resources, are discussed. The team's expert farmers suggested that demonstration activities be conducted using two other forms of social gatherings. The first, called *mutirão*, are shared labour groups organized by members of households to help each other with activities like making fields, planting, and other production or management activities. The second type is *visitas*, which are typically gatherings of families or close friends. In all three events expert farmers are the leading figures and the ones who invite participants to visit demonstration sites. The numbers of *ribeirinho* participants in these demonstration activities are shown in Table 3.4.

Most participating farmers have begun testing the techniques that they learned and observed. They do not necessarily copy the technologies but combine these ideas with their own and create new and original systems and techniques. *Ribeirinhos* usually incorporate the learned technologies only after a long process of experimentation, and they have increased the diversity of technologies used. At the Amapá site during the five years since the first four production systems were demonstrated, participant farmers developed multiple new systems (Table 3.5).

Demonstration activities have helped farmers and communities find solutions to specific problems. Farmers have applied enrichment and other systems to restore land degraded by buffalo and other activities. Production of beans and other annual crops has increased and the fertility of levee soils was improved by farmers from Santarém planting murin grasses. At all three sites, house gardens have been enriched with species that are flood

Table 3.4 Number of demonstration activities and farmer participants

Demonstration activities	Average number per year	Average participants per year	Average participants per event
Encontros	15	975	72
Mutirãos	104	1,890	19
Visitas	82	1,240	21

Table 3.5 Systems and techniques demonstrated by expert farmers and modified by participant farmers

Demonstrated techniques	Objective	Recommended techniques	Main adaptive components
Banana *emcapoeirada* agroforestry system	Managing moko disease in bananas	*Sororoca*; *pariri*; banana	*Açaí*; banana *Fruteiras*; banana *Madeira*; banana Combinations of the above with banana
Building up soils above tide level	Production of cassava and other crops less tolerant to tidal flooding	Keep sediments and organic matter from eroding during high tides using fences	Use of logs rather than fences Placing palm leaves around the highest sections of the field Accumulation of soils around tree trunks Accumulation of wood residues from sawmills
Enriching fallows	Production of fruits and timber	Thinning and removal of vines	Thinning; planting Removal of vines; broadcasting seeds Thinning; broadcasting seeds Combining all above
Managing forests	Production of fruits, timber, and medicines	Removal of vines and formation of gaps (*clareras*)	Gaps and broadcasting seed Removal of vines and transplanting seedlings along trails Gaps and managing of seed dispersal during high tide Combinations of the above techniques

tolerant and produce fruit for fish, agoutis, and other wildlife during flood periods.

Another important result is the planning and execution of collective action in the communities to restore degraded vegetation around lakes and floating meadows. Farmers from the villages located in Ilha Ituqui (Santarém) have successfully restored lake vegetation in their communities. Similarly, farmers from Ilha Marajó enlarged and diversified their agroforestry sites. Perhaps the most significant result of collective or community actions that emerged as a result of demonstration activities is the establishment of family, village, or inter-village lake and forest reserves in the three

PLEC sites. Farmers have used these reserves for the protection and reproduction of endangered, overexploited, or rare wildlife, birds, and plant
species. One important result is the reintroduction of the giant river turtle
into the lakes of the communities in Ilha Ituqui from Ilha Saõ Miguel. In
Amapá farmers protected and managed the resting and reproduction
grounds of migratory and resident aquatic birds, locally known as *ninhaes*.

Farmers' participation was greatly facilitated by maintaining a very flexible structure and direction to demonstration activities. Excessive formality
in establishing partnerships with expert farmers limited the success of
demonstration activities at the beginning of the project. It was learned that
exchange of most knowledge and experiences among farmers takes place in
an informal environment.

Based on successes in the three sites, PLEC-Amazonia organized four
demonstration activities at the regional level. *Ribeirinhos* from *várzea*
regions as far away as Peru participated in these events. Residents from
protected areas such as the Mamirauá Sustainable Development Reserve
also attended.

Other capacity-building activities

Beginning in the second year of the project PLEC-Amazonia conducted
demonstration activities for youths at community-based "family schools"
and other publicly run schools in and near the PLEC sites. From 2000–2001
a series of demonstration activities for rural extension agents, students from
Amazonian universities, researchers, and politicians were successfully conducted. Data collection was an important component of student training
over the five years. Fifty-seven undergraduates, 10 masters' students, and six
Brazilian and four foreign PhD students have been trained since 1998.

PLEC-Amazonia also organized training activities for supervisors working in environmental agencies, rural extension agents, politicians, and
researchers. The training activities included on-farm training at the demonstrations sites, sessions with expert farmers on household surveys and in-
field observations, week-long training sessions in field methods, database
organization and data analysis, and workshops. The majority of the training
activities were organized for rural extension agents and supervisors.[3]

Agrobiodiversity in a dynamic landscape

PLEC-Amazonia continued monitoring changes in agrobiodiversity
throughout the five years of the project. The picture of the *várzea* as a very
dynamic environment was confirmed and these data were stored in the
database. There are clear trends in the levels of agrobiodiversity that are
produced, managed, and conserved at the three *várzea* sites. Farmers are

Table 3.6 Changes in agrobiodiversity, number, and size of fields of 40 sampled families

Categories	1998	2001
Species planted	18	33
Varieties planted	49	72
Average number of fields made	3	1
Average size of fields made (ha)	2.8	0.5

continually responding to environmental and socio-economic changes by varying what they plant, manage, and conserve. Agrobiodiversity increased from 1998 to 2001 (Table 3.6).

Agricultural products are produced in large industrial plantations in the south of Brazil, and are generally cheap and of higher quality than those produced in Amazonia. These flood urban markets in Amazonia and small-holders find they cannot compete with falling prices for rice, beans, and other crops. Household income in all sites is in a transitional phase, shifting from a dependence on agricultural products to agroforestry and forest products. By planting more species and varieties of crops in their small fields, *ribeirinhos* increased agrobiodiversity and introduced to the market new and fresh products not sold in the supermarkets, including a large variety of spices, fruits, roots, grains, and other products.

Rural Amazonians plant and manage large numbers of fruit, timber, medicinal plants, and tree crops in their house gardens, fallows, and forests. Results of inventories of all trees with DBH (diameter at breast height) greater than or equal to 2.5 cm conducted in 20 ha each of managed and unmanaged fallows showed a larger number of species per hectare in the managed (72) compared with the unmanaged (41) fallows. Similar variation was found when managed (84 species) and unmanaged (55 species) forests were inventoried (all trees with DBH greater than or equal to 10 cm in landholdings of 48 families).

The general trend is that smallholders tend to increase levels of bio-diversity as part of a strategy to increase the number of outputs available. The aggregated use-values explain the differences in species composition among managed and unmanaged fallows and forest. Based on these and other results, it was found that despite widespread assumptions to the contrary, *ribeirinhos* are increasing rather than reducing levels of biodiversity in *várzea* environments.

Changes in the forests and fallows

Diverse and complex agroforestry and forest management systems are con-tinually developed to change the composition and structure of forests and fallows. The transformation of the vegetation and innovation of technologies is facilitated by the increased value of forest and fallow products in the markets. Many farmers manage and extract some timbers and conduct pre-harvest operations to avoid excessive damage to the forests, thus enhancing production. They tend to remove vines at least three months before cutting a tree for timber and broadcast seeds or plant seedlings of valuable species in areas where timber was extracted. In all three sites farmers are making small openings (*clareiras*) in their fallows for planting semi-perennial species such as bananas.

PLEC-Amazonia found that the forest areas that are part of the landholdings of smallholders reflect successive management operations that begin at the field stage and continue into fallow and forest stages. Under this land-use system agriculture, agoforestry, and forest activities are closely linked and difficult to differentiate. Expert farmers explained on several occasions that this integrated and multiphased system allows them to produce and conserve resources. By understanding the farmer's logic of production PLEC-Amazonia managed to look beyond the use-values of biodiversity and incorporate various ecological values, particularly the multiple functions of maintaining healthy and productive *várzea* ecosystems and landscapes.

Biodiversity indices estimated for selected forests, fallows, and house gardens show that *ribeirinhos* maintain biodiversity-rich landholdings (Table 3.7). Based on the estimated diversity indices, fallows have values ($H' = 0.92$) that indicate more even distribution of species than forests and house gardens. The presence of a large number of semi-perennial crops such as banana, yams, and pineapples is one of the reasons why managed fallows show such "evenness". Inventory data showed that people also maintain a low number of individuals of several non-commercial species to create habitat for wildlife, particularly agoutis and several species of land birds.

PLEC-Amazonia found great variation in agrobiodiversity and other forms of biological diversity produced, managed, or conserved by smallholders. Each landholding contains different numbers of species and den-

Table 3.7 Biodiversity indicators per land-use stage in *ribeirinhos'* landholdings

Land-use stage	Number of samples	Avg. sample size (ha)	Avg. number individuals	Avg. number species	Shannon index (H')
Fallows	110	0.3	1,108	69	0.92
Forests	22	1.5	862	105	1.05
House gardens	125	0.5	743	53	1.16

Note: All individuals greater than or equal to 2.5 cm DBH were inventoried.

JOLIET JUNIOR COLLEGE LIBRARY
JOLIET, ILLINOIS

sities of individuals. This diversity is an important resource. Farmers see the use-values of biodiversity and its multifunctionality in the ecosystem and landscape. The presence of several pioneer species in fallows and house gardens helps control light intensity for the regeneration and growth of several shade-tolerant species. Likewise, the management of fallows is critical to the composition and structure of subsequent forests.

House gardens are one of the most important sources of germplasm and have enormous conservation value because most of them contain individuals of tropical cedar and other overexploited species. Fallow, house gardens, and forest vegetation management for income and ecological services explains why *ribeirinho* landholdings contain high levels of biodiversity in contrast to other land uses such as ranching.

Species richness estimated for a sample of fallows and house gardens showed *ribeirinho* landholdings are very diverse (Figure 3.2). Fallows and house gardens with low values have high densities of one species, such as *açai* in the case of Amapá and Ilha Marajó, and mango trees in the case of Santarém (Ilha Saõ Miguel). House gardens and fallows with high values of species richness usually belonged to expert farmers and were the ones selected as demonstration sites. By quantifying the levels of biodiversity, PLEC-Amazonia recognized smallholders as stewards of biodiversity.

Impacts of demonstration activities

Although the results are still preliminary, PLEC demonstration activities have had a major impact on household income and other aspects of the livelihood of *ribeirinhos*. At a different level, expert farmers of PLEC are becoming major players in planning and implementing integrated development and conservation programmes. The PLEC approach of working with expert farmers and promoting their technologies is an innovative idea that has opened new opportunities for farmers to be represented in influential political circles and to express their concerns and ideas on how conservation and rural development should be done. By participating in the mainstream of political decisions, expert farmers are not only changing conventional approaches to rural development and conservation, but also educating politicians, technocrats, and the rest of society. For instance, politicians are appreciating the link between biodiversity and the livelihoods of rural populations.

Impacts on biodiversity levels

An increase in the levels of agrobiodiversity and other forms of biological diversity in the landholdings of *ribeirinhos* is one of the main impacts pro-

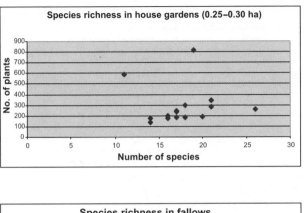

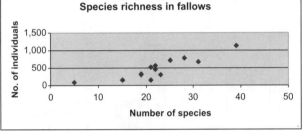

Figure 3.2 Variation in individuals versus species richness among house gardens and fallows

duced by the demonstration activities conducted in the last five years. Bio-diversity inventories show an increase in numbers of species and varieties (Table 3.8). Exchange of germplasm and incorporations of new species, par-ticularly from forests, have facilitated this.

Another important impact is the enrichment of young and old forests with valuable species, including the overexploited tropical cedar. Forest inventories conducted in a sample of 15 ha of managed young and old forests and in an equal sample area of unmanaged young and mature forests owned by 48 families showed a higher number of species in man-aged as compared to unmanaged forests (Figure 3.3).

The implementation of PLEC demonstration activities has also had a major impact on conservation and the number of areas protected by vil-lagers. Family forest reserves have increased from 68 ha to 260 ha, forests from 212 to 507 ha, and the number of lakes from seven to 32 (940 ha). The establishment of family and village reserves is helping to restore the popu-lation of several overexploited and endangered species (Table 3.9). For instance, in a sample of nine lake reserves the adult populations of the endangered giant pirarucu fish (more than 1.5 m size) and giant river turtle

Table 3.8 Increase in levels of biodiversity in the landholdings of 72 *ribeirinhos* who participated in demonstration activities

Land-use type	1998		2001–2002	
	Species	Varieties	Species	Varieties
Fields	14	45	31	83
Fallows	27	39	58	92
Forests	78	95	117	134
House gardens	22	42	46	92

Note: The 72 sample *ribeirinho* families were selected from among the participants at demonstration activities where expert farmers demonstrated the 19 selected production and management systems.

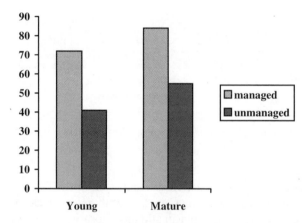

Figure 3.3 Average number of tree species per hectare found in managed and unmanaged young and mature forests

Table 3.9 Changes in population of endangered and overexploited species from 1998 to 2001–2002

Species	1998	2001–2002
Giant pirarucu fish (endangered)	32	170
Giant river turtle (endangered)	19	220
Tropical cedar tree	24	72
Virola tree	18	125

Note: The average area of the selected landholdings was 32 ha. Each landholding contained an average area of 0.6 ha of fields, 13 ha of fallow, 1.4 ha of house garden, and 17 ha of forest.

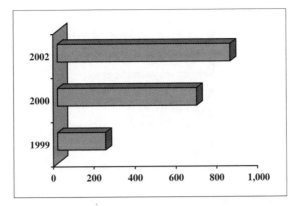

Figure 3.4 Average annual income (US$) from harvesting fruits, construction materials, and other products
Note: Sampled from 68 managed fallows owned by 32 families who participated in demonstration activities where the *enriquecimento de capoeira* forest system was demonstrated. Average was estimated from data collected between January 1999 and January 2002.

(more than 45 kg) increased greatly by 2001–2002. Similarly, the average number of juveniles per hectare of cedar and virola trees has increased in the sample of 15 forest reserves.

Impacts on household income

The adoption and adaptation of farming technologies and conservation practices demonstrated by expert farmers are having direct impacts on household economies and livelihoods. The assimilation or adaptation of the *enriquecimento de capoeira* agroforestry system, for instance, has had a distinct impact. The income of 32 surveyed families practising the system more than tripled from 1999 to 2001–2002 (Figure 3.4).

The increase in household incomes created a major impact on their neighbours. In the three PLEC sites most *ribeirinhos* considered fallows to be unproductive and they never expected to earn money by managing them. This perception is gradually changing. Those participating in the *enriquecimento de capoeira* system are now producing several fruits, medicinal plants, and even timber in their fallows.

The promotion of the banana *emcapoeirada* agroforestry system has increased the income of 34 surveyed families by more than seven times from the sale of bananas (Figure 3.5). Farmers manage moko disease rather than trying to eliminate it. At the same time they are increasing the levels of agrobiodiversity and other forms of biodiversity by producing bananas in

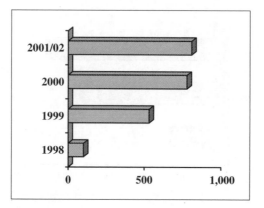

Figure 3.5 Average annual income (US$) of 34 households who participated in demonstration activities of the banana *emcapoeirada* system

agroforestry plots rather than in agricultural fields. The numbers of products for home consumption and the market are augmented, and families are earning income by selling bananas, sugar cane, yams, palm leaves, and other products. This agroforestry system also helps farmers create and maintain habitat for large rodents such as agoutis and capybaras which are an important source of protein.

The banana *emcapoeirada* system promotion has also had major impacts at a regional scale. The Amapá *várzea* region was the main centre for banana production in Amazonia until moko disease destroyed all banana plantations approximately 15 years ago. Production in the state of Amapá in the late 1970s averaged 150 tonnes/month. After moko disease appeared in the early 1980s this declined to an average of 16 tonnes/month. Data collected in Amapá show a major increase in the production of bananas from the region since the system was promoted in demonstration activities (Figure 3.6). Currently, the average monthly production of bananas is more than 90 tonnes/month, which is nearing pre-moko disease levels.

Impacts on behaviour

PLEC-Amazonia's demonstration activities have impacted on the behaviour of farmers, extension agents, politicians, and other social groups in relation to *várzea* environments and biodiversity. For instance, the patterns of land use among smallholders are changing (Figure 3.7). *Ribeirinhos* are making smaller and fewer fields and managing their fallows and forests more for the production of a variety of products. By converting their landholdings into agroforestry plots and managed forest areas, farmers are increasing habitats for wildlife, fish, shrimp, and other organisms. With less

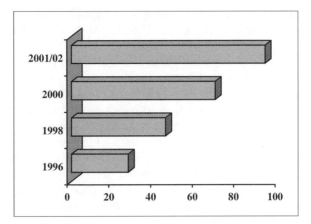

Figure 3.6 Average tonnes of banana produced using the banana *emcapoeirada* system in Amapá

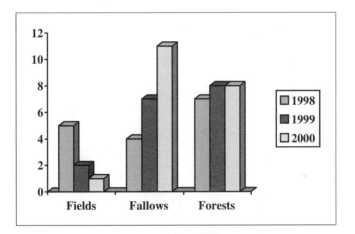

Figure 3.7 Changes in area of fields, managed fallows, and forests in the landholdings
Note: Survey of landholdings of 78 farmers who participated in demonstration activities where the natural regeneration system was demonstrated by the expert farmer. The average property size was 28 ha.

forest areas converted to agricultural fields there is less burning of slashed vegetation and a reduction in the amount of CO_2 produced.

The promotion of economically rewarding and biodiversity-friendly systems has also impacted on the number of farmers engaged in sustainable use of *várzea* biodiversity. The majority of farmers from the three PLEC sites have been practising the *enriquecimento de capoeira* system since it was demonstrated by the expert farmer (Figure 3.8). Most of them are close friends and family members of the expert farmer. When their neighbours saw that they were making money they also quickly adopted the system.

The PLEC-Amazonia work has had major impacts on conservation and development agencies. The model of environmental education programmes conducted as part of demonstration activities by PLEC members in Santarém has been adopted by governmental and non-governmental agencies. Similarly, government agencies in the state of Amapá are adopting the demonstration model for conducting rural extension. PLEC-Amazonia also has impacted on how politicians consider developing rural Amazonia. Politicians and government officials consult members of the team on development and conservation issues that affect biodiversity and the livelihood of rural populations. PLEC-Amazonia has presented several proposals using smallholder technologies and conservation practices as a basis for development and conservation activities in *várzea* communities.

Biodiversity at the Amapá sites[4]

Mazagão and Ipixuna

The Amazonia cluster tested the hypothesis that biodiversity is the result of complex interactions of natural and anthropogenic processes. It measured

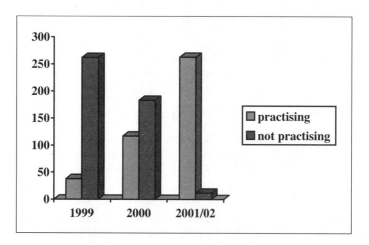

Figure 3.8 Increase in the number of farmers practising the *enriquecimento de capoeira* system after participating in demonstration activities
Note: 300 households have been monitored since 1999.

and monitored the levels of biodiversity produced, managed, maintained, or conserved by smallholders within their landholdings. The identification, quantification, and classification of the existing land-use stages (LUSs) and field types (FTs) were done using information collected from a sample of 50 landholdings: 26 in Mazagão and 24 in Ipixuna. Data were gathered during an average of two visits per year to each landholding (at the beginning and end of the agriculture season) for five years. For each landholding PLEC recorded the number, area, and location, in relation to the river or house, of LUSs and FTs. With members of the families (men, women, and children), researchers made hand-drafted maps for each landholding representing its location within the landscape. The average area of the selected landholdings was 32 ha. Each landholding contained an average area of 0.6 ha of fields, 13 ha of fallow, 1.4 ha of house garden, and 17 ha of forest. The increase in demand for *açai* fruit and timber in the market as well as the decline in prices for agricultural products have changed the role of agriculture, agroforestry, and forest extraction in the household economy.

Management in the fields

In 1998 there were 25 and 23 fields respectively within the landholdings at Ipixuna and Mazagão. The data from 1999 show that the number of fields declined to 12 and 18. In both cases fields were left to become fallows for the production of several agroforestry and forest products such as *açai* fruit and *pau mulato* (*Calycophyllum spruceanum*), a valuable fast-growing timber species.

While the number of fields declined, the average size of fields remained at 0.6 ha and the levels of agrobiodiversity remained constant. Farmers were planting crops, but also protecting the seedlings and saplings of several forest and agroforest species. While a similar number of species and varieties were planted in both sites, smallholders from Mazagão protected more than twice the number of species and varieties than the farmers of Ipixuna (Table 3.10).

Species and varieties observed in fields include grains, tubers, fruit, and medicinal and timber species. A considerable number are perennial. The average number of species and varieties of crops found in each of the sampled fields is higher than those reported in fields owned by smallholders within colonization projects and areas owned by cattle ranchers (Anderson and Ioris 1992).

The protection or planting of timber, fruit, and other forest or agroforestry species in the fields is changing the agrodiversity and other farming technologies used. Although fields are still made using swidden techniques, researchers observed that most farmers are opting not to burn the slash. They can see that seeds of valuable agroforestry species such as *maracuja do mato* and forest species such as tropical cedar are destroyed by

Table 3.10 Number of species and varieties planted and protected in fields by small-holders in Mazagão and Ipixuna

| | 1998 | | 1999 | |
	Mazagão	Ipixuna	Mazagão	Ipixuna
Sampled fields	28	22	36	25
Planted annuals				
Number of species	15	19	21	19
Number of varieties	60	53	66	58
Planted perennials				
Number of species	10	14	16	14
Number of varieties	21	26	38	26
Protected annuals				
Number of species	8	3	8	5
Number of varieties	12	5	12	8
Protected perennials				
Number of species	22	10	25	12
Number of varieties	38	15	41	17

Note: The reported numbers of species and varieties for 1999 are accumulative, including the values from 1998 and the new data from 1999.

the fire, preventing natural regeneration. Similarly, weeding operations tend to be more selective and less intensive. When growing maize, beans, and other annual crops the majority of farmers do not weed.

Changes in farming operations and technologies are helping small-holders to manage seedlings and saplings of tree and shrub species in their fields. In agricultural fields it is common to find protected agroforestry and forest species naturally regenerating, both randomly and in clusters. Most farmers explain that they are protecting the seedlings of timber species, *açai* palm, and other valuable species to enrich their future fallows and forests.

Management of the fallows

Based on the performance of the protected seedlings in fields, farmers produce two main fallow types: unmanaged fallows (*capoeiras com mato*), where vegetation is low in valuable species; and enriched fallows (*capoeiras contaminadas*), where vegetation is dominated by valuable species. Small-holders use the unmanaged fallows for making fields and manage the enriched fallows for the production of agroforestry and forest products.

Despite the assumption that human intervention in fallows lowers their species richness (Anderson and Ioris 1992), researchers found that the enriched fallows contain similar levels of plant diversity to unmanaged fallows. Inventory results show human intervention in fallow vegetation does not necessarily result in the reduction of plant diversity (Table 3.11). The general trend observed is that smallholders maintain or in some cases

Table 3.11 Average number of species and individuals found in eight enriched fallows and eight unmanaged fallows

Sampled fallows	Area inventoried (ha)		Number of species		Number of individuals	
	Enriched	Unmanaged	Enriched	Unmanaged	Enriched	Unmanaged
Alvino	0.30	0.30	39	23	1,120	528
Hilario	0.25	0.25	22	27	460	321
Juracy	0.30	0.25	19	24	297	317
Nonato	0.25	0.25	19	21	330	314
Tomé 1	0.25	0.30	31	23	674	325
Tomé 2	0.25	0.25	25	19	715	364
Tomé 3	0.25	0.25	23	25	305	298
Zinho	0.25	0.25	22	19	555	312

increase levels of biodiversity as part of a strategy to increase the number of outputs available from the fallows. Of the eight sampled households, six maintain more species in their enriched fallows than in their unmanaged ones and only two have fewer species in their enriched fallows than in their unmanaged ones.

While the difference in the average species richness between enriched (25) and unmanaged (22) fallows is just three species, differences in species composition among enriched fallows are greater than among unmanaged fallows. Such differences in species composition among enriched fallows demonstrate that biodiversity levels vary considerably with the intensity and frequency of the owners' interventions. Alvino maintains over two times more species (39) than Juracy in the same size (0.3 ha) of fallow, while in their unmanaged fallows they maintain similar numbers of species.

The contrast between enriched and unmanaged fallows is also apparent when considering the density of individuals per area and species richness (Table 3.12). Smallholders maintain more individuals of species in enriched (average 557 in 0.26 ha) than in unmanaged (average 347 in 0.26 ha) fallows. Differences among the enriched fallows are greater than among the wild ones (Table 3.11). For instance, Alvino maintained over three times more individuals (1,120) per species than Juracy in the same size (0.3 ha) fallow. Differences in density of individuals are even present in fallows owned by a single family. For example, Tomé maintains varying densities of individuals in his three sampled enriched fallows.

Plant diversity and number of individuals per area and species are clearly influenced by the intensity and frequency of management operations as well as the degree to which the seedlings and saplings of valuable species are managed in the field stage. The results obtained from the floristic and structural analysis are consistent with field observations. Individuals of *imbauba* (*Cecropia membraneaceae*) and other early pioneer species dominate vegetation of unmanaged fallows. Most enriched fallows contain agroforestry species including bananas and several species and varieties of

Table 3.12 Estimated biodiversity indices for enriched fallows

Sampled fallows	Area (ha)	Number of individuals	Number of species	Dmn	Shannon's index (H')
Alvino	0.30	1,120	39	1.17	2.09
Hilario	0.25	460	22	1.03	2.14
Juracy	0.30	297	19	1.10	1.24
Nonato	0.25	330	19	1.05	0.84
Tomé 1	0.25	674	31	1.19	1.85
Tomé 2	0.25	715	25	0.93	1.69
Tomé 3	0.25	305	23	1.32	1.64
Zinho	0.25	555	22	0.89	1.88

citrus. Field observations also show that farmers maintain individuals of economic species at different stages of growth in the same fallows and fields. There are adult *pau mulato* trees near other individuals of the same species in the sapling and seedling stages. These uneven-aged stands create a multiplicity of habitats for other species.

Of the eight sampled enriched fallows only two (Tomé 2 and Tomé 3) had an estimated species richness index (Dmn = 0.93 and 0.89) of less than one, while only one fallow (Nonato) had an estimated Shannon index (H' = 0.84) of less than one (Table 3.12). However, the proximity of the estimated indices to one indicates that there is a correlation (r = 0.94) between the distribution of individuals and species in the enriched fallows.

The rates of abundance and dominance of species in fallows reflect the smallholders' intensive use and management of fallows. Species richness in the enriched fallows shows a strong correlation (r = 0.88) between number of species and number of individuals. The number of trees per area increases when the number of species increases in the fallows.

Although thinning and removal of vines are the main management operations applied to fallows, smallholders are adapting or developing new management techniques. This transformation and innovation of technologies is facilitated by the increased value of forest and fallow products in the markets. In both sites farmers are making small openings (*clareiras*) in their fallows for planting semi-perennial species such as bananas. *Clareiras* are also made to transplant seedlings of desirable species. Seeds of several species, such as tropical cedar and *açai* palm, are collected to broadcast in the fallows. The frequency and intensity of removing termite nests and other operations to control pests are also increasing as a result of the farmers' economic dependence on fallow products. The farmers' decisions to convert fallows into fields or forests are based on several factors, including how well their production of agroforestry products, such as bananas, is faring, or whether forest species, such as *açai* palm, are dominating the vegetation.

Management in the forests

In both sites it was found that forest areas within the landholdings of smallholders are the results of successive management operations that began in the field stage and continued into the fallow and forest stages. Inventories conducted in a sample of 10 ha (five in Mazagão and five in Ipixuna) show a great diversity of species (Table 3.13). In both sites the forests contain high levels of species richness and evenness, but the average number of species (51) found in the Mazagão forests is higher than the average (36) found in Ipixuna (Table 3.13). In contrast, the sampled forests of Ipixuna have more trees (average 1,117) than those of Mazagão (average 1,041). These results reflect the histories of management and resource extraction.

Table 3.13 Diversity in forest samples comparing the number of species, number of individuals, and Shannon index (H′)

	Mazagão				Ipixuna		
Sample plots	Number of species	Number of individuals	H′	Sample plots	Number of species	Number of individuals	H′
1	48	892	2.96	6	26	623	1.66
2	55	1,096	2.66	7	41	1,032	1.91
3	54	1,118	2.43	8	38	1,610	1.68
4	45	778	2.66	9	43	1,696	1.80
5	55	1,322	2.26	10	34	923	1.80

In Mazagão people engage more in forest activities and continually enrich their forest with desirable species of timber, medicinal plants, and fruit. Farmers in Ipixuna concentrate more on agroforestry and the collection of fruit and medicinal products than on timber extraction. Despite the differences, forests in both sites show very high diversity on the Shannon index (Table 3.13). Based on the estimated diversity indices, forests in Mazagão have higher values (average H′ = 2.59) than forests in Ipixuna (average H′ = 1.77).

While forests in Mazagão are richer in species than those in Ipixuna, the two most commercially valued species (*Euterpe oleraceae* and *Calycophyllum spruceanum*) are some of the most dominant and abundant species in both sites. This indicates that people are encouraging the establishment and growth of these and other valuable species in their forests. Similarly, the presence of a high number of timber, fruit, and medicinal species suggests an intensity and frequency of management by local people in both sites. The inventory data also show that people maintain a low number of individuals of several non-commercial species. Among these are pioneer species such as *C. palmata* and *Croton* spp. that play an important role in attracting game animals.

The estimated importance value index (IVI) shows that eight of the 10 most important species found in the forests of Mazagão and Ipixuna produce commercial products. As in the case of managing fallows, people are adapting and developing new and innovative management technologies that correspond to specific environmental and economic conditions and promote the regeneration of species under different light and environmental conditions. For instance, the majority of farmers conduct pre-harvest operations to avoid excessive damage to the forests, thus optimizing production. Among the most recent and innovative pre-harvest operations is the broadcasting of seeds or planting of seedlings of valuable species before cutting timber. Most seedlings are collected from other parts of the forests, though *andiroba* seedlings (*Carapa guianensis*) are mainly produced in house gardens.

Management of the house gardens

Within the house garden category the inhabitants of Mazagão and Ipixuna include orchards, nurseries, medicinal species, vegetables, ornamentals, spices, grasses, and vines, as well as areas for raising domestic animals. The sampled house gardens included most of these categories and all vegetation in them was inventoried. They are rich in species and produce a large variety of products. Little variation in the numbers of species and individuals maintained was observed between sites. Variation becomes apparent when individual house gardens are compared. Based on these observations researchers decided to perform the biodiversity analysis on the pooled sample (Table 3.14). Although results show that house gardens contain high biodiversity, there is a significant difference ($CV = -0.02$) in the number of species and individuals found in each garden. The average number of species found was 17, the maximum number belongs to Nicolau (26) and the minimum to Rudinaldo (11) (Table 3.14). Similarly, results show that the number of individuals found in the house gardens varies from 136 (Pedro D) to 815 (Alziro). Most of the species found in Alziro's house garden are herbs, grasses, or vines that he plants for medicinal, ornamental, spice, and food uses. The majority of species inventoried in Pedro D's house garden are palms and trees.

Table 3.14 Number of species and individuals and the values for species richness (Dmn) and diversity (Shannon index, H') found in the 16 house gardens

House garden	Area (ha)	Number of individuals	Number of species	Dmn	H'
Alziro	0.28	815	19	0.67	0.79
Amilton	0.25	189	20	1.45	1.33
Antonio	0.29	340	21	1.14	2.03
Elias	0.24	296	18	1.10	1.91
Gilma	0.26	174	16	1.21	1.39
Gilmar	0.27	201	16	1.13	1.44
Hernandes	0.27	185	17	1.25	2.05
João	0.25	174	14	1.06	1.65
Florindo	0.26	280	21	1.26	1.63
Juraci A	0.27	238	17	1.10	1.25
Juraci Az	0.27	238	17	1.10	1.25
Manoel	0.28	186	18	1.32	1.34
Nicolau	0.28	260	26	1.61	2.83
Pedro	0.27	245	17	1.09	1.83
Pedro D	0.26	136	14	1.20	1.25
Rudinaldo	0.27	586	11	0.45	0.97

Despite the differences in species composition and individuals, the estimated species richness index shows that all farmers are maintaining high
levels of biodiversity in their house gardens. Only Rudinaldo's house garden has a low species richness index (Dmn = 0.45). The estimated diversity
and Shannon indices indicate that all sampled house gardens feature high
species diversity. Two house gardens, Nicolau (H' = 2.83) and Hernandes
(H' = 2.05), contain the highest diversity of species.

While the levels of biodiversity in fields, fallows, and forests are strongly
dependent on the intensity and frequency of production and management
technologies, the number of species in house gardens depends more on
their uses. For example, house gardens that are composed of orchards, nurseries, and gardens together have a greater number of species than those
that are composed of only one field type.

The Santarém sites[5]

PLEC work around Santarém was carried out in two subsites, islands in the
river containing lakes that were important for fisheries. Aracampina on Ilha
Ituqui and Ilha Saõ Miguel are respectively downstream and upstream
from the city. The people of both sites depend very heavily on fish. The
major early emphasis of the project was to assist them in managing their
lake resources, and helping them limit access to outsiders. One of the later
principal subprojects of PLEC concerned regeneration of the ecology of a
small lake on Aracampina. The two islands represent low and high *várzea*
(levee) situations, giving them different sets of problems.

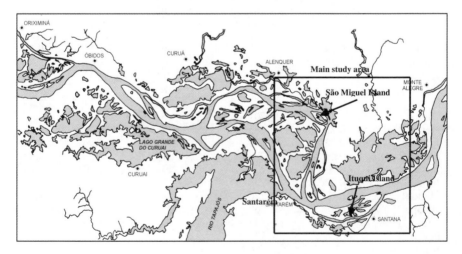

Figure 3.9 Demonstration sites in the Santarém region

The relative unimportance of agriculture

While agriculture has played a central role in the floodplain economy since the beginning of Portuguese settlement, the situation in the lower Amazon near Santarém is quite different today. Formerly the main income source for smallholders, agriculture is now largely supplementary to fishing and small-scale ranching. The average area planted by smallholders is a fraction of that cultivated by their upland counterparts. There has also been a change in the kinds of crops cultivated. Whereas in the past perennial crops, especially cocoa, predominated, the emphasis today is on annual crops. The most promising trend from a strictly commercial standpoint has been the growth of semi-intensive vegetable production. This is restricted to a narrow zone around the region's major urban centres, but the farmers often face glutted markets, low prices, and limited access to agricultural credit.

Environment and constraints

The lower Amazon floodplain consists of four main components: river channels, forested levees, seasonally inundated grasslands, and wide, shallow lakes. River channels divide the floodplain into islands whose outside margins are bordered by levees. On the inland side, levees slope gently downward to form networks of shallow lakes that occupy much of the interior of the floodplain. Vegetation patterns are closely associated with the topography. Levee forests grade into shrubs and then grasses as elevations decline towards the floodplain interior.

In the latter half of the twentieth century, the Amazon floodplain, like the uplands, has undergone a series of resource transformations. In the 1940s cacao, a mainstay of the lower Amazon floodplain since the beginning of colonial settlement, was definitively eclipsed as the main cash crop by jute. In the next two decades jute spread rapidly over the regional floodplain. Frequently the cacao groves themselves were cut down to make way for jute. With the introduction of synthetic fibres in the 1960s the jute market stagnated, and by the mid-1980s had given way to extensive cattle ranching and commercial fishing, now the basis of the floodplain economy. Today the lower Amazon floodplain population consists of two main groups, ranchers grazing cattle and water buffalo on floodplain grasslands, and smallholders engaged in varying combinations of annual and perennial cropping, fishing, small animal husbandry, and cattle raising.

The settlement system consists of smallholder households clustered in communities of 35–100 families, and ranches. Settlements are located on the levees bordering the river, and usually consist of a central area where the school, Catholic church and community centre, and one or more football fields are located, plus individual lots extending away in either direction along the river. Floodplain properties are measured in terms of metres of frontage rather than area, and extend inland to the shores of permanent lakes or channels in the middle of the island. In the study area smallholder properties average about 100 m of frontage by 2,000 m in depth for a total area of about 20 ha, most of which is under water during much of the year. It should be noted, though, that 25 per cent of properties are up to 50 m of frontage, and 50 per cent up to 100 m. A handful of properties account for more than 50 per cent of island frontage.

Most families rely primarily on household labour and exchange of labour between families, and only about a third of families employ any day labour. When the three largest users of wage labour are removed from the sample, household labour accounts for 88 per cent of the total. Within the household, male family members account for about 75 per cent of labour invested in agricultural activities, with fathers contributing almost half the total. Female members contribute the remaining 25 per cent, with mothers contributing the major share. This pattern of labour allocation was surprising because the team's subjective impression was that men and women contributed about equally to farming activities, as men also dedicate a considerable amount of their time to fishing. While family labour predominates, the need to harvest before the flood reaches crops or to plant as quickly as possible to take advantage of the time available may cause families to seek additional labour. Farmers market much of their harvest, with the proportion sold ranging from 93 per cent for beans to 63 per cent for cassava and maize.

Cropping system and land use

Smallholder farming systems consist of three main components: annual crops produced via shifting cultivation, perennials, usually grown around the house, and planting boxes for herbs and medicinal plants. Annual crops are usually produced in fields prepared by clearing and burning grassy or forested areas of the levee. The main crops grown in the two communities include beans (77 per cent of families), maize (73 per cent), water-melon (62 per cent), and vegetables (96 per cent), of which the most important is the tomato (46 per cent). Semi-perennials and perennials are less widely planted. Bananas, for example, were planted by 46 per cent of households and cassava by 27 per cent. Perennials are cultivated by 35 per cent of the families sampled. Some 30 species are grown, few of which represent a significant income source. Planting boxes raised above maximum flood level and filled with a planting medium composed of cow manure, soil, and rotted wood are used for growing herbs, medicinal plants, and ornamentals.

The agricultural season begins when the water recedes, exposing the land. Depending on the site chosen, land is cleared either by hoe and fire if grassy or used the previous year, or by clearing and burning if forested. In some cases the site is cleared before it is covered by flood so it emerges ready for planting. Depending on timing and the crop, one or two harvests can be obtained from the same site before flooding. Farmers select different sites for each crop, taking into account soil texture and length of time the site is likely to be water-free on the one hand, and crop moisture needs and maturation time on the other. Fast-maturing, fairly drought-resistant crops like beans tend to be planted on sandier sites such as beaches and sand bars. Maize is usually planted on levee sites with siltier soils where two crops may be possible. Water-melon is often planted on higher parts of the backslope where soils are more dense. Crops that take a long time to mature, such as cassava, are planted on the highest levees. Bananas and perennials are also grown on the highest levee sites available.

Contrasts between the two communities

Net annual household income from farming ranged from $17 to $680, with an average of $239 for the sample as a whole. Within this range net income tended to be skewed towards the lower end. There were significant differences between communities, with about 70 per cent of farmers in Aracampina earning between $300 and $700 while 50 per cent of farmers in Ilha Saõ Miguel earned less than $100. The difference in income is even greater than these numbers indicate because farmers in Ilha Saõ Miguel dedicated almost 76 per cent more time to farming than their counterparts in Aracampina, a result of their emphasis on labour-intensive crops such as jute, cassava, and banana. This translates into a significantly lower return on farm labour: $14 per day in Aracampina compared to $7 per day in Ilha Saõ Miguel.

The development of agriculture in the two communities over the last decade illustrates both the trade-offs between high and low sites and the general state of floodplain agriculture in the lower Amazon during this period. The first difference between the two can be seen in the kinds of crops grown. Farmers in Aracampina tend to concentrate on fast-maturing annuals best suited to the shorter growing season of the low *várzea*. Farmers in both locations plant beans, maize, and squash; cassava, which needs at least six months to mature, was grown exclusively by farmers in Ilha Saõ Miguel. Bananas were also widely cultivated in Ilha Saõ Miguel but not by Aracampina farmers.

One important difference between the two communities was the continued cultivation of jute in Ilha Saõ Miguel, long after it had been abandoned by Aracampina farmers, who had turned to water-melon and commercial fishing for their cash income. The dismal performance of jute, generating a return to labour of only one dollar a day compared to $6–$13/day for the other major crops, is perhaps the best indicator of why jute has been largely eclipsed by commercial fishing.

One of the best indicators of the height of the *várzea* is the presence of fruit trees such as mangoes, common on high *várzea* sites but absent from low *várzea* where the frequency and duration of flooding are greater. Ilha Saõ Miguel farmers cultivate some 29 species, compared to just nine for the Aracampina sample. Not only were more species cultivated in Ilha Saõ Miguel, but larger numbers of each were found in the house gardens (299 versus 24 individuals). Perennial production is also more market-oriented in Ilha Saõ Miguel, with 85 per cent of output destined for the market, while the small quantities produced in Aracampina are consumed almost exclusively by the family.

While the diversity of crops grown on high *várzea* sites is greater, there are trade-offs in terms of soil fertility. Because high sites flood less frequently, they also receive fewer infusions of fresh sediment and this has consequences for soil fertility and cropping frequency. Low levees, on the other hand, flood almost every year and so receive annual infusions of sediment that rejuvenate soils. Consequently, farmers in Aracampina are able to cultivate fields more or less continuously, while farmers in Ilha Saõ Miguel must fallow their fields for several years after a year or two of cultivation. This means the farmers in Ilha Saõ Miguel need more land to maintain any given level of production than Aracampina farmers. Their farms are also more vulnerable to fertility decline if soils are not managed appropriately or are heavily trampled by livestock.

The greater vulnerability of high levee soils to loss of fertility seems to have been a major factor in the decline of agriculture in Ilha Saõ Miguel during the 1990s. This decline has involved both annual and perennial crops. While farmers attribute the decline of annual cropping to loss of soil fertility, this process has been compounded by a shift to cattle. The total number of cattle and water buffalo grazed on the island has grown considerably. Farmers have cleared the levee for cattle and in the process have eliminated many fruit trees and also retarded recovery of levee soils. While the immediate cause of this shift may be attributed to declining soil fertility, the moribund state of the local market for agricultural products has clearly discouraged investments to augment soil productivity. Farmers in Aracampina, on the other hand, with a lower levee, have been able to maintain the farming strategies observed a decade ago.

High and low sites face different degrees of risk from flood and drought. High *várzea* sites are exposed for planting earlier than low sites so they have more time for growing crops before the driest period of the year. Since they are higher they also have more time until flood waters cover fields; consequently, farmers on high *várzea* have a greater likelihood of obtaining two crops per season from their fields than low *várzea* farmers. On the other hand, because they are higher and flood less frequently and for less time, high *várzea* sites such as Ilha Saõ Miguel can be more vulnerable to drought. In this study, for example, a slightly larger proportion of farmers suffered crop loss due to drought in Ilha Saõ Miguel than in Aracampina (56 per cent versus 60 per cent in the first year and 22 per cent versus 0 per cent in the second). Flooding, on the other hand, is a much more serious problem for farmers on low *várzea* sites such as Aracampina. Ninety per cent of the farmers in Aracampina, 20 per cent in the first year and 70 per cent in the second, lost crops to flooding, while none in Ilha Saõ Miguel suffered flood-related crop losses.

Markets represent both risks and opportunities for all farmers, but what is interesting in the present context is how the interaction between market and floodplain dynamics affects farmers' strategies on high and low *várzea* sites. Three aspects of the Santarém market are relevant here. First, Santarém is integrated into the national market and local products face stiff competition from products produced in other regions of the country, especially the central south. Second, local products have very limited access to markets outside Santarém. Consequently, the capacity of the Santarém market to absorb local output can be quite limited. A third characteristic of the regional marketing system is the existence of two agricultural zones, *várzea* and *terra firme*, which produce somewhat overlapping repertoires of crops. The main difference is the greater importance of cassava and perennials on the *terra firme* and of annual crops on the *várzea*. Despite a similar mix of crops, competition between the two zones is limited by the fact that *várzea* crops are harvested towards the end of the dry season and the beginning of the rainy season, while *terra firme* crops are harvested towards the end of the rainy season. Consequently, the two zones have complementary rather than competitive agricultural cycles.

Notes

1. Moko disease of banana, caused by the bacterium *Ralstonia solanacearum* race 2 (biovar 1), is endemic to the Philippines and Central and South America. Moko disease potentially poses a greater threat to both commercial and subsistence farmers than sigatoka and fusarium diseases. Among edible bananas there is no known resistance and insect transmission enables the disease to spread rapidly. External symptoms resemble those of fusarium wilt and blood disease of banana, characterized by yellowing of the leaves, followed by wilting of the plant. In some cases no external symptoms may be evident until the fruit bunch is produced, when the fruit appears distorted and the pulp exhibits a characteristic dark brown discolouration (Cooperative Research Centre for Tropical Plant Protection, www.tpp.uq.edu.au/disease/moko.htm).
2. In Amazonia management information was integrated into the agrobiodiversity database.
3. Based on the results of these experiences, expansion of training activities to other regions of Amazonia is planned as part of the new phase of PLEC in Amazonia. As part of training

the team will participate in curriculum writing for undergraduates, technical schools, high schools, and schools in the villages. The plan is to test how the demonstration model can be expanded to train technicians and other people working in rural extension and conservation programmes.

4. The following is a substantial extract from the main report (Pinedo-Vasquez *et al.* 2000). Some additional information is provided in Pinedo-Vasquez *et al.* (2001).

5. Extract from a report by D. G. McGrath.

REFERENCES

Anderson, A. and E. Ioris. 1992. "The logic of extraction: Resource management and resource generation by extractive producers in the estuary", in K. Redford and C. Padoch (eds) *Conservation of Neotropical Forests*. New York: Columbia University Press, pp. 175–199.

Pinedo-Vasquez, M., C. Padoch, D. McGrath, and T. Ximenes. 2000. "Biodiversity as a product of smallholders' stratregies for overcoming changes in their natural and social landscapes", *PLEC News and Views*, No. 15, pp. 9–19.

Pinedo-Vasquez, M., D. J. Zarin, K. Coffey, C. Padoch, and F. Rabelo. 2001. "Post-boom logging in Amazonia", *Human Ecology*, Vol. 29, No. 2, pp. 219–239.

4

Ghana

Edwin A. Gyasi, William Oduro, Gordana Kranjac-Berisavljevic', J. Saa Dittoh, and William Asante

Introduction

On the opposite side of the Atlantic, a little further north than Amazonia, is the landmass of West Africa, an ancient dissected plateau of metamorphosed and sedimentary rocks. It lies south of the Sahara and is a heterogeneous area of 6 million square kilometres, with some 200 million inhabitants and a 3 per cent annual population growth rate. The climate and terrain of the two West African PLEC countries, Ghana and Guinée, are totally dissimilar to those of Amazonia.

Ghana is one of the world's biodiversity hotspots because of its high and endangered biodiversity. In former centuries, forests are said to have covered much of the southern part of the country. Current satellite pictures of southern Ghana show little forest; what remains is a mosaic of remnant woodlands interspersed between cultivated areas.[1] This is the general scenario where PLEC activities take place.

The project works in three main areas in a climatic and vegetation gradient that stretches from the savannas in the relatively arid north to the forest/savanna transition in the more humid south. The ethnic and cultural scene is vivid and varied. The country has a long colonial history, many forms of land tenure, large numbers of migrant peoples, and increasing population pressure. In spite of these differences, the farmers of the West African cluster of PLEC have some of the same basic livelihood problems as the Amazonian farmers. Food security is one of them.

79

The first stage

The Ghana cluster was formed in 1993. Its brief was to assess what agro-biodiversity existed after a century of great change, and in what way the local farmers could be assisted to conserve biodiversity and maintain and improve sustainable incomes. A pilot study by six scientists began in the south. In 1994 further sites were set up in two more northerly regions when more local scientists joined PLEC.[2] A link was also established with francophone West Africa based at the Université de Conakry in Guinée. Chapter 5 details their findings.

Preparatory work in Ghana was based on 1974 aerial photographs, because satellite imagery was too expensive in the early days of PLEC. Initially, sites had to be found within reasonable travelling distance of the scientists' workplace. In southern Ghana, PLEC work focused on three pilot sites, Gyamfiase-Adenya, Sekesua-Osonson, and Amanase-Whanabenya, all in the eastern region. The sites (Figure 4.1) have several cultural differences. Gyamfiase and Adenya are in the Akuapem district, the "cradle" of Ghana's crucially important cocoa industry. The villages are occupied predominantly by the native Akuapem and Ayigbe people and Ewe migrant tenants. Amanase and Whanabenya are juxtaposed villages in a former cocoa district, and were settled by migrant Akuapem and Siade/Shai landowners and other migrants, including Ayigbe and Ewe tenants. Sekesua and Osonson are in a migrant Krobo district.

In central Ghana the original plan in 1993 was to work concurrently at four scattered sites (Jachie, Nyameani, Boabeng-Fiema, and Bofie, all in the Ashanti region). This quickly proved to be overambitious. Effort was then concentrated at Jachie and, later, extended to Tano-Odumasi. In northern Ghana, work started in 1994 in the far north at Bawku-Manga (redesignated Nyorigu-Benguri-Gonre) in the upper east region. From about 1998–1999, work there was de-emphasized in favour of the more readily accessible second site at Bongnayili-Dugu-Song in the northern region.

Possible field sites were to be sampled by the transect and quadrat method, and for this it was crucial for the scientists to obtain the cooperation of the local people. In Ghana it is especially important to have agreement first from the chiefs and other leaders, who often also have good knowledge of the agro-environmental history of the area. These key personalities can often serve as facilitators in any applied work.

Meetings with the chiefs and discussion groups with the local farmers were arranged, and the intentions of the PLEC teams explained. In all sites people agreed to cooperate, and surveys were done in the company of the relevant farmers. With their participation, mapping of fields and settlements was carried out. This later helped create a standardized database for demonstration sites (Abdulai, Gyasi, and Kufogbe 1999).

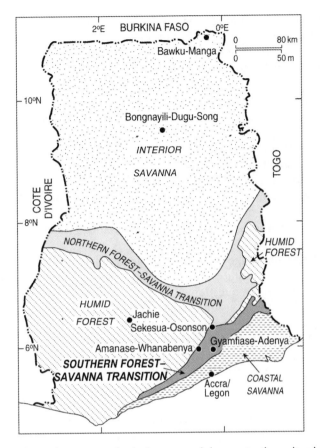

Figure 4.1 The major agro-ecological zones and demonstrations sites in Ghana

These early discussions led eventually to the formation of farmers associations, some of which put on fairs and displays of crops and traditional foods. The associations included some for women. Women farmers predominate in central Ghana, and the scientists spent many hours not only on the farms but also at weddings and funerals and other community events. This helped in understanding village dynamics, and specific issues relating to women such as child marriages, single mothers, and multiple marriages. Soil erosion and poverty were found to be widespread.

The initial participatory fieldwork was essential to better understanding between scientists and farmers, and both groups later admitted that they learned a lot from each other. The PLEC team knew that indigenous knowledge had been of great use in the former cocoa period, when the local farmers had worked out the best row width for cocoa plants, contrary to official advice (Amanor 1994). The ability of the Africans' expertise to cope with especially demanding environments and the damage done by the transfer of unmodified Western technologies have been described by Pacey (1990). It was smallholder farmers who successfully solved production problems that PLEC was seeking to resolve.

The period after 1994 and before funds were awarded by the GEF was a time of strengthening contacts by regular visits. Farmers were asked what they thought was the current state of agriculture, and what problems they faced. There was general concern about the decline in yields since the 1960s, and increasing production pressure. This had led to a shortening of fallows to between one and four years. The women were worried about the disappearance of wild mushrooms, the difficulties of finding firewood, and the increasing demands on their time. This was due in part to the use of women for labour in commercial crop production, in addition to their duties in their home gardens. Hiring outside labour was too expensive for many families.

In the fields, the range of crops and agrobiodiversity, the possibilities of conservation, and the state of the soil were assessed, and selected farmers gave useful answers to questionnaires. Progressive and expert farmers who could contribute to the second stage of PLEC were identified, and the scientists began to publish preliminary findings. One of the interesting discoveries was that there were considerable reserves of biodiversity in the sacred groves, of which there are a large number. Some of these were originally places of burial for chiefs, and plants that have grown there have been left undisturbed.

After a major workshop in 1994 with international and political guests, a book on the West African environment (Gyasi and Uitto 1997) was published by the UNU, highlighting the significance of some of the local farming strategies.

The demonstration sites

The four-year period 1998/1999–2001/2002 witnessed a phenomenal increase in PLEC activities. This positive trend was mainly a result of a substantial infusion of GEF funding. Five demonstration sites have been progressively developed from the pilot phase (Figure 4.1):
- Gyamfiase-Adenya, Sekesua-Osonson, and Amanase-Whanabenya in south-eastern Ghana
- Jachie, with its subsidiary site Tano-Odumasi in central Ghana
- Bongnayili-Dugu-Song, with Nyorigu-Benguri-Gonre as a subsidiary located in the northern interior savanna zone.

A major characteristic of the sites is the considerable pressure exerted on biophysical resources by the predominantly agricultural population, who are mostly subsistence farmers. Their farms have become smaller and smaller as the population pressure has intensified. In the southern Ghana sites estimated densities range from 105 to over 180 people/km², compared to a national average of 70. In central Ghana the range is from 80 to more than 165 people/km². At Bongnayili-Dugu-Song and Nyorigu-Benguri-Gonre in the north there are 100 and 120 people/km² respectively. Numbers of people per household average seven in central Ghana, nine in the south, and as many as 14.5 in the north. The exceptionally high figures for northern Ghana reflect in part the compound houses that contain more than one household. In southern Ghana numbers of people below 18 years of age average four per household. In the central sector those below 14 years of age and those aged more than 65 years together comprise 39.3 per cent of the population. In the northern sector 42.1 per cent of the population is made up of those aged below 14 and above 60 years. All these household statistics indicate a high dependency ratio.

In northern Ghana large numbers of cattle, goats, and sheep exacerbate pressure on biophysical resources. At all sites a major source of pressure on resources is demand for foodstuffs, firewood, and other primary commodities from nearby urban centres (Tamale and Bawku in northern Ghana, Kumasi in the central sector, and Accra and other coastal towns in the south). In the past much of the production pressure placed on the southern and central sectors originated from outside Ghana, when exports of palm oil, cocoa, and timber were sought. The effects persist, especially in the form of deforestation, soil deterioration, and changing agrodiversity. One of PLEC's chief aims was to find out how farmers currently managed their land, what variety occurred, and which practices gave the best hope of achieving sustainable goals.

Agrodiversity in the demonstration sites

The agrodiversity findings set the framework within which the PLEC teams worked.[3] Land-use stages and field types were determined in all areas. In southern and central Ghana the principal land-use stages were annual cropping, agroforest, house/home garden, and fallow, with smaller areas of orchard, natural forest, woodlot, and edges or hedgerows. Northern Ghana has a more complex pattern, described later.

South-east Ghana: Gyamfiase-Adenya, Sekesua-Osonson, and Amanase-Whanabenya

These sites are in the southern forest-savanna transition zone. Average annual rainfall ranges between 1,200 and 1,450 mm and is bimodal. Soils are predominantly ochrosols. Natural vegetation is characterized by a mosaic of forest and savanna species. The dominance of herbaceous species interspersed by few trees is a measure of the floristic change (Gyasi *et al.* 1995; Enu-Kwesi 1997).

Farming by smallholders is the principal occupation. They grow mainly food crops and have some free-ranging livestock. Home gardens, either with or without agroforestry, provide most of their food. Men and women share the work of farming, but men do more of the heavy land clearance and women do most of the marketing. Cassava is the dominant crop, followed by maize.

This is the area where cocoa became the principal cash crop, supplemented by oil palm, in a period of major commercial expansion by the Akuapem and Krobo people between the 1890s and 1920. From the 1930s cocoa was devastated by disease, especially the swollen shoot virus, but also by the mirid bug (or *akate* in Akan) associated with fungal disease and planting in unfavourable soil conditions. Subsequently there was a shift to staple food crop production based on traditional as well as modern management practices. The latter included some use of the tractor as well as the cutlass (bush knife or machete) and other manual tools, monoculture, the use of agrochemicals and hybrid seeds, and row planting. Recently there has been an increased use of leguminous crops, especially cowpeas (*Vigna unguiculata*), which benefit the soil.

Site preparation and tools

Sites for cropping are prepared by slashing using the cutlass and burning the slashed vegetation. Trees having economic, medicinal, ecological, or some other value are often left standing and even nurtured. The hoe is used to turn the soil and make mounds, ridges, and drainage channels. Together with the cutlass, the hoe is the tool most commonly used for sowing and weeding.

Extensive and indiscriminate burning of vegetation and the resultant destruction of faunal habitat contributes significantly towards biodiversity erosion in periodically cropped areas. Similarly, because of its damaging effects on plant propagules or seed stock in the soil, extensive use of the hoe is suspected of being a major cause of biodiversity loss, especially in areas farmed by tenants who rely heavily on this implement. The cutlass by contrast exerts a less damaging effect on biodiversity. An even less damaging effect is achieved by *oprowka*, a land preparation method discussed below.

Water conservation

Crop farming is rain-fed. In Sekesua-Osonson, four farmers used water from nearby streams for their vegetable farms during dry spells. Often, moist or seasonally flooded depressions are used for water-loving perennial crops such as sugarcane and for vegetables during dry periods. Some farmers make drainage channels to drain excess water. A few use stone linings to trap rain-water and minimize its soil erosion, but a PLEC initiative to popularize this has had limited success.

A common water conservation practice is mulching. Cassava sticks and maize stalks are used for trash lines and mulching. The biomass is hoed under later to enrich the soil. Some farmers preserve trees and other plants such as *lelo, sablatso, ayisatso, nyabatso, awamba, kumelo, agbatafotso,* and *makotso* (Dangbe names) that are indicative of soil quality. This enhances soil moisture and provides shade for yams and other shade-tolerant crops.

Crop management

Typically the agricultural holdings are fragmented into fallow and cropped plots. Few individual farms exceeded 2 ha, but the total range was from less than a hectare to about 300 ha. Table 4.1 provides a summary of farm management practices. Since the mid-late twentieth century fallows have been dominated by invasive *Chromolaena odorata*, and woodlots are mostly made up of introduced *Cassia siamea*.

Cocoa was initially planted under a partly cleared forest canopy, and as trees were replaced, food crops were planted among the cocoa. After cocoa had gone from most areas, a mainly land-rotational system was adopted with fallows as the main means of restoring fertility. Cassava was central to this agricultural transition because it was tolerant of the increasingly acidic soils and seasonally dry climate that disfavoured cocoa. It is high-yielding, affordable, and able to meet the food requirements of a rapidly expanding population. Fourteen cassava types have been identified by their local names in surveys since 1994. The most popular are *ankra, agbelitomo, katawire, abontem, asramnsia, tuaka, trainwusiw, bankye nsantom, gbezey, agbeliatsilakpa* or *kable,* and *biafra* or *agege*. The last three are introductions from Benin, Togo, and Nigeria. Some of the varieties were introduced only recently by immigrants and returned Ghanaian migrants.

The nitrogen-fixing cowpea has become an important second cash crop. Less dramatic, but nonetheless significant, has been an increased emphasis on maize, vegetables, and legumes. Cultivation is gradually involving hand irrigation, manuring, agrochemicals, and other forms of intensification. The forest-savanna ecozone has consolidated its role as a major producer of food crops and vegetables for the nearby coastal urban areas and other settlements in Ghana.

The home garden agroforests still include some cocoa. Other common crops include peppers (*Capsicum annuum*), condiments, leafy vegetables, plantains and bananas, fruit trees such as mango, avocado, citrus, coconut, and *Chrysophyllum albidum* (called *adesaa* by Twi-speaking Akan people and *alatsa* by Adangbe-speaking Krobo and Shai people), and yams and

Table 4.1 Selected management regimes/practices and their advantages in PLEC demonstration sites in southern Ghana

Practices	Major characteristics and advantages
Bush/fallow land rotation, using fire to clear land	A means of regenerating soil fertility and conserving plants in the wild
Minimal tillage and controlled use of fire for vegetation clearance	Minimal disturbance of soil and biota
Mixed cropping, crop rotation, and mixed farming	Maximizes soil nutrient usage; maintains crop biodiversity; spreads risk of complete crop loss; enhances a diversity of food types and nutrition; favours soil regeneration
Traditional agroforestry: cultivating crops among trees left *in situ*	Conserves trees; regenerates soil fertility through biomass litter; some trees add to productive capacity of soil by nitrogen fixation
Oprowka, a no-burn farming practice that involves mulching by leaving slashed vegetation to decompose *in situ*	Maintains soil fertility by conserving and stimulating microbes and by humus addition through the decomposing vegetation; conserves plant propagules, including those in the soil, by the avoidance of fire
Usage of household refuse and manure in home gardens	Sustains soil productivity
Use of *nyabatso* (*Neubouldia laevis*) as live stake for yams	The basically vertical rooting system of *nyabatso* favours expansion of yam tubers, while the canopy provides shade and the leaf litter mulch and humus; it also is suspected that *nyabatso* fixes nitrogen
Staggered harvesting of crops	Ensures food availability over the long haul
Storage of crops, notably some species of yam, *in situ* in the soil for future harvesting	Enhances food security and secures seed stock
Conservation of forest in the back yard	Conserves forest species; source of medicinal plants at short notice; favours apiculture, snail farming, and shade-loving crops such as yams

taro that thrive in the shady and humid conditions created by the tree canopy.

Yams have been cultivated in West Africa for centuries, and Blay (2002) has found 140 different yam cultivars in southern Ghana. Some are heirloom varieties that have been grown at the same spot for decades. Cultivated yams are a prestigious food in many communities, and are associated with customs and ceremonies across the country. They occur in all land-use types. Six main types of cultivated yam and one wild type are general favourites in this area, each having its own merit of palatability or ease of storage or cultivation. Species include *Dioscorea rotundata* (and a wild yam of this species), *D. alata, D. cayenensis, D. dumetorum, D. esculenta,* and *D. bulbifera.* Fifty-four named yam varieties were grown in 2000 in Sekesua-Osonson and Gyamfiase-Adenya, and 36 varieties in Amanase-Whanabenya. Farmers usually grow from five to eight different types of yam, according to land-use type. Some varieties are planted in holes among trees rather than being mounded.

There still is high agrobiodiversity. This reflects the transitional nature of the ecosystem, which permits cultivation of crops adapted to humid and dry conditions. It also reflects the great ethnic and cultural diversity resulting from migration (Gyasi 2002).

Land tenure and tenancy

There are two main types of land allocation in the region. In Gyamfiase-Adenya, and in parts of Amanase-Whanabenya, the land is owned almost exclusively by extended families of the native Akuapem people on the basis of the matrilineal kinship principle. Under this arrangement, members of the landowning group have free access to the land, which they may also grant out permanently or temporarily to the growing number of tenants. The plots in these areas show a mosaic pattern. In other areas of Amanase-Whanabenya, and in Sekesua-Osonson, the land is inherited on the patri-lineal principle and the land divided according to linear *zugba* strips, following the *huza* arrangement developed by the Krobo. Access to land in all areas is achieved in two principal ways: based on kinship and involving no payment since the members of the family enjoy free usufruct; or by grants that involve payment in cash or kind by contract (customarily unwritten) between landlord and tenant. There are two tenancy practices, namely share cropping and renting or leasing. Leaseholds are variable in duration and cost.

In 1996–1997 mapping of landholding patterns showed 269 farmers in Gyamfiase-Adenya were operating agricultural fields. Sixty-five per cent were tenants who farmed a mere 20 per cent of the total of 1,863 ha. A more recent PLEC survey, carried out in 1999 over a much greater area within the Sekesua-Osonson demonstration site, underscored the importance of tenancy. All 13 farmers interviewed farmed freely on family *zugba* inherited from their forebears. However, 23 per cent of them farmed also as tenants on other people's land because of the insufficiency of family land. Sixty-two per cent of them were hosting tenants on their land.

Sharecropping arrangements are the most common form of tenancy. Table 4.2 summarizes these arrangements for different food crops. In Amanase-Whanabenya and Gyamfiase-Adenya sharecropping ratios are similar. When the tenant farmer provides most of the seedlings, two-thirds of the produce for maize goes to him/her (*abusa* arrangement), while for cassava and taro harvests it is shared on an equal basis between owner and

Table 4.2 Tenurial arrangements in Amanase-Whanabenya and Gyamfiase-Adenya

Main crop	Owner proportion	Tenant proportion	Comment
Maize	$\frac{1}{3}$	$\frac{2}{3}$	Tenant provides the seeds
Cassava	$\frac{1}{2}$	$\frac{1}{2}$	Tenant provides the seeds
Plantain	$\frac{1}{2}$ or $\frac{1}{3}$	$\frac{1}{2}$ or $\frac{2}{3}$	Proportion varies among landowners
Yam			Shared at the discretion of the planter
Taro	$\frac{1}{2}$	$\frac{1}{2}$	Pertains to Gyamfiase-Adenya
Cocoa	$\frac{1}{2}$	$\frac{1}{2}$	Tenant provides seedlings
	$\frac{2}{3}$	$\frac{1}{3}$	Owner provides seedlings
Oil palm and other trees	All		Gives the tenant a small portion if the palms are naturally growing ones
Naturally growing firewood trees			Proportion varies between landowners; while some owners share with tenants, others do not

tenant farmer (*abunu*). In Sekesua-Osonson additional arrangements exist. The *ape ni agba* arrangement literally translates as "do and let's share". It mainly involves the starchy staples, maize and cassava, which are shared in the ratio of two-thirds to the landowner and one-third to the tenant, with the landlord bearing the cost of initial land clearing and supplying seeds or planting material. *Hu ni agba* translates as "farm or crop and let us share". With this the landowner provides only the land, and the crop, typically maize and cassava, is shared half each.

Central Ghana: Jachie and Tano-Odumasi

Jachie and Tano-Odumasi are in the Ashanti region, in the moist semi-deciduous forest zone. The major rainfall season is from March to July, and the minor season begins in September and ends in November. During the dry season (November to March) winds from the Sahara blow across the country bringing harmattan conditions. Jachie is hilly, and Tano-Odumasi hilly to undulating. Soil erosion is a severe problem within the town and villages.

Climatic and biophysical characteristics are similar to those in southern Ghana. The bimodal annual rainfall ranges between 1,500 and 1,600 mm, and the natural vegetation is of the moist semi-deciduous type. Herbaceous species are expanding at the expense of trees, as land is cleared and burned for more intensive farming. Soils are predominantly savanna ochrosols and ochrosols-oxysols integrade.

Women farmers

In these two communities many men work in the nearby city of Kumasi, but still clear and prepare land for cropping. A high proportion of farm management is in the hands of women, and in Jachie 74 per cent of farmers are women. They have incorporated knowledge, work, and responsibilities that were formerly in the male domain. Now they are leaders in the conservation of agrobiodiversity.

Production here has been less commercially oriented than in the south-east. The farmers practise both mono- and multiple cropping. In multiple cropping, the crops are plantain, cassava, maize, and vegetables, especially eggplant and pepper. In monocropping the crops alternate between maize and cassava. Maize is preferred because of its shorter cropping period. Yams are grown in separate plots and are mounded. There are a number of mixed crop fields in which taro (mainly *Xanthosoma* spp.) is important. Sometimes wetter patches are selected for concentrated planting of *Colocasia* taro.

Home gardens

Both men and women have home gardens where a variety of food crops and medicinal plants are cultivated as a source of food for household needs, especially in emergency situations. Some women manage their gardens jointly with their husbands, mostly in monogamous families. In polygamous families, each wife may operate a home garden separately. Usually the family members do all the work in the gardens, because home garden work is considered light work which does not require hired labour.

Home gardens are more complex than in the south-east. Each observed garden differed in composition and structure from the next. Most home gardens could be described as extensively managed multistoreyed gardens, with tree crops covering 61 per cent of farmland at Jachie and Tano-Odumasi. They varied from a monoculture of *Musa* spp. with cleared undergrowth to a dense tangle of many different species. Intensively cultivated compound farms were few in Jachie (3.2 per cent), and there was none in Tano-Odumasi. In the larger home gardens there was a greater number of traditional annual or perennial staple foods. Household refuse is often dumped in the garden.

The planting designs were mostly haphazard for tree crops, vegetables, and fruit crops. Other traditional crops were sometimes spaced or planted in rows. The arrangement was determined by farmers' traditional knowledge of optimizing crop production as well as by food preference.

Multipurpose trees are preferred. They are used for windbreaks, fodder, food, timber, medicine, or ornament and shade. They include teak, *Morinda lucida*, mango, citrus, and avocado. The ground may be dense with tangles of many different species, less covered, or totally cleared of undergrowth. Crop species may be annuals or biennials, including plantain and banana, cassava, taro, and vegetables. The staple cereal or tuber crops are more common than vegetables in both villages. Citrus, bananas, and some staple crops are sold for cash income.

Land, sacred groves, and tree tenure

The household is the basic farming unit. Most of the land is owned by individual families. About 60 per cent of farmers gain access to some of their farm land on *abunu* and *abusa* sharecropping bases, but tenancy is less common than in the south-east. Tracts of land vary in size. Every member of the family has access to land but not in equal amounts, and land disputes are increasing. Other forms of land acquisition for agricultural activities are hiring, gift, and purchase.

There are individual and community rights to use of trees. Trees on individual land give the owner of the land exclusive rights to products and services provided by that tree. Trees on community land such as sacred groves, meeting places, and cemeteries are for use by the entire community. Sacred groves fall under category seven of the IUCN/UNESCO protected areas. Local people believe that their ancestors reside in the forest. Even in the case of individual lands, the community may benefit if the tree is of medicinal value. The rights to trees have been recognized under the new Forestry Law which requires that before anyone cuts down a tree, a contract must be agreed with the tree owner. Any economic benefit goes to the owner of the land which nurtured the tree.

Soil preparation and the oprowka system

Fallows are nowadays slashed and burned by most farmers as a method of soil preparation for crops. This gives the short-term benefit of the addition of ash to the soil for planting, and destroys weed seeds, pathogens, pests, and snakes. But it also destroys a certain amount of biodiversity, and enhances insolation and soil temperatures that affect useful soil microbes and do not sustain higher yields in the long term (Quansah and Oduro 2002).

PLEC scientists have investigated a traditional system, *oprowka*, sometimes called *proka*, and described by Bakang (2002). This practice was formerly more widely used in south and central Ghana. It is a slash-and-no-burn method of ground preparation, and has been demonstrated for PLEC in Jachie by the charismatic expert farmer Cecilia Osei. When tree-dominated fallow is cleared, the vegetation is slashed and then left on the ground as mulch. The Akan term means "cut and leave to rot". Crops are planted through the mulch, so that they benefit from the moisture conserved and humus generated.

This method of land preparation usually begins in August with slashing of shrubs and small trees, and the felling or killing by fire of particular big trees. Further clearing continues in the dry season (December/January) to create the necessary spaces for planting while awaiting the onset of the rains in February/March. Planting of crops (plantains, taro, cassava, fruits, and vegetables) is done after the rains are well established. Traditionally, taro grew naturally and profusely in *oprowka* without being planted by farmers.

This mix of crops, together with the trees deliberately left on the field by the farmer, results in what has been described elsewhere as traditional small peasant farms under the general land-use stage of agroforestry. It is also this mix of crops that farmers in Tano-Odumasi refer to as *afupa* ("the real farm"), meaning the old traditional small peasant farm which aims to satisfy all subsistence or food-security needs of the household (Bakang 2002). It is "a field on which one can depend to provide the food needs of the household, or a field that provides everything we need" (Yaw Bio, Tano-Odumasi). Consequently, the traditional *afupa* has always been associated with the most fertile lands of the household, but these are now further and further away from the settlement. Another feature of *afupa* is its symbolic position. Generally, every family of the landowning group and a few immigrants of good standing possess it. In central Ghana *oprowka* is used principally on *afupa*.[4] Quansah *et al.* (1998) and Quansah and Oduro (2002) have shown that *oprowka* as a land management practice conserves biodiversity and enhances soil biota, moisture, and fertility. It can be improved by the addition of organic manure, and chicken manure is used locally.

In south-eastern Ghana three botanists have begun a controlled field experiment on this conservation system, comparing it with the slash-and-burn technique under identical conditions (Asafo, Laing, and Enu-Kwesi 2002). The first yield of maize after only seven weeks showed only minor differences that may not be statistically significant, and the investigation is continuing. It is likely that the *oprowka* system may enhance crop growth and yield in subsequent years after the decomposition of the slash-no-burn matter results in the release of mineral materials in the soil. However, this release of mineral nutrient from decomposed litter can be a very slow process.

Northern Ghana

The two northern Ghana sites are in the savanna, with no surviving forest.[5] There is a single rainfall maximum and a very long dry season. Bongnayili-Dugu-Song (population 1,648) is within the Guinea savanna zone, which is associated with an annual rainfall of about 1,000–1,300 mm, but with high variability. The rainy season is 140–190 days, while the estimated annual evaporation is about 2,000 mm, creating a great seasonal deficit every dry season. The peak rainfall period is usually late August or early September. About 60 per cent of the rainfall occurs within the three months of July to September, with torrential rains creating serious drainage problems.

In the far north-east, in Nyorigu-Benguri-Gonre the population is 764 with a growth rate of over 3 per cent. This site lies in the more arid Sudan-type savanna, with an average rainfall of 800 mm. Settlement is in compounds, with farms around the homesteads. Cash cropping is limited, and there is widespread poverty. Small-scale agriculture engages 62.5 per cent of those employed in Bongnayili-Dugu-Song, and 72.1 per cent in Nyorigu-Benguri-Gonre. Field types are different from those in the south. Intensive intercropped farms are adjacent to living compounds and sustained by household refuse. Small home gardens are distinct from bush fields.

Because of high population densities many farmers in both sites maintain "distant" farms, often many kilometres away from the home village and worked by a family member who lives on the farm during the growing season (Table 4.3). Some land is used only for grazing, more than in the southern sites. Low-lying areas with irrigation or longer-lasting soil moisture are a third field type, useful in the dry, hot "harmattan" season. There are only small community forests and sacred groves.

Population densities at both sites are above the regional average, and in both areas there are more females than males. Based on a sample survey, total size of agricultural holdings per household range in size from approximately 1.6 to 3.2 ha and 0.3 to 2.2 ha respectively. Landholdings are larger than in southern and central Ghana. Farm work is shared in about equal proportions between men and women, with the men doing the heaviest

Table 4.3 Data on farms in northern Ghana

Farm (field) type and characteristics	Bongnayili-Dugu-Song	Nyorigu-Benguri-Gonre
Compound farms		
Average number of plots per household	2.20	5.10
Average area (ha per household)	1.46	2.23
Distant farms		
Average number of plots per household	3.00	2.90
Average area (ha per household)	1.34	1.34
Bush farms		
Average number of plots per household	3.60	1.40
Average area (ha per household)	3.16	1.21
Lowland/irrigated farms		
Average number of plots per household	0.40	1.20
Average area (ha per household)	0.24	0.32

work of ground preparation. Harvesting of the sheanut and *dawadawa*, and their processing into sheabutter and food condiments respectively, are the primary responsibility of women, as is the processing of groundnuts into oil. Many male children are shepherds, while girls help their mothers with household duties.

Population pressure has led to severe land degradation and soil erosion. Overgrazing, deforestation, declining soil fertility, and low agricultural productivity are evident. One result is outmigration of the most able labour, predominantly young girls, who move out to serve mainly as *kayayei*, porters or carriers, especially in Accra. In Nyorigu-Benguri-Gonre, prospects of optimal land resource management are threatened by ethnic conflicts.

Trading is the second most important occupation for the local people. It involves mainly selling of farm produce and items of food and drink prepared by the traders themselves and peddling of other items bought. Dressmaking and hairdressing, carving, carpentry, masonry, and other artisanal work are also important.

The demonstration site in the Dagomba region: Bongnayili-Dugu-Song

Bongnayili-Dugu-Song demonstration site is situated in the Tolon/Kumbungu district of the northern region. The ethnic group is Dagomba, one of the most widespread and numerous peoples of northern Ghana, and their language is Dagbani. There are two principal towns, Yendi and Kumbungu, in the northern region, and Tamale is the regional capital. Subsistence agriculture is the main occupation.

Crop management

Compound farms usually have higher fertility, as a result of using household waste and livestock droppings as compost. The compound farms are normally planted by May, immediately after the first heavy rains and before the bush farms are planted. The bush farms are not manured and the land is allowed to rest for some years. The fallow system is always part of the sequence, but fallow periods in recent times have been drastically reduced to between two and four years. The prevalent farming system is mixed cropping, but there are plots of sole maize, yam, or groundnut. Where cotton is grown the usual practice is monocropping.

The principal crops are yam, maize, cassava, rice, sorghum, cowpea, millet, tobacco, cotton, groundnuts, and vegetables. Animals are reared by most households, and include sheep and goats, with some farmers owning cattle. The animals are kept for security reasons, or as capital investment. They are rarely slaughtered for consumption, except for ceremonial occasions. Most households also keep chickens and guinea-fowl.

Yams are one of the most important traditional crops and many varieties exist. They are often planted on newly broken land, to be followed by maize and sorghum. Grown on large mounds a metre high, the yams are frequently interplanted with bulrush millet and other crops between the mounds. Twenty-four types of yam were recorded at Bongnayili-Dugu-Song during the 1999 growing season (Kranjac-Berisavljevic' and Gandaa 2000). Men do all the work on yam farms. In the second year, the same field site provides most of the grain and pulse requirements. A wet-season visit in 1996 showed that mounding and ridging practices are very responsive to variations in soil moisture. Some rice is grown in wetter patches.

The Dagomba farming system, described in detail by Lynn (1937; 1942) and by Allan (1965: 236–240), remains remarkably little changed except in detail. Land use is affected by reduced fallow periods, low soil fertility, erratic rainfall, annual bush fires, firewood and fodder shortages, and water bodies silting at very fast rates. Traditional methods of maintaining soil fertility are few and animal manure is equally used for fuel, while both women and men are engaged in cultivating crops other than yams.

Land tenure, tree tenure, and the chiefs

Land tenure is one of the most important factors affecting use of resources. In northern Ghana, although land ownership is communal almost everywhere, the administration of the land depends on the tribe. In the northern region in general the chief only leases land-use rights to the household, while in upper east and upper west regions the power to dispose of land belongs to the earth priests (*tindana, totina, teng-nyono*).

Dagomba society is strongly patrilineal and highly stratified. Each village has a chief who is given authority by higher chiefs leading back to the Yaa Naa, the King of Dagbon, based in Yendi. All the land in the Bongnayili-Dugu-Song demonstration site area is vested in the Voggu paramountcy. Any request for land for agricultural activities is channelled through the chiefs in the individual communities. Some family lands exist in certain communities. Land can be acquired by an individual (an indigene or a stranger) by presenting kola nuts to the local chief. Rents are not paid for land use, but at the end of the production season tenants are obliged to send token portions of their produce to the chief.

The economic trees on the land are also vested in chiefs by Dagomba tradition. The locals have a wide knowledge of certain indigenous tree species and use them in many ways. Common tree species found growing in the wild include *dawadawa* (*Parkia biglobosa*), shea (*Vitellaria paradoxa*), kapok (*Ceiba pentandra*), and ebony (*Diospyros mespiliformis*). Trees are managed by the appointment of tree chiefs who are responsible for particular tree species, for example a *dawadawa* chief. A tree chief monitors the harvesting of the fruits of that species in a particular locality and checks for indiscriminate cutting or felling. All this is geared towards increased yield of the species. Only dead trees or dead wood of economic trees can be harvested for firewood. Interestingly, in the event of the death of a tree chief, it is only firewood produced from that particular tree species that can be used in preparing the funeral meals.

For Dagomba, the land is far more than an economic resource. Both land and trees are the habitat of supernatural beings. To farm or gather fruits or other tree products is to negotiate with such beings and to be aware of both the prohibitions they place on certain behaviours and the dangers they pose. The spirits tend to be found around particular species of tree and are more likely to be present where trees are dense, for instance in the sacred groves.

Through a combination of taboos and religious prohibitions, the communities have preserved sacred groves. In Jaagbo the grove is located near the PLEC demonstration site. It is owned by two communities: Jagriguyili and Yoggu. Some common tree species found in the grove include *Diospyros mespiliformis* (ebony), shea, *Acacia dudgeoni*, *Anogeissus leiocarpus*, *Sterculia setigera*, and *Securidaca longipedunculata*. The chiefs and the community leaders have made declarations and devised methods to control and prevent bush fires.

Soil management

Farmers in most parts of the northern Ghana region classify soils according to their location in the topography. They recognize soils of the uplands, the transition, and the lowland or valley-bottom soils. They identify certain crop species with the soils on which they grow best: cereals are farmed on upland soils, deep-rooted crops like yams and cassava in the transition zone, and rice and water-tolerating crops on the valley-bottom soils.

Ridging, mounding, and bunding are used. The ridges are often made perpendicular to the contours to enhance runoff and control excess water during the rainy season. They are also used in the valley bottoms for some rice varieties and the cultivation of millet. The mounds are large because of relatively deep soils and are used for yam and cassava. The cassava mounds are usually on the uplands and are smaller than yam mounds. Bunding was introduced in the mid-1980s as a conservation measure in the valley bottoms and has since been improved in design. The bunds are normally about 40 cm high at the lowest point of the valley and decrease in height towards the uplands.

Far north-east Ghana: Nyorigu-Benguri-Gonre

This subsidiary site is in the Bawku-East district of the upper east region of Ghana. The ethnic groups are mainly Kusasi, and there are some Busanga,

Moshi (major ethnic groups in Burkina Faso), and Frafra. The Nyorigu-Benguri-Gonre site is characterized by highly degraded soils and many silted water bodies. There is considerable outmigration. While the settlements in Bongnayili-Dugu-Song are largely nucleated, in Nyorigu-Benguri-Gonre they are dispersed. Allan (1965) described the local agriculture as a set of concentric circles around the household settlements, with home gardens close to the houses, manured fields beyond this, and unmanured fields further out. In the home gardens and the annual cropping fields the land is cleared with the hoe and the debris burned.

Crops include early and late millet (*Pennisetum* spp.) and sorghum (*Sorghum bicolor*). Yams are not cultivated. Cereals and legumes are grown on ridges and in home gardens where only organic fertilizer, including wood ash, crop residues, and cow dung, is used.

Onions for sale are grown on raised beds on irrigated lands, depending on the availability of water. Both organic and chemical fertilizers are used. Both introduced *Oryza sativa* and the indigenous *O. glaberrima* rice are grown in the valleys. There are 12 varieties of *O. glaberrima* (Anane-Sakyi and Dittoh 2001). The crop is harvested by hand.

Soils and soil management

Detailed soil information was obtained in 1999. Various soil types in the area belong to clegosols, lixisols, and leptosols. The lixisols are generally sandy loams, clegosols are clays, and leptosols are sandy loams with a lot of laterite. Lixisols are the main soils where the cereals and legumes are planted, while clegosols are used for rice and vegetable production. Leptosols are found to be not very suitable for agricultural production and are mostly left for grazing. Chemical properties of the soils among the field types vary, depending on the land-use stage and field type. Under the continuous cropping of land with millet and sorghum pH values were found to be low (pH 4.5). Home gardens had favourable pH values of between 5.0 and 6.0. Low pH values were accompanied by low organic carbon (0.9 per cent) as well as low quantities of available phosphorus and potassium (4.7 and 10.8 mg/kg^{-1} respectively).

Land is prepared around May in the uplands. In the Bawku area the soil layer is thin, and to encourage moisture retention, small conical mounds are made with a base of about 50 cm diameter and 30 cm in height for seeding with millet and sorghum. When seeding on flat land, small mounds are made around the plants during the first weeding. This enhances moisture retention and suppresses weeds. The mounds slow runoff, facilitate percolation, and function as mini-compost heaps. This technology is purely local and has not been modified in the last century.

Ridging is especially used in the uplands. Soil is raised in the form of a line along the slope of the terrain. Some of the ridges are made down the slope of the land to help drain the field. Placing stones across the slope in a straight line is common. Stone lines slow down the flow of rain-water, enhance infiltration, and facilitate the deposition of debris and fine soil particles which increase soil fertility in the long term. The size of the stone lines normally depends on available material. Stone terracing is used in places with slopes of about 10 per cent. The usual upland crops of millet, sorghum, beans, and groundnuts are sown on the terraced fields.

Basins are constructed in the valley bottoms and are mostly surrounded by irregularly shaped ridges. They are made to retain runoff during rainstorms to offset water deficit during dry spells. The basins are made by hoe using the available soil, mostly clay loam, and are reinforced during the weeding period with the uprooted weeds. Rice is the main crop, followed by sorghum. A second crop can be produced using residual moisture after the rice has been harvested.

Activities at demonstration sites

PLEC teams realized early on that farmers are not able to sustain biodiversity conservation unless their livelihoods are stabilized or improved. They therefore sought to promote economic activities that generate more value from conserved biodiversity, or that generate income in other ways, to make the conservation possible. Even so, frustrations arose when the teams could not meet the overly high expectation of some farmers that PLEC would rapidly end the endemic poverty. Better understanding of what was possible was spread through the farmers' associations.

Farmers' associations

The first step in convincing local farmers that the PLEC approach could benefit them was to get their cooperation in setting up a workable infrastructure. One of the most successful outcomes has been the growth of a population of participating farmers and several farmers' associations. In 1993 when PLEC work started, 10 farmers in the south agreed to collaborate. Four years later, the figure had increased to nearly 400, with representation in all three sectors – southern, central, and northern. By 2001–2002 membership had increased to nearly 1,400, with the highest concentration in central Ghana. The women farmers' association in Jachie has grown from 45 members in 1996 to 600 in 2002. Women farmers have been empowered by being able to open savings accounts, whereas traditionally they had no control over their income. Generally female membership shows a rising trend. In sites of mixed membership, female members are organized into subgroups, such as the Gyamfiase-Adenya Bowohommoden Kuw, to address issues that primarily concern them.

The associations each have a constitution (either written or unwritten), an elected executive (chairman, secretary, financial secretary, treasurer, women's organizer, etc.), and patron. They serve in the demonstration sites as the medium for:

- farmer-scientist interactions and collaborative work
- farmer-to-farmer interactions including exchange of knowledge and germplasm
- reaching out to farmers and sensitizing them to issues of conservation and development
- mobilizing the latent knowledge, energy, and other resources of farmers for the purpose of conservation and development
- tapping or accessing external support for farmers
- carrying out demonstrations
- in general, empowering farmers politically, socially, and economically.

Capacity-building

Capacity of the associations is strengthened by bank and savings accounts opened by them with the advice of PLEC, and by links developed with government as well as NGOs. In all the three sectors there are links with district assemblies, the Ministry of Food and Agriculture, the Ministry of Lands, Forestry, and Mines (including its Savanna Resources Management Project), the Ministry of Education, and the Environmental Protection Agency of the Ministry of Environment and Science. Collaboration with NGOs is also growing. In southern Ghana, PLEC is involved with the Ghana Rural Reconstruction Movement, Heifer Project International, and the Roman Catholic Church. The principal collaborating NGO in central Ghana is the Ghana Association for the Conservation of Nature, and in northern Ghana it is the Information Centre for Low-External-Input and Sustainable Agriculture Working Group.

There is also collaboration with schools, especially junior secondary schools. PLEC scientists realized that with the very high proportion of children in the country, it is essential for this future generation to understand the importance of preserving and nurturing the natural biodiversity.

Biodiversity and agrodiversity assessment

The role of the farmers' associations was pivotal in popular understanding of the purpose of the field surveys and studies, identification of the expert farmers, and encouraging involvement of over 50 local ethno-botanist experts in the actual survey and verification of results. Documenting the biodiversity and agrodiversity has improved knowledge of local diversity, distribution, and uses of plants, and increased the self-esteem of farmers through explicit recognition of the value of their ethno-botanical knowledge and a growing awareness of a need to conserve rare biotic species. The surveys have helped bridge the gap between systematic scientific knowledge and traditional knowledge.

One measure of the impact is the integration into the local vocabulary of scientific terms such as "transect", "biodiverse", "biodiversity", "agrodiversity", "value addition", and "*in situ*".[6] Initially, however, the new terms were a big problem for many people.

Promoting conservation

Mobilization of farmers for biodiversity conservation is a key PLEC activity, and has proved catalytic. Over 30 demonstrations in traditional as well as modern ways of management were given in 2001 in southern Ghana alone. They involved over 20 expert farmers, including those sponsored by PLEC for training in modern farm management at the University of Ghana Agricultural Research Station at Okumaning. Over 1,000 farmers and schoolchildren attended demonstrations, which were often accompanied by video shows. Extension agents of various ministries also attended.

Foremost among the conservational management practices is *oprowka*. Others are shown in Table 4.4. A successful outcome of the original demonstration activity is subsequent demonstrations for the benefit of other farmers, in a spontaneous and informal farmer-to-farmer arrangement. The expert farmers move not only within demonstration sites but also between sites, and occasionally between regions. Movements often involve an exchange of germplasm.

Some PLEC farmers have already produced good results. George Amponsah Kissiedu, the pioneer PLEC-Ghana farmer at Adenya, has a highly biodiverse home garden, developed on traditional and modern management principles. He uses row planting and balanced use of soil nutrients by a diversity of crops, increasing both food and economic security. This has enabled him to integrate cattle into his farming practice and to diversify on a second farm.

Income-generation activities motivate biodiversity conservation

Table 4.5 summarizes the key PLEC-sponsored value-generating activities. Those that have had the greatest impact are beekeeping in southern Ghana, woodlots, semi-intensive commercial raising of breeds of rare local domestic fowl (central Ghana), processing of cassava into flour in central Ghana, and spinning and weaving of cotton in northern Ghana.

Table 4.4 Management practices used as demonstration activities

Southern Ghana	Central Ghana	Northern Ghana
Management of citrus and oil palms	Management of rare local breeds of domestic fowl under semi-intensive conditions	Management of yams within agroforestry systems
Split-corm technique of propagating plantain and other crops	Management of medicinal plants within conserved forest or arboretum	Establishment of a plot for propagating yams and demonstrating their management
Management of medicinal plants within conserved forest or arboretum	Management of woodlots	Conservation and management of indigenous varieties of rice, *Oryza glaberrima*
Management of trees within farms under food crops	Management of trees within farms under food crops	Management of trees within farms under food crops
Grafting and budding of plants; management of plants in nurseries	Grafting and budding of plants; management of plants in nurseries	Grafting and budding of plants; management of plants in nurseries
Composting	Composting	Composting
Regeneration of forest		

Beekeeping

Beekeeping for honey and wax has caught on the most at Sekesua-Osonson. PLEC sought to expand this enterprise on a commercial scale by supplying wooden hives to replace traditional and fragile earthen ones, and to generate more value from the secondary forest and agroforestry patches located immediately behind many houses. In 2000–2001 25 wooden hives were constructed and distributed between six households and the farmers' association. Beekeeping training and equipment, including boots, protective clothing, and over 300 wooden hives, were provided by the NGO Heifer Project International which collaborates with PLEC. Beekeeping expanded to approximately 70 households. The initial harvest amounted to 25 gallons valued at ¢1,250,000 (US$170 approximately).

Woodlots and plant nurseries

In Jachie the association of female farmers in 1994 initiated a 10 ha woodlot of teak (*Tectona grandis*) for poles and *Cidrella* for firewood. It now generates income principally from sales of poles. According to one report:

Today the woodlot has become one of the major breakthroughs for the [PLEC] project. Increased availability of adequate electric poles and fuel wood has estab-

Table 4.5 PLEC-sponsored value-generation activities carried out through farmers' associations in Ghana

Activity	Ownership and operation	Location	Output/impact status
Plant nursery operation	Farmers' association Privately by individuals	All sites	Income from selling seedlings Contributes to floral diversity
Snail farming	Farmers' association Privately by individuals	Southern and central Ghana	Commercial output expected Enriches faunal diversity; former wild supplies were decimated
Dry-season vegetables using irrigation	Farmers' association	Nyorigu-Benguri-Gonre, northern Ghana	Off-farm seasonal employment and income Enhancement of crop biodiversity
Woodlot operation	Farmers' association	Jachie, central Ghana, and Bongnayili-Dugu-Song	Income from selling of poles: fodder for live-stock; time saved by avoiding need to fetch wood from far away; impoverished soils can still be put to productive use; raised popular esteem of PLEC
Piggery	Initially by farmers' association Eventually to involve private individuals	Gyamfiase-Adenya, southern Ghana	Popular income generation through planned nuclear swine dispersal arrangement Adds to faunal diversity
Sheep	Initially by farmers' association Eventually to involve private individuals	Amanase-Whanabenya, southern Ghana	Income generation Adds to faunal diversity
Semi-intensive commercial raising of rare and local fowl	Farmers' association Privately by individuals	Jachie, central Ghana	Already income yielding Adds to faunal diversity
Beekeeping	Privately by individuals	All sites except Nyorigu-Benguri-Gonre, northern Ghana	Already yielding honey; eventually yield wax; pollination capacity increased; value addition to conserved forest
Processing of cassava into flour for bread and pastries	Privately by individuals	All sites except Nyorigu-Benguri-Gonre, northern Ghana	Improved income; value added to cassava; market for cassava
Spinning and weaving of cotton	Privately by individuals	Bongnayili-Dugu-Song	Employment and income for young women; market for cotton

lished goodwill for the project in the eyes of the villagers, winning their trust ..."
(Oduro 2002b)

Women who formerly needed five hours to collect one headload of firewood now need only two hours. They also participate in watershed design
and management. Impoverished soils are improving and rare medicinal
plants from the wild are being conserved by the women in a medicinal plant
arboretum.

Women from the farmers' associations are organized into groups numbering four to 10, and produce seedlings in the associations' nurseries. At
Bongnayili-Dugu-Song, by the end of 2001, over 40 members of the association had acquired proficiency in plant grafting and budding and pruning
under a PLEC-sponsored training programme. At Nyorigu-Benguri-Gonre,
through PLEC-sponsored female farmer-led demonstrations, growing of
the rare local varieties of rice is spreading among farmers.

In all the three sectors income from sales of assorted seedlings is growing. During one farming season at Gyamfiase-Adenya, sales of oil palm
seedlings from a nursery operated privately by the farmer George Amponsah Kissiedu raised a reported profit of more than ¢1,000,000 (US$140).
Profit from sales of a mix of oil palm and other seedlings from another
PLEC nursery operated by a farmers' association amounted to over
¢2,000,000 (US$280 approximately).

Other value-adding projects

In central Ghana the PLEC-supported project of breeding local varieties of
domestic fowl generates income for the farmers' association as well as for
its individual female members. The other successful project is processing
cassava, the main cash crop, into flour for bread and pastries.

In northern Ghana a PLEC-sponsored programme aims at providing
employment skills to stem outmigration of young women by training them
in spinning and weaving. This draws on the experience of the elderly
women. As at March 2001, 42 young women from four communities had
benefited from the scheme, which operates under the auspices of the Dugu
Suglo Mali Nyori Ginning Association, the women's branch of the PLEC
farmers' association in Bongnayili-Dugu-Song. In Nyorigu-Benguri-Gonre
the women's group obtained profit from PLEC-supported dry-season vegetable gardening to supplement revenue from the cultivation of rare varieties of local rice.

Other income ventures managed by farmers' associations have yet to
yield. They include the piggery which is planned to serve as the nucleus of
a "swine dispersal project" for farmers in Gyamfiase-Adenya. A sheep project at Aboabo aims at producing rams for public sale and parent stock for
supply to PLEC farmers on a credit basis, to stimulate the livestock indus-

try as a supplementary activity to food farming. Other relevant ventures involve snail, fish, and mushroom farming.

Management of agrobiodiversity

The three southern demonstration sites

The PLEC-supported practice of using home gardens and forests conserved near houses to keep bees for honey and wax represents a significant development because it entails enrichment of biodiversity and a rise in its value by increased plant pollination and utilization of nectar.

An arboretum, a secondary forest of rich species of medicinal plants conserved by ex-army sergeant Osom Djeagbo, expert farmer at Sekesua-Osonson, is one of the more significant land-use types. It is a primary source of herbs for traditional medicine in the Bormase community and germplasm for conservationists there and elsewhere. His resolve to conserve the arboretum is strengthened by PLEC's keen interest in it and recognition of its value, and by the increased numbers of visiting researchers and other visitors. His model is inspiring similar arboretum development elsewhere, and the National Centre for Scientific Research into Plant Medicine is collaborating.

Cultivation of assorted yams on the basis of traditional agroforestry principles is highly developed among the Krobo farmers of Sekesua-Osonson (Blay 2002). One expert tenant farmer who manages an agricultural holding within a grassy landscape formerly dominated by forest near Bewase combines elements of the traditional Krobo agroforestry system with the *oprowka* mulching and no-burn practice. He has increased plant biodiversity, grows yams in a way that is apparently enriching soils, and has reported income improvement.

A major crop diversification programme is the promotion of integration of citrus and oil palms into food cropping. Over 40 PLEC farmers grow citrus or oil palms or both with a mix of traditional crops. Some have small mushroom farms to replace the loss of wild fungi.

A further PLEC strategy discourages monocultures in favour of combining traditional intercropping practices with modern cropping practices, such as planting in rows. Diversity of crops ensures both food and economic security by spreading risk of production failure. Schoolchildren are using some of these techniques in their school gardens.

Another biodiversity-enhancing intervention focuses on improving and propagating the threatened traditional agroforestry practice of growing a mix of food crops among trees left *in situ* in periodically cropped fields. The following are key elements of the effort:

- trees-and-food-crop compatibility experiment and studies on optimal spacing of crops relative to trees (Owusu-Bennoah and Enu-Kwesi 2000; Asafo, Laing, and Enu-Kwesi 2002)
- a biodiverse model farm of endemic and exotic species, which is managed along traditional and modern principles by the Gyamfiase-Adenya PLEC Farmers' Association with the support of PLEC scientists
- campaigns through PLEC farmers' associations urging farmers to practise agroforestry.

Central and northern Ghana

Data on the impact of PLEC interventions on biodiversity are still being analysed. Positive feedback reveals that diversity of livestock is being improved through a programme focused on promoting the rearing of local chickens, goats, and sheep as well as rabbits. A water-pond rehabilitation programme is adding to fish supplies. In central Ghana watersheds are being strengthened through the use of plants from farmers' nurseries for rehabilitation of degraded portions. This is helping to enrich the flora and improve soils through increased biomass. It is hoped to check erosion by planting more trees. Tano-Odumasi has a reported 25 per cent increase in the number of biodiverse home gardens.

In northern Ghana the greatest impact appears to have been in the area of yams and rice biodiversity. At the Bongnayili-Dugu-Song site the scientists tapped into the great store of indigenous knowledge about yams, and carried out a detailed morphological characterization of 23 types of yam. Then a farmer member of PLEC CAMP (Collaborative Agroecosystems Management Project) donated land for a yam farm. The plantation is used to demonstrate yam management and propagation of various types and germplasm (Kranjac-Berisavljevic' and Gandaa 2000, 2002), and interested farmers occasionally bring in new types from the wild. There is greatly enhanced popular awareness of rare species and knowledge of types with the highest protein content. A follow-up is the commitment to conservation by farmers.

At Nyorigu-Benguri-Gonre (Bawku-Manga) women are leading conservation of indigenous varieties of African rice, *Oryza glaberrima* (Anane-Sakyi and Dittoh 2001). The women farmers of Gonre have been cultivating many of the 12 local varieties for years, whereas male farmers had switched to introduced "improved" rice and had largely forgotten the names of indigenous species. It was explained to farmers that plant genetic diversity is a key ingredient for sustainable development, and that it would help buffer them against environmental, market, pest, and disease hazards. On-farm trials have since been made by participating farmers, and two of the indigenous varieties have proved to have high yield potential and to compare well with the introduced varieties. Some indigenous varieties have unique properties that women prefer, such as being a good baby food, cooking easily, and keeping well overnight. Availability of seed can be a problem, as the normal seed exchange does not provide enough of the indigenous varieties. The PLEC team has encouraged the women to set up a community seed plot to multiply seed of the six indigenous varieties they prefer and also to work towards improved storage management.

Some of the PLEC-supported activities are ubiquitous as they occur at all sites. They include operation of plant nurseries and conservation of forests, including those regarded as sacred. Sacred groves are protected and improved by vigilance, sanctions, firebelts, buffer zones, and replanting with PLEC support. From their analysis of biodiversity and agrodiversity in southern Ghana, Enu-Kwesi and Vordzogbe (2002) inferred that "protection confers a lower change in species composition in any land use stage, particularly a native forest, provided the area is not disturbed".

Seedlings from nurseries owned and managed by associations of PLEC farmers are used to rehabilitate watersheds, ponds, and even waterfalls. Deforested areas are being rehabilitated. At Jachie in 1994, nearly 20,000 seedlings were raised by the PLEC women's group: the period 1996–2001 saw an 80 per cent increase in the number of seedlings. At all sites integration of a variety of seedlings from nurseries into food-crop farms is enriching biodiversity. The trees include teak, *Cassia siamea*, neem, cedar, citrus, mangoes, and oil palms.

An occasional failure

The PLEC-Ghana effort is not all a success story. In a hilly area near Ebedwo, a village in Gyamfiase-Adenya, an attempt to strengthen the basis of agriculture and biodiversity and to check erosion with the cooperation of a local farmer through the use of *Vetiveria fulvibarbis* grass failed. This was so partly because of weather failure. A more fundamental reason was the objection of landowners to the introduction of a foreign grass in an environment they traditionally perceive as forest.

An attempt at using stone lines to check soil erosion near the same village and at the Sekesua site could also not be sustained despite a positive and visible significant accumulation of soil behind the stone filters. It failed mainly because farmers were not used to the drudgery of carrying stones and lining them systematically along hill contours with the aid of an "A-frame", a device which is simple to construct but ponderous to use.

A major constraint on work was the inability of scientists to visit the field as frequently as they would have liked in order to sustain interactions with farmers, due to their other work obligations and the long trekking distance to farmed areas. The work was also constrained by lack of taxonomists, social anthropologists, and experts in environmental economics. The solutions lie in capacity enhancement through training.

It has been difficult to convince farmers to sacrifice short-term higher monetary gains expected from monoculture for the long-term security that agricultural diversification can offer. This constraint can only be removed by demonstrating the value of diversification.

Other outcomes

Visits by policy-makers, especially those of the government of Ghana, are a growing feature. District-level agents, most especially agricultural extension, occur in all PLEC areas.

In 1995 a former chief of Gyamfiase, the late Nana Oduro Darko II, who was patron and a founding and inspiring member of Gyamfiase-Adenya PLEC Farmers' Association, made a memorable visit to the PLEC office and various departments in the University of Ghana at Legon. He was accompanied by an eight-member entourage including a linguist and farmers. Other spontaneous visits by farmers to PLEC offices have since become routine. Similarly, through telephone calls and occasionally faxed messages, farmers maintain regular contacts with the PLEC administrative office at Legon.

An important initiative of the farmers was their participation in Ghana's first International Food and Agriculture Trade Fair (AGRIFEX), which was organized by the Ministry of Food and Agriculture in conjunction with the Ghana Trade Fair Company in December 2001 at Accra. The diversity of plants and photographs of activities exhibited by farmers' associations from south, central, and northern Ghana attracted considerable interest from policy-makers. Songs by schoolchildren included one specifically composed in honour of PLEC farmers.

PLEC farmers have themselves arranged to be featured on radio and TV programmes. Farmers' associations have established links with government organizations, including the National Plant Genetic Resources Centre, through exchange of visits and germplasm, the Ministry of Food and Agriculture, Forestry Department and other government establishments for seedlings and technical advice, Adventist Development and Relief Agency, and rural banks.

Three graduate students have taken advantage of their association as research assistants with PLEC to produce theses. Foremost is one on "Adaptation of farmers to climate change" by Felix Asante. The thesis provides new useful insights into the kinds of strategies pursued by farmers to cope with climatic variations, especially in capricious environments such as the forest-savanna ecozone. Students for bachelors degrees have also drawn significantly on PLEC information.

Publications

Publications based upon research findings of scientists are an important feature of PLEC work output in Ghana. They feature mostly in *PLEC News and Views*, and need to be developed for publication in peer-reviewed scientific journals and books.

Notes

1. Fairhead and Leach (1998) present evidence that fluctuating agricultural populations, followed by some forest regeneration on formerly cultivated land, have been the norm for centuries.
2. Those who volunteered to work with PLEC at this time were drawn principally from the following institutions: University of Ghana, Legon, Legon/Accra, in southern Ghana; Kwame Nkrumah University of Science and Technology, Kumasi, in central Ghana; and the University for Development Studies, Tamale, in the northern region.
3. Material is drawn from book chapters by Enu-Kwesi (1997), Gyasi (2002), Oduro (2002b), Quansah *et al.* (1998); from final general reports by Gyasi, Asante, and Gyasi (2002), Kranjac-Berisavljevic' (2002), Oduro (2002a); from articles in *PLEC News and News*; and from numerous reports (see References and Bibliography). Comparative material is also drawn from Allan (1965) and Lynn (1937, 1942).
4. It is interesting to note that any other fields (no matter the size of the farm) with plant species compositions that do not correspond to the mix of crops described, including the most popular maize/cassava intercrops or monocrops, are considered to be not "real farms". When one is informed that a farmer has left for "his/her farm" without any further information, it means, to the people of Tano Odumasi, that the farmer has actually gone to the "real farm" or *afupa*. However, when one is informed that a farmer has gone to "the farm" (*afuom*), further questions are needed to ascertain which particular field is being referred to. This minor distinction in the words of the people has important household food security implications embedded in the definition of *afupa*.
5. A now-abandoned experiment of leaving a tract of land unused and unburned for a number of years revealed that almost all trees found only in a more humid region over 100 km to the south would emerge and flourish here (Enu-Kwesi, personal communication, 1996).
6. In fact, the nickname used by children for the coordinating leader, Edwin Gyasi, is Professor Insitu.

REFERENCES

Abdulai, A. S., E. A. Gyasi, and S. K. Kufogbe, with assistance from P. K. Adraki, F. Asante, M. A. Asumah, B. Z. Gandaa, B. D. Ofori, and A. S. Sumani. 1999. "Mapping of settlements in an evolving PLEC demonstration site in northern Ghana: An example in collaborative and participatory work", *PLEC News and Views*, No. 14, pp. 19–24.

Allan, W. 1965. *The African Husbandman*. Edinburgh: Oliver & Boyd.

Amanor, K. S. 1994. *The New Frontier. Farmers' Response to Land Degradation*. London: Zed Books and UNRISD.

Anane-Sakyi, C. and S. Dittoh. 2001. "Agrobiodiversity conservation: Preliminary work on *in situ* conservation and management of indigenous rice varieties in the interior savanna zone of Ghana", *PLEC News and Views*, No. 17, pp. 31–33.

Asafo, L., E. Laing, and L. Enu-Kwesi. 2002. "Effect of some traditional farming practices on the growth and yield of some crops", unpublished manuscript.

Bakang, J. A. 2002. "The system of resource access and distribution and the use of land in central Ghana: A case study of Tano-Odumasi", unpublished manuscript.

Blay, E. T. 2002. "Diversity of yams in PLEC demonstration sites in southern Ghana", *PLEC News and Views*, No. 20, pp. 25–35.

Enu-Kwesi, L. 1997. "Floral and faunal diversity", in E. A. Gyasi and J. I. Uitto (eds) *Environment, Biodiversity and Agricultural Change in West Africa: Perspectives from Ghana*. Tokyo: United Nations University Press, pp. 64–75.

Enu-Kwesi, L. and V. V. Vordzogbe. 2002. "Biodiversity and agrodiversity inventory (with review of causes of land degradation in southern Ghana)", unpublished manuscript.

Fairhead, J. and M. Leach. 1998. *Reframing Deforestation. Global Analyses and Local Realities: Studies in West Africa*. London: Routledge.

Gyasi, E. A. 2002. "Traditional systems of conserving biodiversity within agriculture: Their changing character and relevance to food security", in H. Brookfield, C. Padoch, H. Parsons, and M. Stocking (eds) *Cultivating Biodiversity: Understanding, Analysing and Using Agricultural Diversity*. London: ITDG Publications, pp. 245–255.

Gyasi, E. A., G. T. Agyepong, E. Ardayfio-Schandorf, L. Enu-Kwesi, J. S. Nabila, and E. Owusu-Bennoah. 1995. "Production pressure and environmental change in the forest-savanna zone of Ghana", *Global Environment Change: Human and Policy Dimensions*, Vol. 5, No. 4, pp. 355–366.

Gyasi, E. A., F. Asante, and Y. A. Gyasi. 2002. "Integrated final report of PLEC work in Ghana, August 1992–February 2002", unpublished manuscript.

Gyasi, E. A. and J. I. Uitto (eds). 1997. *Environment, Biodiversity and Agricultural Change in West Africa: Perspectives from Ghana*. Tokyo: United Nations University Press.

Kranjac-Berisavljevic', G. 2002. "Summary report of PLEC work with special reference to history, demonstration site development/activities and achievements in northern Ghana", unpublished manuscript.

Kranjac-Berisavljevic', G. and B. Z. Gandaa. 2000. "Collection of yam types at Bongnayili-Dugu-Song main demonstration site in northern Ghana", *PLEC News and Views*, No. 15, pp. 27–30.

Kranjac-Berisavljevic', G. and B. Z. Gandaa. 2002. "Sustaining diversity of yams in northern Ghana", *PLEC News and Views*, No. 20, pp. 36–43.

Lynn, C. W. 1937. *Agriculture in North Mamprusi*. Accra: Department of Agriculture Bulletin 34.

Lynn, C. W. 1942. "Agriculture in North Mamprusi: A review of a decade's progress", *Farm and Forest*, No. 3, pp. 78–83.

Oduro, W. 2002a. "Summary report of PLEC-GEF work with special reference to history, demonstration site development/activities and achievements in central Ghana." PLEC-Ghana, unpublished manuscript.

Oduro, W. 2002b. "Genesis and purpose of the women farmers' group at Jachie, central Ghana", in H. Brookfield, C. Padoch, H. Parsons, and M. Stocking (eds) *Cultivating Biodiversity: Understanding, Analysing and Using Agricultural Diversity*. London: ITDG Publications, pp. 145–152.

Owusu-Bennoah, E. and L. Enu-Kwesi. 2000. "Investigating into trees that combine effectively with field crops", *PLEC News and Views*, No. 15, pp. 20–22.

Pacey, A. 1990. *Technology in World Civilization: A Thousand-Year History*. Oxford: Basil Blackwell.

Quansah, C., E. Asare, E. Y. Safo, E. O. Amontuah, N. Kyei-Baffour, and J. A. Balang. 1998. "The effect of poultry manure and mineral fertilizer on a maize/cassava intercrop in peri-urban Kumasi, Ghana", in P. Dreschel and L. Gyiele (eds) *On-farm Research on Sustainable Land Management in Sub-Saharan Africa*. Bangkok: IBSRAM.

Quansah, C. and W. Oduro. 2002. "The '*proka*' mulching and no-burn systems: A case study of Tano-Odumasi and Jachie", unpublished manuscript.

5

Guinée

Ibrahima Boiro, A. Karim Barry, and Amadou Diallo

Background

Guinée was the first francophone country and the second country in West Africa to become independent. Having voted against de Gaulle's French Community plan in 1958, it was immediately given independence but cut off by France from aid, which first came from Ghana and then in larger volume from the former USSR and its allies. From 1958 until the 1980s Guinée was governed by a nominally socialist regime which made few lasting economic changes in rural areas, but which did effect a number of social changes that were of significance. These changes did not, however, go so far as to overturn inequalities in access to land in areas such as the Fouta Djallon, in which PLEC worked.

Evolution of the cluster and its work

The idea of developing a PLEC cluster in Guinée arose at the first major workshop in Ghana in 1994, where it was proposed to develop work in other West African countries. The meeting was attended by English anthropologists Melissa Leach and James Fairhead, who had done substantial work in Guinée. They provided the West African PLEC leader with advice on whom to contact in Conakry. In 1995 Professor Ibrahima Boiro of the Centre d'Études et de Recherche en Environnement at Conakry and Dr

Sidafa Camara of the Université de Conakry (Faculté des Lettres et Sciences Humaines) attended a Ghana-PLEC meeting at Kumasi in central Ghana. Subsequently a core team was formed in Guinée, and it proposed areas on the Fouta Djallon upland and in the semi-arid region near Kouroussa as sites for work. The Fouta Djallon was to come first.

In 1995 the team evaluated the agro-ecological conditions of each zone of the Fouta Djallon and met with the relevant ministries. Bantignel (Pita), located in the central Fouta Djallon in the Guetoya sub-basin, was chosen as the study site because of a survey produced by the FAO accompanying the reforestation of 42 ha of degraded land there. The preliminary research involved the farmers of Kollangui and Hadiya as well as local rural development authorities at Pita, especially the agricultural research station at Bareng. A preliminary phase report was completed at the end of 1996 (Barry et al. 1996). Work was expanded to a group of localities lying further to the south-east in the Guetoya Basin. By 1998 PLEC concentrated in five main communities, Missidè Héïré, Tioukoungol, Goloya, Dar ès Salam, and Lari, over a linear distance of about five kilometres. The group also initiated work at Moussaya near Kouroussa in the north-east of the country. At 600 km from Conakry, it proved hard to sustain this site and the situation became more critical after a core member of the team, Sékou Fofana, was seconded from the Centre d'Études et de Recherche en Environnement in 2000. Following advice, arrangements were made with scientists from the Université de Kankan, only about 80–100 km from Moussaya, to manage most of the work at that site.

The Fouta Djallon (Pita-Bantignel)

The area is a group of plateaux with deep valleys at altitudes varying between 600 and 1,500 m. There are three main geomorphological divisions of the Fouta Djallon (Diallo et al. 1987): the central plateau (600–1500 m); the intermountain zones (300–600 m); and plains and foothills. The entire area of the Fouta Djallon region is about 56,000 square kilometres, or approximately 22 per cent of the total land area of Guinée. It is geologically ancient and has a history of least a thousand years of human occupation, largely for livestock husbandry. Such woody forest as remains is secondary and comprised of stunted and distorted trees, especially *Parinari excelsa* and *Parkia biglobosa*. Grass covers a large part of the degraded areas. The radiating pattern of rivers, which flow heavily during the May–October rainy season, make the Fouta Djallon the "watershed of West Africa". The Guetoya River basin covers approximately 77 square kilometres, with an average altitude between 800 and 1,000 m. By the national census of 1999, the population of the basin was 7,846 inhabitants with a population density

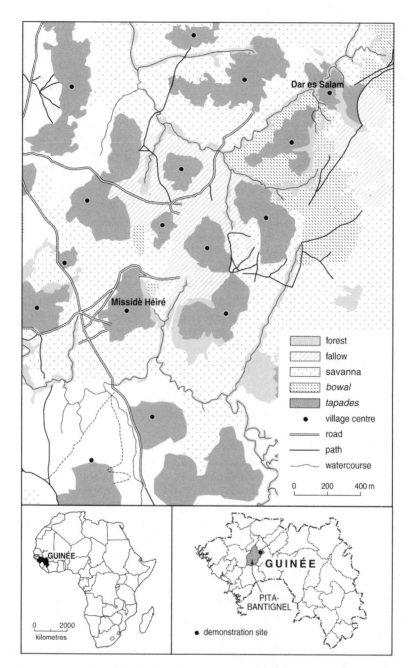

Figure 5.1 Land use in the Bantignel region of the Fouta Djallon in Guinée

of 60/km². There are around 3,442 inhabitants in the demonstration site villages, of whom 70 per cent are farmers. There are also traders, Koranic teachers, and some craftsmen, but only around 27 per cent of the people can read and write in Arabic script or French.

The landscape consists of a succession of hardpans (*bowal*) separated by largely open areas; two lithographic units are sandstone and dolerite. Three main types of soils have been identified: ferralitic soils, hydromorphic soils, and skeletal soils. More information is obtained from the vernacular typology used by Fulbe people to classify their soils; it integrates relief, texture, and hydromorphy. The Fulbe names designating the different types of soils are very convenient to use, and are also pertinent and efficient for fieldwork due to their clear separation and relation to agronomic utility. Each main soil type corresponds with a different part of the complex series of catenas which link the higher and lower areas. Table 5.1 is modified from Maignien (1960) to incorporate the Fulbe classification. All these soils are variably characterized by acidity (pH is below 5.0), are poor in organic matter, and have low base saturation. Nitrogen, calcium, available phosphorous, and micro-nutrients are low and there is low cation exchange capacity.

Table 5.2 is derived from interpretation of 1978 air photographs of the area of concentrated work, and shows the percentage of the different land types encountered. Within the demonstration sites vegetation is mainly woody, with community forests around villages and gallery forests along watercourses. This table shows that about a third of all land is in fallow, while village land occupies 26.5 per cent of the measured area.

The people and their land use

Fulbe (Fulani) people first entered the area as pastoralists in the thirteenth century, and a later fully Islamic wave conquered the area from its formerly dominant Djallonké holders in the eighteenth century. Many Djallonké became slaves, and the Fulbe also obtained other slaves during their wars of conquest. By the late nineteenth century, slaves and their descendants formed the large majority of the population, ruled by the Fulbe who, until French conquest, governed the area as a centralized, theocratic state. Slavery was abolished during the colonial period, but the effect was only that the former slaves became serfs, still obliged to work for their former masters and obtaining land only from them. The serfs lived in separate communities, and could be evicted and relocated at will.

Fulbe, originally pastoralists, are now a fully agricultural people, although cattle remain important. Since the political reforms of the early independence period, the former serfs now also regard themselves as Fulbe, using the family names of their former masters. Although labour obligations were abolished in 1949, successive post-colonial land reforms have not greatly

Table 5.1 Description of soils within the Bantignel demonstration sites

Soil types	Vernacular names	Texture	Depth	Lithology	Topography
Ferralitic soils (yellowish)	*N'Dantari*	Silty-clay	50–100 cm	Sandy	Slope 3–5%
Hydromorphic soils	*Hollandè*	Sandy-silt and silty-clay	50–120 cm	Sandy	Slope 2–3%
Gravelly ferralitic soils	*Wossourè* and *hansanghèrè*	Boulder or gravel mixed with silt	About 100 cm	Sandy, stony	Slope 5–30%
Rich soils	*Dounkiré*	Sandy-silt or clay	More than 150 cm	Low terrace	Lowland slope 3%
Red ferralitic soils	*N'Danta pada*	Clay-silt > 60%	Variable 50–100 cm	Sandstone oligomectic	Weak slope
Top ferralitic soils	*Bowal*	Hardpan	Weak	Hardpan thick laterite	Irregular slope 4–10%

114

Table 5.2 Classification of the landscape shown in Figure 5.1 (Bantignel)

Land-use types	Area (ha)	%
Bowal	200.49	3.30
Community forests	76.87	1.30
Woody savanna	1,367.34	22.80
Fallow – 7 years	1,468.46	24.50
Grassland fallow	23.89	0.40
Grassland savanna	266.49	4.40
Forest grove	4.65	0.07
Woody fallow	408.91	6.80
Degraded area	4.44	0.07
Woody land	192.46	3.20
Bushy savanna	74.25	1.20
Fields in cultivation	27.14	0.40
Gallery forest	265.66	4.40
Villages and *tapades*	1,586.59	26.50
Forest	21.73	0.40
Total	5,989.40	99.97

changed the structure of access to land in this region. Some 80 per cent of the land is held by only about 10 per cent of the people, being mainly those Fulbe who are descended from the conquerors and who occupy only a minority of the villages. Commoner Fulbe own their land within their village areas, but not the outlying fields. Some former serfs have acquired land within their own village areas, but many still pay a rent of 10 per cent of produce to the Fulbe owners.

There is a common pattern of settlement and land use, constituting an almost classic infield-outfield system. PLEC work cannot be understood except in the context of this system, which evolved between one and three centuries ago. It has two main elements, and a small area which does not fall into either.[1]

The tapades *(infields)*

The *tapade* is at once the village, the core of the system of landholding and allocation, and the intensively cultivated infields. The *tapades* contain the houses of landholders and their wives, usually with one concession (about 0.25 up to 0.5 ha) per wife. The wife "owns" her concession while she remains married, but inheritance and transfer are only to male descendants. In the former-slave *tapades*, family or joint-family residence is common. The family concessions, combining the allocations of different wives of the same husband where there is more than one (*sunturés*), are each enclosed by a fence and form a network.

Certainly, from as long ago as the nineteenth century, the *sunturés* were intensively cultivated with large imports of manure and recycling of vegetable and other wastes. The manure was supplied by the small *n'dama* cattle of the Fulbe, as well as goats and sheep, the proportion of which has increased through time. The livestock are pastured without supervision on the open lands outside the *tapades*, as well as being stall-fed within them. Cattle are normally corralled at night just inside the boundary fences, while goats and sheep have pens within the enclosure that are approached by narrow runways from the boundary fences. Some fences are live hedges, while others are built of dead wood. Fencing is a male task, although formerly the women had to collect the wood from a distance. There are fences around all *tapades*. In some villages there are many developed fenced paths, as in Missidè Héïré, Goloya, Nyafouya, Tioukoungol, and Dar ès Salam. Within former-slave villages the expansion of *tapades* develops as an aggregation: new families (who do not have kinship relations with established families) create new enclosures around villages. In Fulbe villages development has been by internal growth. Expansion takes place like an ordinary extension of the community dwelling.

All *tapades* have the appearance of orchards due to the density of trees, which include *Parinari excelsa*, *Parkia biglobosa*, and *Erythrophleum guineense*, many fruit trees (citrus and mango), and *Ficus* spp. Men plant and own the fruit trees within the *tapades*. Women and children do almost all other work. Before the rains have begun, and after taro and cassava remaining from the previous year are lifted, manure is collected, dried, spread on the ground, and hoed in. Taro is immediately replanted. As soon as the rains begin maize is planted, followed by cassava, groundnuts, and sweet potatoes. A number of other plants, some of them recent introductions, are also planted. These include tomatoes, *courge* (*Cucurbita pepo*), *niébé* (cowpea, *Vigna unguicalata*), pea aubergine (*Solanum torvum*), chilli (*Capsicum frutescens*), *gombo* (*Hibiscus esculenta*), yam (*Dioscorea alata*), haricot beans (*Phaseolus vulgaris*), and potatoes. Then the whole surface between the growing crops is covered in leaves, collected from within the *tapade* and outside, mostly for mulch but sometimes composted together with animal manure. Weeding and further spreading of ash, manure, and domestic refuse on the land continue through the year. Small quantities of chemical fertilizer, if available, are applied on a precision basis to the plant sites.

Maize is harvested at the end of the wet season, and the *tapades* yield mainly root crops and fruit until the following wet season. In the *tapade* at Missidè Héïré, PLEC has measured yields on 6.5 ha and found that maize yielded up to seven tonnes/ha, cassava 21 tonnes/ha, sweet potatoes 19 tonnes/ha, and groundnuts about eight tonnes/ha.

There are two types of *tapades*. One is old-established and matches the criteria of crop association and the mulch-based restitution of soil fertility using animal manure. The second is a preparatory extension of the *tapade* where monocultures such as groundnut, fonio, or cassava are predominant.

Depending on fertilizer input, it takes 10 years or longer before a *sunturé* achieves full production, with input of nutrients fully replacing the harvest. When maturity has been achieved, the pH within the tapade is up to 1.5 points higher than in the open land outside. Soil structure and chemical content, except phosphorus, reach satisfactory levels. Although heavy application of manure can override the natural differences, *tapades* on *hansaghèré* (upper catena) soils, such as those of Missidè Héïré, often do better than those on *n'dantari* (lower catena) soils. The majority of *tapades* – and especially those of the Fulbe as opposed to the former serfs – have been made on the former. The *n'dantari* lands are mainly devoted to rotational use in external fields.

The external fields (outfields)

In the characteristic infield-outfield manner, the fields outside the *tapades* are deprived of nutrients in favour of the infields. The outfields are cultivated from three to five or seven years, then fallowed for at least six or seven years, and sometimes longer. They are not allocated to individuals as are the enclosures within the *tapades*, nor are they collectively owned as are the small reserved areas around the Fulbe villages. Even now, large external areas, comprising two-thirds of all the land, remain owned by the descendants of those who held them at the time the settlement pattern was established. These are the highest class among the Fulbe of Hindé and Bantignel Maounde, situated some kilometres away. At the Fulbe village of Missidè Héïré the core families own almost all the land within their *tapade*. Although a good deal of this land has been bought and sold in modern times, the holders of land within the *tapade* own none of the surrounding land, and their external fields are from two to as much as 10 kilometres away. External land may sometimes be rented for a single payment covering the five years or so of cultivation, but most land is rented annually on sharecropping tenancies at an annual fee of 10 per cent of the crop. Because of land shortage in this densely populated area, individual plots in the external fields are seldom larger than one hectare.

Work in the outlying fields is also done mainly by the women and children, except for some of the heavier hoeing work and use of an ox-plough where this is possible. Clearing and burning are dry-season jobs, and planting begins as early in the wet season as the prior demands of establishing the maize and other crops in the *tapades* will allow. Often three weedings are necessary, and the women do all these. The undemanding fonio (*Digitaria exilis*), grown mainly in these outfields, is the basic grain crop in Fulbe subsistence.

The type of cultivation and fallow cover depend on the soil. The stony but more fertile *wossourè* and *hansaghèré* soils permit longer periods of cultivation, and support a low, woody fallow. Those on steeper slopes can be cultivated only by hand. The *hansaghèrè* soils will support four crops – upland rice, then groundnuts and two crops of fonio – before being fallowed. It is only on these soils that upland rice, formerly a more important crop on the Fouta Djallon, is still sown. Cultivation on the sloping and more stony areas is considerably reduced because of the large but mainly temporary out-migration of men.[2]

Larger field areas are developed on the *n'dantari* soils. Their stone-free constitution permits use of the ox-drawn plough; these soils will support only two or three crops, sometimes all fonio. There are limited areas of nitrogen-fixing groundnuts. On the smaller areas of hydromorphic (*hollandé*) soils, lowland rice (as a dry crop) is possible as the first and even third crop in a four-year cycle.

Since livestock pasture freely by day outside the *tapades*, the cropped areas in the external fields must be fenced. Cattle can break through weak fences, which last only one year before they have to be rebuilt. Previous fences are employed as a source of increasingly scarce firewood. The productivity of most of the external fields is extremely low, and is declining due to heavy use with insufficient fallow, collection of dung from them for use on more intensively cultivated land, and their liability to sheet erosion, especially on the *n'dantari* soils. The lower part of the Guetoya River basin (Hadiya, Kollangui) is less populated, and some of the land now carries *Acacia mangium* and *Acacia auriculiformis* introduced in 1990 by the FAO project. Formerly this area was very depleted and even fonio failed, but there is some improvement in the last decade.

The alluvial areas along the streams

These small areas have year-round use, which their clayey *dounkiré* soils will support. They are cultivated for unirrigated lowland rice and maize in the wet season. In the dry season, with daily hand irrigation, they support a variety of vegetable crops for sale in the nearby weekly markets. Some are fertilized with urea and other products bought in those markets. Organic manures are also applied, especially on seedbeds. Dry-season farming in the valleys is less labour intensive than in the *tapades*, but not by a wide margin. Some alluvial areas remain under gallery forest, but usually of a degraded type except where carefully reserved close to villages.

North-east region (Moussaya)

Moussaya is in the upper Niger watershed, on a low plateau, with uplands around 500 m and valleys falling to around 350 m. The surrounding area is a wooded savanna. As in the Fouta Djallon, there is a single wet season. The settlement was founded by Malinké-speaking people who were originally hunters, and hunting for small game remains a seasonal activity. Society is patrilineal, with four founding lineages at its core. The village has about 1,200 inhabitants. Land is a collective property, but is worked by lineages. Individual members of the community may farm anywhere, and hold the land so long as they are using it. Permanent possession is confined to small enclosed areas for house gardens. A stranger seeking land must approach the lineage heads.

There are four main field types: bush fields, house gardens, lowland rice fields, and fallows. The bush fields, spread at some distance from the village on higher land, grow upland rice, maize, and fonio, together with cassava, yams, and groundnuts, commonly intermingled. Cotton is also cultivated. Land is cleared using fire, and the men do all tillage work, principally with hoes but also some with ox-drawn ploughs. Women are responsible for weeding and harvesting. Bush fields are cultivated for from two to five years, and sometimes even up to 10 years, and are then fallowed for from 10 to 30 years, becoming forested during this longer time. Fallows are pastured by livestock and fruit trees are planted. Firewood is collected from the fallow. The families who formerly cultivated the site are responsible for the fallow land, but no individual ownership persists into a following cultivation cycle. House gardens, mostly in shallow valleys close to the village, are family property, worked mainly by women. Vegetables and tubers are cultivated in the wet season and fruit trees are sometimes planted. Cultivation in the dry season is limited because the water table falls as the season advances. The rice fields are 12 km from the village close to the Niger River. Inundation is natural, without diversionary or water-retaining works, and a series of dry years has reduced production. The land is cultivated using ploughs.

Livestock are pastured on all types of land, and close to the village fencing is needed to protect crops. The community also depends on hunting, a substantial amount of craft work, and the collection of honey. The area lies close to the buffer zone of the Parc National du Niger and the people participate in the management of this zone, in collaboration with the authorities.

PLEC activities in the demonstration sites

PLEC-Guinée has strengthened collaboration between the scientists, farmers, and decision-makers at all levels, from local to national. This allowed the team to get good results in areas such as combating soil exhaustion, encouraging agroforestry, safeguarding the environment, and improving the rural population welfare and people's awareness on the state of the environment. The PLEC project approach conforms closely to the government strategy to reduce poverty through the rural development sector and the development and management of natural resources.

Immediately after the final choice of the sites, fieldwork started by making all stakeholders aware of the objectives of the project. In Bantignel, 10 meetings of scientists, farmers, rural development and NGO agents, and local and prefectural authorities were held at prefecture and community levels. At the beginning there was a certain fear and reserve from the Fulbe notables and some farmers, but as activities progressed and were shown to be profitable, the people fully participated. At the village community level 52 groupings were distributed in the eight districts of the Bantignel subprefecture. PLEC-Guinée was asked by the farmers' associations for collaboration or material, moral, and technical assistance.

Identification and choice of expert farmers

Given the highly stratified social system in the Fouta Djallon, it was not easy to select expert farmers. The team looked specifically for particularly good farmers who, in this case unlike in other clusters, had previous experience of project work, were able to communicate with others and transmit their knowledge to their colleagues, and had the status to do this. After the first meetings at Missidè Héïré, Dar ès Salam, Goloya, and Tioukoungol in 1998, and on the advice from an NGO, the Association des Volontaires pour le Développement et Protection de l'Environnement (AVODEP), Mamadou Aliou Kane from Héïré and Mody Oumar Barry from Dar ès Salam were chosen. Later, in 1999, the late Mamadou Diallo and Aïssatou Barry from Goloya and Tioukoungol were added on the basis of their experiences and their abilities in human as well as natural resource management.

None of these people was a leader in the political sense or was a principal landholder, yet they were required to exercise leadership among and beyond their own communities. Because there is also a stratification among the communities themselves, principal reliance was placed on the two farmers from Héïré and Dar ès Salam, both of which are mosque villages, senior to others around them. The team also placed considerable reliance on technicians from the Agricultural Research Station at Bareng (Pita), and on specialists from AVODEP. Expert farmers were also identified at Moussaya, but only limited use was made of their services.

Demonstration activities

The activities carried out in the demonstration sites varied. Some were initiated by the scientists, some by technicians, and some were based on farmers' own initiatives. Especially in the earlier years, technicians led many of the demonstration activities. The expert farmers acted more as conduits and leaders of farmer groupings than as initiators. The team gave particular emphasis to activities that would improve soil and water management.

Diverse themes related to endogenous and modern technologies have been developed for an exchange of ideas to find out what the farmers know and do not know. This approach was initiated by the demonstrators, followed by questions and answers. The development of topics allowed the team to collect information related to the traditional knowledge in the field of biodiversity in the agricultural systems of the demonstration sites, and to integrate this with modern knowledge. The collection and comparison of information later helped to formulate policy and technical recommendations at local and national levels.

The total of participants in PLEC-Guinée demonstrations numbered 438, among whom 68 per cent were farmers and 32 per cent were scientists and technicians. Table 5.3 sets out activities between 1998 and 2001.

Compost-making above ground

This has been one of the main activities in the demonstration sites in Bantignel. It started in 1998, with the objective of using agricultural residue and animal waste to increase yield with organic inputs at low cost. The technician in charge of the demonstration first indicated all the technical details of compost-making, the input quality, and the composting requirements during the dry and rainy seasons. Inputs must be easily biodegradable, with strong concentrations of nitrogen, phosphorus, calcium, and potash. He explained the composting technique, showed the tools used, the raw materials (straw, animal wastes, harvest by-products, grass, domestic wastes) and their possible sources, and the technique of creating different layers, which was new to the farmers. Subsequently, these farmers have demonstrated the method throughout the participating communities and beyond.

In Moussaya the technician demonstrated compost preparation using agricultural by-products and domestic wastes, and explained how it helps manage the biomass. A comparative study of compost prepared with these raw materials showed the importance of using this type of compost.

Tapade *cropping: Preparation, sowing, harvest, and product conservation (Pita-Bantignel)*

The *tapade*, once created and enriched, is cultivated every year after the harvest of cassava, potato, and groundnuts. During the dry season organic fertilizers such as animal manure, agricultural wastes, dry straw, and household wastes are put on the ground, or burned so that the ash can be used at the start of the new cultivation season. The two expert farmers showed all the inputs necessary for fertilizing the *tapade*, and spoke about pest control.

Table 5.3 List of demonstration activities

Activity	Demonstrator	Participants
Missidè Héïré area		
Preparation of compost (at Missidè Héïré)	Technician	15 farmers and 5 scientists
Tapade farming (at Héïré and Goloya)	2 expert farmers	30 farmers and 6 scientists
Extension of *tapade* (Héïré and Dar ès Salam)	Expert farmer	20 farmers and 4 scientists
Outfield clearing (at Dianguel)	3 expert farmers	4 scientists and 8 farmers
Establishment of a local plant species nursery (at Héïré and Tioukoungol)	2 expert farmers	6 scientists and 6 farmers
Mulching in the gardens and under tree plantation (at Héïré and Dar ès Salam)	2 expert farmers	5 farmers, 4 scientists, and 3 technicians
Moussaya		
Rice farming in rows	Technician	5 scientists, 10 farmers, and 2 technicians
Fabrication and setting of a traditional hive	Expert farmer	5 farmers and 6 scientists
Preparation of compost by using refuse and agricultural waste	Technician	5 farmers and 6 scientists
Traditional method of honey harvest	Expert farmer	6 farmers, 4 scientists, and 2 technicians
Post-harvest conservation	Expert farmer	23 farmers, 7 scientists, and 7 technicians
Bantignel		
Agrobiodiversity inventory	2 scientists	5 farmers, 6 scientists, and 4 technicians
Proper management of cowsheds	2 scientists	6 farmers and 3 technicians
Transplantation of local plant species	Farmer	5 farmers and 5 scientists
Advantages of live fences compared to dead-wood fences	Technician	36 farmers, 6 scientists, and 6 technicians
Planting coffee under canopy	Farmer and technician	12 farmers and 6 scientists
Setting firebelt around villages and plantations	Technician	13 farmers, 4 scientists, and 5 technicians
Community forest management	2 farmers	23 farmers, 6 scientists, and 4 technicians

Table 5.3 (cont.)

Activity	Demonstrator	Participants
Production of fodder by using agricultural waste	Breeder	22 farmers, 4 scientists, and 7 technicians
Identification of good soil through field indicators	Farmer	23 farmers, 8 scientists, and 8 technicians
Restoration of outfield fertility (fallow system)	2 farmers	5 farmers, 4 scientists, and 3 technicians
Plantation of *Anacardium occidentalis*	Technician	23 farmers, 5 scientists, and 4 technicians

They also indicated the cultivation techniques on the outer parts of the *tapades* where soil fertility is much less than in the areas close to the houses which benefit most from inputs. The farmers enumerated the tools used in soil preparation, sowing, maintenance, and harvesting. They showed which varieties are best sown at what period of the agricultural calendar, and the possibilities of introducing new varieties that are economically and agro-ecologically suited.

Mulching in the gardens and under trees (Pita-Bantignel)

Garden mulching allows maintenance of humidity and nutrients to ensure the rapid growth of the plants. This practice also helps to avoid or diminish soil erosion and controls weeds. It uses branches cut from within the garden or outside. Tree pruning readily gives leafy branches to cover the ground around the plants, as excessive shade is not good for the young plants. This practice is currently ongoing in the coffee-tree plantations.

Management of cowshed manure (Pita-Bantignel)

In 1998 PLEC and AVODEP combined in the construction of the first modern cowshed at Héïré in the Pita-Bantignel area. Several cowsheds have since been built in other demonstration site villages, and the expert farmers have repeated the message widely. Cowshed management is important to animals and farmers. It consists of frequently providing litter for the animals, protecting the urine channel, and ensuring that incoming water does not bring in non-fermentable matter. Dry straw, the stover of fonio and rice, is recommended as litter. The cowshed should have a small slope to facilitate the urine flow. The litter in the urine canal should be refreshed frequently to get compost rich in fertilizing elements.

Agrobiodiversity inventory (Pita-Bantignel and Moussaya)

The scientists who led this demonstration started by explaining the importance of making an inventory of the flora, fauna, and crops on a scientific basis. They showed the method of inventory according to the vegetation type and field type. To form the subplots of one square metre they used iron bars and explained the method of random sampling of the subplots and the numbering technique of each plant species in the sample. The farmers understood that inventory is necessary in order to determine the endangered status of the species. The expert farmers noted the importance of the work for the conservation and reforestation of the degraded areas by local species.

Importance of quickset live fences (Pita-Bantignel)

During this demonstration the agricultural engineer showed the four types of fences found in the Fouta Djallon: built barriers (dead-wood fences) or palisades of dead wood or prickly plants; live fences; fences of bricks, cement, or stone; and barbed or wire netting. The quickset hedges are constituted in different ways according to their economic use (firewood, construction wood, fruit, medicinal, mulching, or fodder species), their ecological use (windbreak, soil fertility, shelter for small wildlife, or conservation value), and their life cycle.

As quickset fence material he mentioned three plant categories: cuttings, planted tree species, and spontaneous species. The fence used for the demonstration had eight species planted from cuttings, four planted species, and six wild species. The demonstrator also explained the reason for the choice of forest species to prevent invasion by domestic animals. He estimated the volume of wood needed to build 100 m of fence (about 15 m^3) compared with the volume of wood (4 m^3) necessary to fire 2,500 bricks to make an enclosure of 100 m. This allowed farmers to understand the impact of dead-wood fences on the environment. The demonstration convinced the farmers of the necessity to replace the dead-wood fences by quickset hedges to save time, reduce work, and restore fallows.

The PLEC-Guinée researchers initiated a further activity of replacing wooden fences with wire, preferably supported by live hedge species. One advantage is the significant reduction of wood-cutting, allowing better restoration of fallows, pasture, and the fauna shelters. New fencing of 3,000 m and 800 m, at Héïré and Dar ès Salam respectively, saved much woodland and also saved two months of work in construction and maintenance.

Coffee-tree plantation under canopy (Pita-Bantignel)

The demonstration indicated the different varieties of coffee (*Robusta* and *Arabica*). *Robusta* does not do as well under shade as *Arabica*. The very knowledgeable demonstrator explained nursery and transplantation techniques. Coffee planting under the canopy is expanding in Bantignel, where it ensures a good microclimate, provides for the daily consumption of coffee, and generates income. Some institutions encourage this activity as a means to reduce poverty, and they subsidize farmers with large coffee plantations.

Early fires around houses and forest and fruit plantations (Pita-Bantignel)

This activity constitutes a security measure that the farmers take at the beginning of the dry season to avoid fires that could consume houses with straw roofs or the plantations or orchards. The forest and water service agents have recommended this technique since the colonial era. The demonstrator showed the measures to be taken before setting the fire. It is not necessary to wait until all the grass dries when clearing a band of 10–20 m. In setting the fire, it is important to watch it from the beginning to the end.

Three farmers were trained in this environmental protection technique by two rural development agents, with the aim of promoting fire management techniques throughout the villages. The process is very beneficial as it avoids deforestation and protects gallery and other managed forests. Productive activities like agroforestry introduced by PLEC also help to manage resources better, especially in limiting damage by bush fires which formerly ravaged many hectares during the dry seasons.

Management of the community forests (Pita-Bantignel)

The two farmers who led the demonstration explained the historical, cultural, and economic reasons for the forest reserve. The advantages and disadvantages of the forests were discussed, with emphasis on the need to provide windbreaks. The forest is a reserve of medicinal plants, food plants, and fodder. These resources are extracted with the advice of knowledgeable men. Reforestation along the edges prevents animals from gaining access and wandering, and thus provides manure to the villagers.

Product conservation after harvest (Moussaya)

After threshing fonio and rice, the grain is dried and put in bags. The demonstrating farmer explained the "preservatives" that can be added to prevent insect attacks. The tubers (such as cassava) are peeled and dried before being put in bags to conserve on shelves in the cooking house, where they receive heat. Some cassava varieties need to be treated to eliminate cyanide toxicity.

Field indicators of rich and poor soils (Pita-Bantignel)

The demonstrating farmer used the soil morphological structures and the biological diversity they support to differentiate rich from poor soils. He explained that the same plant species grow differently according to the soil types, and this may require a modification of crop varieties. The farmer selected farms that were several kilometres distant. During this demonstration he showed woody and herbaceous species that indicate soil fertility. The presence of worms indicates soil fertility, especially for upland rice. Natural conditions are the cause of differences in species growth. Soil depth and land slope, percentage of stones, and differences in permeability are particularly significant. The degree of aluminium toxicity, the organic matter content, and the carbon/nitrogen ratio also denote fundamental differences. To validate the expert farmer's ideas, soil samples taken from different soil types were analysed at the laboratory. The results confirmed the traditional knowledge.

Fallow fertility restoration (Pita-Bantignel)

In the Fouta Djallon, and also in Moussaya, fallow restoration depends on natural processes. Some farmers mix crops of the last year with *Harungana madagascariensis*, *Erythrophleum guineense*, or *Uvaria*, which accelerate fertility restoration. Bush fires are also avoided. The demonstrator explained the plants used for soil restoration of fallows and the nitrogen-fixing plants. Controlled pasturing of livestock during the early fallow years is also important.

Other activities and experimentation

Responding to the government preoccupation with new economic policies, as well as to PLEC goals, the researchers committed themselves to group training in the demonstration sites. This support contributed to fertility restoration and to development of income-generating activities. All the activities indicated in Table 5.4 were initiated and led by farmers, with the technical, material, and scientific support of PLEC, rural development agents, and NGOs working in the locality. Before the project began the dry season was an inactive period that led to rural-urban migration after the harvest period.

Dyeing (Pita-Bantignel)

The revival of this ancient trade has been initiated to derive value from biodiversity through dyeing. It is an activity of the village women of Missidè Héïré and neighbouring villages. The local plants used are *Indigofera tinctoria*, *Morinda geminata*, *Nauclea latifolia*, and *Lawsonia inermis*. In 2002 the president of the women's dyer group tried cotton planting in her *tapade*. For the women this is an activity of major economic importance, bringing in a significant income. Because of increased pressure on tree resources, assistance in planting the principal species has now become a part of PLEC support. By 2001 the local market for the striking blue clothing was becoming

Table 5.4 Results of demonstration activities and experiments

Activity	Pita-Bantignel				Moussaya		
	1998	1999	2000	2001	1999	2000	2001
Market production of vegetables (kg)	8,000	17,500	22,750	21,600	–	–	–
Apiculture (litres of honey)	–	–	–	–	40	56	100
Collection of *néré* (*Parkia biglobosa*) and *karité* (*Vitellaria paradoxa*) (kg)	–	–	–	–	500	1,200	2,600
Cultivation of grain and root crops (kg)		11,000	16,500	29,500	7,500	13,600	23,700
Manure sheds	–	2	–	16	–	–	–
Clothes dyed	75	153	350	475	–		

saturated, and efforts were being made to market the product in more distant areas.

Soap-making (Pita-Bantignel)

This activity is exclusively conducted by the Goloya, Hindé, Héïré, Tioukoungol, and Dar ès Salam women's associations. These associations depend on individual contributions, PLEC-Guinée support, and since 2000 World Food Programme support. PLEC provided material to the groups. It is an income-generating activity using local plants, and saves the women buying soap from markets several kilometres away.

Literacy training for women

When PLEC arrived there were almost no literate women in these communities, yet they needed to be able to read and write to conduct business. Starting in 1999, regular classes to impart literacy in French were begun at Missidè Héïré, and have drawn participants from other villages. By 2002, 27 women had learned to read and write.

Giving agriculture new impetus (Pita-Bantignel)

Two groups of women farmers are led by expert farmers Mamadou Aliou Kane at Missidè Héïré and Mody Oumar Barry at Dar ès Salam. Both of them are specialists in compost-making. The groups grow maize, fonio, and rice, and market tomatoes, cabbage, onion, lettuce, aubergine, and other garden crops, potatoes, sweet potatoes, cassava, and groundnuts. The harvest and the income contribute to meeting the needs of the group members.

With the advice of PLEC and NGO workers, the compost was mixed with mineral fertilizers. Yields increased significantly: tomato from 5 to 20 t/ha; onion from 10 to 25 t/ha; cassava from 7 to 20 t/ha; maize from 1.5 to 5 t/ha; and potato from 1.5 to 15 t/ha. This increase was achieved by the rational management of the cowshed manure and compost, used in conformity to the agricultural calendar. The produce is marketed at Bantignel and Pita for the benefit of the women farmers' groups, which gain income to invest in new activities.[3]

Results of income-generating activities are summarized in Table 5.4.

Agroforestry at Pita-Bantignel

Reforestation and the development of *in situ* conservation of the flora resources are major activities of the Bantignel expert farmers. These experts have developed fruit and forest species nurseries since 1998. Now the young plants have been transplanted to strengthen or replace dry-wood fences. There are local as well as exotic species. Table 5.5 shows the nurseries' results by 2001.

Survey on traditional knowledge at Pita-Bantignel and Moussaya

To appreciate the traditional knowledge of natural resources management, the West African PLEC researchers conducted interviews and applied par-

Table 5.5 Progress of agroforestry production

Species	Missidè Héïré		Dar ès Salam	
	Numbers of plants in nurseries	Numbers of plants transplanted	Numbers of plants in nurseries	Numbers of plants transplanted
Fruit trees				
Orange	1,250	458	1,300	612
Coffee	1,275	600	860	575
Avocado	125	78	56	45
Mango	1,230	689	1,250	756
Banana	–	158	–	89
Oil palm	56	21	–	–
Local plants				
Lingué	245	120	200	71
Gobi	125	65	97	57
Caécidra	56	23	64	29
Indigotier	80	42	62	33
Exotic plant species				
Acacia mangium	644	253	384	178
Acacia auriculiformis	1,100	500	860	568

ticipatory observation methodology. For the scientists it was a knowledge-sharing, then hypothesis-formulating, experience. The people gave surprising answers, for example "the bush is a storehouse for us; it gives us all we need (food, firewood, construction wood, medicines, and meat) but certain people abuse it" (casual cutting of wood, late fires). Farmers distinguish and classify soils, improve the agricultural calendar, and are very well aware of the dangers of fire. Sometimes they tend to interpret natural phenomena according to religious beliefs, for example attributing the drying of streams to evil spirits or to acts of God. This is not surprising in view of the low degree of literacy.

These enquiries were not exhaustive. The principal lesson was the necessity to transfer knowledge to other farmers in order to have a better management of natural resources, better work organization, learning of methods such as compost-making using local raw materials, and the creation of permanent hedges or fences. According to the scientists and rural development workers, improvement in these areas could diminish or even end rural-urban migration, and increase productivity and improve livelihoods.

Biodiversity analysis

The agrobiodiversity data were collected and analysed according to the principal guidelines of the project. The results were satisfactory, and some conclusions have served as a basic model for guiding farmers and local authorities interested and involved in the management of biological diversity for a better use of natural resources. Table 5.6 presents the Shannon diversity indices for the land-use stages at study sites.

Diversity of vegetation is almost the same at Pita-Bantignel and Moussaya, with large savanna areas at the first site and large dry forests at the second. Agroforestry has been introduced at Pita, but not at Moussaya. In observing the inventory of biodiversity, the Shannon indices for shrub savanna at Missidè Héïré (3.48) and fallow at Goloya (3.32) are higher than at other sites, and the richness of species is important within these zones. The indices show a significant heterogeneity and diversity. At Moussaya herbaceous species are very important and contribute to biodiversity richness (67 species).

Management of outfield fallow lands at Pita-Bantignel

Established fallows are characterized by a high biodiversity. In the early stages there is a high diversity of herbaceous species. As the fallow gets older, taller species appear progressively. The inventory results show that the biological diversity in these areas varies according to the zone and espe-

Table 5.6 Species abundance, diversity (Shannon index, H') and richness (Margalef, Dmg) of different land-use stages in the demonstration sites

Location	Land-use stage	Species abundance	H'	Dmg
Dar ès Salam	Fallow	52	3.20	8.3
Missidè Héïré	Forest	47	2.90	7.5
Missidè Héïré	Fallow	35	2.99	6.0
Missidè Héïré	Shrub savanna	64	3.48	9.4
Goloya	House garden	17	2.17	2.8
Goloya	Fallow	52	3.32	8.5
Goloya	Orchard	39	2.69	5.9
Missidè Héïré	House garden	33	2.65	5.3
Dar ès Salam	Household	19	2.05	3.2
Tioukoungol	House garden	17	2.04	2.8
Dar ès Salam	House garden	21	2.27	3.5
Tioukoungol	Fallow	39	2.69	5.9
Moussaya	Household	67	2.11	9.7
Moussaya	Forest	44	3.16	8.0
Moussaya	Woody savanna	52	2.66	7.4
Missidè Héïré	Agroforestry	25	2.38	4.7
Dar ès Salam	Forest	38	2.55	6.5

cially to the age of the fallow. The team found 52 species in the oldest fallows versus 35–39 species in the youngest ones (see Table 5.6). The diversity indices obtained during the study were variable, and closely dependent on the specific richness and the number of individuals in the field units sampled.

Fallow management is principally based on bush fire control in the initial stages. Some farmers add to their last crops the seeds of *Harungana madagascariensis* and *Uvaria chamae* in order to accelerate fallow recovery. In recent years they have also used *Erythropheum guineense* because of its rapid growth, and *Carapa procera* which also grows rapidly and is used in soap-making. In addition, preservation of useful trees such as *Parinari excelsa*, *Parkia biglobosa*, and *E. guineense* during clearing creates conditions for quick recovery of cover. Leguminous plants are indicators of fertile soils. For land being brought back into agriculture, the presence of species like *Pericopsis laxiflora* is a decisive factor. Similarly, groundnut planting in the *tapade* extension parcels is not by chance – it is explicitly known by farmers that legumes are useful soil improvers and are valuable in reducing the period for establishing a mature *tapade*.

Differences in management within the *tapades* at Pita-Bantignel

Within the studied *tapades*, the PLEC team has observed differences between one family and another. Maize farms are dominant in households having access to local labour. The spaces occupied by crops in the old infields are logically distributed. Near huts and houses where intensive practices are ongoing, maize is associated with cowpeas with 0.7 × 0.8 m distance between holes within 15 to 20 m² squares. The space between the holes are used to plant cassava, with 0.5 × 0.7 m between plants. This technique of cassava planting has been developed by the farmers of Bantignel, who know that maize and cassava are not compatible in close proximity and must be planted with care. Cassava or groundnuts are the main crop in the newer areas which receive less care. Taro is generally planted under trees, but nowadays few families cultivate it.

Within the demonstration sites, the hedges of *tapades* are formed of mixed agroforest species of rapid growth, fortified by dead trees. The species commonly used for live hedges are *Jatropha curcas*, *Carapa procera*, *Ficus thonningii*, *Mangifera indica*, *Margaritaria discoidea*, *Afzelia africana*, *Parinari excelsa*, *Parkia biglobosa*, *Ceiba pentandra*, *Cassia sieberiana*, *Holarrhena floribunda*, *Detarium senegalense*, *Anthocleista nobilis*, and *Jatropha gossypifolia*. In addition exotic species introduced by the FAO restoration project are planted, such as *Acacia mangium*, *A. auriculiformus*, and *Grewia* spp. The Shannon diversity indices are high, being above 2.0 for most *tapades* inventoried. There is also high heterogeneity.

Forest management

For centuries Guinéean traditional societies have practised systems of management that protect land cover, water resources, and soils. These apply especially to heads of watercourses, gallery forests, and hill slopes. The "wise men", particularly the Koranic "*marabouts*" or the fetish guardians, would keep warning that such sites are haunted, or inhabited by devils. Whoever cut trees in such areas would quickly go mad or die. By these means, vegetation along the watercourses was conserved, allowing the growth of big trees. The creation of a new settlement took into account the availability of watercourses and forests. Forests serve as toilet areas and sources of firewood. The current small areas of forest around villages are due to these traditional methods of environmental management. Also, the notion of sacred forest has been made use of in certain villages, helping to build richness in species.

It is now time to recall these old ways, and apply them in order to save and conserve the environment for future generations. During the inventory it was noted that there was an exceptional diversity of tree species within the demonstration sites. Species richness varies from one forest to another, ranging between 38 and 47 species. Shannon indices were consequently significant, indicating the impact of these traditional management tools. Many rare plant species retain high importance value, because they are represented by large individuals. In contrast, the more common species have low importance value.

Conclusions

The work of PLEC at Pita-Bantignel and Kouroussa has done much to raise the level of consciousness among farmers and encourage a dynamic approach to sustainable resource management. The approach brings together traditional and modern knowledge related to the management of village lands. Unlike many projects carried out before in these areas, PLEC distinguished itself by supporting farmers' actions. International organizations like the FAO and the World Food Programme have assisted rural people by supplying food in the name of tackling poverty. When PLEC was implemented many farmers familiar with such aid had difficulties with the team's emphasis on simply assisting farmers in the resolution of their daily problems. Despite the novelty of this approach, the farmer members of PLEC have concluded that this is a better way of combating poverty. Today, all the groups established by PLEC have found ways of generating funds to serve the needs of the group as a whole.

With the increase in the number of cowsheds and the popularization of compost-making, many more families are now able to provide for their needs throughout the year, improving management of small areas. People move less, understanding the need to bring to the soil all those elements that are indispensable for good agricultural production. Yields have increased, and resources, formerly subject to uncontrolled degradation, are conserved. One important introduction is that perennial coffee farming is taking place at both Missidè Héïré and Dar ès Salam.

Income-generating activities like cloth dyeing and soap production have provided all-season employment. Formerly the women worked only on the harvest within the *tapades* during the dry season; today they can be active in either farming or artisanal work all 12 months of the year.

The project has made people much more aware of sustainable management of resources. Everyone is now keen, and the farmers have become both the users and the guardians of their resources. With the new approach, a start has been made on reforesting certain areas with *Anacardium occidentale*. Another species being tried is *Stylosanthes guianensis*, a fodder plant of high value.

All these ongoing activities are reinforcing the capacity-building of expert farmers, young scientists, decision-makers, and rural development agents trained by PLEC scientists. PLEC-Guinée has been particularly interested in initiating undergraduates and postgraduate students in the methodology of research; and in the specialization of expert farmers who can then popularize agricultural techniques for sustainable resource management. This also involves the rural development agents. Decision-makers at local level (prefectural and subprefectural) have also participated in PLEC demonstrations. PLEC has witnessed a revolution of consciousness regarding sustainable management in all the villages in which the project has worked. The former ways of doing things are tending to disappear, giving place to viable ways of managing and enhancing the environment.

Notes

1. The system is more fully described by Boiro *et al.* (2002).
2. Outmigration of young men is very common to Sierra Leone and Sénégal as well as to the towns of Guinée. Some of this is seasonal, but many stay away for much of their adult lives. They do, however, provide funds for community innovations such as rebuilding mosques and digging wells, and for the reconstruction of their own houses in durable materials with tiled roofs. Many return home to live after about the age of 50.
3. There is a weekly market at Bantignel and a daily market at Pita, but only the former is easily reached on foot.

REFERENCES

Barry, A. K., S. Fofana, A. Diallo, and I. Boiro. 1996. *Systèmes de production et changements de l'environnement dans le sous-bassin de Kollangui-Pita*. Conakry: WAPLEC-Guinée.

Boiro, I., A. K. Barry, A. Diallo, S. Fofana, F. Mara, A. Baldé, M. A. Kane, and O. Barry. 2002. "Improvement of production and livelihood in the Fouta Djallon, République de Guinée", in H. Brookfield, C. Padoch, H. Parsons, and M. Stocking (eds) *Cultivating Biodiversity: Understanding, Analysing and Using Agricultural Diversity*. London: ITDG Publications, pp. 233–244.

Diallo, A. G., A. Bah, H. Jover, and Diridollou. 1987. *Géographie de la Guinée et de l'Afrique*. Conakry: Hatier Guinée.

Maignien, R. 1960. *Le Fouta Djallon dans l'Ouest Africain. Recherches Africaines*, Études Guinéennes No. 4. Conakry: Institut National de Recherches et de Documentation.

6

Uganda

Joy Tumuhairwe, Charles Nkwiine, and John Kawongolo

Introduction

Background

East Africa (Uganda, Kenya, and Tanzania) has much greater environmental variety in detail than the countries of West Africa. A large proportion of the region is upland or highland, with considerable geological diversity due to faulting, uplift, and vulcanism. Climatic conditions vary greatly over short distances, giving rise to the complex mosaic of "agro-ecological zones", terminology inherited from late-colonial research and still used for classification in all three countries. PLEC intended from the outset to develop a cluster in East Africa, but it was only after Michael Stocking became an associate scientific coordinator that suitable core people were identified in each of three countries of Kenya, Uganda, and Tanzania (Figure 6.1). A single cluster with three subgroups was formed in 1995 under the leadership of Dr Kiome of the Kenya Agricultural Research Institute.[1] Over time these three groups have come to be separately managed, with only occasional regional meetings to provide harmonization.

The initial objective in Uganda was to study the effects of biophysical, socio-economic, and demographic change on land degradation and the environment, and to develop feasible approaches to sustainable agriculture in the diverse agro-ecosystems of the region. The south-western region of Uganda was selected for study because of the dynamism and richness of its

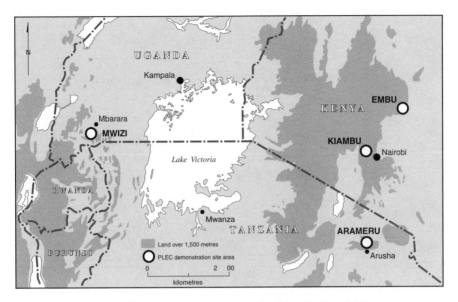

Figure 6.1 Location of demonstration sites in East Africa

biodiversity. In addition to the spontaneously growing species, the different ethnic groups have introduced a diversity of crops and conservationist management practices. Mbarara district, in particular, has several ethnic groups and high agrodiversity, but significant demographic and socio-economic changes have resulted in drastic changes in land cover and use. Between 1954 and 1993, with pressure on resources from an increasing population, most of the hills have changed from scrublands to annual crop land, and the valleys from thickets and natural forest to perennial crop lands and settlements. Scattered patches of scrub and bush remain only on uncultivable slopes. Some natural forests were gazetted, but most of these have been replaced already with planted softwood forests. The uncultivable grazed hill slopes are greatly eroded, resulting in what is known commonly as the "bare hills of Rwampara". Under the successive rules of Presidents Idi Amin and Milton Obote there was little constructive government activity in this rural area, and fighting occurred in the Mbarara area during the Tanzanian invasion that overthrew Idi Amin.

The PLEC cluster spent most of its initial two years examining a wide range of sites. In 1997 two were selected for study, based on agro-ecological zone, receptivity of the people, ethnic diversity, accessibility, diversity of land-use types, and the number of crop combinations:

- Bushwere parish in Mwizi subcounty in the tall grassland/banana/coffee/ annuals zone

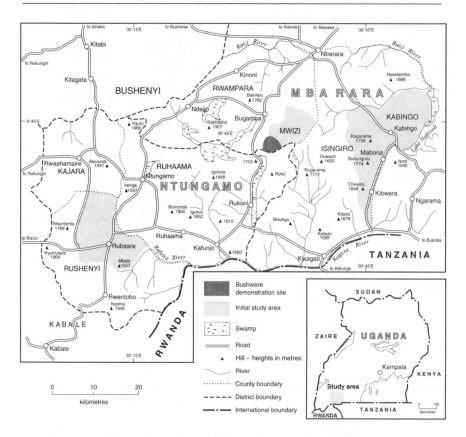

Figure 6.2 The demonstration site region of Uganda

- Kamuri parish in Kabingo subcounty in the pastoral semi-arid range-lands zone.

The two subcounties are located in the southern part of Mbarara district, south of Mbarara town and a few kilometres from the border with Tanzania. Demonstration activities were later concentrated only at Bushwere due to financial and personnel constraints (Figure 6.2).

Characterization of the area began with a review of literature, consultation with local officials, and field observations at landscape level along transects in an area of 50 km by 5 km. The physical features of the study area (relief, rivers, and land cover) are shown in Figure 6.2, interpreted from 1964 topographic maps. Consultations were held with the local agricultural extension officers and local council authorities. The area was traversed along eight two-kilometre transects positioned across selected broad land-use systems and the most representative catchments. Land-use types (later land-use stages) were identified along the lines, while the biophysical diversity and resources within each land-use type were assessed in a belt 20 m wide along the transect line.

Bushwere demonstration site

Bushwere is the most southerly of the five parishes of Mwizi subcounty, bordering two government-gazetted lands being developed for commercial softwood forests (Figure 6.2). The area is 3,116 km², with a population of 4,081 people in the Uganda census of 1991, and recently projected to 5,235 people and 793 households. The population density has increased from about 90 to over 250 persons/km² during the last three decades (1959–2001).

Inhabitants are of four ethnic groups. Bakiga form the majority (55 per cent), followed by the Banyankole (30 per cent). The Banyarwanda and Baganda comprise 10 per cent and 5 per cent respectively. This diverse mix of groups arose from migrations spurred by rapid population increase in bordering areas, civil wars, and economic opportunities. The first Bakiga came in small numbers voluntarily in the early 1940s, and larger numbers came later from the district of Kabale (formerly part of Kigezi) under government resettlement schemes in the 1950s. More recent (1970–1999) arrivals of young Bakiga have come from neighbouring Bushenyi district (Tumuhairwe *et al.* 1999).

The Bakiga found Mwizi subcounty to be very similar to their home, and there was vacant land because the rugged terrain and the presence of wild animals and tsetse fly infestations had limited settlement by the Banyankole. The Banyarwanda came from Rwanda in the 1950s and 1960s as refugees, and are mostly Tutsis who kept cattle. The Baganda came from Buganda from the southern-central regions of Uganda during British rule, mostly as traders and colonial administrators. Although high mobility of ethnic groups has ceased, the region is still undergoing rapid socio-economic transformations through intermarriages and both in- and outmigration as people search for land for cultivation or employment opportunities.

Ethnic tradition has influenced land use and cropping systems, and with the integration of settlements the different groups have adopted practices from one another. The subsistence crop of the Banyankole was millet, but during the last 50 years bananas have supplanted it. The Bakiga, who are skilled in annual crop cultivation and never grew bananas, have adopted them as a source of livelihood and food security. Similarly, traditional cultivators have adopted cattle-keeping, even though the opportunities in Bushwere are limited.

Bushwere farmers' main source of income is from the sale of agricultural farm produce, especially potatoes, beans, bananas, and coffee (67 per cent).

Farmers also earn income (33 per cent) from trading, off-farm employment, or by selling grains, timber, furniture, and handicrafts made of local materials. The poorer farmers earn income from sale of their labour. Apiculture is gradually expanding, mostly using traditional systems. Processing of local foods and drinks follows traditional systems, and sale of local brews is a common trade.

Physical characteristics

The landscape is an elevated, dissected plateau with very steep slopes. Altitudes rise to 1,800 m in Bushwere. The terrain is rugged, dissected by V-shaped steeply sloping upland valleys draining into narrow U-shaped lower valleys that get broader eastwards. The area drains eastwards into Lake Nakivali, northwards into the River Rwizi and Lake Mburo, and southwards into the River Kagera (see Figure 6.2). The climate is humid, but tending to subhumid because of strong desiccating winds most of the year. Rainfall is bimodal, with an annual mean of 1,150 mm. The temperature range is 15–20°C.

Farmers divide their landscape into four land types, named *ekibungo* (ridge tops), *ahamushozi* (backslopes), *empanga* (valleys), and *obuhanga* (ravines). Each land type is known to be suited to different crops, and the farmers attribute this to the different soil characteristics. Because of the highly dissected plateau landscape, most of the available land for agricultural production is on the long, broad ridge tops (50 per cent) and on backslopes (42 per cent). Most annual crop gardens are on hilltops and shoulders. Some are on the steeper backslopes, only a few of which are terraced. Almost all valleys in Bushwere are under crop cover (mostly bananas).

The soils are predominantly ferrallitic with laterite crusts and granules on the ridge tops. Most dominant are the sandy clay loams fully developed from Karagwe-Ankolean phyllites (Bugamba series) or schists and quartzites (Mbarara catena), which are of medium to low productive potential. The highest areas, above 1,600 m, have the more productive red sandy clay loam, called the Rugaga series. Soil fertility levels are generally moderate to high, but water-holding capacity is poor due to low clay percentages (23 per cent) in most places.

Farmers name six soil types differentiated by their physical properties, using mostly colour, gravelliness, and soil consistency. Dark-coloured and loamy soils are considered more fertile and suited to a wider range of crops compared to the red clayey soils that support only sweet potatoes and cassava. Farmers identify declining soil fertility by declining crop yields, yellowing and stunted plants, abundance of certain weeds like *murasha* (*Bidens* sp.), or dominance of stunted weeds that are difficult to uproot by hand. Their remedy is to rest the land by fallowing or to plant hardy crops like cassava. Since nutrient-deficiency symptoms manifest only in some crop species, farmers interpret them to mean that the soil is unsuitable for that particular crop and so they grow the crop in more "suitable" areas, or inter-crop to spread the risk of yield loss if the "unsuitable" crop fails.

The vegetation has been greatly altered by clearing, uncontrolled burning, and overgrazing. The original vegetation was a grassland savanna association of *Themeda* and *Combretum molle* together with medium-altitude moist semi-deciduous forests of *Albizia* spp. and *Markhamia* in the valleys. The common remaining trees on the hills are *Acacia abyssinica*, *Acacia hockii*, and *Combretum molle*. Along the valleys the common species are *Markhamia lutea*, *Erythrina abyssinica*, *Croton*, *Acanthus*, and *Vernonia* species.

The land use is a small-scale annual cropping system. Currently cultivated land covers 63 per cent, fallows cover 22 per cent, grassland 11 per cent, and forest, thickets, and bushes only 5 per cent. Crop diversity is high, maintained through seed selection and management to match not only market demands but also food preference and seasonal variability. The most widely grown crop is maize, followed by bananas, beans (*Phaseolus vulgaris*), and potato.[2]

There is great variability in the way farmers manage their cropping system. The total number of field types identified in Bushwere during the major growing season, known as *itumba*, was 194 (Table 6.1). There were 70 in the perennial land-use stage, 80 in annual cropping, nine in natural grassland, eight in bushlands or woodlands, 10 in the land-use stage gazetted for conversion to forest and used under the *taungya* system, and 16 home garden field types. The most common field types were banana-based, potato-based, beans-based, and peas. The banana plantations usually occupy the more fertile land in the valleys and ravines that receive sediments and moisture from the surrounding catchments. However, bananas, beans, and maize occurred on all parts of the landscape from hilltops to valleys, while potatoes, peas, and sweet potatoes were limited to hilltops and backslopes. Inter-

Table 6.1 Field types in Bushwere

Land-use stage	Number of field types
Perennial crops	70
Annual crops	80
Home gardens	16
Natural grasslands	9
Natural bushlands	8
Gazetted forest land	10
Hedges	1
Total	194

cropping is widespread and intensive. Sorghum and millet have largely given way to maize, the preferred non-banana staple, because it has high market value and lower labour and soil fertility requirements.

Species diversity and abundance are influenced by agronomic practices. For example, 50.4 per cent of surveyed farmers planted peas after the fallow. During field preparation they simply broadcast the seed, then roughly till without harrowing. Usually the crop is not weeded, hence the high species diversity and abundance. Potato and maize fields also had high species diversity, as the soil mixing during land preparation encourages weed germination. While most of the food and commercial crops are planted, some weeds are also used as food, medicines, fodder, and for cultural purposes. Other medicinal, fodder, and cultural species are deliberately planted or conserved.

Home gardens around individual homesteads include the compound, hedges, vegetables, and banana gardens. Although there are several different banana-based field types, every homestead has a banana home garden. Additional banana plots may be at varying distances from the homestead.

Natural bushland and grasslands occur only in patches on very steep slopes and lateritic hilltops. These field types had the highest species diversity, probably because they are little used apart from some grazing and occasional bush fires. Species diversity is highest on backslopes, and lower on hilltops which are more intensively grazed *Loudetia* grasslands. All of *Pteridium*-based field types are on the backslopes, which have slopes of 26 per cent or more. Farmers associate *Pteridium* with degraded soils of low productivity which only support root crops such as sweet potatoes and cassava. Beans usually fail.

Remnants of natural high forest are extremely small, and occur only in ravines bordering gazetted forest reserve area. Farmers have been permitted access to gazetted forests only for non-destructive harvesting of medicines, dry firewood, and sawmill wastes. Woodlots are few and very small in size (less than 0.3 ha), ranging from 10 to 1,000 trees per plot and mostly composed of *Eucalyptus* species. Only two farmers had larger woodlots of different tree species. Trees planted on farmland and around homesteads are usually *Eucalyptus* and *Pinus patula*. Species used for construction are conserved in the woodlots or on boundaries. Indigenous species, especially *Combretum*, *Markhamia*, and *Acacia* species, are left scattered in grasslands and bushlands, and a few in crop gardens and fallows. These are harvested indiscriminately and are mostly highly degraded. Agroforestry other than in homesteads is rare. Apiculture, which relies on a variety of tree species, is a growing industry. It is being transformed from a subsistence system with traditional methods to a more commercial system with modern beehives under the influence of expert farmers.

In general, Bushwere is experiencing a decline of the natural resource base. Indicators include reduced fallow length, declining crop yields, intensification of intercropping, and increased erosion of soil and biodiversity.

Banana growing is expanding at the expense of annual cropping. Production of some crops, like millet and sorghum and local potato varieties, has drastically declined. There is an increasing shortage of arable land available, and young families migrate to other districts. Farmers attributed these trends to high population growth and changes in market demands. Other important constraints on production and resource management are land fragmentation and gender imbalance in control of resources and benefits.

Management of the land

The major conservationist management practices identified were bench terracing, contour bands, and trenches. Terraces were used by 36 per cent of surveyed farmers for erosion control on the steep slopes, mainly backslopes. Other practices are trashlines, ridges, and mounding. Ridges are constructed along the contours and trap water while the buried organic materials decompose to release nutrients and improve water-holding capacity. Trenches and grass strips are commonly used in perennial crops, especially banana fields. Other practices used for soil management include weed-heaping, trash burning, mulching, fallowing, crop rotation, manuring, and bunding. On steep stony slopes, stone heaps are common. They function as a place to put stones, somewhere to dry noxious weeds, and as an erosion barrier. Certain species of perennial plants, such as *Lantana camara* and *Dracaena fragrans*, are planted for live hedges to shelter houses and crops of higher economic value against wind and rain damage.

Most farmers cultivate previously cropped fields (79 per cent), a few use fallowed fields (20 per cent), and only 1 per cent cultivated previously uncleared land as there is hardly any available. The traditional practice of land clearing of the overgrown fallows is slash and burn. Primary rough tillage (*okubanjura*) and then fine tillage (*okuchonkya*) are used to prepare fields. Crops with small seeds such as millet and sorghum require a fine seedbed. In general, the Bakiga people are known to use more rough tillage (even for sorghum) and leave plant residues on the surface. The Banyankole mostly create fine tilth for all crops except peas, separating all the plant residues and big stones. The Banyankole always criticize the Bakiga for their "dirty" gardens which are difficult to weed due to the stubble, although they learned from the Bakiga that peas grow better with rough tillage.

Trash removed during land clearing and secondary tillage was traditionally heaped and burnt or thrown to the field edges. Many farmers now collect the trash after drying and carry it to mulch bananas or use it to make trash lines along contours. One farmer and his family manage weeds by differentiating non-rhizomatous weeds, which they bury, and those that are noxious or stubborn, which they dry and burn. Trash burning, although discouraged due to its adverse long-term effects on soil fertility and biodiversity, is often preferred to heaping trash or even making trash lines. The trash harbours rodents, especially fieldmice, that eventually increase and cause crop damage in the fields and losses during storage.

Ridging and mounding are used for planting sweet potato and potatoes to increase soil volume to grow large tubers. The depth and width of ridges vary with each farmer's method of cultivating, the soil thickness and workability, and the type of crop planted. The depth ranges from 10 to 30 cm and width from 30 to 55 cm, with bigger ridges for sweet potato than potatoes. The sweet potatoes stay for five to nine months in the field with minimum disturbance to the soil, being weeded only once at an early stage as the crop provides good surface cover.

The planting methods used for annual crops by the majority of farmers are broadcasting and dibbling (chop and plant). Broadcasting small-seeded crops saves time and labour, but requires skill and experience to ensure uniform and appropriate spacing. Other crops that are sometimes broadcast include beans and maize, especially when the farmer is late to plant or is working alone. Dibbling is mainly used for planting potatoes, cassava, beans, and maize, being crops that require wider spacing for better yield. Most perennials, especially bananas, coffee, and all types of trees, are planted by suckers or seedlings in holes 60–100 cm in depth and diameter with compost or farmyard manure mixed with the soil in the hole.

Row planting allows room for intercropping. The main crops planted in rows are cassava, potatoes, and sweet potatoes. Potatoes are usually interplanted with beans or maize, with the potatoes on the ridges and the beans or maize in the troughs. This maximizes use of space and reduces the labour required for land preparation and weeding. Generally farmers do more intercropping during the *itumba* season than in the short cropping season (*ekyanda*). The abundance of soil moisture and flushing of soil nutrients allow higher plant density during *itumba*.

Intercropping beans, maize, and cassava in newly planted banana and coffee fields is the normal practice during the first 12–18 months while the perennial crop is establishing. Intercropping is reduced or discontinued as the perennial crop matures to allow for mulching and management. Bananas are very susceptible to competition, but local varieties of pumpkins, eggplants, and tomatoes are grown amongst them. It is believed that these intercrops do not affect yield if carefully managed by thinning and directing them to creep in open spaces. Due to land shortage intercropping in established plantations is becoming more common. The crops planted include beans, maize, coffee, taro, papaya, pepper, and fodder, but good farmers are particular about the spatial arrangements to avoid compromising banana bunch yields. Sugarcane, taro, and grasses are often grown at the edges of the banana plantation. Fodder grasses have been introduced recently on conservation trenches.

Crop rotation sequences vary with the farmer. Usually beans are the first or second crop and cassava the last in the rotation sequence. Farmers tend to have multiple crop combinations during the third season of cropping when productivity declines and intercropping becomes a strategy for coping with the risk of getting low yields. Cassava is introduced at this time and no other crops are planted once its full canopy develops. Since cassava stays in the field for over three seasons and can withstand competition from most weeds except couch grass, it acts as a fallow for farmers with small landholdings.

All crops grown in Bushwere have several varieties. They are grown either singly or mixed. All farmers said that mixtures yield better than single-variety crops, especially during the short rains (*ekyanda*). Mixtures of varieties are less common in the long rains of the *itumba* season when farmers focus on production for market.

Farmers know the water requirements of each crop and use this to decide which season is suitable for growing each crop or crop combination. Maize, millet, and sorghum are mostly grown during the long rains while peas, sweet potatoes, and cassava dominate in the short rains. Potatoes and beans mature in two to three months and are grown in both seasons, but have to be planted early at the onset of rains because of their high moisture requirements during the vegetative stages.

Most surveyed farmers (74 per cent) practise short fallow to restore soil fertility. More fallowing is done during the short rains (20 per cent) than in the *itumba* season (4 per cent). Some farmers did not fallow because they had inadequate land, and others felt that their land was still fertile enough to support continuous cropping. Most cultivate for three or four seasons then fallow for one or two seasons, but some farmers plant one season and fallow the next. Farmers who fallowed their fields for more than four years were quite few (12 per cent), as were those who could crop for more than eight seasons or over four years continuously (6 per cent).

Resource tenure and access

Land tenure is mainly by customary and freehold systems whereby an individual acquires land through inheritance or purchase and has full ownership and user rights. Most holdings are small, 1–5 ha per household, with an average of 3 ha. Land fragmentation is a major characteristic of the agricultural lands throughout Mwizi. This creates the mosaic pattern of gardening visible across the landscapes, especially on the hilltops and backslopes. Even the expanses of banana comprise plots belonging to different farmers that are clearly demarcated with boundary markers like *Dracaena fragrans* (*omugorora*).

The few farmers (mostly the early settlers) who own more land still have gardens scattered in different parts and planted according to the suitability of crops. They also rent or lend small parcels to less fortunate relatives. When the elderly subdivide land among their offspring, each male child is given pieces scattered in different locations. This is to ensure equitable distribution of lands with different productive potential among all sons.

While most of the gardens (94.4 per cent) are on owned land, 5.6 per cent of farmers hire or borrow land for annual crops. There is always negotiation between the landowner and the tenant. A tenant uses the land for one or more seasons and after harvest gives the landlord an agreed portion of the harvest. There is no written agreement. Most of the land borrowers are relatives, usually sons who have not yet been granted full ownership by parents, and unmarried daughters or daughters married to men who do not own adequate land. Some borrowers and renters are new settlers.

Although the majority of farmers in Bushwere have small holdings, most of those with inadequate land take advantage of access to gazetted forest land granted to the Bushwere community by the Uganda Government Forestry Department. Farmers are allowed to grow annual crops in areas being cleared for reforestation until the planted trees establish a canopy that stops the crops growing. Some farmers, especially the young, put the little land they own under perennial crops and depend on the gazetted land for annual crops. They sell most of the produce from gazetted land and are eventually able to raise enough capital to buy more pieces of land.

Within the household, a woman's rights to land are determined by her husband or father. Women generally access household land for growing annual food crops to meet the household needs, but rarely for cash. Although women grow and manage almost all the annual crops, with or without the participation of their husbands or fathers, the male makes the decision to sell the produce and controls the commercial proceeds. Commonly, if a wife has been using a field for annual crops for some time and her husband decides to plant a perennial crop, the woman has to leave it. Women also have access to forests, bushlands, gazetted lands, and household woodlots from which they collect firewood, medicinal herbs, and raw materials for handicraft making, but if bushland is cleared by the husband or father, the woman has to look for these materials elsewhere.

Potatoes are the main source of household income for most families, and many potato gardens belong to both husband and wife and are managed jointly for joint benefit. Some plots of sorghum, maize, beans, and bananas are similarly managed. The household head, usually a man except for widows, is the only person in a household who can own a tree, livestock, or poultry. They own the coffee, bananas, woodlots, and the patches of natural grasslands or bushland, determining the use, purchase, and sale of trees and animals. Even if a woman or child gets an animal as a gift, it is under the control of the husband or father. The recipient has no right to sell or slaughter it without his permission. However, the husband or father may slaughter or sell it without consultation except out of courtesy. Despite the fact that it is the women and children who do the day-to-day management of land, crops, and livestock, the gender imbalance in access and control hinders efforts of women and children to invest in conservation of resources.

Resource endowment and distance of fields from home were the most important factors influencing use of biodiversity, and indirectly influencing farmers' capacity to conserve it. The poorer farmers who generally cultivate borrowed land are not able to conserve much biodiversity in their gardens. They have crops for food and brewing local beer. The moderately rich and intermediate income categories cultivate owned land and have many uses for biodiversity. On the other hand, the very rich farmers are able to plant woodlots and grow species for construction timber, but they do not use as many different species because they are usually traders, with no time to invest in conservation management.

Management of banana plantations

Bananas are highly valued. They provide food and cash income, and are an indicator of social status. A local proverb counsels youths planning marriage, "*Attaine rutookye n'ente tashwera*", meaning "one without a banana plantation and cows does not qualify, for he won't sustain a family".

A typical banana garden relates closely to a multistorey natural forest. A few scattered trees form the upper canopy above the banana plants, and shrubs like eggplant, castor oil, or coffee and maize in a few cases comprise a lower storey. Vegetables, spices, beans, pumpkins, and other plants are grown below. The bananas are always planted in rows, but these gradually disappear as suckers spread out. De-suckering and pruning are needed to maintain spacing.

Management of bananas, especially weed management and density and type of intercropping, varies from farmer to farmer depending on labour availability and preference. Generally there is less species diversity in the banana field due to weeding and mulching. The traditional belief is that bananas require plenty of manure and cleaning to be able to look good and yield well – the visual appearance of a banana plantation and size of bunches reflect the "seriousness" of its manager. Crop residues, domestic wastes, and often compost and farmyard manure are brought into banana gardens at the expense of other fields.

Varietal diversity of bananas is large. In one survey of 45 farmers, equally divided into groups farming hilltops, backslopes, and valleys, 54 banana varieties were found, of which 29 were cooking varieties, 20 were for beer brewing, three for sweet (dessert) use, and two for roasting. Each farmer grew on average 9.8 cooking varieties and 3.6 for beer brewing. The management of diversity is extremely complex, but certain features are apparent.

- Varieties often planted at the fringes of the banana plantation because of their resistance to being toppled by winds, especially on ridge crests, are *Musa paradisiaca*, especially the *kabaragara* variety.
- Size and marketability of bunches determines choice. *Enyarunyonga*, for example, needs supporting props when carrying a bunch.
- Some varieties are planted for other uses as well as for food. Twine is made from *enzirabushera* fibres to support heavy bunches on adjacent plants and to construct houses.
- Some varieties, *enyabutembe* and *enhenyi* for instance, are planted because they produce prolific suckers that can be sold or used to expand plantations quickly.

Banana varietal diversity is also matched in the diversity of uses of plant parts. After harvesting, the pseudostems are chopped or shredded and used as mulch. The staple food made from the cooking bananas is the mashed *matooke*. Specific varieties have other uses, including for cooking with meat or vegetable sauces (*akatogo*), for making pancakes, fresh unfermented juice (*eshande*), *tonto* (local beer), and *waragi* (local gin), and for thatching, ropes, handicrafts, food wrapping, packing materials, animal feed, and soap (from the inside of rotting stems). The corm is used as a temporary cooking stone for ceremonies and sometimes as the base of a pulley system for digging pit latrines. Pseudostems are used for shading, mulch, chairs, fodder, and fencing material. Sheaths of banana plants are used as simple water-harvesting devices. The fibres have multiple uses, including toilet covers, roofing, scare dolls in agricultural fields, toys, hats, windbreaks, and walls for urinals and bath sheds. The leaves are typically used for roofing (dry), but also for plates, wrapping material, and school lunch boxes. The most commonly used head-load support is a ring made of banana leaves and fibres. Untorn leaves are often used as an emergency umbrella. Male buds, stalks, fingers, banana peels, and young whole plants uprooted during pruning are fed to livestock. Young whole plants are commonly used as decorations along the guest routes as a symbol of a warm welcome.

Demonstration activities

Working with farmers

The population of collaborating farmers gradually grew following the initial consultations and community workshops. Before 1998 the collaborating farmers consisted of only two expert farmers identified for having high biodiversity conserved on their land. When these two were visited by PLEC scientists other community members became curious and enquired more about PLEC, and many were motivated to attend the workshops. As the demonstration activities started and with more regular field visits by PLEC scientists, the number of collaborators increased to 40, including 10 field assistants, five local leaders, and 25 owners of gardens. By the end of first year 120 landowners had participated in the biodiversity inventory, including two more expert farmers. During the third year, 280 farmers participated.

Common-interest groups

Common-interest groups developed from demonstrations and are engaged in integration of crop and animal diversity, diversification of nursery and home garden plants, and holistic approaches to community development with an emphasis on the promotion of agrodiversity using multipurpose trees, goats, and beekeeping. The groups coordinate, organize, and monitor training activities, rotating their meetings between the homes of members. Each group encourages member households to host meetings, field-days, and demonstrations and to monitor improvement in household income and welfare through farm record-keeping and analysis. PLEC support was in the form of technical back-up, coordination and transportation of participants, and remuneration of the demonstrators. PLEC facilitated formalizing the new associations (for example by giving technical guidance on writing constitutions and registration) and assisted in writing proposals soliciting financial support.

These groups have acted as a vehicle for encouraging conservationist agrodiversity management. The demonstration and exhibition activities have been publicized nationally through radio and television, and some members from each group have participated in the development of PLEC policy recommendations. Leaders of the associations have met with high-level stakeholders at subcounty, district, national, regional, and international levels.

Expert farmers

Expert farmers were selected using a number of criteria. Their management practices promoted biodiversity conservation, with many different crops and varieties. They were innovators who used traditional or modern management techniques to benefit from and preserve agrodiversity. They were able to spare time to prepare for and participate in demonstration activities, were known to welcome people to their home and freely share experiences with others, and had willingness to experiment with new techniques.

Initially, community leaders and extension workers identified 16 potential expert farmers. Only two of the 16 people were suitable as expert farmers and they pioneered the PLEC demonstrations. The first experts demonstrated biodiversity conservation for herbal medicine and integration of zero-grazing with crop production.

The number of expert farmers increased, motivated by attendance at farmer-to-farmer demonstration activities and sharing experiences. Over the course of the project individual farmers demonstrated on their farms:
- banana-based agroforestry for enhancement of beekeeping and livestock
- the use of setaria grass to stabilize soil
- water conservation in *fanya juu* bands in banana plantations, and annual cropping techniques
- timeliness of planting, weeding, and harvesting
- diversification and storage of harvests
- using the diversity of forest trees for fallowing arable land and efficiently using other land
- maximization of land productivity by staking beans intercropped in the banana plantation and selective weeding
- using the products of agrobiodiversity to construct traditional granaries and modern cribs for drying and storing crop harvests
- *in situ* preservation of different varieties of potatoes for better marketing opportunities
- enriching biodiversity in the home garden with an emphasis on indigenous vegetables
- the value of banana diversity other than for food and income
- diversity of varieties and use of potatoes
- biodiversity enrichment on a smallholding (less than 0.2 ha)
- importance of conserving indigenous trees (*Combretum* spp.) in annual fields on very steep slopes
- importance of farm record-keeping and doing a cost-benefit analysis of the agricultural enterprises of smallholders.

Participating farmers learned from the expert farmers and experimented with the practices. One farmer adopted the practice of trenches with setaria grass stabilizers from another. He experimented on management of the grass bands to test whether grass consumes rather than conserves soil moisture, leading to reduced banana yields. From his successful results he demonstrated to others, and became an expert farmer as well as an experimenting farmer. In this way there was an increase in the numbers of experimenting farmers. One farmer who was expert in conserving crop diversity in annual crop fields became an experimenter in staking beans intercropped in bananas after attending demonstrations at a neighbour's farm. Some of these farmers, together with the expert farmers, formed common-interest groups which acted as a multiplier of adoption. Other groups of farmers who did not initially attend demonstration activities, like cultural groups and the Kisirira women's group, joined in PLEC activities through their participation in exhibitions and advocacy programmes. In addition, individual members befriended PLEC farmers and scientists and were then invited to PLEC activities.

Examples of demonstration activities

Diversity in banana gardens

The late Fred Tuhimbisibwe was the first expert farmer. He knew the direct and indirect benefits of rich biodiversity. He had high species diversity and abundance in his banana gardens, although bananas yields were low due to competition. He earned most of his income from apiculture. The many tree and herb species he cultivated were to meet the requirements of his apiary enterprise with flowers for nectar and pollen, sap for beehive repairs, and branching trees for stands. The household used other species as food, fruits, vegetables, and medicines and there were tall trees for windbreaks. He became known at district, national, and regional levels as a PLEC model farmer on agrodiversity conservation for enhancement of apiculture production. He also experimented with the integration of zero-grazing cattle in the apiculture agroforestry system, and advanced the demonstration site approach by allowing his farm to be used for training for the Bushwere Beekeepers Association.

Fred improved the productivity of his crops without compromising biodiversity while working with PLEC. Some species were thinned where they were too abundant (such as setaria grass); spacing between larger plants was increased; highly competitive plants like eucalyptus were removed; manuring was used for fruit trees and grass as well as bananas; plants were regularly pruned; setaria bands were changed to the upper side of trenches; and fodder and agroforestry legumes like *Calliandra* and *Sesbania* were added. In addition he changed the spatial arrangement by moving some species to the edges of the garden, weeding for beans was changed from hoeing to notching with a panga and hand pulling, and systematic mulching of all parts was adopted. *Grevillea* was introduced for windbreaks on boundaries instead of eucalyptus.

Results were dramatic, with visual evidence of improved crop vigour and increased banana bunch sizes. After one year there was a significant increase in bunch numbers and honey yield. After two years the farmer reported increased fodder for his livestock (Tuhimbisibwe 2001), and he advanced from supplementing grazing of goats with cut-and-carry fodder to acquiring a dairy cow under zero-grazing. He planted more fodder species in the edge of the same banana garden and in other gardens, including grass strips along contours in annual crop fields for soil and water conservation. Other farmers learned from Fred through demonstration activities and are also improving management of their fields for better yields.

Post-harvest handling and storage of farm produce

Improvement of storage through construction of rat-proof and well-ventilated outdoor and indoor cribs was developed together with two innovative farmers in response to the general outcry of collaborating farmers about high post-harvest losses. The demonstration activity showed how to preserve maize, beans, and potatoes through drying and storage to improve seed quality and timeliness of planting and marketing, while also controlling vermin and other pests in stores. It was an opportunity to demonstrate the multiple benefits and uses of different species used in preservation of farm produce.

Demonstrations attracted the enthusiasm of many farmers. Within a period of 16 months 50 per cent of those who attended the training adopted the construction of outdoor maize cribs. The maize crib was adapted to store beans and other grains except millet, sorghum, and potatoes. It has good ventilation that permits more effective drying, and rat guards for vermin protection. In order to avoid light and thefts, modifications were made to the design for storing potato indoors. More than 10 farmers experimented with the indoor cribs for potato storage and five for maize and beans. Some farmers constructed indoor cribs for small quantities of maize.

Home gardens

Households traditionally plant many different vegetable and fruit species and varieties in home gardens. They grow indigenous and introduced species. Some traditional species have become rare, like *eshwiga* (*Solanum nigrum*), *ekituruguma*, and *eshogi*. Home garden demonstration activities were most popular among women, who eventually formed the Bushwere Nursery and Homegarden Farmers' Association. It was initiated by two households, who mobilized 20 others within two months. The association consists of 24 women and five men. Skilled older members train others in processing and use of rare traditional species. Demonstrations focus on diversification of vegetable and fruit species for improved household nutrition and cash income. Every household has grown at least 10 different species in small home gardens of less than 0.2 ha. The association promotes the household approach and gender balance in agrodiversity management. Membership and participation involves both husband and wife where possible, or alternately in other cases.

Integration of stall-fed livestock

Livestock keeping in the parish has always been constrained by water shortage. There are only four watering points in four distant valley bottoms. Livestock production has been constrained further during the last 15 years by an increasing shortage of grazing land due to the rapid expansion of bananas and annual cropping. The few animals have to walk long distances in search of food from the remnant natural grasslands and bushlands, fallows, and crop residues in fields. Fallows are communally grazed from the time of harvest up to the time of next cultivation.

Farmers keep local breeds of cattle and goats. They are grazed mostly on a communal system. Some farmers supplement pastures with banana peelings, particularly for milking cows. At the beginning of the project only one farmer had four Friesian-cross dairy cows, which he kept by a combination of communal grazing, paddocking, and stall-feeding systems. Stall-fed livestock are usually a dairy breed (Friesian) or the offspring of a Friesian crossed with local Ankole or Nganda cows. These give higher milk yields and make the stall-feeding system economically viable. Some collaborating farmers got together and formed the Bushwere Zero-grazing Crop Integration Association, with the aim of facilitating training, fundraising, and monitoring to acquire an improved breed of livestock and establish a commercially viable project. The number of members who have adopted the system increased from one to four within one year. Farmers are able to have both crop and livestock enterprises on their farms in a complementary manner, as opposed to the traditional mixed-farming systems where the two competed for available resources.

There was a series of demonstration activities on zero-grazing crop integration. Expert farmers strategically plant fodder species along boundaries and contour trenches, in contour bands or scattered within fields as appropriate: A number of farmers are planting more diverse fodder species, especially legumes like *Calliandra*, *Canavalia*, *Sesbania*, and *Desmodium* and grasses like napier, setaria, *Chloris gayana*, and *Cynadon* within or at the edges of banana plantations. Some farmers have planted fodder on contour bands in annual crop fields in preparation for starting zero-grazing units. Farmers with crops on sloping land use grassed contour bands for soil and water conservation, but are now motivated to do stall feeding by utilizing this fodder resource.

Developing the methodology

At the start of the project there was low interest among local leaders in technical meetings and workshops, so developing a relationship with the community took longer than anticipated. PLEC deliberately encouraged participation through personal invitations. Initially, farmers did the listening while scientists introduced the PLEC project and its concepts of agrodiversity and agrobiodiversity conservation. In subsequent workshops participation increased, and farmers gave information about the area and the population and were involved in biodiversity assessment as owners of monitored gardens. They also assisted in identifying and counting the species.

Young field assistants from the area assisted scientists, and the presence of graduate and postgraduate students at the site helped sustain communication. They left an impact, motivating some farmers to set ambitions for higher education. A teacher, the husband of a collaborating farmer, is now in the third year of a university degree. Another expert and experimental farmer recently completed his first year in college upgrading his professional qualification.

Field demonstrations by expert farmers were the most effective method used, and the attendance was usually 100 per cent of the invited farmers. Expert farmers took the lead in most of the training activities, including preparation. They also participated in mobilization, while scientists facilitated through encouragement and providing field materials, transport, refreshments, technical back-up, documentation, and evaluation. Curiosity meant that individual participation in activities was always high.

Field visits and tours outside the site fostered farmer involvement. Farmers in neighbouring subcounties and the Uganda National Farmers Association hosted field tours for Bushwere farmers. The hosts and visitors exchanged knowledge and experiences. Listening to the histories and progress of the hosting farmers and their families and discussing their challenges, innovations, and victories were very inspiring. Thirty per cent of farmers who visited two model farmers returned with new plant species obtained from the hosts after being convinced of their uses and benefits. About 50 per cent of the participants started experimenting with the various new practices shortly after.

Farmers' reasons for adoption

It is important that appropriate demonstration activities be chosen. The first expert farmer in Bushwere had many medicinal herbs, shrubs, trees, and rare species conserved on his farm. Several other farmers learnt skills from him but could only plant a few of the medicinal plants that are easy to grow and use. Their priority is production for food and cash, and they allocate more resources to crops that meet those needs. Medicinal plants require special skills and do not earn significant regular income. Different people in the community have a few medicinal species but hardly any household has as many as the expert farmer. A few have up to 60 per cent of what the expert grows; one man has special skills and interest but is commercially minded and charges for his services (unlike the expert farmer). Charging limits the number of beneficiaries.

Some farmers adopted the demonstrated practices entirely, especially in the case of maize cribs, where a local artisan was accessible for consultation on issues such as ventilation, orientation, and size for efficiency. Other farmers adopted some components of the demonstration or modified others. The general trend observed is that the majority use alternative materials and blended approaches, with various methods from different demonstrators as deemed appropriate. They first adopt practices that give tangible benefits.

There was initially significant gender imbalance, with especially low involvement of women in workshops, farmer exchange visits, and demonstrations. Through PLEC activities, however, women have participated more effectively than ever before. This has enhanced women's empowerment and harmony in families as the workloads are now shared amongst members, reducing women's burdens.

PLEC activities "opened eyes" for farmers to appreciate and cherish the abundant natural resources around them, the medicinal species, and alternative income-generating activities. There was increased community awareness of the importance of agrodiversity and biodiversity conservation not only for environmental protection but also for socio-economic benefits. Diversity of management regimes and biophysical and economic factors influence selection, management, productivity, and species richness and diversity. The resilience of the banana system to environmental, economic, and social pressures is high. The banana growing and eating culture in Uganda offers great potential for sustainable agrodiversity, especially agro-biodiversity conservation.

Notes

1. Dr Kiome became Director-General of KARI in 2000.
2. Data on biodiversity and agrobiodiversity were included in the database supplied to the scientific technical and advisory team. Except in terms of the land-use stages and field types, they are not discussed in the final general report on which this chapter is based.

REFERENCES

Tuhimbisibwe, F. 2001. "Agrobiodiversity conservation for promotion of apiculture and household welfare", paper prepared for the East Africa PLEC annual general meeting, Arusha, Tanzania, 26–28 November.

Tumuhairwe, J. K., C. Nkwiine, E. N. Nsubuga, and F. Kahembwe. 1999. "Agrodiversity of Bakiga and Banyankole peoples of southwest Uganda", unpublished manuscript.

7

Kenya

John N. Kang'ara, Ezekiel H. Ngoroi, Charles M. Rimui, Kajuju Kaburu, and Barrack O. Okoba[1]

Introduction

The background to PLEC work in Kenya is described in Chapter 6. Work began with a country planning meeting in mid-1998 at the Kenya Agricultural Research Institute (KARI). The meeting discussed the activities and work plans for the cluster. Initially two multidisciplinary teams were formed to carry out activities in two ethnic communities in different agro-ecological zones: the Lari division of Kiambu district of central Kenya and the Embu and Mbeere districts of eastern Kenya.

The core PLEC team was initially made up of an agronomist, a soil scientist, and a livestock scientist, together with one technician. From time to time specialists from other disciplines were involved for a particular purpose. In 1999 a soil surveyor, a demographer, a PRA socio-economist, a veterinary officer, and two herbalists were involved in surveys. A biometrician was involved during the regular monitoring of farmer experiments and demonstrations. At the beginning of 2000 the need for a home economist/nutritionist was felt and the first female member of the PLEC team was recruited.

One of the main difficulties encountered was experienced by the scientists themselves. The KARI orientation is towards the farming systems approach to research, extension, and training, where problems are identified and prioritized, and intervention made either through research or extension. The scientist and the extension workers are the experts and the source of technology. The PLEC approach is different and the roles are reversed: to appreciate the farmers as the experts, while the researcher and the extension worker learn from them and use them to teach other farmers. It took a very long time for the researchers and extension officers from the Ministry of Agriculture and Rural Development to adjust to the PLEC approach.

Moreover, promotions for scientists in Kenya are based on the number of scientific papers published in refereed journals and presented at conferences based on hard science. Where the farmer is the expert and the scientist a student, the fear was that papers emanating from this work might not qualify for publication in recognized journals and therefore may not contribute to the career advancement of the scientist. However, KARI has now developed an evaluation scheme that recognizes such publications.[2]

A further problem is historical. Non-governmental organizations made extension by government institutions very difficult because the NGOs issue hand-outs in the form of tools, seeds, food, and even money to farmers as they disseminate technologies. The extension officers from the Ministry of Agriculture who came after the NGOs were ignored by farming communities since they had nothing to offer. The Ministry adopted the policy of not giving anything free to the farmers to discourage the dependency syndrome. It was difficult for a PLEC team composed mainly of government scientists to break out of this mode of working and develop strong relationships with farmers, motivating them to spend some of their farm time rendering service to other farmers, scientists, and their community. PLEC therefore had a slow start working with the expert farmers. Although many successful conservationist practices of expert farmers were identified and recorded, there was less time to develop the demonstration activities fully. Farmer-to-farmer training proceeded mainly through meetings and informal networks.

Site selection

Study sites were selected based on population pressure, ethnicity, richness in biodiversity, and the agro-ecological zone, which is characterized by agricultural potential, soil types, climate, and agrobiodiversity. Socio-economic factors and proximity to the market were also considered. Initially a quick reconnaissance was made. In Embu this initially included two sites with high biodiversity: an area from the Njukiri Forest to Gachoka traversing five agro-ecological zones; and the area from the Kirimiri Forest to the Gitaru and Kamburu Dams on the Tana River. Data were also collected at Kiambu along two transects: one ran along the Kamae Forest/Kijabe axis while the other started at Kimende to Maai Mahiu on the old Nairobi-Naivasha road. A PRA (participatory rural appraisal) was conducted early in 1999, but by the end of the year it was decided that work should concentrate on the Embu site in which PLEC activities were more advanced, and that work at the Kiambu site should be discontinued. The Embu-Mbeere site initially was to cover a large area of 450 km², from the lower Kirimiri volcanic footridges (1,790 m) in Embu district to the Gitaru and Kamburu Dams on the Tana River in Mbeere district (793 m). It was scaled down and activities were concentrated on the northern end of the site at the Nduuri sublocation as the demonstration site (Figure 7.1).

The initial survey of Embu in 1998 was by a PRA conducted along the transects. The different land-use and management systems were recorded using land-use maps, informants, and observations. The upland mid-altitude area had cover of indigenous, well-preserved forest, with a form of the *taungya/shamba* system of cultivation (planted with exotic trees), and diverse land-use systems along the altitudinal gradient. At lower altitudes various strategies were being developed by farmers in response to decreasing land availability and an increasing population. The lower section is bounded by the recently built Kamburu and Gitaru Dams, which have a great influence on the people. The dams affect the surface hydrology and provide fishing activities. People are changing from being purely subsistence cultivators and extensive livestock keepers to practising supplemen-

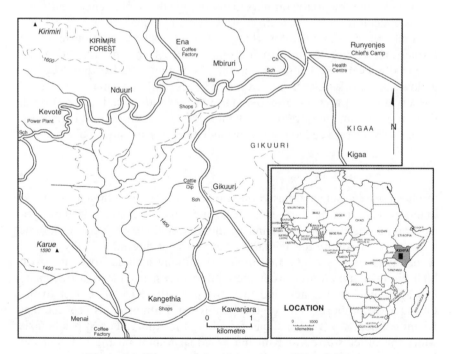

Figure 7.1 Demonstration site region at Nduuri, Kenya

tary fishing and horticulture using irrigation. Since the 1950s coffee has been extensively planted as a cash crop on bench terraces. Macadamia nuts are also a cash crop. Maize, potatoes, and beans are grown on thrown-up (*fanya juu*) terraces or on unmodified slopes. Bananas are grown close to houses and in clumps elsewhere. Sugarcane, arrowroot, and a range of horticultural crops are grown in valley bottoms. Biophysical evaluation of the land involved literature reviews, aerial photo interpretation, and conventional soil survey.

Demonstration site

The Nduuri demonstration site is located at Nduuri village, 0°25'S and 37°33'E in the Upper Midlands 2 agro-ecological zone (AEZ), as classified by Jaetzold and Schmidt (1983), within the Kirimiri-Karue catchment. Administratively, Nduuri falls under Mukuuri sublocation, Kagaari South location, Runyenjes division, in the Embu district of Eastern Province. The nearest urban centre is the town of Runyenjes, three kilometres east of Nduuri village, while the town of Embu, the provincial capital, is 25 km to the west. Two major landmarks dominate the area – the forested Kirimiri hill (1,790 m) in the north and Karue hill (1,591 m) in the south (Figure 7.1). These are volcanic cones on the lower slopes of Mount Kenya. The vegetation, major land use, land management practices, cropping systems, and household characteristics of this area were surveyed. The team included researchers from Embu Regional Research Centre in collaboration with extension personnel from the Ministry of Agriculture, a forester, herbalists, and the farmers in the area.

Mukuuri sublocation has a total population of 5,978 inhabitants (Central Bureau of Statistics 1999), comprising 2,928 males and 3,050 females. Within an area of 11.2 square kilometres, Mukuuri has a population density of 534 inhabitants per square kilometre. There are 1,235 households. The inhabitants of the area are of the Embu ethnic group. In 1998 surveys, the Nduuri household family sizes were between two and 15, with a mean of 6.8. The family provides most of the labour, although 55 per cent of families hired labour for coffee-related operations. Family income is wholly dependent on farm income. Sixty-four per cent of families are headed by males. Household landholdings vary between 0.2 and 2 ha (0.92 ha is the average size). Population pressure has led to a subdivision of land, to the extent that over 50 per cent of households farm less than one hectare, and only 13.5 per cent have two hectares or more. Sixty-nine per cent of households own and cultivate their own land, while 29 per cent cultivate undivided family land and about 2 per cent rent land.

The demonstration site topography ranges from gentle slopes at the top of ridges to steep slopes of between 15 and 50 per cent (Figure 7.1). Altitude ranges between 1,200 and 1,790 m. The area is endowed with permanent streams originating from Kirimiri hill and Mount Kenya forests about seven kilometres to the north. Soils at the demonstration site are classified as humic nitosols developed on tertiary basic igneous rocks, but there is variation in soil type from one village subunit to another. Soils are well-drained, extremely deep, darkish-brown friable clay. They are considerably acidified, with pH between 4.4 and 4.1, and organic carbon measured in the Nduuri area ranges from 1.78 per cent to 0.69 per cent. Rainfall has a bimodal pattern with the amount varying between 1,000 and 2,000 mm per annum; the long rains are from March to April, and the short rains from October to December. The vegetation ranges from conserved natural forest to agroforestry farmlands. Both exotic and indigenous trees make a dense cover.

The land-use system

Most of the farmers settled in the area 40 years ago when landholdings were consolidated and registered. Before this period the community practised shifting cultivation. Significant changes have taken place in the cropping system as the years have passed. Earlier, dolichos beans (*Dolichos lablab*) were planted during the long rains and millet and sorghum during the short rains. With the introduction of coffee, maize and short-maturity legumes replaced the millet and dolichos beans. The short-rains season is still referred to as the *mbura ya mwere*, the millet season, although millet is no longer grown. Maize and beans are now grown during both seasons. Most of the income in the study area has for decades been generated from coffee, dairy cows, and sale of food crops such as maize and beans. Coffee has provided investment income as payments are made up to four times a year and farmers are able to obtain money and pay for school or medical fees and invest in housing or other agricultural enterprises without taking out loans. However, as a result of low coffee prices and poor cooperative society management, returns from coffee sales have decreased and farmers are paying less attention to its cultivation and maintenance.

Changes in farmers' management systems have enabled more intensive and diversified use of land for food crops, but without compromising the larger portion devoted to coffee. Surveys found that coffee is commonly associated not only with cultivated crops but semi-cultivated and wild species of trees, shrubs, annual and perennial herbs, and grasses. Thirty-three cropping systems were recorded in Nduuri, with 40 per cent based on coffee in various combinations, for example as sole coffee, coffee-cassava, coffee-banana, coffee-sweet potatoes, coffee-banana-macadamia, coffee-cowpeas, coffee-tobacco, coffee-passionfruit, coffee-*miraa*-banana,[3] and coffee-pumpkin. Other crops like maize and beans are intercropped with sorghum, cassava, bananas, and macadamia. *Miraa (Catha edulis)* is a crop that is becoming more prominent within the coffee fields. Macadamia is another established cash crop in the area. Taro, sugarcane, bananas, kale, and onions are concentrated in the valley bottoms. Sugarcane and taro occupy the largest area. There is increasing use of edges, especially the terrace risers, for planting supplementary crops. These evolving adaptions have ensured that, while remaining coffee farmers, the Nduuri farmers have obtained better incomes from the same land.

Of the farms visited more than half had open-stall-type dairy cowsheds. Other livestock included goats and pigs that were also kept in open-stall sheds. Poultry were predominantly local types purely for home consumption. Beehives were encountered mostly in valley bottoms. Timber and fruit trees are predominant in the farms. *Grevillea robusta* is the most common exotic tree, followed by macadamia, mangoes (unimproved varieties), and avocados. Twenty agroforestry trees were identified. Seventeen indigenous trees were recorded, some of which are becoming very rare within the area (Table 7.1).

Table 7.1 Agroforestry trees and shrubs at Nduuri

Indigenous species		Exotic species
Local name	Scientific name	
Mururi	*Commiphora zimmermannii*	*Grevillea* (mukima)
Mukuyu	*Ficus sycomorus*	Macadamia
Mutundu	*Neoboutonia macrocalyx*	Mango
Muringa	*Cordia africana*	Avocado
Mukwego	*Bridelia micrantha*	Pawpaw
Muu	*Markhamia lutea*	Guava
Mugumo	*Ficus thonningii*	Passionfruit
Kariaria	*Euphorbia tirucalli*	Castor
Mukambura	*Dovyalis abyssinica*	Eucalyptus
Muvuti	*Erythrina abyssinica*	Cypress
Mubuthi	*Caesalpinia volkensii*	Mukinduri (*Croton megalocarpus*)
Murubaine	Not identified botanically	*Miraa (Catha edulis)*
Muthiriti	*Lippia javanica*	Loquat
Murerema	*Basella alba*	Nandi flame
Mukeu	*Dombeya burgessiae*	Euphorbia
Mubiru	*Vangueria madagascariensis*	Mulberry
Muchakuthe	Not identified botanically	Lemon
		Calliandra
		Acacia
		Jackfruit

Production constraints

The principal production constraints identified are:
• declining soil productivity (due to continuous cultivation, especially on steep slopes without adequate conservation)
• shortage of livestock feeds, especially during the dry season
• inadequate tree-crop interactions
• cultivation and exploitation of the Kirimiri Forest has affected the water catchment for the Karii, Kamiugu, and Nthungu streams, which could adversely affect planned irrigation activities; a government ban was imposed on further exploitation in 2000.

The conventional measures recommended to overcome these constraints include the use of inorganic fertilizers and farmyard manures, implementation of conservation measures such as grass strips, planting fodder banks along farm boundaries, use of pure-stand cash-crop trees, and crop rotation to overcome pests and disease. The farmers are mostly unable to adopt the recommended measures, and some have modified and also introduced other measures that are compatible with their knowledge and ability.

Demonstration activities

Demonstration site activities began by the local chief first mobilizing the community for a meeting with a team of researchers, agricultural and forestry extension personnel, and renowned herbalists. Virtually all the farmers in the village turned up for this first meeting. The PLEC concept was explained to the farmers and other collaborators. A reconnaissance walk was undertaken along the Kirimiri-Karue axis with the aim of identifying the vegetation, major land use, land management practices, cropping systems, and general household characteristics. From this survey several farmers were identified, and the diversity of the vegetation and management techniques was noted.

The first innovative management practice to be identified was using fig trees for shade and soil fertility replenishment. Farmers used several other methods of improving soil fertility in coffee farms, for example by the use of sweet potatoes in rotation, and the use of farmyard manure and crop residues. Other successful practices identified were the use of irrigation for vegetable production; introduction of *miraa* into the cropping system; planting of indigenous trees; mulching coffee with banana and *Grevillea* leaves; intercropping coffee with irrigated vegetables, bananas, sweet potato, or potatoes; modifying bench terraces into basins for irrigation; and using banana pseudostems and leaves, maize, and sugarcane stover for fertility enhancement. Some farmers were controlling soil erosion and maintaining soil fertility by mulching without the use of bench terraces. Other farmers were using trash lines of banana leaves and pseudostems for soil erosion control.

Expert farmers

Expert farmers were selected after several visits to their farms where they demonstrated their practices. Preliminary findings were reported to the farmer community at one of the several demonstration meetings held. In meetings expert farmers described the practices they were demonstrating. Farmers were encouraged to visit and learn from those farmers. Expert farmers recorded all visiting farmers who came on a learning mission. More contact was also achieved between expert farmers and the rest of the community during seminars organized at Nduuri primary school.

From the initial three expert farmers more farmer practices were identified and the number of collaborating farmers rose to 32. By the end of the project PLEC had drawn together 14 expert farmers and a cluster of 60 farmers with enthusiasm for PLEC activities. During one of the activities investigating the botanical knowledge gap between age groups, the whole of the Nduuri community was involved, including the younger members.

Use of fig trees (Ficus sycomorus) as a shade tree in coffee

PLEC initially identified three farmers who had planted fig trees in their coffee farms. The farmers claimed the fig tree modified the microclimate and improved soil fertility. Later six other farmers using this technique were included in the monitoring. Although the research results indicated no statistically significant difference between yield and soil quality under the fig trees and outside, there was a strong indication of benefits, especially during the severe drought in 2000. Coffee berries developed only under the fig tree canopy. This practice is also contributing to the conservation of biodiversity.

The use of fig trees as a shade tree in coffee generated interest among farmers. During expert farmer demonstration, useful exchanges took place and most farmers agreed that the practice was beneficial to coffee. Expert farmers allayed fears expressed by their colleagues about the possible increase in coffee-berry disease, leaf rust, and coffee thrips as a result of shading. The participating farmers showed that trimming away the lower branches of the fig tree and leaving the canopy high over the coffee trees reduced humidity. They observed that in July and August when the weather is cold and conducive to disease outbreak the fig tree has shed its leaves, leaving bare twigs, and the shading effect is minimal. During one of the meetings, interested farmers requested fig tree seedlings which some of the expert farmers were willing to provide.

Control of stem borers in coffee

In the recent past coffee pests such as the white borer (*Anthores leucotonus*), black borer (*Apate monacha*), and yellow-headed borer (*Dirphya nigricornis*) have multiplied due to no spraying of the crop as a result of low financial returns from coffee. Farmers have devised a technique of plant-to-plant inspection and spot application of paraffin or other chemicals to destroy these devastating borers. They check for the symptoms, such as yellowing of leaves, frass, and tunnelling made by the borer. Soil is excavated from the base of the stems of the suspect plants and when tunnels are noticed a piece of cotton wool soaked in insecticide or paraffin is inserted into the tunnel using a bicycle spoke; the larvae die on contact or through the fumigative effect of the insecticide. Spot application of the chemical, according to the farmers, is cheaper and avoids environmental pollution. Many farmers adopted the control of stem borers in coffee, as expert farmers demonstrated that there was low recurrence of borers after the treatment.

Top working Ruiru 11 on to SL34 coffee

Successful coffee cultivation is dependent on disease control of coffee-berry disease caused by *Colletotrichum coffeanum*, leaf rust caused by *Hemileia vastatrix*, and bacterial blight caused by *Pseudomonas syringae*. If these diseases are not controlled, field losses can be very high. Spray programmes using various fungicides are recommended, and the number of sprays can range from eight to 14 depending on weather conditions and the disease (Coffee Board of Kenya 1996). Other recommended practices to reduce the incidence of these diseases include pruning and use of shade trees. Bacterial blight does not occur in Nduuri, and the farmers have only to contend with the fungal diseases.

One of the Nduuri farmers was dealing with the problem of disease by top working the disease-tolerant Ruiru 11, a new hybrid cultivar introduced in 1985, on to the susceptible variety SL34. Ruiru 11 is a compact variety, with a higher yield per unit area than the traditional varieties. Its quality is as good as that of the traditional varieties SL28 and SL34. With the scarcity of land and the prohibitive cost of chemicals, top working quickly converts mature trees of traditional varieties without the cost and delay in production of uprooting old trees and replanting. The grafted suckers start bearing in one or two years.

The farmer began grafting Ruiru 11 scions in 1998 using root suckers from a neighbour. These suckers would otherwise be destroyed during pruning. The farmer got the idea from his father, who had a citrus nursery. His father would graft orange scions on to lemon rootstocks. The farmer selects healthy and well-placed suckers and grafts these with scions bearing a pair of leaves. The joint is tied with a polythene tape. A light polythene tube is lowered over the grafted sucker and the lower open end is tightly tied below the joint to maintain high relative humidity for faster healing. The polythene tubing is from used sugar and rice packages. The sucker is left to grow for between 45 and 60 days, after which the tapes and tubing are removed. The grafted sucker grows until bearing starts and then the old stem is removed.

By 2002, of his 946 coffee trees the farmer had grafted 500 and 300 had taken. The first plants to be grafted in 1998 have come into production. Four other farmers from Nduuri and its neighbourhood have started to adopt the technology, and many others are waiting to see the results before making a decision on adoption.

Intercropping

Conventionally, coffee is planted as a monocrop because regulations do not allow farmers to intercrop. Uprooting of coffee is also prohibited except with the express authority of the Director of Agriculture, which is usually cumbersome to obtain due to bureaucratic red tape. This leaves the farmer with few options for making a change to other more profitable crops. Farmers are able to bear the loss of income from poor prices up to a certain level, after which they ignore regulations imposed by the Ministry of Agriculture or the industry body, and try all sorts of experiments which are likely to improve their income.

On the other hand, the coffee regulations do allow for coppicing as a management tool. This involves cutting the coffee plant, leaving a stump of about 20–30 cm. Several new shoots arise from the stump. Some are removed, retaining two or three healthy shoots. The resulting plants are robust and more productive than the older trees. During this change of cycle, it is acceptable to plant annual crops in order to reduce loss of income while waiting for the shoots to mature. This is one of the main strategies adopted by farmers to reduce the coffee canopy to favour more profitable crops. Farmers have developed numerous intercropping systems, and most of these have resulted in improved household income and welfare, increased agrobiodiversity, and reduced land degradation. The crops grown include peppers, tomatoes, kales, and cabbages. These are planted on flat basins or tied ridges, and are heavily fertilized with manure or inorganic fertilizers. The crop in most cases is irrigated, but in some farms it is rain-fed. Some farmers simply plant beans, potato, or sweet potato. Although these are not such high-value crops they contribute substantially to the household food security.

Initially only one expert farmer was identified intercropping pumpkins. By the end of the project six farmers had adopted using pumpkin as a cover crop in coffee and augmenting their income through sale of the pumpkins. In this technology, beans (*Phaseolous vulgaris*) and an initially slow-growing local variety of pumpkin are planted at the same time under coffee. As the season progresses the beans mature faster, providing a ground cover which enhances water percolation, reduces soil and moisture loss, and smothers weeds. Meanwhile, pumpkins catch up and start to spread on the surface just when beans are ready for harvesting. After the beans are removed the pumpkins spread and continue to provide ground cover. The expert farmer harvested 500 pumpkins from 0.4 ha of land. These were sold locally in a roadside kiosk or to buyers who took them to the capital city 150 km away. The pumpkin also has the added value of increasing the organic matter in the soil as the residues decompose. Thus from a plot of land which originally produced only coffee the farmer harvests three crops, enhances household food security and income, and improves soil fertility.

Instead of deliberately neglecting their coffee, some farmers ignore the regulations against intercropping and reduce the canopy of the mature trees by cutting them back to one stem with a few laterals. The most common intercrops include maize, beans, cassava, and macadamia, but those who have benefited most plant high-value crops like kales, tomatoes, spinach, chillies, and bananas. The crops are rain-fed but are sometimes also irrigated, especially when planted before the rains or just before the end of rains.

One expert farmer is synchronizing intercrops produced under irrigation in coffee with peak market prices. The farmer lops the coffee and plants maize in the off season. The maize matures during a period of maize scarcity and is harvested green to fetch premium prices. The land is prepared immediately and planted with kale, tomatoes, chillies, spinach, and onions in the middle of the rainy season. The vegetables mature under irrigation and are sold during a period of scarcity and good prices in the local market.

Miraa cultivation, as demonstrated by another farmer, was found to be a good alternative source of income given the prevailing low coffee prices. However, adoption of the crop was subject to socio-religious complications since this stimulating drug was not acceptable to some members of the community.

In most intercropping systems the space between two rows of coffee is dug, levelled, and weeded to make it easier to irrigate. The seedbed is heavily fertilized with manure and inorganic fertilizer before planting. Some farmers plant in basins, pits, ridges, or furrows. Creating bench terraces and using manure in pits, ridges, and furrows has increased water percolation and reduced soil and water loss and general soil degradation. After planting, crops are weeded and pests and diseases controlled. Coffee yields per stem are higher with the increased fertility, and this compensates for the reduced canopy.

Irrigation

Farmers expanded irrigation after a PLEC-organized tour to Meru district, where an expert farmer demonstrated his technique of growing out-of-season maize and vegetables. Farmers formed four self-help irrigation groups. The Nduuri water project used the Ena River and the Kamiugu irrigation project tapped and reticulated water from the Kamiugu River. Other farmers use water from the national water pipeline supply, although it is unreliable. Those farmers living next to the rivers extract water directly.

Enhancing biodiversity

The agrobiodiversity assessment revealed that farmers are important agents of biodiversity conservation. In sample plots, annual crop fields had 12 species, grass- and shrub-dominated fallows had more than 30 species, while *shamba*-system agroforestry plots had more than 25 species. There is evidence that the community has some successful crop variety selectors, especially for the traditional food crops. They conserve old varieties that have tolerated adverse biotic conditions for many decades and have special uses. Diversity conserved in the major food crops included 20 varieties of banana, four varieties of sweet potato, nine varieties of yam, and six varieties each of sugarcane and cassava.

Detailed study was made of selected home gardens. The portion of land spared for the homestead ranged from 0.04 to 0.3 ha, with an average of 0.14 ha, and varied according to family size, the number and species of livestock, and total landholding. Those with more land or larger families had larger home gardens. The gardens are rich in biodiversity. In the surveyed home gardens the study recorded 46 species of food plant, 23 species used for fodder, 29 species used for fuelwood, 15 for construction, 13 species with commercial use, and 22 species used for medicines. Plants were also used for soil fertility enhancement, yam support, oil, mulching, art, ornament, and spices. The most popular food plants were bananas and 10 varieties were recorded. Tomatoes, passionfruit, sugarcane, avocado, *nduuma* (arrowroot), macadamia, mango, cassava, and yams were also popular. Herbs and spices included onion, chillies, and rosemary. Farmers made use of wetter areas, such as near water taps or in trenches dug along a wall to capture rainwater runoff from the roof, to grow arrowroot, sugarcane, and kale. Weeds such as *Commelina benghalensis* and natural grasses were not removed from the garden immediately, but were allowed to grow and weeded later to provide feed for livestock. Sixty per cent of the homesteads had a perimeter live fence (hedge), sometimes reinforced with barbed wire, and many also had smaller internal hedges. While there were only seven hedge species, a total of 30 species were found in the hedges with 10 different uses, including fodder, fuel, construction, food, and medicine.

PLEC also introduced diversity in crop production by exposing farmers to new crops and new varieties during field-days at the local primary school. Due to the very high incidence of potato blight, fungicide spraying was a common and expensive practice, and the two late blight-tolerant varieties of potatoes, Asante and Tigoni, were introduced. Several varieties of climbing beans tolerant to bean fly and anthracnose were introduced as they occupy a small area and are suitable to smallholder farms. From a visit to a farmer in another district farmers learned other uses of various tree species for fruit, medicine, and specialized purposes such as water purification. This experience motivated a tree nursery team, who were eager to add more tree species to their collection. PLEC demonstration has popularized increased agrobiodiversity in the coffee land-use system.

Investigation into the botanical knowledge gap

A study was made to assess whether there were differences in botanical knowledge between age groups among the Nduuri community. Seventy-three members from the village subunits representing four age groups participated in the study. The participants identified many uses of plants, ranging from food, fodder, medicine, and fuelwood to more unusual uses such as banana ripening, mole trapping, oil for cosmetics, pesticides, construction of beehives, and pot cleaners. Some species have very specialized uses. The investigation revealed apparent gaps and age-related differences in general knowledge of plant species' names as well as in utilization of the species (Table 7.2). Those born between 1940 and 1959 could name the most species, whereas the older age group named more medicinal plants and plants with more specialized uses. The study generated great interest

Table 7.2 Number of plants named by each age group in various use categories

Number of plants named	Age groups (year of birth)			
	1920–1939	1940–1959	1960–1979	1980–1990
Total	180	195	153	135
In recent fallow	68	69	62	51
Medicinal plants	65	53	46	24
Fuelwood	73	90	62	43
Fodder	39	56	33	34
Ripen bananas	4	4	3	2
Trapping moles	5	3	1	2
Roof thatch	6	5	2	1
Tool handles	8	4	4	2
Pesticide	2	2	1	1
Beehive support	8	4	3	–
Fibre	9	7	6	3

among the community and raised awareness of the need for a concerted effort towards conservation. Participants resolved to plant herbaria in schools so that children could become acquainted with various species, especially those that are rare or threatened.

Livestock

Livestock have become substantially more important, with at least 90 per cent of farmers keeping one type or more, and patches of spare land taken up for cut-and-carry fodder production. Of the farms visited 54 per cent had open-stall cowsheds, 71 per cent of households had chickens, and 69 per cent had dairy cattle. Cross-breeds between the native Zebu and exotic breeds (mainly Ayrshire) are preferred. Other livestock included goats and pigs, which are also kept in open-stall sheds. Chickens are free range except during critical times of the year when they might damage food crops. Poultry production for income, which requires relatively high capital investment, has also increased in years when coffee prices are high. Livestock also have an important insurance role during periods of low coffee prices as they can be sold to meet short-term cash demands.

Livestock take up very little land and are fed mainly on maize stover, banana pseudostems, and other collected fodder. Napier grass is grown on terrace risers in the coffee gardens. Farmers identified 56 species of plants used for fodder for cattle. Up to 66 species of local forage plants were offered to goats. Grain supplements are also bought in.

Livestock are becoming a much more important contributor to local nutrient cycles. Zero-grazing is a large generator of manure, with 65 per cent of households in Nduuri getting between 0.9 and 20 tonnes of manure per season. It is usually composted with crop residues. Towards the end of the dry season it is removed from the stall area and heaped to decompose, and then is spread mainly on coffee lands. This has meant a decrease in purchased inputs of fertilizer. The manure generated by animals has also brought substantial nutrients into small areas, especially near the compost heaps. Biodiversity has flourished and is now used by farmers who harvest species that include *Amaranthus* spp., *Solanum nigrum*, and *Pennisetum clandestinum* (kikuyu grass).

Notes

1. The authors gratefully acknowledge the contributions of others cited in the references at the end of the chapter.
2. Scientists from the University of Nairobi were also initially involved, but because of severe pressures in the Kenyan universities in the 1990s they were unable to continue participation. This was one of the main reasons for the delayed start.

3. *Miraa* is a mild narcotic stimulant, and it is exported to countries in the Middle East as well as being used in Kenya.

REFERENCES

Central Bureau of Statistics. 1999. *1999 Population and Housing Census*. Nairobi: Central Bureau of Statistics, Ministry of Finance and Planning.

Coffee Board of Kenya. 1996. "Disease control in coffee", *Kenya Coffee*, Vol. 61, No. 722, pp. 2345–2346.

Jaetzold, R. and M. Schmidt. 1983. *Farm Management Handbook of Kenya*, Vol. 2. Nairobi: Ministry of Agriculture.

1. Brazil.
   Farmers of the floodplain locate their houses on the levee banks of the river. Perennials are grown around the house and planting boxes above the flood level are used for herbs and medicinal plants.
   (Photo: C. Padoch)

2. Brazil.
   Innovative Amazonian farmers in the floodplain have developed diverse agroforestry systems to minimize the impact of the Moko disease in bananas. PLEC-Amazonia has been demonstrating and disseminating this technology.
   (Photo: C. Padoch)

3. Guinée, Fouta Djallon.
   Expert farmer demonstrating his method of aboveground compost
   making to PLEC scientists.
   (Photo: H. Brookfield)

4. Guinée, Fouta Djallon.
   Women farmers' group with a display of cloth they have dyed using
   local plants.
   (Photo: H. Brookfield)

5. Guinée, Moussaya.
   A group of women weeding rice.
   (Photo: H. Brookfield)

6. Southern Ghana.
   A village display of yam diversity (PLEC scientist at the right).
   (Photo: H. Brookfield)

7. Southern Ghana, Jachie.
   Expert farmer and demonstration site leader, Cecelia Osei, discussing a
   group of cultivated plants.
   (Photo: H. Brookfield)

8. Southern Ghana, Gyamfiase.
   A PLEC play. The 'scientist' is seeking to persuade a dubious farmer to
   plant trees on his land.
   (Photo: H. Brookfield)

9. Uganda.
   PLEC scientists and farmers learning about medicinal plants from
   woman specialist
   (Photo: H. Brookfield)

10. Tanzania.
    Expert farmer demonstrating planting methods to a visiting group of
    scientists and fellow farmers.
    (Photo: H. Brookfield)

11. China, Xishuangbanna.
Wet rice fields under winter
vegetable crops, with community
forest and shifting cultivation in
the background.
(Photo: H. Brookfield)

12. China, Gaoligongshan.
A meal prepared by farm
families for PLEC visitors,
using only wild and cultivated
local plants.
(Photo: H. Brookfield)

13. Peru, Santa Ana de Muyuy.
Ephemeral sand bars are available to farmers for planting for about 5 months.
(Photo: R. Sears)

14. Peru, Santa Ana de Muyuy.
During high water only the levees are cultivable for the concurrent production of timber, banana and other fruit tree crops.
(Photo: R. Sears)

15. Jamaica.
Expert farmer addressing a 'work-experience day' on his farm.
(Photo: E. Thomas Hope)

16. Thailand.
Soil-restoring *Macaranga denticulata* (pada) emerging after the rice harvest.
(Photo: H. Brookfield)

8

Tanzania

Fidelis Kaihura, Edward Kaitaba,[1] *Edina Kahembe, and Charles Ngilorit*

Introduction

Farmers consider PLEC as a project that touches the real day to day problems of the farmers in daily life and facilitates them to manage successfully. It has made some improve production, others have become powerful heads of their own families by meeting the real basic daily needs of the family and some have been exposed to knowledge they did not have before as a tool to struggle with nature. (Kaihura 2002a)

Farmers in Arumeru have developed an extraordinary diversity of crops and cropping systems. By formally valuing the human resources at the local level and appreciating the agrodiversity that farmers have developed themselves, PLEC in Tanzania has brought to the fore the heterogeneity of rural society and empowered farmers. Some farmers practise sustainable use of biodiversity using many varieties and landraces that are now rare, and their sustainable and productive management practices provide food security. There are innovative and expert farmers who carry on agricultural activities that have substantial scope for replication, and farmer-to-farmer training through demonstrations has been particularly successful. Women have begun teaching each other, swapping planting material, and enthusiastically engaging in community works. The PLEC experience has also highlighted the beneficial and mutual understanding between professionals, field workers, and farmers. Working closely together on demonstration sites, they have come to appreciate each other's different kind of knowledge.

169

History of the cluster

Tanzania was first associated with PLEC in 1993, when initiatives were taken for forming the East African PLEC cluster together with Kenya and Uganda (Chapter 6). Land degradation was a major focus, but plans also included the analysis of agricultural systems and biological and socio-economic changes. The main objective of the pilot phase was to develop and test methodologies to research issues in relation to human ecology, land management, and environmental change. The theme for PLEC-Tanzania was "farming systems' response, biodiversity, and adaptation to conservation". Two districts, Arumeru in Arusha region and Lushoto in Tanga region, were selected because they have high population density, diverse land-use systems, different processes and stages of land degradation, in- and outmigration, and other projects working on natural resources management in the districts. Due to logistical problems, Lushoto district was later dropped from the study.

Arumeru district is one of nine districts in the Arusha region of northern Tanzania. It has an area of 2,966 km². Mount Meru, the second highest mountain in the country at 4,585 m, is situated in the northern part of the district. Initially two areas, one on the windward side and another on the leeward side, were selected and studied by transect method. The transects ran from the lower slopes of Mount Meru to the lowlands, from subhumid to semi-arid ecozones, covering a range of land-use systems, soils, and climate and with different impacts of population and degradation. The windward side normally receives more rain than the leeward side. The windward transect included Olgilai/Ng'iresi (upper slope position and subhumid), Moshono (mid-slope and intermediate), and Kiserian (lower slope and semi-arid) villages. The leeward transect included Engorika (upper slope) and Olkokola/Lengijave (lower slope). When the pilot phase was concluded it was agreed that work should continue only on the windward side and in only the upper and lower sites, to concentrate efforts more effectively in a smaller area for development of demonstration work. This was done rapidly in 1997–1998.

Methodology

The initial research team included a socio-economist, agronomist, herbarium technician, demographer, soil scientist, livestock specialist, soil conservationists, community development staff, and agricultural extensionists. Different methods were used to collect information, including semi-structured group interviews, participatory diagramming, timeline history, use of key local indicators, and shared discussions between experts and villagers along the transects. Aerial photographs were used to establish mapping units along the eastern (windward) transect. Temporal and spatial changes in land use and cover were established, mainly using ethno-historical information from the elderly as time-series remote-sensing data were not available.

Assessment of biophysical diversity and crop, land, and livestock management diversity used a checklist as a guideline (Brookfield, Stocking, and Brookfield 1999). Land-use stages and field types were established. In farmers' fields, the current field types were identified (Kaihura, Ndondi, and Kemikimba 2000). The study was conducted in collaboration with key informants in the case of public lands, and with farm owners and key informants on farms. For each field type farm ownership, farmer category, location, land form, vegetation, drainage and percentage slope, soil fertility rating, and evidence of major deficiency symptoms on plants were described. Mini-pits of 10×50 cm^2 were excavated to describe soils. Local and scientific names were recorded, and other descriptive parameters included topsoil depth, surface (0–20 cm) and sub-surface (30–50 cm) soil properties of colour, texture, structure, pore size, and distribution, and root size and abundance. Soil samples were taken for laboratory analysis.

Agrobiodiversity was assessed following PLEC BAG guidelines (Zarin, Guo, and Enu-Kwesi 1999). Biased sample plots were used except in native forests. The aim was to collect data representative of the most species-diverse examples in each field type. The minimum number of sample plots depended on the type of land-use stage, with five plots selected in native forests, 10 plots in house gardens and edges, and three plots each in selected annual cropping fields, planted forests, woodlots, micro-catchment, and agroforestry fields. Presence, abundance, ethno-botanical value of plant species, use category such as food, medicine, construction, fuelwood, or fodder, and whether a species was an indicator of water, drought, or salinity were recorded. Sampling was carried out in 1999 between May and June, just after the main rainy season.

Land degradation assessment was also conducted for each field type. It described erosion type, presence of micro-pedestals, exposed tree trunks or mounds and estimates of erosion rate, colour contrast of bare and covered surface patches, surface signs of crusting, sealing, or stone remnants, evidence of deposition and its rate, and evidence of soil accumulation against obstructions or landslides. Evidence of sodicity or salinity was checked by the presence or absence of indicator plants and was later confirmed by laboratory analysis. For each field type, major degradation agents were also described.

Farmers willing to work with PLEC were identified. These farmers were grouped into three resource-endowment categories based on criteria set by the farmers themselves. Criteria included the number of wives, house type (brick with iron roof versus mud with grass roof), number and type of livestock, farm size, and tillage method used (ox, tractor, or hand).

Farmers participated from the beginning through a participatory rural appraisal (PRA) of natural resource management and in establishing criteria for farmer categorization, and most importantly in the identification of land-use stages and field types. In addition they were involved in development and implementation of the exchange of knowledge and demonstrations of management practices, conducting experiments and taking part in outreach programmes within the village and outside PLEC sites. Many PLEC farmers also participated with other organizations and projects in the village. The activities of other projects were complementary in addressing rural livelihoods, but none of them addressed biodiversity.

The Arumeru demonstration sites

The area around Mount Meru is dominated by volcanic cone hills, dissected footslopes, and undulating plains. In general the volcanic cones have steep and long slopes which become gentle to almost flat at the lower end of the footslopes. The footslopes merge to form wide and sometimes extensive U-shaped valleys. The long, steep slopes have a high erosion potential and land use has to go hand in hand with a number of diverse soil and water conservation measures. There are seven major perennial rivers in the area, and most drain through Arusha district, including the Nduruma, Ngaramtoni, Maji ya Chai, and Tengeru. All these rivers originate from forest surrounding Mount Meru. The rivers contribute to economic development as they are utilized intensively for irrigation.

The subhumid site of Olgilai/Ng'iresi is located at an altitude of about 1,900 m along the footslopes of Kivesi hill, one of the volcanic cones of Mount Meru. Agroforestry is the major land-use system in this subhumid area. The semi-arid site of Kiserian is located in the lowlands on an extended plain below Mount Meru where agro-pastoralism is the dominant land use. The altitude is 1,200 m. Rainfall is bimodal, with long rains from about March to May and short rains in November and December. Annual average rainfall for Olgilai/Ng'iresi is 2,000 mm and in Kiserian it is 500 mm. Temperature range for both sites is 12–30°C. There is one dependable growing season per year, with the duration decreasing southward from six months to 10 weeks.

Soils are well-drained dark sandy loams and loams developed on volcanic ash and pumice. They are of moderate to high natural fertility with favourable moisture-holding properties. The soils are, however, very susceptible to both water and wind erosion even on gentle slopes, and require careful management. Declining productivity is seen as a major problem. The major criteria used by farmers for classifying soils were soil colour,

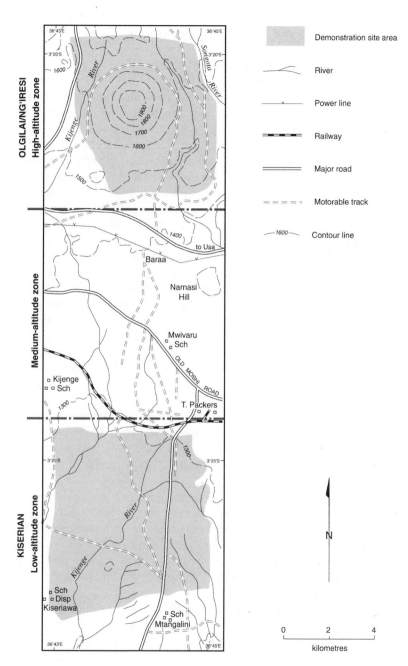

Figure 8.1. The Arumeru demonstration sites

workability, susceptibility to wind and water erosion, and fertility with reference to crop yield and water-holding capacity (Kaihura, Ndondi, and Kemikimba 2000).

About 60 per cent of the land is under cultivation, 30 per cent under grassland, and 10 per cent under forest. In Olgilai and Ng'iresi farmers use different parts of the landscape in different ways, matching crop suitability to the land, taking into consideration not only the biological suitability but also the value of the crop, labour requirements, and the risk of crop failure. High-value crops are planted near the home for more careful management, less distance to carry manure and crop residues, and to reduce the risk of theft. Hillside plots are planted with sweet potato to reduce soil loss, and field borders are planted with bananas and trees to mark boundaries. Some older farmers have a deep understanding of soils. They select crops and planting dates for each soil type to make the best use of available nutrients and moisture and reduce the risk of crop failure.

A checklist of 143 species in 53 families was compiled following the agro-biodiversity assessment of plots at the demonstration sites. High species diversity was found in natural forest systems. Thirty-eight species were recorded in the least disturbed forest. Highly disturbed forest had a larger number of understorey species recorded in the small plots and fewer large trees than in the less disturbed forest plots. Overall, human influence on the environment was associated with a loss in biodiversity. Soil management practices like soil and water conservation using physical and biological structures and fertility improvement using organic inputs increased on-farm biodiversity. Land tenure was also observed to affect species richness. Private plots had significantly higher species richness compared with similar communal plots, and many of the species are used. Forty-three species were recorded in a *Terminalia-Combretum* private woodland and 58 in the woodland of another expert farmer. Table 8.1 shows some of the utilized species found in the area.

Poor farmers had higher species diversity than rich and middle-income farmers. In order to spread risk, poor farmers plant as many crops as possible on a small piece of land and take advantage of whatever grows on the plot, including volunteer crops. Poor farmers also have less choice in what to remove and what to maintain on their farms. For the two plots of rich farmers studied, the more fertile plot showed more diverse plant growth than the less fertile field.

Within the main crops a high diversity of varieties is grown. Selection is a continuous process. Some varieties are tried and become part of the farmer's collection, whereas others disappear from the field. Farmers consider more than high yields and pest resistance when selecting varieties. They select for characteristics such as taste, intercropping compatibility, labour requirements, drought tolerance, and market value. Bush beans, for

Table 8.1 Some useful species recorded in Arumeru

Timber, fuelwood, and catchment value species		
Species name	Uses	Habit
Wood		
Albizia gummifera	timber and poles	T
Olea africana	timber	T
Maesa lanceolata	poles	T
Cordia abyssinica	poles	T
Croton macrostachyus	poles	T
Neobotonia macrocalyx	poles	T
Nuxia floribunda	poles	T
Rauvolfia caffra	fuelwood	T
Albizia gummifera	catchment and fuelwood	T
Ficus thonningii	catchment	T
Maesa lanceolata	fuelwood	T
Ficus sur	catchment	T
Wild fruits and food		
Ficus sur	fruits for animal	T
Piper capense	animal fodder	H
Basella alba	vegetable/animal fodder	CL
Vangueria tomentosa	fruits	S
Rubus pinnatus	fruits	S
Albizia gummifera	animal fodder	T
Rytigynia schumannii	fruits	S
Tools, ornamental, and hedge		
Maesa lanceolata	tools	T
Caesalpinia decapetala	hedge/ornamental	CL
Crassocephalum mannii	hedge	S
Aspilia spp.	ornamental	H
Rubus spp.	hedge	S
Tagetes minuta	roofing	H
Themeda triandra	roofing	G
Croton macrostachyus	storage for maize	T
Medicinal species		
Bidens pilosa	heartburn and cough	H
Rauvolvia caffra	anti-diarrhoea	T
Croton macrostachyus	anti-haemorrhagic	T
Crassocephalum mannii	arrest stomach pain	S
Albizia gummifera	arrest tooth ache	T
Aspilia africana	releaves lumbago	H
Maesa lanceolata	removes stomach worms	T

T: tree H: herb, S: shrub, CL: climber, G: grass

example, are preferred over climbing beans, which get tangled in the maize intercrop so that they are more difficult to harvest and pods are lost. Table 8.2 lists some of the varieties of the main food crops grown.

Table 8.2 Varieties of the main food crops in Arumeru

Crop varieties	Plant characteristics and crop uses
Maize varieties	All are used for food, income, and crop residues fed to animals
Kienyeji	Not very sweet, low yielding, drought susceptible, tolerant to storage pests, good milling quality
Katumani	Drought tolerant, early maturing, low yielding, good milling quality, tolerant of storage pests
CG4141 (lowlands)	Good milling quality, drought tolerant
UCA (highlands)	Good milling quality, drought tolerant
Kilima	High yielding, high water demand, susceptible to storage pests, good milling quality, high-quality flour
Bean varieties	All are used as food, most residues are fed to livestock, and some are used for income
Soya kijivu	Income, high price, good taste, "no gases after eating", early maturing, sweet, grey climbing type
Kachina	Income, high price, early maturing, spoils quickly after cooking
Lovirondo	Climbing type, "gases after eating", laborious to harvest, low market price
Bwanashamba	Most popular in Kiserian, high yielding, good taste, susceptible to diseases and aphids
Maasai red ndogo (namira)	High yielding, good taste, "no gases after eating", needs wide spacing for high production
Maasai red kubwa (namriri)	Income, high price, early maturing, bush type, susceptible to diseases, good flavour
Karanga	High yielding, good flavour
Lyamungu 90	Income, high price, good flavours, early maturing, drought tolerant, high yielding
Kiburu	Drought tolerant, grows well on soils with poor fertility
Engichumba	Income, very high yielding, violet bean
Engichumba-ng'iro	High yielding, sweet, grey bean used in *loshoro*
Engichumba-narok	Income, similar to Engichumba-ng'iro, black bean
Moshi	Income, very high yielding, sweetest, yellow bean
Kibumulu	Income, fast cooking, high price, dark red bean
Banana varieties	
Kisimiti	Early maturing, drought tolerant, used for income, brewing, fodder (stem)
Ng'ombe	Hard when cooked; used for *loshoro*, brewing, income, roofing, fodder
Mshale	Long and thick fingers; used for roasting, *matendela***, income
Uganda fupi	Early maturing, susceptible to pests and diseases; used for soup (*mtori*), fruit, income, fodder (peels)
Uganda ndefu	Large with few fingers, susceptible to pests and disease; used for soup, fruit, fodder (peels)
Kisukari	Very sweet, drought and disease tolerant, low nutrient demand; used for fruit, income, fodder (stems)
Mzuzu	Tolerant to drought and disease; roasted for tea

Table 8.2 (cont.)

Crop varieties	Plant characteristics and crop uses
Malindi	Drought tolerant; used for food (*matendela*), fodder
Mnanambu	Used for shade, soup, roasting
Mkonosi	Disease tolerant; roasted
Mkono wa tembo	Disease tolerant; roasted
Ndishi	Susceptible to diseases; used for *loshoro*, income
Olmuririko	Modest tolerance to diseases; used for *loshoro*, brewing

* *Loshoro*: traditional Waarusha, Wameru, and Wamasai food made of maize, beans, and milk
** *Matendela*: traditional Waarusha and Wameru food made of vegetables, milk, banana, and beans

Olgilai/Ng'iresi

The five dominant land-use stages identified in the Olgilai/Ng'iresi subhumid site were natural forest, planted forest (*taungya* system), agroforest, water source micro-catchments, and pasture fallows. Agroforest was the dominant land-use stage, covering 80 per cent of the site with eight field types identified. Coffee, banana, and other trees are intercropped with maize and beans together or as monocrops, with potatoes often in rotation with vegetables, or with other plants in house gardens and on boundaries and field edges. A single coffee/banana agroforest may have more than six varieties of bananas and several varieties of beans and maize, depending on the production objectives, the use of each variety, the plant characteristics, and farmers' taste preferences – the latter may be influenced by socio-cultural considerations specific to the tribe. Most field types were on farmers' fields, but some were in gazetted forest and in open common grazing lands.

A total of 42 different field types was found in Olgilai/Ng'iresi, with nine on one farm in Ng'iresi. The boundary and house garden field types had the greatest frequency, reflecting the importance of demarcations of land under conditions of land scarcity. House gardens were an important immediate source of household vegetables. The most common vegetables grown were cabbage, onions, tomatoes, spinach, *Amaranthus*, eggplants, and peppers. As a general rule, the field type in an individual farmer's field changes with the season. On the contour bunds they plant Napier and elephant grass (*Pennisetum purpureum*), *Leucaena leucocephala*, and *Grevillea robusta*.

Agroforests are planted randomly. A few farmers use recommended spacing, while others modify spacing to suit their own conditions, personal demands, and crop variety. The crops planted for the long rains include potatoes, tomatoes, coffee, and fodder (both grass and trees). Forest trees are also planted. Maize, bananas, sugarcane, beans, and sweet potatoes are planted for the short rains. Vegetables (cabbage) and fodder are planted during both seasons. Boundary trees, shrubs, and yams are also planted throughout the year. Most vegetables are planted using seedlings raised in farmers' own or commercial nurseries. Potato-growers use seed tubers from the previous crop or buy from the local markets. Coffee seedlings and bananas suckers are usually obtained from the farmers' own farms.

Bananas are a source of food and income. There is a very strong emphasis on the *mshale* variety because it is more marketable, although there are several traditional varieties grown – these include *indishi, mdadau, engiondo, emboo, umuririko, engamalindi, endusugari,* and *mkojozi.* An attempt to replace the traditional varieties with new varieties such as *Uganda* (a soft variety) had failed because the new varieties were not disease resistant. Bananas are consumed when they ripen or are cooked. In recent years roast bananas have become very common in urban areas, where they are consumed with *nyama choma* (roast meat). Despite heavy local consumption, bananas also have a good market outside the Arusha region and are transported as far as Dar ès Salam, Singida, and Dodoma, where prices are much higher.

Some indigenous forests are protected as national, district, or village forest reserves. Since colonial farm extension programmes promoted monocropping and discouraged tree planting on farmlands, forest reserves remain the only source of fuelwood, fruits, timber, and some fodder. Government forests and reserves lack adequate protection and proper management, having less involvement of the local leadership, and the neighbouring people benefit very little if at all from these reserves. Fire outbreaks are common, as neighbours take no trouble to prevent them. Encroachment into the forest reserves, shifting of the boundaries, and indiscriminate lumbering have occurred. During drought periods, livestock grazing in the forest reserve area is still common. All these activities have reduced forest density, diversity, and size, and have degraded other resources. Some indigenous forests have been replaced by state-owned forest plantations.

Local ownership and sharing of resources has encouraged communities to protect their forests. Yet even with legal or community protection, community forest reserves too are being gradually depleted and degraded. In contrast, conservation of remnant natural forest patches is an important activity for some farmers, particularly elderly farmers. Different types of trees and shrubs are found in complex mixtures, each of which has a particular use value. Most remnant forest woodlots were found in ravines or seasonal river valleys. They have been conserved as gene banks for plants used for traditional medicine, building poles, firewood, soil fertility improvement, and wood for making carvings. Other economic uses of the trees include fruit production, dyeing materials, shade, windbreaks, and drought insurance. Farmers understand the growth habits of each type of tree and manage them differently. Trees least attacked by pests and diseases receive less attention than more vulnerable types.

Kiserian

The lowlands are used for agricultural crop production and livestock keeping. The majority of farmers are agro-pastoralists with large herds of free-grazing cattle. Livestock include cows, goats, sheep, pigs, and donkeys. With Kiserian's larger farms, primary tillage for most annual crops is by ox-ploughing, in contrast with Olgilai/Ng'iresi where ox-ploughing is almost non-existent. Tillage is normally preceded by spot application of manure, which is incorporated together with crop residues and weeds.

The seven land-use stages identified in Kiserian are *mbuga*,[2] mixed-cropping fields, neglected fallows, woodlots, agroforests, stony hilltops, and quarries. *Mbuga* is dominant, covering 68 per cent of the area, and is mainly used for grazing. The team identified 29 field types. Maize and bean intercrops and natural pasture were the most frequent. Both local and introduced maize varieties are grown. Introduced varieties are *Kilima*, mainly for home consumption and occupying less area, and CG4141 for marketing. The major crops are maize, beans, millet, and pigeon peas. Minor crops include cowpea, finger millet, pigeon pea, sunflower, tobacco, sweet potato, and pumpkin, which are all local varieties. Sisal is planted as a live fence, and is also a source of ropes and building poles. Cassava, sweet potatoes, and sunflower were previously grown but had disappeared and were reintroduced by PLEC. There are fewer trees than in Olgilai/Ng'iresi. Farmers grow papaya and citrus for fruits around the homestead. Other trees include newly introduced *Cassia* spp. and various indigenous trees are grown near the homestead as windbreaks. Although there are communal woodlots that are less carefully managed in Kiserian, most woodlots are privately owned.

At Kiserian, maize is planted just before the beginning of the main rainy season, which starts between mid-February and early March. Beans are planted at the same time, although a few farmers plant beans after maize germination. During the middle of the season sweet potato cuttings are planted, but mainly in outlying fields. This later planting is to avoid tuber rot caused by heavy rains. Other crops planted are onions and a local *Amaranthus* species grown as a vegetable. Maize and beans are sown in rows, and bean rows are generally two or three times more numerous. They are planted more densely because the crops stand a greater chance of survival if rains are inadequate, and fetch a much higher price at markets. In some farms pigeon peas or cowpeas are broadcast before the maize and beans are planted. Seeds of local varieties are obtained from farmers' previous crops, while improved seeds are obtained from commercial farmers and the Agricultural Research Institute.

The vegetation in the lowlands is dominated by grasses and herbs, with scattered or isolated patches of shrubs and trees. The area is highly disturbed due to heavy grazing, as indicated by the presence of *Ajuga remota* and *Sida schimperiana*. The acacia bushland has an assemblage of woody plants, most of them being shrubby with a canopy of less than six metres and occupying about 20 per cent of the ground cover. The vegetation is dominated by *Acacia megacephala* and *Acacia seyal*. Thorny acacia is cut and used as fences for the cattle *bomas*. Indicator species of drought tolerance such as *Opuntia vulgaris* are also common.

Household characteristics

The area has three major ethnic groups: the more sedentary Wameru and Waarusha and the pastoralist Maasai. The Wamasai and Waarusha are still organized on the *boma* system where the whole clan settles in one cluster called a *boma*, comprising several houses enclosed in a fence, leaving the centre open for keeping livestock. The *boma* pattern of settlement is still followed by the four main Waarusha and Wamasai clans, namely Laizer, Mollel, Kipuyo, and Lukumayi, but the settlement pattern has started to disappear in the densely populated areas in the highlands. The rate of change is very rapid in peri-urban areas where traditional houses are replaced by houses built out of bricks and roofed by either corrugated iron sheets or tiles. However, the *boma* system emerges again when the Waarusha migrate from the densely populated highlands to marginal lowland areas where land is not a limiting factor.

In 1998 the village population in Olgilai/Ng'iresi was 2,158 and in Kiserian it was 3,330. The annual population growth rate is estimated to be 3.8 per cent, slightly higher than the average regional rate of 3.5 per cent. The population density, at 137 per square kilometre, is one of the highest in the country, but varies from the highly populated slopes to the lower plains which have a scattered population. Population growth rates in Arumeru were slightly higher in the 1960s, and decreased from the 1970s to the 1990s. During the later years there was outmigration to other parts of the region and to other areas of Tanzania due to land scarcity. Life expectancy is estimated to be 60–65 years, although it may change now following the outbreak of HIV/AIDS.

In Olgilai/Ng'iresi the average family size in 1999 was 5.0 people, compared with 7.1 in 1998 (Mbonile 1998). There were 350 households in 1999 and 305 in 1998. The change may be due to the difference in definition of a household. In the 1999 survey, families that lived in separate accommodation and farmed their own land were treated as separate households, even though several houses may be physically situated in the same *boma* or compound. In the 1998 survey all people living in the *boma* were included as a single household. There are some quite large families – over 30 per cent of the families in Ng'iresi have seven or more family members. Kiserian family sizes are generally larger because many men have two or more wives. The poor categories have the smallest family size. All households in the rich categories have large families, and in Olgilai/Ng'iresi the number of adult males in rich households was significantly higher than in poor households.

The average farm size is lower in the high-altitude zone, but in both areas farm sizes have been decreasing. In Ng'iresi in 1998 the average farm size was 1.9 ha, whereas in 1999 it was 1.1 ha. In Kiserian it dropped from an average size of 5 ha to 2.7 ha. The rich category of farmers constitutes about 5 per cent of the village population in both sites. Rich farmers in Olgilai/Ng'iresi own more than 1.2 ha of land, between three and eight head of cattle, and obtain their main income from crops such as maize, coffee, bananas, beans, and potato. Some farmers have more cattle but keep them in the lowlands. In Kiserian rich farmers own more than 4 ha of land and keep more than 30 head of cattle, 60 or more goats, and about 10 sheep. The main income is from maize and beans. Farmers also obtain income from off-farm activities which contribute about 60 per cent of total household income for most farmers in Olgilai/Ng'iresi and Kiserian, unlike other rural areas further removed from urban employment possibilities.

Average farmers in Olgilai/Ng'iresi own between 0.4 and 1.2 ha of land, two or three head of cattle, and a few sheep and chickens. Income is obtained from crops, but is lower than that of rich farmers. This category makes up about 15 per cent of the village population. In Kiserian average farmers own between 2 ha and 4 ha of land and keep 10–25 head of cattle, 10–15 goats, and between two and five sheep. Average farmers constitute 60 per cent of the village population. Poor farmers in Olgilai/Ng'iresi have on average less than 0.4 ha of land, none or up to two head of cattle, and sell very small quantities of maize, coffee, and potato. Bananas are not enough even for home consumption. In Kiserian, poor farmers own less than 2 ha of land, keep fewer than eight head of cattle, and do not own small livestock. Income obtained is very low and mostly from maize. Poor farmers constitute 80 per cent of the village population in Olgilai/Ng'iresi and 35 per cent in Kiserian.

Education of heads of household ranges between standards 1 and 4 in Olgilai/Ng'iresi and standards 5 and 8 in Kiserian. Heads of households in rich categories have more education (often above primary school) and are older than average and poor household heads. Male members of the family are relatively more educated than the female members.

According to farmers, while crops are the major source of income, changes in weather patterns, declining soil fertility, and farm sizes have affected crop production. Most farmers sell their crops from home, but some sell in Arusha town and prices are highly variable. Livestock are not sold regularly because they have both social and economic value, but are sold only as a last option when farmers cannot get income from other sources. They sell their animals because of urgent cash requirements for school fees or preventing food shortage. Sheep, goats, and chickens are sold in higher numbers, but in value the sale of cattle is more important. Cattle are the savings account and are important as working animals. However, the price for live cattle is very low during periods of food shortage and increases when there is enough food. Other income-generating activities include brewing, pottery, food vending, carpentry, tailoring, shoe-making and repair, charcoal-making, iron and tin smithery, masonry, weaving, all sorts of retailing business, oil processing, and flour milling. In some villages the pressing of sugarcane to get *jaggery* and the use of milling machines are popular income-generating activities. Both males and females are involved in most of these activities. A few people have part-time work in town. Although off-farm·activities are limited, most farmers, particularly in average and poor households, consider them important for their livelihood. In some households the youth seek off-farm activities at a greater distance and send some money back home.

Family expenditure is on food, clothing, school fees, house construction, taxes and levies, and, to a limited extent, medicine. Food shortage before the harvest is more widespread in Kiserian. Livestock purchases are another major expenditure item, indicating that cattle are still considered a good investment. Expenditure on agricultural inputs to improve the returns from agriculture is minimal. January to June is the most difficult period for cash income, although a few indicated July to September also to be difficult months. The major reason given is because no crops are sold during these months, whereas from July to December crops are harvested and sold. A few farmers, mainly in the poor category, mentioned borrowing from friends and relatives as a solution to cash shortage.

Land degradation and soil management in Arumeru

Arumeru is one of the two districts in Arusha severely affected by soil erosion, and the farming practices of the majority of farmers have in the past encouraged and promoted soil erosion. Some communities were originally pastoralists, and farming became a supporting activity to supplement livelihood from cattle. It was often done with poor skills. As livestock were grazed in the valleys, hilltops considered unsuitable for grazing were used for subsistence farming. Cultivation was done along slopes without any soil conservation measures. Forests on the hilltops were cleared to acquire more farming land and to drive away vermin and wild animals. This opened the way to erosion and increased overland flow. Soil conservation began during the colonial era, but some farmers believed that soil conservation structures reduced the farming area while others associated them with rodents and other vermin. Extension services were and still are strictly confined to disciplinary specialisms. Extension staff have good knowledge concerning their own fields and to some extent are ignorant of or unwilling to address other fields. For many years farmers believed that soil erosion and land degradation were a result of frequent monocropping alone, and were not aware of other causes. They were advised to apply fertilizer or to leave land fallow for some time. Both practices were not easily adopted: fertilizer is expensive, and fallowing is impossible as people are short of land due to population pressure. A demand for feasible control measures existed but no immediate solutions were at hand.

The zone has to a great extent adopted recent improved soil conservation interventions. Methods adopted include *fanya juu* (thrown-up) terraces on the steepest slopes (30–50 per cent) and *fanya chini* (narrow, cut-down) terraces on slopes up to 35 per cent. Other physical measures of soil conservation include stones, bunds, grass strips, trash lines, retention ditches or absorption channels, and ridge terraces. Farmers have criticized physical construction of structures such as terraces because they reduce the land available for farming. Others criticize the promotion of intensive use of them for the production of fodder grass when there is no market for the grass.

Olgilai/Ng'iresi

Annual rainfall is high, but intensity is much reduced by the canopy developed under the agroforestry systems that are the dominant land-use stage. Surface cover ranges from 70 to 100 per cent, but the majority of field types have over 95 per cent cover from a combination of tree canopy, crops, weeds, and litter. For annual crops the seedbed is cultivated to smoothness and left bare for a period until covered by the growing crop. Splash, sheet, and rill erosion are evident in most field types. Wrong timing for weeding or poor construction and strengthening of conservation structures may increase erosion. Traditionally farmers used to cut furrows across their farms in the middle or at the top to cut off overland flow from the catchment above the farm or neighbouring farms. In many cases these furrows worked but in other cases they did not. The furrows were constructed based on eye judgement, sometimes aligned to avoid obstacles and crops. Under situations of steep slopes furrows got eroded, and those that discharged into neighbouring farms due to land shortage often created conflicts.

Well-managed fields do not suffer erosion. In some fields trash lines or other structures greatly check the flow speed and the amount of materials transported with runoff. Litter and straw are transported by surface runoff but are obstructed at various places. Mostly the soils have a good structure developed through continued mulching, litter decomposition, and manure application, which increase organic matter and encourage infiltration. Improved microbial soil life and a network of root systems from the complex cropping systems enhance protective processes.

Physical structures for soil conservation include fences and raised beds along boundaries for soil erosion control, *fanya juu* terraces for maize and sweet potatoes, and cut-off ditches in pasture and maize and bean plots. Ditches control both erosion and drainage. *Fanya chini* are usually 0.3–0.6 m deep and 1 m wide, with lengths that vary depending on field size. Trash lines are the most common erosion-control practice. In most cases lines are made across the slopes and sometimes on contour ridges. Crop residues and other plant residues are traditionally used to conserve soil moisture. Natural vegetation on contour ridges is enhanced by planting elephant grass (*Pennisetum purpureum*), sugarcane, fodder grasses, cypress, bananas, *Leucaena, Sesbania, Grevillea*, setaria, and other species. Setaria is also used for erosion control on boundaries and as live fences in vegetable gardens. Sunken beds around coffee trees have a dual purpose of collecting surface litter for soil fertility improvement and reducing surface runoff. Manure and compost are quite heavily applied in the sunken beds.

Kiserian

Rainfall in Kiserian is highly intensive and farms are on variable slopes. The woodlots and natural conserved pastures have 100 per cent canopy cover and are least disturbed. Surface cover on annual crop lands ranges between 40 and 60 per cent. Some fields have natural trees retained, but with intense grazing pressure economic tree species and palatable grass species are disappearing. Non-palatable grasses such as *Vernonia poskeana* are increasing, especially near the homesteads. Erratic rains adversely affect the clayey soils and detachment is easy with low organic matter, while transport is rapid due to small particle size. Sheet erosion was dominant for most field types. *Mbuga* is typified by thorny trees that are indicators of sodic soils, and both sheet and gully erosion were observed. The rate of soil loss was estimated to range from 0.1 cm/year in *mbuga* to 0.9 cm/year in annual cropping fields. Visual assessment of crops indicated deficiencies of major nutrients, in a few cases due to weed competition.

Secondary tillage makes the ploughed layer smooth, except in a few cases where clods from primary tillage are left intact. Such rough surfaces increase infiltration and reduce runoff. On soils with vertic properties cultivation is problematic, especially when it is either too wet or too dry. Occasionally waterlogging is a problem on the dark clay soils. Soil compaction due to animal trampling creates problems for all types of soils in the area. Planting is done along furrows opened by ox ploughs, and women drop seeds as they walk behind the oxen. Ridging and weeding are done using hand hoes. Crops are weeded at least twice during the growing season. Some weeds like couch grass are burned after weeding, and some are fed to livestock. Weeds are controlled in all field types, including pastures.

Physical soil conservation structures are few and are mostly reinforced with trees and grass. They include contour ridges in maize/bean cropping systems, deep trenches 0.2 m deep × 0.7 m wide covering 100 m for soil moisture conservation in natural pastures, and shift-grazing in improved and fenced pastures. Stone lines are used to control soil erosion in woodlots and maize fields, and deep tillage is used for soil moisture conservation in maize and bean cropping systems. In *mbuga* pastures the prohibition of cultivation and burning is important for erosion control.

Demonstration activities

Demonstration activities attracted and involved farmers much more than was foreseen. Participating farmers increased from 80 in 1998 to over 3,000 in 2001. Farmers actively participated in on-site farmer-to-farmer training programmes, outreach programmes, workshops, and meetings. From 2000, farmers from outside Arumeru and the Arusha region started to visit PLEC sites, sometimes even without invitation, to participate in PLEC work or to see the management practices. During 2001 farmers' associations were established in the villages neighbouring PLEC sites.

Selection of expert farmers and the development of farmer-to-farmer training

Expert farmer selection is a continuous process of close and intimate interaction between farmers, researchers, extension staff, and sometimes the village administration. In this process researchers learn directly of the local problems that farmers face, understand their accumulated knowledge and coping strategies, and identify farmers with successful management strategies. Researchers and extension staff also learn the reasons for the success or failure of particular management practices, seeking to understand the value of management models within the cultural and social framework of the area. An evaluation is also made of the communication skills of successful farmers, their willingness to share knowledge with others, and the respect they command among fellow villagers. At this point researchers and extensionists also try to identify areas and types of intervention that may improve existing techniques. Based on these criteria, successful resource managers are selected to train other farmers.

Expert farmers' successful management practices are used as demonstrations to teach other farmers. Village members are informed of the day, time, and venue for training. The training is organized and carried out by the expert farmer at his or her farm. They demonstrate their management practice to other farmers and explain why the practice works. Conditions under which the practice would be a failure are also given. In some cases expert male farmers who work with their wives and children on the farm include them in the training to make it a wife-and-husband trainers' session. Where appropriate, researchers and extension staff contribute to the discussions, particularly with scientific facts that support the practice and possibilities for its improvement. Occasionally, participating farmers may come up with even better examples than the method demonstrated by the expert.

In this way, the demonstration site becomes a class, the farm becomes a chalkboard, the expert farmer a teacher, the experts become facilitators, and participating farmers the modifiers or improvers of the technology. At the same time, since the demonstration site field type is common in the village and different participating farmers manage it differently, individuals choose part or all of the demonstrated practices for implementation on their own farms. Others may gain some information that helps them modify their own practices in their own way, while still others choose not to adopt the practice. When the training is recorded on video, this is used to train other farmers elsewhere or is borrowed by some of the participating farmers to view the training more closely. The demonstration process continues when farmers convene at another expert farmer's demonstration site for training on a different management model on another date.

Examples of demonstration activities

Fertility improvement

The first demonstration activities addressed the problem of soil fertility. Farmers variously use the available inputs (mostly organic) to improve soil fertility. In the past, application of fresh manure has resulted in surface capping and reduced crop yields. Some farmers were sceptical of using manure, saying that it resulted in prolific weed germination that increased labour demand. After long discussions, experts in compost-making convinced others to experiment, and then conducted demonstrations on the techniques involved. They facilitated adoption by additional training on the types, quality, and amounts of organic materials to use, amounts of inorganic fertilizer and ashes to apply, how often to water, and how frequently to load or unload the pile before it matures. The number of farmers throwing away manure on the roadsides, dumping it in plug gullies, or burning it as a waste decreased by over 50 per cent. The use of well-ripened and nutrient-conserved manure instead of fresh manure has improved the size of banana bunches from an average of 30 kg to over 50 kg.

Crop production has improved in various other ways with demonstration activities. Expert farmers have experimented, especially in the subhumid site, with different types of manure and other inputs such as ash and soda for different crops. Effective use of manure in vegetables has improved production, with increased size, quality, and disease tolerance resulting in better market prices. Maize yield has increased in Kiserian from 240 kg per hectare to above 1,450 kg in favourable weather conditions due to soil fertility improvement from using stone lines. After many knowledge-exchange sessions, purposive selection of fodder species for planting on contours for soil fertility improvement and erosion control is now being practised. In the past farmers only planted what was brought to them by various development projects. Currently, some farmers have claimed to have increased milk production as a result of the mix of fodder species.

Experimenting farmers demonstrated the optimal use of fertilizers for potato production and associated increase in yield. Farmers knew that potato production has to be high in order to obtain the desired cash income, but many did not know of the benefits of fertilizer. After seeing the results most farmers no longer grow potatoes without fertilizer, and the new knowledge has encouraged even poor farmers to use fertilizer.

Intensification and diversification

Intensification of farming is common in Olgilai/Ng'iresi, where land is a scarce resource. Farmers have different objectives and different methods of agricultural intensification. One farmer, when surveyed in 1999 on less than 0.5 ha, had 12 field types and 45 varieties of crops, vegetables, and fruits, each with unique characteristics. These included 10 cash and food crops, six tree species, more than 10 medicinal plants capable of curing more than 30 diseases, 17 species of nursery seedlings for propagation and sale, six vegetable crops, 18 fruit trees, and seven ornamental species. The plants have more than 60 uses. He also had three dairy cows but no grasses on his farm. A few trees provided fodder and he earned surplus money to buy fodder from other people (Kaihura 2002b).

This farmer has organized two demonstrations at his home, on potato and maize production. Farmers from his village, neighbouring villages, and from Kiserian discussed extensively his successful practices, and some of the farmers presented some even better practices they have developed. He has participated in five demonstrations conducted by other expert farmers in his village and hosted three expert farmers from outside Ng'iresi. He has also participated in two locally organized workshops, and presented his experiences with farming in Arumeru in a national workshop. Farmers who have been at his home for demonstrations have picked several of his plant materials to plant at their farms. He has himself collected some from other farmers when he attended PLEC demonstration site training.

Through on-farm training by expert farmers effective crop spacing is now used by 20 per cent more farmers. The selection of the types of crops to grow, and the correct management of each crop in the mix for yield optimization, are now concerns for more farmers. The diversity of crops in farm boundaries has increased to include trees for timber, fodder, and crops. Farmers have learned from expert farmers how to optimize production by "making" soils, then planting particular crops and harvesting roots and shoots to be able to feed a family of five for a month from a 6 m² area.

Optimal use of the rains is another approach gaining ground among farmers in land-scarce areas. The *matatu* system of continuous cropping of three crops on the same piece of land throughout the year was developed by one expert farmer and is now a strategy adopted by several farmers. The expert farmer has 0.25 ha near his house that has a perennial crop of coffee and bananas. Instead of planting only the traditional maize/bean intercrop, two crops in demand in the market, cauliflower and potato, are planted in addition to maize. In 1998, for example, the farmer applied manure and planted cauliflower in March. It was harvested in May and then potatoes were planted. Potatoes were harvested in July, manure was applied again, and maize was planted for harvesting in February. Bananas were harvested in July and August and the coffee harvest began in November. Areas of the field where yield was lower received the first manure application and then more manure the following season. Taro, fodder species, *Grevillea robusta*, and yams were planted on the field border.

The farmer's selection of crop species depends on the lengths of the growing season and the rainy period, ease of mixing the crops, and the expected market price. Demonstrations have made more farmers take the market price into consideration when planting. Some farmers sell green maize and buy cheaper dry maize from the market at a later stage, planting a different crop after uprooting the maize stover. They have experimented with new maize varieties and different intercrop combinations (sorghum and millet with soya beans) and planting times. One farmer was experimenting with cross-breeding maize.

Other experts optimize production of crops that are grown to meet the family food and vegetable requirements. They buy nothing from the market as they have no cash. Others intensify to meet the requirements of certain cultural foods such as *loshoro*, popular with Waarusha in Arumeru. *Loshoro* combines maize, beans, milk, and other appetizers, all of which must be in abundant supply at any time of the year.

One expert farmer in Kiserian has a well-developed agroforestry system with cereals, legumes, and trees adapted to the dry conditions that prevail between the rainy seasons. He concentrates on growing for home consumption, as Kiserian is more remote from markets than Olgilai/Ng'iresi. In 1999 he had 10 field types. On 0.3 ha he grew two annual cereal crops and a variety of trees, and tethered cattle and sheep. The cereals were maize and a local variety of millet (*Eleusine indica*). The maize variety is high yielding with good milling qualities, and is easy to intercrop among trees. The millet is used for porridge, brewing, sale, and animal feed and is drought tolerant and stores well. The trees include five varieties of mango, two varieties of papaya, lemon, orange, *zambarau* (*Syzygium guineense*), *ukwaju* (tamarind, *Tamarindus indica*), two varieties of banana, and volunteer *mnafu* (*Solanum nigrum*) and amaranth (*Amaranthus thunbergii*). This farmer had become isolated from the community. After long discussions, the PLEC team convinced him to teach others how to conserve their environment better and be able to harvest crops during the dry season. After PLEC consulted the village government and discussed the farmer's problems with them, villagers attended the demonstrations at his home and the farmer has also participated in outreach activities outside the community (Kaihura 2002b).

Environmental conservation

One farmer in Kiserian has a woodlot with the greatest diversity of trees, shrubs, and grasses in the whole community. Most of the trees are natural, but some were collected from other places to add missing economic and social values to the existing trees. Some of the added tree species were those considered by the farmer to be endangered due to excessive use. Trees and shrubs have more than 300 uses. Besides medicines, the farmer has a planned harvesting and firewood collection system. From his forest he also obtains building poles, and has controlled erosion where trees are growing. The farmer is always ready to share his experiences and knowledge with other farmers through farmer field-days and meetings. He has also convinced some of his neighbours, especially those trespassing in and harvesting from his woodlot, to plant and conserve their own woodlots (Kaihura 2002b). After farmer visits others adopted the practice of raising trees in nurseries, either individually or as groups. They decided, especially in Kiserian, to conserve the environment around their homesteads first. It has been difficult to establish a market for tree seedlings raised by farmers' associations. Instead, farmers have been planting all the seedlings in degraded parts of their villages while both PLEC staff and district extension officers were exploring potential markets. During the study period, water shortage due to drought retarded progress in raising tree nurseries, particularly for farmers' associations. Containers and watering buckets were bought to assist with hand irrigation.

Expert farmers and scientists also trained schoolchildren in tree nursery production and planting in the school compound. Students were each given two seedlings to plant at home and manage to maturity. Where indigenous endangered trees are the principal focus, PLEC expert farmers have trained farmers and members of other organizations on where to get seeds in the forests, how to grow the seeds successfully, and on the appropriate environments in which to plant them. Some of these farmers have even been invited to demonstrate at national agricultural shows and farmers' days on techniques for raising endangered indigenous trees.

Activities were different from site to site depending on the identified constraints, existing management, and the diversity of farmers' access to resources. In Kiserian, for example, farmers wanted to improve water availability during the growing season. The PLEC assessment survey indicated the existence of a plough pan restricting downward movement of water and encouraging runoff. Farmers did not know of the problem of the plough pan. They then adjusted their ploughs for ploughing deeper than 30 cm rather than the traditional depth of 20 cm. Blunt and old ploughs, and the inability of indigenous oxen to pull the deep plough during primary or secondary tillage, also caused a problem. However, deep tillage in combination with the application of large amounts of farmyard manure was adopted by farmers who are interested in harvesting water for increased crop yield.

Other treatments, including tied ridging and applying farmyard manure combined with fertilizer, were rejected during farmer field-days. Tied ridges are an effective method of water harvesting but have a high labour requirement and preclude the use of ploughs. Most of the existing erosion-control structures were ineffective. PLEC, through collaboration with the village soil conservation team, trained farmers on how to use an "A" frame to make contours and establish contour intervals, but the uptake is slow, as farmers want somebody else to make the contours for them.

Crop-livestock interaction

Smallholder livelihoods in Arumeru depend on both livestock and crop production. In the high-altitude area farmers obtain most of the fodder requirements for livestock from the homestead rather than from distant support plots or communal land, unlike the farmers in Kiserian, who source fodder mainly from communal land. Fortunately, some expert farmers in Olgilai/Ng'iresi were aware of how to optimize both crop and livestock production by zero-grazing. Instead of taking maize and bean stover to the field for mulching, it is first fed to animals and later the manure and composted residues are transported. Bean stover improves the nutritional quality of animal feed and increases milk yield. One farmer experimented with collecting the urine from stalls to prepare a pesticide. It is fermented in combination with exudates from plants, then mixed with water and used to control pests in vegetables (such as aphids) and ticks in livestock (Kaihura, Ndondi, and Kemikimba 2000).

Keeping of guinea pigs, encouraged by PLEC to increase the diversity of livestock, helps reduce loss of stored maize in the house by reducing the population of other rodents. They also alarm people if snakes are around, and can be eaten.

Household nutritional improvement

During characterization of field types on farmers' fields it was learned that house gardens play an important role in supporting the family. This is a field type that mothers visit almost every day to collect some vegetables for the next meal. From discussions, farmers highlighted the importance of vegetables. Understanding of the value of house gardens contributed to their improved management and diversity. Increased chicken rearing and regular use of their meat and eggs was a way around the problem of Waarusha keeping livestock but not slaughtering except on special occasions.

Increased farmer interactions and visits

Farmers have come to know each other better through exchange and training visits. They know where to go with a specific problem even in the absence of extensionists. Experience has shown that many farmers had production constraints for which they had been seeking solutions for a long time without success. Solutions to some of these problems came from farmers within the same villages. In this way individual farmer visits to other farms or villages to search for knowledge and materials are now common. The methodology, when further developed, could resolve the technology development and dissemination problems faced by Tanzania as a result of a now non-functional extension service.

Farmers' associations have gradually been established. By the end of 2001 there were eight groups addressing livestock, poultry, and honey production. Farmers subdivided the village communities, so that each has a small number of farmers' associations. Smaller associations can be more responsive to farmers' interests and able to implement the resolutions more effectively. Kiserian farmers split into upper and lower Kiserian, as lower Kiserian has much less rainfall and different requirements. Through the formation of associations very active and enthusiastic farmers have become leaders and a very reliable support to PLEC scientific staff. The main objective is to improve livelihood through increased income, while enhancing and conserving biodiversity in agricultural systems. Groups or the leaders of each association broadly coordinate on-farm demonstration sessions by expert farmers with the extensionists.

Gender sensitivity in community development

One marked impact of the project was to change the customary habit that women cannot interact with the public, or attend and actively participate in public gatherings or community development. At the start in 1994 it was very difficult to get access to female members of the household, and hardly any women would talk if they attended group discussions. Women are now active participants in rural development activities, particularly with PLEC. Various factors contributed to the observed change, including:

- four years of participatory meetings and interaction with farmers of all categories
- using women expert farmers to talk to other women
- inviting all women to workshops and asking them to talk about their problems and management practices in front of men
- educating husbands to involve their wives.

Two associations were established by women in 1999 for small-scale tree nurseries and raising local breeds of poultry. Poultry production has a low establishment cost and provides food, manure, and income. They are the women's "cattle" and women can use them as they please without asking their husbands. After a year five groups had been formed and more than 70 per cent of households kept chickens.

Forming women farmers' associations and training them to become independent in small household requirements, like buying washing soap or body lotion, made even those who were reluctant to cooperate come forward. Almost all the current PLEC village committees that manage the project include women. A notable indicator of change was the women coming, together with their men, to cheer the visiting PLEC management group members at night in Arusha town in 2001. In Waarusha custom women usually do not go out at night, nor do they accompany their husbands even if going to the same place.

Extended support to farmers, and the future

The activities and benefits of PLEC work were not clearly understood by many farmers at the beginning. They saw PLEC as just any other project which would come and go. They only started gaining interest through the spread of farmer-to-farmer training programmes that involved the participation of every interested person. They gained more interest when some of their colleagues were seen on television talking about their work. Many of them were impressed by the outputs of the new farmers' associations. Of greatest importance was the PLEC concept of sharing knowledge with all in need, and they observed that benefits come to those who sustain a keen interest and participate. When in 2000 some obvious positive impacts started being seen, and other farmers talked about the importance of PLEC to their own family well-being, many others started to chase PLEC. They lamented that it was late for them to become part of the project and there was not enough time for them to benefit. They requested that PLEC be extended to support them, particularly the latecomers and those outside PLEC sites who did not have a chance to participate.

Farmers' associations are the driving force, and a tool to bring people together and implement what they plan. Most activities of these associations are aimed at biodiversity enhancement, livelihood improvement, and food security. They are headed by expert farmers and other committed farmers. They also work to bring together women, who for quite a long time have been left behind, so that they can become productive participants in rural development and reduce their dependence on men. The associations are still immature and need to develop. They need both technical and financial support to manage their funds and programmes of work before they continue on their own.

Many farmers recognized the importance of PLEC but joined late. This is not uncommon, as adoption of innovations is usually slow. Other farmers from outside PLEC sites started establishing their own associations and asked to join PLEC. They were visited by the PLEC team to encourage them to continue working based on the experiences of their neighbours. Extension staff also need to develop the skills of working with farmers. They do not get this through formal training but through continued practice. Since the government has limited funds to promote participatory development, a PLEC project already promoting participatory development of sustainable resource management methods with farmers as trainers has been an important resource.

Several of the recommendations made through PLEC annual workshops, and later presented to decision-makers for incorporation into rural development programmes, need to be followed up at both community and national levels to ensure their implementation. It would be meaningless to work for four years and come up with good recommendations for agrodiversity development, and then just leave others to ensure implementation. After the January 2002 technical and policy recommendations meeting, the government is looking for cooperation from PLEC to work towards implementation of the recommendations. The recommendations were a result of PLEC groundwork in the sites. They were developed jointly with farmers and could be followed up by the same farmers and PLEC scientists. The taste of the pudding is in the eating. PLEC must taste the impact of implementation of developed recommendations before letting others eat the pudding.

Notes

1. Sadly, Edward Kaitaba has died since this chapter was written.
2. *Mbugas* are low-lying parts of the landscape, seasonally waterlogged, consisting of peats (histosols or organic material) and vertisols (active clays). In many catchments they are the principal source of dry-season grazing, or, where population density is greater, the main

place where vegetables are grown because of the good moisture and high intrinsic fertility. There are quite a number of types of *mbuga*, depending on characteristics such as the degree of wetness, heaviness of the clay, degree of salinity, and month in which it dries sufficiently to plant vegetables.

REFERENCES

Brookfield, H., M. Stocking, and M. Brookfield. 1999. "Guidelines on agrodiversity in demonstration site areas", *PLEC News and Views*, No. 13, pp. 17–31.

Kaihura, F. B. S. 2002a. *Tanzania: Final Report*. Mwanza: PLEC-Tanzania.

Kaihura, F. B. S. 2002b. "Working with expert farmers: The case of PLEC-Tanzania", in H. Brookfield, C. Padoch, H. Parsons, and M. Stocking (eds) *Cultivating Biodiversity: Understanding, Analysing and Using Agricultural Diversity*. London: ITDG Publications, pp. 132–144.

Kaihura, F. B. S., P. Ndondi, and E. Kemikimba. 2000. "Agrodiversity assessment and analysis in diverse and dynamic small-scale farms in Arumeru, Arusha, Tanzania", *PLEC News and Views*, No. 16, pp. 14–27. (Reprinted in H. Brookfield, C. Padoch, H. Parsons, and M. Stocking (eds) 2002. *Cultivating Biodiversity: Understanding, Analysing and Using Agricultural Diversity*. London, ITGD Publications, pp. 153–166.)

Mbonile, M. J. 1998. *Population Dynamics in Relation to Land Characteristics*. Mwanza: PLEC-Tanzania.

Zarin, D. J., H. Guo, and L. Enu-Kwesi. 1999. "Methods for the assessment of plant species diversity in complex agricultural landscapes: Guidelines for data collection and analysis from the PLEC biodiversity advisory group (BAG)", *PLEC News and Views*, No. 13, pp. 3–16.

9

China

Zhiling Dao, Huijun Guo, Aiguo Chen, and Yongneng Fu

Introduction[1]

Whereas the dynamism of the Amazon River was the dominant consideration governing PLEC work in Brazil, work in China has been dominated by
a dynamic political and social environment more than in any other country.
Work has been wholly in the province of Yunnan, and in communities
having either a majority or a significant proportion of minority peoples.
Remoteness may have partly protected these communities from some of the
damaging disturbances which affected rural China in the period between
1958 and the early 1970s, but all the main policy changes took place here as
elsewhere. After liberation in 1949, landlords and other large landholders
were dispossessed and their land redistributed. Beginning in the late 1950s,
village land was collectivized and land management was centrally directed.
Many upland villages, including both those studied by PLEC in Xishuangbanna, were relocated to more accessible sites. There was a start to the large
expansion of rubber in subtropical Xishuangbanna and of sugarcane in
western Yunnan. In and after 1982, individual decision-making was first
partly then much more widely restored under the "household contract
responsibility system".

The land contracts were allowed to be extended up to 15 years in 1984,
and later were allowed to be extended for another 30 years after the expi-
ration of the previous contract. By the end of the 1990s landholdings,
although still on lease from the collective, had become in many ways as if

they were private. Substantial renting and other forms of transfer were permitted, and although the local government authorities have continued to provide substantial guidance, and at least until lately some commands, the context of most land-use allocation decisions has become the village community and the individual farms within this.[2] In the same period the market economy has flourished greatly, and its influence has extended both widely and quickly, so much so as to destabilize long-term decision-making on land-use allocation. The impact of modern individualization was still working through the village systems during the years of PLEC work from 1993 to 2002. Other changes were imminent in 2002, notably an enormous improvement in accessibility to markets being created by the splendidly engineered new highways extending to the national borders west and south from Kunming which, when complete by 2004, will pass close to both the PLEC areas. Unknown changes in marketing conditions will flow from the accession of China to the World Trade Organization in 2002.

Evolution of the cluster

The work which became that of PLEC-China began in the 1980s, but took off in the 1990s. Mainly with Ford Foundation support, the Traditional Land Management Systems Research Programme was set up, expanding its activities after 1992 as the Yunnan Agroforestry Systems Research Project and Indigenous Land Resources Management Programme (YAF). By 1994 YAF had published 16 working papers. This work, carried out all over Yunnan although focusing ultimately on a small number of main sites, identified four main types of agroforestry in Yunnan, with 82 forms and 220 associations (Guo and Padoch 1995). It also revealed the great dynamism of the systems, in response to both changing economic conditions and the major innovations in national land tenure policy of the period since 1950.

PLEC and YAF were brought into contact late in 1992 by Dr Christine Padoch. From 1993 onwards there was a small group of PLEC researchers in Yunnan, at the Kunming Institute of Botany, in the Xishuangbanna Tropical Botanical Garden, and in other institutes. Until 1997 they collaborated closely with a PLEC group at Chiang Mai in Thailand, and several joint field workshops were organized.[3] Early work was mainly in Xishuangbanna, in a number of villages close to blocks of the Menglun state nature reserve, based on the Xishuangbanna Tropical Botanical Garden of the Chinese Academy of Sciences. In 1995 the same group of researchers successfully sought the interest of the MacArthur Foundation for a project in Baoshan prefecture in the west of Yunnan, on the management of farm and forest land in the buffer zone of the Gaoligongshan state nature reserve, a "biodiversity hotspot" of global significance. MacArthur Foundation funding for what became the Forest Management and Biodiversity Conservation Programme in Gaoligongshan (FMBC) was renewed for a second term until 2000. After 1997, when PLEC gained the support of the Global Environment Facility, the Xishuangbanna and Gaoligongshan work was brought together as the programme of the China cluster of UNU-PLEC. The work reported here has been done within this enlarged project.

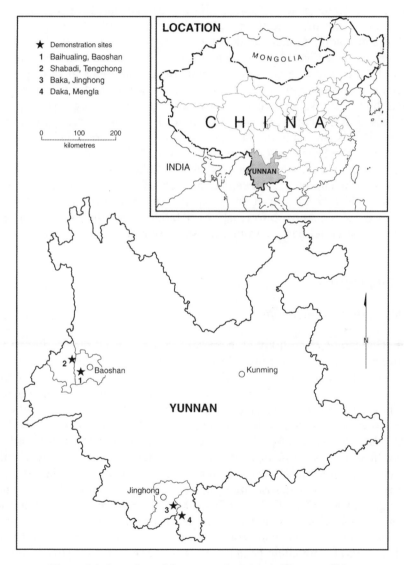

Figure 9.1 Location of demonstration sites in Yunnan, China

Differences within the China cluster

Work at Xishuangbanna has essentially formed a part of a long-term pro-gramme of assistance to regional communities by staff of the Xishuang-banna Tropical Botanical Garden, begun during the 1960s. During the 1970s this already involved assistance to villages relocated from upland to lowland sites. In 1978 and 1983 respectively the state nature reserve was declared and later enlarged, leading to the exclusion of some villagers from a part of their land. These included the people of Baka, one of PLEC's villages.

Work at Gaoligongshan, on the other hand, began in the mid-1990s with the specific objective of encouraging land use that would facilitate protec-tion of the nature reserve. This was an innovative approach involving sup-port for intensification, rather than control measures to exclude farmers from the forest reserve. This innovative aspect of the Gaoligongshan proj-ect goes far in explaining why most China-PLEC initiatives were taken first in Gaoligongshan, while the long period of top-down direction, with assis-tance from the Botanical Garden, in the Xishuangbanna villages probably helps explain why some innovations failed to take root quickly. Successive Gaoligongshan innovations included the successful farmers' association ini-tiated in 1995, the identification of expert farmers between 1995 and 1999 and their subsequent use to teach other farmers, and the initial develop-ment of household-based agrobiodiversity assessment in 1999–2000.

Gaoligongshan

The region and the people

The Gaoligong (Kao-li-kung) mountain range lies in the border area between China and Myanmar (Burma), between the Nujiang (Salween River) and Dulongjiang (Irrawaddy River). The mountains are a south-eastern extension of the Himalayan system, reaching 4,640 m at their high-est point. Geological history since the Mesozoic has created conditions which preserve East Asian endemic plants and allow a fusion of Gondwana and Laurasian species. Botanical survey since the early 1990s has recorded more than 5,000 seed-plant species in the Chinese part of the range. With increases in population and economic development, the relationships between protection and sustainable use of biological resources had become an urgent problem (Li, Guo, and Dao 2000). The principal site chosen was in the accessible Baihualing valley on the eastern slope of the range, a val-ley followed by the ancient "southern Silk Road" which linked China to India. Work at Baihualing began in 1994. A second site was also set up at Shabadi on the western side of the range, but its relative inaccessibility led to its downgrading to a research site after 1999.[4] The administrative village of Baihualing covers 1,810 ha and has a population of 2,180. Its land extends from 850 m to 2,000 m at the edge of the forest reserve. Most people are Han, with smaller numbers of Lisu, Bai, Yi, Hui, Zhuang, and Dai. Fieldwork is mainly in Hanlong, the highest of the 10 natural villages in Baihualing.[5] Hanlong has 128.7 ha of land, including 100 ha of community forest on the upland side, and only 12 ha of upland fields. Its 15 ha of wet-rice fields are between three and five kilometres away in an adjoining valley. They now grow a range of winter crops as well as summer rice. Within this limited area, the project identified seven major land-use stages and 22 field types, following the PLEC methodology (Zarin, Guo, and Enu-Kwesi 1999; Brookfield, Stocking, and Brookfield 1999; Chapter 2 above). These are listed in Table 9.1.

PLEC activity at Baihualing

For many years sugarcane has been the dominant cash crop in all parts of Baihualing village, and a large part of upland fields on the slope below the nature reserve was devoted to sugarcane and maize in rotation, but the pattern is changing. The sugar price is unstable, and the factory demands high-quality sugarcane that should be grown below 1,300 m. Some risk-taking farmers and expert farmers have successfully developed profitable agro-forestry systems of fruits, timber, and coffee by replacing sugarcane on the uplands above 1,300 m. PLEC demonstration activities, including extension of new crops and techniques and farmer-to-farmer exchanges, have facilitated this rapid diffusion of environmentally friendly and profitable systems in Baihualing village. The leadership of Baihualing village has remarked that the PLEC project, especially its farmer training courses, has promoted the development of cash-crop tree plantations, which have increased both farmers' income and the conservation of flora and fauna in and around the nature reserve.

The expert farmers and the farmers' association

Particular attention at Baihualing focuses on the expert farmers and the association of which they are the core members (Dao *et al.* 2001; Liang 2002). The first expert identified was Dayi Li, an almost illiterate Lisu and a former shifting cultivator and hunter. In the 1980s he started experimenting with domestication of a rare timber species found in the forest, *Phoebe puwenensis*, and, although no botanically established means existed, succeeded in two years in growing viable seedlings. He then converted 0.13 ha of maize-growing land allocated to him in 1983 into a tree plantation. PLEC began to support his work in 1995, and he has subsequently extended his technology to 95 of the village farmers.

Table 9.1 Land-use stages and field types of Hanlong village

Land-use stage	Field types	Management
Natural forest	Timber forest	Upper part of community forests close to the nature reserve, usually for timber
	Fuelwood forest	Middle part of community forests for fuelwood
	Scenery forest	Close to village and near the road or path
Cultivated forest	Chinese fir forest	Introduced timber trees, usually planted on steeply sloping upland fields or around them, young trees intercropped with maize before shade formed
	Phoebe puwenensis forest	Native timber species, naturally growing around 1,800 m, planted by locals since the 1980s, seedlings grown by farmers and planted on slightly steep fields
	Toona ciliata forest	Native tree, seedlings obtained from old tree sprouts, cultivated on sloping farmland or in home gardens
Agroforests	Chestnut	Usually intercropped with maize, beans, planted on upland fields
	Persimmon	As above
	Walnut	As above
	Coffee	As above
	Tea	Monocropping or as above
House gardens		Trees planted on the edge, herbs and vegetables in the garden
Fallow		Used for pastures, very small area
Annual cropping on upland field	Maize intercrop	Intercropped with other annual crops in summer
	Pea monocrop	In winter
	Sugarcane monocrop	Change to maize after three years
Annual cropping on wet-rice field	Wet-rice monocrop	In summer
	Sugarcane monocrop	Change to wet rice or other annual crops after three or four years
	Potato monocrop	In winter
	Wheat monocrop	In winter
	Maize intercrop	Both in summer and winter
	Tobacco monocrop	In winter

Supported by the FMBC and PLEC, Mr Li and a number of others came together in 1995 to set up the Gaoligongshan Farmers' Association for Biodiversity Conservation, the first farmer-based conservation association in China. Growing slowly because it restricts its membership to good, conservationist farmers, it had achieved a membership of 115, including 10 women, by early 2002. Progressively, it has become the main organizing body for demonstration site activities, and the main mediator between villagers and the nature reserve authorities. It has attracted considerable regional and also national interest, so that other projects and the authorities have now set up more than 40 similar associations in other areas of Yunnan. Only a proportion of these are developing well, because they did not arise spontaneously as did the Baihualing association.

Ten expert farmers are the core of the association and of PLEC work in Baihualing. Initially, PLEC scientists and the technicians they brought from Baoshan demonstrated agroforestry principles to the farmers, as well as assisting Mr Li. In the process they recognized a wider pool of local expertise, and since 1999 these 10 specialist or generalist expert farmers have been demonstrating mainly agroforestry techniques to others, and by example demonstrating their profitability. A striking case is that of Chaoming Wu, economically the most successful of the group. He has converted a rocky 0.5 ha plot into an agroforest with over 100 species, and in his small home garden does a lot of experimentation. There are 73 species in his gardens, and 71 per cent are useful species. He has grafted many pear, persimmon, and new apple varieties on to local tree varieties, and prepared and grafted seedlings of walnut, chestnut, and cardamom (medicinal use) seedlings. Mr Wu says to the young generation that when you cultivate a tree crop, planting counts for only 30 per cent of the efforts while management absorbs 70 per cent. He often discusses grafting techniques with older farmers, and teaches the young generation both in his house and in the fields.

One farmer, Zhixue Yang, has developed an intercropping system of chestnuts, peach, maize, and peas on steep uplands. The productivity of his agroforestry systems is much higher than the former cropping patterns (Table 9.2).

Table 9.2 Comparison of productivity between monocropping and agroforest in Hanlong village

Farming type	Crop	Yield (kg/mu)	Value (yuan/mu)	Total value
Agroforestry	Chestnuts	45	360	
	Maize	120	96	
	Beans	40	48	504
Mixed crops	Maize	150	120	
	Beans	50	60	180
Chestnut monocrop	Chestnut	30	240	240
Maize monocrop	Maize	150	120	120

Note: 15 trees/mu, trees are five years old; local market price; 15 mu = 1 hectare.

Most of the demonstration is done in the fields, and by 2001 it had reached over 1,000 farmers. Example alone is also important. One of the experts, Shihou Chen, began cultivating a traditional rice variety of high quality instead of hybrid rice in 1999. Now more and more farmers are following his example and cultivating this rice variety because of its high quality and high market value. Several training courses on techniques of planting fruits, such as grafting, pruning, and prevention and cure of plant diseases, were organized to help farmers expand areas of coffee, longan, orange, chestnut, walnut, and persimmon as alternatives to sugarcane. The expansion and diversification have increased farmers' income and reduced the risk arising from market fluctuation. Tree crop cultivation increased nine times and production increased 10.6 times from 1997 to 2000. Up to now, about half the upland farmlands of Baihualing administrative village are managed in agroforestry systems, and the total area is over 330 ha (Table 9.3).

The agroforestry innovations have been demonstrated by the expert farmers to be profitable, as well as providing greater stability of income and a more manageable work year (Liang 2002). Table 9.4 compares the incomes of the 10 expert farmers in 1999 and 2001. All but two show an improvement, and for some the improvement is of a substantial order. Although these are not high incomes by the standards of the more commercial regions of rural China, they are from good to very good incomes in what is generally an impoverished region. The farmers report that many others have followed their example, with beneficial results, but do so less intensively than do the 10 experts, who regard themselves as innovators.

There are also substantial benefits from the point of view of biodiversity. Based on household-level agrobiodiversity assessment, the best agroforestry farmers have average species-richness indices considerably higher than the average. However, the purpose has not simply been to increase biodiversity in particular plots; it has been to disseminate the skills of

Table 9.3 Area and production of the main tree cash crops in 1997 and 2000 in Baihualing village

Crops		Walnut	Chestnut	Coffee	Longan	Persimmon	Orange
Area (mu)	1997	35	50	82	10	4	43
	2000	150	130	1,272	480	4	42
Yield (kg)	1997	500	600	1,200	1	80	172
	2000	3,200	4,400	18,500	120	93	970

Source: Dao *et al.*, 2002 PLEC/China Report No. 4.
Note: Most cash crops are still young seedlings. Data are from the village statistics, and PLEC data suggest that the village statistics underestimate the area under tree crops, which now totals more than 5,000 mu.

Table 9.4 Cash income change of 10 expert farmers between 1999 and 2001

Expert farmer (household)	Annual cash income (yuan)	
	1999	2001
Chaoming Wu	26,840	32,060
Zhixue Yang	12,990	14,170
Denglin Gao	5,600	6,600
Xiubo Yang	29,900	20,100
Shihou Chen	10,090	11,730
Yunheng Mi	17,000	7,300
Chengwu Yang	12,000	14,000
Jiafan Zhen	6,535	14,300
Jiahu Li	15,600	27,000
Dayi Li	12,250	13,450

Note: 8.3 yuan = US$1.

expert farmers, which will help increase biodiversity at all scales and generate a philosophy of conservation. Nonetheless, the area of community forest was found by aerial survey to have decreased by 2001, although how much of this is now agroforest has not been established. Monocropping of newly introduced cash crops, especially coffee, was expanding in 1998–2000, but this ceased in 2001–2002 due to a fall in price. Farmers' decisions are extremely responsive to short-term changes in prices, and it is possible for good long-term investments in tree crops to be uprooted in favour of what is more recently an alternative of higher value. This same pattern is, as is seen below, even more marked in Xishuangbanna. Monocropping could again become the dominant form of production, displacing the biodiversity-rich agroforestry systems and associated native crops, if the environmental and social benefits of these diverse systems are not widely appreciated and supported.

Xishuangbanna

Between 1993 and 1996 the Xishuangbanna group worked in nine villages, ultimately selecting two as demonstration sites. These were Daka and Baka, both fairly easily accessible from Xishuangbanna Tropical Botanical Garden except during periods of flood. The region has considerable similarity to northern Thailand and the intervening land in Laos and Myanmar, with subtropical rainforest and a population including significant numbers of ethnic minority people. Dai, formerly the majority in Xishuangbanna, still constitute 35 per cent of the 993,000 people; Hani are also numerous. Since their immigration as rubber growers, which began in the 1960s, Han now form 30 per cent of the regional population. Until very recently, Xishuang-banna was a region of shifting cultivation, although with a number of agro-forestry systems and, among the Dai people, highly developed and diverse home gardens. These latter have recently declined as the large lower-lying Dai villages have become more urbanized. A particular Dai system that has now become more widespread in the region is the planting of blocks and rows of *Cassia siamea*, used by pollarding every three years for abundant provision of firewood.

Shifting cultivation with long periods of fallow was employed in the past in both villages. Government policy has been to reduce this, and assistance has been provided with the creation of wet-rice fields wherever possible. Some farmers have added to the irrigated area on their own. Hybrid rice is now common, but traditional varieties are still grown. Rice is no longer the only crop. Cultivation of vegetables for the nearby urban market in Menglun is now an important activity. Wild vegetables and other products are collected from the fallow areas, which provide important goods for the village people as well as for sale.

The main economic crops are cultivated on the hillsides, on land that was formerly devoted only to shifting cultivation, or are grown within the old secondary forest. The most important crop is rubber, widely planted since the 1960s. Previously it was intercropped with upland rice, but now is increasingly intercropped with passionfruit, which became as rewarding as rubber in 1999. Since then the price has fallen, and some farmers are now replacing it with teak. Within the secondary forest, tea has been planted beneath the canopy for at least 200–300 years, but in the 1980s it was massively replaced by *Amomum villosum* (Chinese cardamom) which, for a few years until both yields and price declined, offered much greater reward. At the end of the 1990s, rubber, passionfruit, and *Amomum* together provided over 90 per cent of farm income. Other field types included fuelwood plantations and home gardens. Home gardens, copied from the much larger and more elaborate home gardens of nearby Dai people, provide medicinal plants, vegetables, fruit, and ornamentals. The classification of land use at the end of the 1990s is set out in Table 9.5.

Daka, the larger of the two villages, has a population of 332 people, all but a few of whom are Hani (or Akha). Daka was relocated from a former higher-altitude location in the 1960s, when cultivation of wet rice also began. It has 727 ha of land between 540 and 980 m, including almost 20 ha of irrigated rice land, but the main land use is rubber (260 ha). Some of the rubber is planted on land that in 1995 was still community forest or upland dry-crop fields. The dry-crop fields still account for most of the total of 78 ha of rice. *A. villosum* is the second major cash crop after rubber, cultivated under a partial tree canopy in the community forest. More recently, passionfruit and teak have become additional sources of income. The vil-

Table 9.5 Classification and areas of land-use stages and field types of Daka and Baka

| Land-use stage | Field type | Area (ha) | |
		Baka	Daka
Reserved forest	Headwater forest	20.0	26.7
	Holy hill	0.2	6.7
	Scenic forest	–	6.7
	Community forest	–	266.7
House garden	House garden	0.7	5.0
Other cultivation	Fallow	93.3	63.3
	Wet-rice field	15.3	19.7
Multi-year crop gardens	Rubber plantation	42.2	186.7
	Amomum villosum plantation	19.6	16.7
	Passiflora caerulea plantation	13.3	50.0
	Camellia sinensis plantation	1.7	0.3
	Cassia siamea plantation	3.7	2.7
	Citrus grandis plantation	–	2.7
Waters		–	0.3
Other field types		1.0	1.0

lage, at 740 m, is quite spacious, with important home gardens established on the Dai model.

Baka has 269 people, almost all members of the small Jinuo minority group, whose land occupies the steep northern side of the small Manka River valley. They moved from an old location higher in the mountains in 1971 and 1972. All their land south of the river, some 180 ha, was excised to form part of the Menglun state nature reserve in 1978. In 1983 the local government further excised 40 ha of Baka land to establish a new Menglun township rubber farm. On this occasion Baka received the partial compensation of 40 ha of rather mountainous land from the territory of a neighbouring village. Baka village now has only 173 ha, giving much less land per capita than most other villages in the region, and creating serious problems for a fallow-based agriculture. The valley bottom is at around 600 m and the upper margins, in secondary forest, exceed 1,000 m.

About half of the 15 ha of irrigated rice land, in the Manka valley floor, was created with the aid of Botanical Garden staff in the mid-1970s, and there have been more recent additions, assisted financially by the local government. Meanwhile, a major flood at the end of the 1990s damaged or destroyed a good deal of the older irrigation work in the Manka valley. As in Daka, rubber is the main cash crop, now covering 94 ha, some of which is underplanted by rice, passionfruit, and teak. Twenty varieties of upland rice are still grown, and collection of wild vegetables from the secondary forest is an important activity, its market value supplementing the winter cultivation of vegetables in the rice fields (Chen *et al.* 2001). There are 12 ha under *A. villosum* within the community forest. Some *A. villosum* from an earlier period also remains in the nature reserve south of the river. Guan, Dao, and Cui (1995) have shown that there is considerable damage done to forest restoration at Baka by the cultivation of *A. villosum*, but it remains an important source of income. The practice of cutting out forest seedlings to make space for *A. villosum* greatly reduces the lower storey of the forest. A decade or more after *A. villosum* became a major cash crop, there was considerable difference in the diversity of both the lower and intermediate storeys of forest areas with and without *A. villosum*.

The village is very poor and crowded on its steep slope, and its home gardens are small. With insufficient wet-rice land to satisfy the needs of the people, fallowing of upland fields remains very important. The young fallows are now dominated by the invasive *Chromolaena odorata*, widespread in Xishuangbanna since the middle of the twentieth century, but people derive many products from the woody fallows. Table 9.6 shows, for Daka, that the greatest number of utility plants is found in the older fallows, but outside the community forest such fallows exist only in Daka. In Baka, only very small areas of fallow older than five years can be found.

The species-richness indices of fallow plots of different ages at Daka varied from 3.4 to 9.5. The species richness of one-year fallow is high, but there were many herbs and compositae, particularly *Chromolaena odorata*. There were also many young trees and shrubs such as *Maesa indica* in the one-year and two-year fallow fields where local people can collect wild vegetables and medicinal plants. In fallow fields aged between four and six years other dominant species such as *Mallotus macrostachyus* replace *Chromolaena odorata*. In fallow of this age, fuelwood and small building wood can be collected. In 17- and 33-year fallow fields, which are regarded as community forest, local people collect wood for house construction, particularly *Machilus rufipes*.

Table 9.6 The number of useful plants in fallows of different ages in Daka, Xishuangbanna, Yunnan, China

Fallow age (years)	1	2	4	5	6	17	33
Building wood	1	–	3	2	3	5	5
Fuelwood	2	5	2	1	5	2	4
Medicinal plants	4	7	2	5	5	14	6
Animal feed	1	–	–	–	1	–	2
Wild vegetables	6	2	2	1	3	4	3
Wild fruits	1	–	2	3	3	2	3
Other uses	2	2	1	4	1	4	2
Useful species	16	15	10	13	19	24	25
Other species	5	15	6	4	3	9	10

PLEC activity at Daka and Baka

Staff from the Botanical Garden have carried out almost all the PLEC work in these two villages, including extensive biodiversity and agrobiodiversity surveys, and a lot of essentially extension-type work on the land of collaborating farmers. Work has included the promotion of a *taungya* approach to intensification of land use on former shifting cultivation land, using crops first among passionfruit and then under young teak. There has been a particular focus on improvement of home gardens, in which farmers already maintain a variety of domesticated and encouraged wild plants. Work has included removal of undesirable species and introduction of 11 others.

Extension of *Cassia siamea* plantations and introduction of energy-saving wood stoves have been promoted in order to reduce fuelwood depredation in the community forest and the nature reserve. At Baka, a survey of 60 per cent of households concluded that 34.5 per cent of fuelwood consumed is collected from fuelwood plantations, 14.5 per cent from the community forests, 44.2 per cent from the household forests, and 6.7 per cent from the nature reserve. Some 2,500 seedlings were cultivated by the project to ameliorate this situation. New species have been introduced into the agroforestry systems to meet market opportunities, including pomelo, coffee, orange, banana, litchi, and also pumpkin, cucumber, and taro as understorey crops in the rubber groves. Training courses in participatory silviculture have been held for the farmers of both villages, the training being provided at the Botanical Garden.

A particular innovation at Baka has been the promotion of butterfly farming for the tourist market, especially visitors to the Botanical Garden. Collection of wild butterflies had led to endangerment of some species, and butterfly snaring has been included in a general prohibition on wildlife hunting. Since March 1999 investigation into suitable plants for butterfly food has been followed by the establishment of butterfly plots on the land of two farmers. Some 20 other farmers have followed this experiment, but without wide adoption.

With a few exceptions arising from the work on home gardens and butterfly farming, expert farmers have been identified through the household-level agrobiodiversity surveys conducted since the end of 1999. By 2002, 17 "experts" had been recognized. Their skills were not used in a systematic manner for the instruction of other farmers until the last project year. During the same period, efforts were made to encourage the villagers to form farmers' associations for biodiversity protection. These efforts have not been successful. Farmers were initially passive recipients of PLEC innovations, but participation has become more voluntary through time, especially with home garden improvement and agroforestry. Incomes have improved, although not in the dramatic manner recorded at Baihualing.

The work of students

The institutes of the Chinese Academy of Sciences support and train graduate students, and students in botany were involved in PLEC work from an early date. One of these was Yuqin Guan, whose work on the ecological effects of planting *Amomum villosum* within the forests has been noted above. Arrangements were made for Chinese students to be trained in the Faculty of Agriculture at Chiang Mai University in Thailand, but this was not continued. In 1999–2000, after a fairly lengthy period of negotiation, students of the Department of Anthropology at Yunnan University began to work with PLEC, and up to early 2002 seven students had completed or were completing masters' theses on topics involving work at the PLEC sites. There were several benefits to the project from this arrangement: students stay in the field for longer periods than is possible for the scientists, they bring a social science perspective that is otherwise weak in PLEC-China, and the majority are female in an otherwise male-dominated cluster. For the students and their university department, a botanical dimension has been added to anthropological work. During the last two project years the students attended the annual meetings of the cluster, and gave papers which led to valuable discussion. Abbreviated abstracts of their research follow. Some results will be or have been published in *Acta Botanica Yunnanica* (see Bibliography).

Jianqin Li. 2001. Fuelwood forest at Shabadi, Tengchong county (Gaoligongshan)

Using participatory observation, in-depth interview, and household agro-biodiversity assessment, this work surveyed traditional knowledge and practice of *Quercus acutissima* fuelwood forest management in Shabadi. It also investigated means to accelerate the growth of *Quercus* and to economize on fuelwood use through building a methane tank. At present, a large part of the wood needs at Shabadi are still met from within the nature reserve. When demonstration work was being conducted at Shabadi in 1999 and early 2000, one major activity was development of a *Quercus* fuelwood plantation, *Quercus* taking the place at this higher altitude of the *Cassia siamea* that is useful in Xishuangbanna. This student research continued that experiment.

Jiqun Li. 2001. Socio-economic development and biodiversity change in an agro-ecosystem. A case from Baihualing (Gaoligongshan)

The researcher investigated the socio-economic situation of sample households and inventoried 37 sample plots in three natural villages of Baihualing administrative village. Changes were analysed.

Li-wei Yin. 2001. The impacts of different management on biodiversity of community forest

Community forests are managed in different ways, and in Baihualing initial individualization was later replaced by a restoration of collective management and hiring a guard to prevent poaching. Results of agrobiodiversity assessment show that with the intensity of harvesting declining, the indexes of biodiversity are increasing in the tree layer and herb layer, but that of the shrub layer is decreasing. The timber volume is increasing.

Yi-Qun Zeng. 2001. Causes and dynamics of the changing of agroforestry practices in Baka (Xishuangbanna)

Agroforestry systems play a vital role in modern Chinese rural development, especially in tropical upland areas. This dissertation deals with the dynamics of social, technical, and economic elements in agroforestry practices, as alternatives to shifting cultivation. The land-use changes at village and household levels are identified, examining the relationships between fallow systems and agroforestry practices. The dissertation describes farmers' strategies in agroforestry development and their impact on other agricultural systems, the environment, and agrobiodiversity.

Yi-Qun Zeng. 2001. Household-based agrobiodiversity assessment of agroforestry systems in Baka village (Xishuangbanna)

Three types of agroforestry systems of 18 households were selected for agrobiodiversity assessment. Methods used were household-based agrobiodiversity assessment, sampling, on-farm monitoring, PRA, and interviews.

Xue-Fei Du. 2001. Indigenous medicine and agrobiodiversity conservation in Daka (Xishuangbanna)

Indigenous medicine is an important part of indigenous knowledge; about one in five plants are used to cure illness. Indigenous medicinal knowledge leads people to preserve 24 medicinal plants. But the traditional medicine is disappearing, and there is a need for policy measures to conserve its importance.

Xue-Fei Du. Relationship between the nature reserve and the adjacent communities: The case of Menglun nature reserve and Baka village (Xishuangbanna)

This study, using market investigation and questionnaire, focused on the benefits and costs that have arisen from excision of land for the nature reserve. It is found that the local people had obtained a large part of their income from what is now the nature reserve, and have lost opportunities when they were excluded from the reserved land. Suggestions are given for participatory management and development of the reserve.

Zhi-lian Gong. Inventory of existing upland rice varieties in the community: The cases of Baka, Daka, and Manalong villages (Xishuangbanna)

Upland rice varieties were collected in Daka, Baka, and Manalong villages. Thirty-nine per cent of households in each village were investigated using structured and semi-structured interviews followed by household-based agrobiodiversity assessment. The results showed that there was a range of upland rice resources, with diverse morphology and genetics. Some upland rice varieties of good quality are disappearing, but most survive because they are suitable for poor soils. The number and varieties of upland rice which farmers plant are influenced not only by the area of upland rice and swidden but also by farmers' interests, planting techniques, the market, and culture.

Research and publications

Research is the principal activity of scientists in the institutes of the Chinese Academy of Sciences, including the Xishuangbanna Tropical Botanical Garden. It is also the major activity of staff in several Yunnan province institutes. Most of PLEC's scientists are drawn from these institutions, and the only ones for whom research is not a mandatory activity are staff from the Nature Reserve Bureau and other government agencies. In the early days of PLEC, and even as late as 2000, annual meetings of PLEC-China were taken up almost entirely with the presentation of scientific papers. There is substantial published output from all this work, most of it in Chinese. The Bibliography lists first publications in English, including pre-1998 papers cited in the text above, and then publications in Chinese by members of the cluster, staff and students, since 1998.

Notes

1. The editors gratefully acknowledge the considerable assistance received from the managing coordinator, Luohui Liang, in writing this chapter, by translating some materials from Chinese, providing substantial further detail, and commenting on draft versions of the chapter.
2. Decisions were still constrained until quite recently. Even in 1995–1996, the Baoshan prefectural authorities still required of the village collective that 200 ha of upland fields at Baihualing (Gaoligongshan) be allocated to sugarcane to supply the factories in the Nujiang valley. By 2002, decisions on land-use allocation had become almost entirely individual, and depend largely on profitability to the farmers.
3. Because Thailand had not, and still has not, ratified the Convention on Biological Diversity, it was not permissible for the GEF funds that became available in 1998 to be used in support of work in that country. Work in Thailand continued with direct UNU support, but at

a lesser scale than had been planned. The joint cluster originally formed had to be broken up. Work in Thailand is separately described in Chapter 14.

4. Shabadi is both higher than Baihualing and has more people.

5. "Natural" villages in China are grouped into larger administrative villages. The 10 natural villages in Baihualing are fairly closely clustered in the upper part of the valley.

REFERENCES

Brookfield, H., M. Stocking, and M. Brookfield. 1999. "Guidelines on agrodiversity in demonstration site areas", *PLEC News and Views*, No. 13, pp. 17–31.

Chen, A., Z. Dao, H. Guo, and Y. Fu. 2001. "Development and conservation of agro-biodiversity by small farmers: A case study from Yunnan, southeast China", *Acta Botanica Yunnanica Supplement*, Vol. XIII, pp. 59–68.

Dao, Z., X. Du, H. Guo, L. Liang, and Y. Li. 2001. "Promoting sustainable agriculture: The case of Baihualing, Yunnan, China", *PLEC News and Views*, No. 16, pp. 34–40. Reprinted in H. Brookfield, C. Padoch, H. Parsons, and M. Stocking (eds). 2002. *Cultivating Biodiversity: Understanding, Analysing and Using Agricultural Diversity*. London: ITDG Publications, pp. 213–219.

Guan, Y., Z. Dao, and J. Cui. 1995. "Evaluation of the cultivation of *Amomum villosum* under tropical forest in southern Yunnan, China", *PLEC News and Views*, No. 4, pp. 22–28. Reprinted in H. Brookfield, C. Padoch, H. Parsons, and M. Stocking (eds). 2002. *Cultivating Biodiversity: Understanding, Analysing and Using Agricultural Diversity*. London: ITDG Publications, pp. 200–206.

Guo, H. and C. Padoch. 1995. "Patterns and land management of agroforestry systems in Yunnan: An approach to upland rural development", *Global Environmental Change*, Vol. 5, No. 4, pp. 273–279.

Li, H., H. Guo, and Z. Dao (eds). 2000. *Flora of Gaoligong Mountains*. Beijing: Science Press.

Liang, L. 2002. "A discussion with some Chinese expert farmers", *PLEC News and Views*, No. 19, pp. 25–26.

Zarin, D. J., H. Guo, and L. Enu-Kwesi. 1999. "Methods for the assessment of plant species diversity in complex agricultural landscapes: Guidelines for data collection and analysis from the PLEC biodiversity advisory group (BAG)", *PLEC News and Views*, No. 13, pp. 3–16.

10

Papua New Guinea

John Sowei and Bryant Allen

General

Papua New Guinea (PNG) is a country of great biophysical diversity and also great cultural diversity, with some 800 distinct languages spoken among its 5 million people. Most rural people are semi-subsistence farmers, and all but 3 per cent of land is owned by the farming people under customary title, occupied at densities ranging from under one to several hundred persons per square kilometre. There are also great contrasts in agricultural systems and in access to resources and services. There is no fully integrated surface-transport network and, unfortunately, the quality as well as quantity of many services have declined since the 1980s (Hanson *et al.* 2001).

Logistical problems are among the reasons why PLEC in Papua New Guinea did not develop a single integrated programme comparable with those developed in some other countries. Others include a series of unfortunate events, as outlined below.

History of the cluster

Plans for formation of the cluster were drawn up in 1992–1993, intending to bring together work by Japanese anthropologists and Australian geographers. The latter had some good linkages with local scientists. Local

212

leadership was sought in the University of Papua New Guinea, then in the National Research Institute (NRI) which was working with a British-based project at Ossima in the far north-west of the country. Both the first two leaders moved to other posts where they were unable to continue work with PLEC. Only in 1998 was a new leader, an agricultural scientist (Sowei), found and appointed at the NRI. It was another year before he had recruited a small national staff. By that time it was becoming clear that the remote Ossima site had little to offer PLEC.

The Japanese and Australian scientists had meantime begun work in two areas where they had established experience, in the mountainous valleys near Tari in the Southern Highlands and at Tumam in the uplands north of the Sepik River. Valuable data were collected in the period 1996–1998. Then, in 1999, a major outbreak of tribal warfare in the Southern Highlands led to a cessation of PLEC work at Tari, a decision confirmed in 2000. In 1999 it was decided to focus work on Tumam, and comparatively at nearby Miko. In place of Ossima a more accessible site at Ogotana on the plateau inland from the capital, Port Moresby, was developed in 2000. Work at Miko had to be broken off when the site became somewhat dangerous because of crime. Then a final disaster occurred in 2001, when the very successful national site officer at Tumam, around whom substantial plans had been developed, died suddenly on his way back there from a spell of data analysis in Australia.

Although a major amount of work was done at Tari and Miko, especially in the former area, and some early work was done by PNG national personnel at Ossima, none of this could be followed through. Substantial material on Tari has been published by the Japanese scientists (Umezaki, Yamauchi, and Ohtsuka 1999; Umezaki *et al.* 2000; Yamauchi, Umezaki, and Ohtsuka 2001), and the cluster final report describes Miko in some detail. Discussion in this chapter concentrates only on Ogotana and Tumam, where work continued until the end of the project.

Ogotana

The site and the agricultural system

Ogotana is a village of the Koiari people of central Papua, located at around 700 m on the Sogeri Plateau between the coastal lowlands and the main Owen Stanley range. Soils are based on volcanic formations uplifted and eroded during and since the Pleistocene, but appear to be low in natural fertility and are often shallow. The area has a well-marked drier season between May and October, and over time fire has replaced a good deal of the original forest with grassland. The landscape includes both savanna

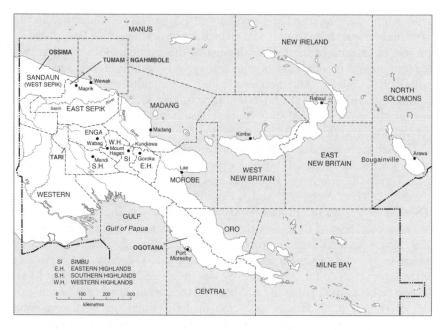

Figure 10.1 The Papua New Guinea sites

grassland and secondary forest regrowth, usually with sharp boundaries between the two formations.

Describing a nearby part of the plateau where forest remains extensive, Allen *et al.* (1996: 53–55) describe a long-fallow system in which on average land is cultivated for only two years in about each quarter-century. Banana is the dominant staple, and the greater yam (*Dioscorea alata*) is the second most important staple. Other staples include cassava, *Xanthosoma* taro, sweet potato (*Ipomoea batatas*), the lesser yam (*D. esculenta*), and *Amorphallus* taro. Important vegetables include *aibika* (*Abelmoschus manihot*), common beans (*Phaseolus vulgaris*), *choko* tips (*Sechium edule*), maize, cucumbers, *kangkong* (*Ipomea aquatica*), lowland *pitpit* (*Saccharum edule*), peanuts, pumpkin tips, and *karakap* (*Solanum nigrum*). Fruits and nuts that are cultivated include mangoes, *marita pandanus*, oranges, papaya, pineapples, watermelon, pomelo, breadfruit, *okari* (*Terminalia* spp.), and coconuts.

At Ogotana there are now comparatively few fields made in the forest because of the ravages of the introduced giant African snail (*Achatina fulica*), which eats the leaves, stems, and tubers of several crops. Most fields are now made in the grassland, where yam, banana, and sweet potato are the main crops. The giant African snail is more readily managed in the grassland areas where there is less plant matter on the ground for its habitation. Nearby commercial farming activities include cattle ranching and rubber plantations. Labourers from other provinces were recruited to work on the plantations and farms, and many have settled on local village land on the plateau. The commercial farmers (mainly large companies), the settlers, and the local landowners compete for available resources. Ogotana village is made up of three clans of the Koiari tribe. There are 51 households in the village with a total population of 260 people. Twenty-eight per cent of families are composed of local women married to men from other parts of the country who have decided to settle in Ogotana. There are home gardens near the village.

Demonstration activity: Restoring forest

The Ogotana area is not densely populated, but there is concern over the recent spread of grassland, which has advanced significantly at the expense of forest in recent decades. In preliminary discussions in 1999, this was the problem on which help was particularly sought. Grassland rehabilitation has been developed from farmers' own experience. The demonstration activity tested an intervention approach to landscape rehabilitation using the agroforestry concept and fallow management.

The initial aim was to propagate seedlings of local tree species to be used in the rehabilitation demonstration site. A nursery was established in 2000, and became a demonstration activity for the community and stakeholders to raise useful local and introduced tree species. To determine what species should be used and where, biodiversity surveys were undertaken in forest fallow of close-spaced ages. After only two years of work no firm results have yet been established, but it has been determined that the requirements for agricultural production in grassland environments cannot be met by the practices of shifting cultivation employed in the forest. Therefore, alternative crops have to be introduced and production systems adopted to replace the traditional crops and provide food security under the grassland agricultural system.

The advantage of the Ogotana demonstration site has been its proximity to Port Moresby, where many NGOs and agencies are located. This has enabled the project to involve many stakeholders to disseminate through networking the importance of biodiversity conservation issues. This has strengthened the sharing of information and experiences with different approaches to biodiversity conservation in Papua New Guinea.

Tumam-Nghambole[1]

A different place and a different purpose

Unlike in Ogotana, work at Tumam-Nghambole (hereafter Tumam) began in the 1970s with Allen's doctoral thesis, and did not have the initial purpose of dealing with a locally perceived problem. It was because of the long data record (updated in 1989), as well as the obvious interest of the place, that it was chosen by a cluster meeting in 1999 to be the principal site for work in PNG. The perceived problem was viewed externally, resting on population growth and a growing shortage of land for cultivation. Internally, answers seemed to have been found which met these problems up to the end of the twentieth century, and the specific aim was to record these adaptations with a view to their wider dissemination in the region. One of the national staff recruited in 1999, Chris Tokomeyeh, had been born at Nghambole and returned to adjacent Tumam after several years in employment to become the site officer for PLEC.

No attempt was made to encourage instruction of others by the more expert farmers within the community, who were recognized from the outset of work in the 1970s. In pre-colonial and colonial times agricultural production was closely linked to highly competitive, even aggressive, exchanges of food. Group leaders cajoled their followers into producing more than their ritual competitors. The techniques for growing more and better yams, bananas, taro, sugar, and *pitpit* were jealously guarded and included spells, magical potions, abstinence from sexual contacts with women, and a number of other practices. Furthermore, in a society in which there are no chiefs and no inherited offices, any leader can be challenged at any time, and frequently is. The challenge may be physical, social, or magical, and there is a widespread belief in sorcery. There is a marked reluctance to give up knowledge to potential rivals who may use it against one. Farmer-to-farmer training is a foreign concept in such an environment.

In place of farmer-to-farmer training, the PNG-PLEC group focused on field-days in which everyone could be informed of PLEC work and findings in public, and on visits between the farmers from distantly located PLEC sites. So Tumam farmers visited Miko and Ogotana and vice versa. These visits to other areas, although expensive because of the high cost of travel, were very successful. In all three areas yams and bananas are important and the farmers found much to discuss. The environmental degradation at Ogotana, and even at Miko, was a shock to Tumam farmers, and they held meetings in the village on their return to discuss what could happen if they did not take measures. The exotic giant African snail, only recently encountered in the Sepik region but endemic and a serious problem at Ogotana, was also a topic of many conversations.

No attempts were made to form farmers' associations at Tumam. This area has a colonial history of several forms of cooperatives, all of which collapsed in various states of bankruptcy. New churches sweep through the area about once every decade and, after a short, sharp, and ecstatic frenzy of activity, people are left feeling depressed and let down. Political parties also come and go. People are generally suspicious of new organizations.

What was next planned was that site officer Chris Tokomeyeh, who was running for the elected position of council chairman, would, if successful, try and get an agreement between a number of local Urat-speaking villages through their councillors to refrain from clearing the remaining corridors of rainforest that still exist along the boundaries of village lands. Posters of the PLEC work that illustrated the impact of shifting cultivation on the land and the biodiversity value of these forests were in preparation for this programme. From a position as council chairman Chris would have been influential in working at the intervillage level, but his untimely death in 2001 brought the plans to an end.

The site and its farming system

Tumam is located in Dreikikir-Ambunti district, on the southern or Sepik fall of the Torricelli Mountains. The Torricelli Mountains are part of a mountain range that runs parallel to the coast of north-western New Guinea, reaching a little over 2,000 m at the highest point. South from near the watershed on the main range, Tertiary sediments, mudstone, sandstone, and conglomerates form a wide band of foothill country which falls south to merge into the alluvial sediments of the Sepik plain. South-flowing streams have dissected the soft Tertiary materials into an intricate ridge and valley pattern, with relative relief between 200 m and 300 m in the north and less in the south. There are no roads from the coast inland, except for a road that leaves Wewak in the east, crosses the range, and then runs east–west along the foothills. Parts of this road are in very bad condition.

The hill slopes are characterized by moderate to strong slumping, which has given rise to a pattern of emergent crests and steep slopes near the top of the ridges, generally concave upper slopes, and mounds of slumped material which create swampy patches midway between ridge and valley bottom. Below these, convex lower slopes border incised streams. The complexity of the slope forms precludes using them as a major landscape division. The study area lies in a major earthquake zone, and two large shocks occurred in the area in the first half of the twentieth century. Soils are determined by the site conditions of an unstable area and, while mainly of the brown forest soil type, vary enormously over small areas.

Climatic records for the area are limited, but show that for a six-year period 60 per cent of the rain fell between October and March. During the rainy season, damp, heavy mists are common in the mornings. Thunderstorm activity is frequent. The knowledge that heavy falls of rain can be expected from late September onwards influences agricultural activity. New gardens are cleared and burned during August and September, and gardens are planted to catch the rains.[2] The early or late arrival of the rain causes concern, as does too much or too little rain. Droughts are not unknown but appear to be rare, and do not give rise to as much concern as wet periods.

A tall lowland hill forest with an irregular canopy is the most common vegetation. However, even apparently untouched areas of forest are said to have been the site of former settlements, and would therefore have been cut and cultivated at some time. Below 600 m the majority of ridges have patches of *Imperata* and *Themeda* grasses. Tumam men relate how before the introduction of steel axes gardens were smaller and followed their ridge tops, rather than running from the ridge down into the valleys as they do now. Steel axes enabled larger trees to be cleared further down the slope, causing a change in the shape of gardens as well as an increase in their area. It seems likely that this factor, combined with less soil moisture on the ridge tops, has allowed the grasses to become dominant on the ridges. Sago is planted in groves of up to 10 palms in valley bottoms, and all over the slopes in small swampy areas formed by slumping.

The people of Tumam speak the Urat language, and there are both genetic and linguistic differences between the Urat and their neighbours. The resident population at the two demonstration site comunities has doubled since 1970 from 250 to 500 persons. The overall pattern of population change since the first full census in 1941 has been one of a sharp fall during the Second World War (from deaths, a fall in the birth rate, and migration), followed by a slow increase to 1970 and a more rapid increase since then. Healthcare standards are in decline at present, but it will take some time for increased death rates to slow population growth. At the same time, living conditions are improving, with sawn timber and roofing iron being used to construct houses and rain-water being used increasingly for drinking. This may offset the impact of the failure of the healthcare system on demographic change.

The two villages share a common area of 1,450 ha. Although most of the land is covered in forest and regrowth, it is closely subdivided. The subdivision boundaries are marked with cordyline plants (*tanget*) or are known by landmarks, streams, and other natural features. Every subdivision has a name, usually a personal name of an ancestor who is said to have first cleared or cultivated the land, or who wrested the land from the control of a previously occupying group. The population does not see simply a forest around them, but a landscape of former fields. A complex history of fighting and occupation and reoccupation of land characterizes pre-colonial times. In order to provide a common reference point for PLEC staff and village farmers, a GPS survey of all ridge lines was carried out, recording and mapping the names of blocks of land. Approximately 400 names were recorded. These names have been used for the agrodiversity and biodiversity surveys and in investigations into land tenure and use in the period 1994–2001.

The selection of any particular site for cultivation depends upon a number of social, environmental, and locational factors. The site must be, in the Urat language, literally "ripe" – the forest successions must have proceeded to the point where a number of known tree species have reached maturity. This set of trees is known collectively as the *loumbure*, the "good trees". If the forest has not reached this stage it is considered poor management to clear it. On the other hand, if the forest proceeds beyond this stage the increasing size of the trees begins to give concern because clearing "overripe" forest is dangerous and difficult.

The owner of a garden site that is "ripening" will begin actively to seek participants in a gardening operation. He cannot clear the land without assistance, and will exchange access to the land for up to three years for the labour of other people willing to cultivate with him. He will cite family relationships, precedent (parents gardening together, for example), good site and soil characteristics, and proven past production from this land. Those he approaches will take into consideration the location of the site relative to existing gardens and the village, and other offers of land being made to them. Kinship is often the explanation given as to why any individual is cultivating another's land. But in a village of 500 people in which marriage within so-called descent groups is allowed and in some circumstances cross-cousin marriage is encouraged, where sister exchange is practised, and there is a high incidence of adopting individuals into the groups, it is possible to prove a kinship relationship of some sort between almost everyone in the village. Often kinship links seem to be little more than a legitimization of a relationship based on friendship or good neighbourliness.

Previous surveys in the 1970s found around 45 per cent of people at Tumam were cultivating land directly inherited from their fathers. A further 20 per cent were occupying land given to them by an agnate, a relative on their father's side of the family, often a father's brother. Only 10 per cent were gardening land given to them by non-agnatic cognates, relatives on their mother's side of the family. Eighteen per cent were on land given to them by an affine, a relative on their wife's side of the family. The remaining 7 per cent were on land owned by a special friend, an exchange partner, a moiety "brother", or just a close neighbour. These data have been collected again for the period 1995–2000. They are expected to confirm popular belief that there has been a "tightening" of land tenure and an increasing reluctance to let non-agnates use land.

The progress of farm work at Tumam

At Tumam the system is a well-elaborated form of shifting cultivation, mainly for subsistence. Cash crops, cocoa and coffee, are grown in clearings near the villages. All species cultivated or used for food were documented before carrying out a survey of agrobiodiversity. A survey of all species and varieties growing in the gardens of 49 Tumam and Nghambole farmers was conducted in 1999. The purpose of the survey was discussed with two experts identified in earlier work, Joel Ngemgutu and Albert Yilumbu, who have a detailed knowledge of plants. Chris Tokomeyeh and the experts drew the sample of 49 farmers to include, at their insistence, "old" men, "middle-aged" men, "young" men, and women gardening alone, usually older widows. The men were divided into "good" gardeners and "poor" gardeners. There was some reluctance to include "poor" gardeners in the sample on the grounds that they do not properly represent how gardening should be done. Tokomeyeh counted the number of species observed, ideally in four 10 m × 10 m quadrats (top, side, centre, and bottom of garden). Two local experts identified the species and varieties. Where the gardens were small, one or two of the quadrats were not used. The survey was carried out three times, beginning in 1999 with the newly cleared gardens and again in 2000 and 2001. A small number of farmers were lost from the survey because of death or illness.

The field or garden stages

Most people have two blocks under cultivation: the *wah* (which literally means "work") is newly cleared and planted; and the *yekene* is a garden in the second year of cultivation. Most people cultivate a third garden, known as *nerekase*, which is also the name of the first stage of the fallow (*ngere* being the name of the saccharum cane grass which begins to invade at this time). The name reflects the recent extension to a third crop. The yam crops produced from these gardens are known respectively as *hau wah*, *hau mbisionge*, and *hau yom* or *hau ka*. Gardens are on average 0.1 ha in area. The mean area under cultivation per person is 0.06 ha.

Forest clearing begins in August towards the end of the dry season. Undergrowth is slashed by men and women. Men, especially young men, climb high into taller trees to pollard them, trimming all the branches off. The fallen debris is cut into smaller pieces by men and women and spread evenly over the garden site to dry. Men fell some large trees within the site that cannot be pollarded, and trees around the perimeter are felled outwards into the surrounding forest to open up the garden to sunlight. Slashed species known for their poor burning qualities are carried from the site.

When the slashed material is dry and the weather is fine and hot, the site is burned. A good burn is essential to a good garden, and it is not unknown for a site to be abandoned if a burn is poor. Only men should conduct a burn, because, they say, women will become confused by the smoke and flames and possibly get burned to death. However, there are many examples of women successfully conducting a burn. After a good burn the site is tidied up by heaping unburned material and burning it. Women sweep the garden surface with brooms made from coconut palms, forming the fine ash and rubbish into small heaps. They use the heaps to plant particular varieties of yams reserved for their use, because they are forbidden to break the soil with their digging sticks in a new garden site.

Even before the burn, some species are planted. Taro (*Colocasia esculenta*) is planted around the edge of the site, along with sugarcane. Clearing reveals numbers of two naturally occurring species, *Ficus copiosa* and *Ficus wassa*. The new leaves of these species are an important source of greens. They are heavily pruned. The fire destroys the taro tops and burns all the remaining leaves from the *Ficus* trees. The young sugarcane appears unaffected by the heat. The taro quickly reshoots and the *Ficus* produce new leaves. As well as the usually quoted benefits of the burn, the fire probably has a sterilizing effect on already planted species, destroying fungal infections and insects. Pre-fire planting is said by villagers to be just a matter of "getting the garden going early". After the fire, taro planting continues and banana planting begins. This work is always done by men. Women may be occupied planting introduced crops such as *Xanthosoma* taro or sweet potato in last year's gardens, where restrictions on them do not apply.[3]

Men, women, and children spend most of their time in their gardens. Most build at least one house nearby in which to store yams and gardening equipment, and if the garden is some distance from the village they build a house in which they may live for some days at a time during periods of heavy work. Gardens were previously fenced against pigs and people, but this practice disappeared in the 1960s when shotguns reduced the numbers of pigs and competitive food exchanges became less important. The introduction of steel bush-knives and axes in the 1940s and the decision to cease fencing must have released considerable amounts of labour, some of which was invested into planting cash crops, in particular *Robusta* coffee. The first coffee was planted in 1961. Cocoa was not planted in any amount until 1990 but is now more important than coffee, mainly because the labour required for a family to produce an equivalent income is considerably lower.

Edible species are planted in the newly cleared garden in well-established sequences (Table 10.1). Seven months after clearing more than

Table 10.1 Survey details and number of species and varieties per hectare, by garden stage

Garden stage	Months from clearing	Number of 10 m² plots surveyed	Total area surveyed (ha)	Number of edible species	Number of edible varieties	Number of weed species
Wah	7	125	1.25	41	195	559
Yekene	20	135	1.35	43	177	1,198
Nerakase	33	116	1.16	19	70	No data*

*Regrowth was so thick in many plots at this stage that weeds were not counted.

195 varieties of 41 edible species have been planted into the garden. A year later the number of species is about the same, although there is some loss of varieties. A further year later the garden is allowed to slip back into fallow, no further weeding is undertaken, and the number of edible species is half what it was at the beginning of the cultivation sequence.

Of the staple species, *Colocasia esculenta* (taro), *Dioscorea esculenta* (lesser yam or *mami*), and *Xanthosoma sagittifolium* (Chinese taro or taro *kongkong*, introduced in the 1940s) predominate in the *wah* stage. The other most important species in this stage is banana, of which there are a large number of cultivars. Many of the bananas planted at this stage continue to produce food through all stages and into the early part of the fallow.

As the cultivated site progresses from stage to stage, the species composition changes. The two main yam species, which are replanted in the second year, decrease in number, bananas remain about the same for at least two years, while the density of sweet potato increases in the final stages. Maize and sugarcane are important early-producing *wah* crops which are reduced by the second year and gone by the third, but *Saccharum esculentum* (a tall, edible grass known as *pitpit* in pidgin) increases sharply in the final stage of cultivation when it is planted all over the garden and left to fend for itself.

As well as species composition changing during the gardening stages, the composition of cultivars of individual species also changes. The most important root crop, *D. esculenta*, illustrates this point. The most abundant varieties planted in the *wah* garden continue to be the most abundant in all stages, but a number of varieties, such as *hau glame*, are planted in greater numbers in the later stages of cultivation than in the earlier stages. Individual gardeners have their favourite varieties which they feel they can grow best. Some varieties appear to be common to all gardens and are valued for certain characteristics, such as lack of fibre, firmness when cooked, or tuber size, for example. The less important varieties are constantly changing as new varieties are brought in and tried and unpopular varieties cease to be planted. A systematic loss of some varieties appears to be occurring, in particular the *wuye'* varieties that require the construction of a low fence. Older men find planting them too much work. Younger men, no longer pressed to compete in yam exchanges where not being able to present or return *wuye'* varieties would be shameful, are also not planting them.

Some varieties are always kept physically apart because it is said that if brought together one variety will lose favoured characteristics and take on the less favourable characteristics of the other variety. For example, *mwariyai* and *mwarisepeli* tubers, which have particularly desirable taste and texture characteristics, are never brought into contact with or allowed to rest beneath *mwarasenge*, the most common variety, because they will become contaminated and will "revert" to the characteristics of *mwarasenge*.[4]

Some varieties are cultivated only by women. They are placed in the heaped-up ash and rubbish within the new garden, above the soil surface. In this way women can cultivate yams without breaking the soil with sticks. The restriction does not apply to later stages. Men consider the varieties planted by women inferior. But a listing (not reproduced) suggests that despite this disparagement they are an important group. Some *D. alata* varieties are genderized and are known as "male" or "female" tubers, because although their vines are indistinguishable the tubers produced are suggestive of human genitalia. Both are cultivated only by men.

A locally unique feature of yam-planting techniques is the use of the leaves of the *ton* or *yah* tree, *Pometia pinnata*. The *Pometia* is a tall, handsome fruit tree of the *Sapindaciae* family, a close relative of the litchi. It is deliberately encouraged in the secondary forest by the planting of hundreds of seedlings along the upper edges of the new gardens, many of which survive to form orchards along all the main ridges. *Canarium*, *Artocarpus*, *Gnetnum*, and *Areca* are also planted in this manner. *Pometia* fruit ripen from January to March and villagers gorge themselves on the fruit. Later, in August and September, women collect the now dry leaves into large bundles and carry them to the newly prepared gardens.

Pometia leaves (known as *yah hikor* when used for this purpose) are placed in a shallow, 30 cm hole with the seed yam or set, beneath the seed tuber in the case of the *hau* varieties and on top of the tuber in the case of the *wuye'* and *bwa'* varieties. Gardeners say this gives the young developing tubers "room to move" and results in a smoother, more aesthetically pleasing shaped tuber.[5]

Pometia leaves are not used with *D. alata*, which is cultivated using similar techniques to the Abelam and Wosera who grow yams up to 3 m long. Urat gardeners dig a hole only up to 1 m deep. Soil removed from the hole is crumbled into a fine tilth and replaced around a stick held vertically in the hole. The stick is then removed and the seed yam (which is usually only the top part of a tuber) is placed above the hole left by the stick. Commonly the seed tuber is placed in a shallow trench dug across the slope immediately adjacent to the hole. Special techniques are used with some varieties, such as hollowing out the seed tuber and packing it with soil to "irritate" or "stimulate" it and make it grow faster and fatter.

Within a garden, some varieties are placed on steeper slopes, others on flatter areas. *Wuye'* varieties are always planted on slopes of up to 25 degrees behind a low soil-retaining barrier constructed from a single tree branch (called *louluingah*, literally "tree-path") held in place by stakes hammered into the soil on the downslope side. Small channels are made to allow water running down the slope to pass through the *louluingah*. If water ponds behind the barrier it will cause the tubers to rot.

An important task is the tying up of the yam vines. Vines from a nearby fallow are used to train the developing vines on to standing trees or 3 m long stakes. The correct tension on the line attached to the vine is important. An approximation to a catenary curve is required to ensure that rainwater running down the vine will drop off before reaching the hole occupied by the tubers or the yams will rot. Taro is planted beneath the point where the water drops off. Skilful use is made of the many pollarded trees left standing in the gardens when the layout of the rows of yams is being planned. The staking or training of the yam vine was found by Enyi (1972) to be the most important factor influencing total tuber production. Urat gardeners invest a lot of labour in staking their yams and spend much time in maintaining the stakes and the lines securing the vines to them.

Harvesting takes place about six months after planting. It is associated with more behavioural restrictions and magic to ensure the irascible tubers do not burrow down into the ground to escape the harvest. The tubers are lifted using sticks and hands, despite the thorns, and great care is taken not to damage the skins to avoid decay in the storehouse. The tubers are stored in a cool, dark house, built specially for the purpose, either in the garden or nearby.

The only yield figures available for Tumam yams are those from 50 *D. esculenta* vines and seven *D. alata* vines. The *D. alata* tubers averaged 4.1 kg each. The *D. esculenta* produced 174 tubers with a mean weight of 2.25 kg and a mean yield per vine of 4.4 kg. The 174 tubers were produced from 133 m² of garden, a yield of 16.4 tonnes/ha. Comparative figures from the Abelam are 21 tonnes/ha from Yenigo and 16.3 tonnes/ha from Stapikum (Lea 1964). At Ohuru village near Yagaum, Madang, on good alluvial soils, 44 *D. esculenta* vines (variety *gasin*, or "white yam") yielded 16.6 tonnes/ha (according to fieldnotes recorded by Allen in 1998). It would seems that Tumam yields are well within acceptable village yield ranges for other parts of Papua New Guinea.

After the yam crop is planted other vegetables follow, including winged beans (*Phosphocarpus*), an introduced *Phaseolus* bean, tobacco (introduced about 200 years ago), and *Xanthosoma* or taro *kongkong*, which is planted on only the lowest parts of the garden or on steep slopes not used for anything else, because its large leaves shade other young plants. Also planted is a large variety of green-leaved vegetables, including the traditional greens: *Amaranthus* (*wuripinu*), *Abelmoschus* (*bisiem*), *Nustertium* (*hoholi*), *Deeringia* (*nihnang*), and *Grantophyllum* (*sarindai*). In a protein-poor diet, these plants are nutritionally very important. They are universally liked and valued and eaten with every meal.

As soon as the *hauwah* crop is safely in store, a second or *haumbisionge* crop is planted back into the holes left by the removal of the first and the garden becomes *yekene*. Many restrictions on it are lifted. More introduced crops are now planted among the yams, including papaya, maize, spring onions, tomatoes, pumpkin, cucumber, Chinese cabbage, sweet potato, and cassava. Once established the *yekene* garden is left largely in the care of the women.

Shortly after the *hauwah* harvest, misshapened or damaged yams are sorted out and consumed immediately, undersized tubers are marked for replanting in the *yekene*, and, until recently, the best tubers were selected for exchanges. Up until around 1990 yams were exchanged between "moieties" – two groups of men who exchanged food and initiation responsibilities. These ceremonies appear to have been abandoned as a result of fundamentalist Christian teaching. However, the exchanges have twice been "abandoned" before, only to be revived again. Following the exchanges, tubers were divided into those to be eaten over the next six months and those to be held as planting material for the next year's *wah* garden. Nowadays this division takes place after the harvest. Those tubers put aside for planting are not touched, even when the food tubers have all been eaten. Tumam people cannot recall a time in the past when the seed yams had to be eaten because of famine, although this is not unknown in other yam-growing areas in Papua New Guinea. Previously, when the eating yams were all consumed, sago was used until the first yams became available from the new plantings. In the past this period was called the "hungry time", although sago was available. It appears to have been a time of poorer health. Today, *Xanthosoma* and sweet potato tubers largely take the place of the sago and there is no hardship.

The *haumbisionge* harvest takes place in the same way as the *hauwah* harvest but with less fuss. The tubers are smaller and they are all eaten. Until about 10 years ago the harvesting of the *yekene* garden normally ended the cultivation period. *Pitpit* was planted all over the garden and some further *Xanthosoma* planting sometimes occurred. The garden was rapidly overwhelmed by weeds and creepers. Bananas were harvested for a short time and taro and *pitpit* for longer, but by nine to 12 months cane grass (*Saccharum robustum*) regrowth had taken over the garden and it became known as *nerakase*, the first stage in the fallow sequence.

Two significant contemporary developments

Presently two significant changes are under way. Firstly, many people plant a third yam crop, the *hau yom* or *hau ka* crop. This garden is still known as *nerakase*, although it is no longer the first stage of the fallow. Sweet potato is also increasingly planted all over the garden. This practice began ostensibly as a means to control weed growth in the third yam crop, but in fact sweet potato provides an increasingly important source of food. The demand for food created by the increase in population over the last 20 years is met by extending the cultivation period by 30 per cent. Sweet potato is planted by merely pushing vines taken from a nearby garden into the soil behind the blade of a digging stick or bush knife. *Hau yom* tubers are consumed straight from the garden.

Secondly, a number of farmers are planting coffee or cocoa seedlings into the garden during the *wah* and *yekene* stages. Until around 1990 the only cash crop in the area was *Robusta* coffee, grown in small plots averaging 150 trees per plot, surrounded by secondary forest, and shaded by *Leucaena*. The layout and location of these plots was very much influenced by the colonial government extension service of the 1960s. Very little additional coffee was planted after the initial enthusiasm when all families planted at least one plot and often two. However, between 1990 and 2001 more than 70,000 cocoa trees were planted, and three local fermentaries and driers have been established in the two villages, two owned by village "business groups" and one by an individual previously employed as an agricultural extension assistant. Two large areas were planted with over 10,000 cocoa trees by the business groups, and individual plots similar to the coffee plots were also planted, shaded by *Gliricidia* rather than *Leucaena*. The business group plots have been neglected because they require constant and dominant leadership to manage them, whereas individual plots planted by almost all farmers are kept clear of undergrowth.

Of major interest is the experimentation that is occurring in the integration of cocoa, and to a lesser extent coffee, into the shifting cultivation cycle of food-crop gardens. Farmers are planting cocoa seedlings into the late *wah* and *yekene* stage gardens in order to increase their cash incomes. During the *nerakase* stage sweet potato controls weeds and fallow tree species and tall grasses are weeded out. *Gliricidia* is also planted in the third year from clearing. Thus the food garden is transformed into a cash-crop garden. Farmers argue that in 20 years they will clear the cocoa and plant food again. They know that land cleared from cocoa and *Gliricidia* or *Leucaena* grows food crops as well as a 20-year forest fallow, so the consequences of this practice will not be a reduction in food production; rather it will be, over 20 years, a significant loss of natural successional fallow species. Farmers recognize this problem but believe the loss will not be significant, because not every site cleared for food crops will be converted into cocoa or coffee. They will not have the labour to harvest and process this amount of cocoa or coffee.

Agrobiodiversity in the food gardens

This analysis of agrobiodiversity is based on the number of varieties of all species that are cultivated and not just on the number of species. Agrobiodiversity is highest in the first or *wah* stage. That is the stage when there is a greatest abundance of both species and varieties. However the *yekene*, or

Table 10.2 Agrobiodiversity by garden stage, Tumam

Garden stage	*Wah*	*Yekene*	*Nerakase*
Number of species	195	176	69
Number of individuals	14,774	7,381	1,740
Margalef index	20.2	19.6	9.1
Shannon index	3.77	3.89	2.93

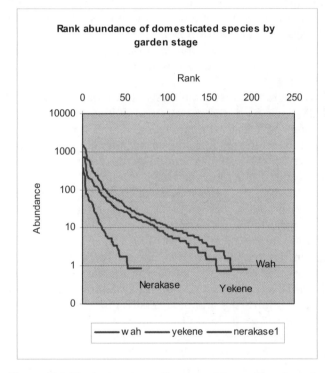

Figure 10.2 Rank abundance diagram of domesticated species

second year, stage is not much less diverse (Table 10.2, Figure 10.2). After 24 months from clearing, crop diversity falls considerably as the fallow begins. *Saccharum esculentum* is planted over the whole garden area and only bananas are kept clear of vines and weeds.

The fallows

After cultivation ceases, a continuous process of natural regrowth begins and continues for between 25 to 30 years until the site is again cleared for cultivation. Tumam people recognize that the process of regrowth is complex and continuous. However, like "scientific" observers everywhere, they simplify the process by classifying the vegetation communities into four stages. They base their classification on observed features of the vegetation and not on time. The stages are as follows.

- *Nerakase*, which lasts from the third year after clearing for about six to eight years.
- *Banande*, lasting from around six to eight years to 15 years from the cessation of cultivation. The term is a reference to the fast-growing softwoods that dominate this period and die and fall after about 15 years. In its later stages it is also known as the "trees which die" stage, or *kupyi-hope*, a general term derived from the disappearance of *kukup* (*Geunisa*) trees which have been replaced by slower-growing tree species by the end of this stage.
- *Loumbure*, literally "trees-good" stage. In the latter parts of this stage, around 25 years from the cessation of cultivation, the garden site is judged to be again ready for cultivation. At this time, the *loumbure* forest is sometimes referred to as *hipwurieu*, literally "black and brown", a reference to the loss of sunlight caused by the closing of the forest canopy.

If it is not cleared the previous stage continues into a fourth stage, *loutinginde* (literally "trees-forest"), in which the secondary trees increase to their full height and species normally only found in the undisturbed forest begin to appear in the succession.

During 1999 a botanical survey was undertaken to establish the biodiversity contained in the fallow sites at Tumam. This survey built on a previous less intensive survey in the 1970s. The regular and systematic use of forest sites for cultivation raises a number of interesting questions for the assessment of agrodiversity and biodiversity. First, how should the garden sites under regrowth be defined? The Tumam people view them as "fields" or garden sites which at the moment have natural vegetation growing on them. They appear to see clearly both the fields themselves and the countryside with its ridges and streams, bare of the trees, in much the same way as those of us who have not grown up in forest view fields of wheat or potatoes. Second, species appear and disappear through the regrowth phase, in a series of complex successions of plant (and probably micro- and macrofaunal) communities. This situation justifies the use of the fallow stage as a field type and sampling for biodiversity on that basis. The analysis includes only woody stems – further analysis will take place of the grasses, vines, and other herbaceous plants when time allows. Three rainforest sites (sites that have never been cultivated within the communal memory and oral history) were also observed to provide some sort of baseline or background measure of biodiversity – only three plots do not adequately represent the true level of biodiversity of these sites.

Table 10.3 Biodiversity by fallow stage, woody stems only, Tumam

	Nerakase	Banande	Loumbure	Loutinginde	Rainforest
Fallow stage and age	Up to 5 years	10–15 years	15–20 years	20–50 years	
Number of species	88	171	72	88	88
Number of individuals	510	4,683	4,656	5,036	1,758
Margalef index	14.0	20.1	8.4	10.2	9.3
Shannon index	3.63	4.64	3.46	3.53	3.53

The analysis looks at the fallow stages as they were identified by the farmer experts (Table 10.3). The years have been added to show the age range of the fallows in each stage. An interesting pattern emerges in which biodiversity appears to be greatest during the second stage of the fallow, the *banande* stage, between 10 and 15 years from clearing. This stage is characterized by maturing of a number of fast-growing softwood trees species, dominated by *Leucaena*, a large number of *Ficus* species, *F. damaropsis*, *F. gul*, *F. wassa*, *F. hispicoides*, and *F. calopina* in particular, *Melanolepsis*, and *Premna*. *Althoffia* is a particular fast-growing species which reaches 15 m before it matures and dies at around 15 years from the beginning of the fallow. The *loumbure* and *loutinginde* stages are dominated by slower-growing trees, including *Kleinhovia*, *Oreocnide*, *Leea*, *Artocarpus*, and *Pometia*.

An analysis of useful species in the Tumam fallows by McCoy (2000), based on total vegetation cover, finds that species which are eaten by humans and important game animals (mainly birds, bandicoots, and bats) occur at a higher proportion in the earlier fallow stages (between *banande* and *loumbure*) than in the later stages. On the other hand species used for construction and house building tend to occur most commonly in the later fallow stages. The dominance of the *Ficus* genera is of particular interest. They appear early in the fallow sequence and remain through two stages, but are not present after about 40 years. They have been shown to be important in the maintenance of insects – 792 herbivorous species of insects have been collected from 15 species of *Ficus* in New Guinea (Novotny *et al.* 2002). Tumam hunters state that *F. pungens*, *F. borycarpa*, *F. congesta*, and *F. hispicoides* in particular are very important for attracting game (McCoy 2000). The dominance of this genus would appear to be the outcome of a long period of adaptation to prevailing conditions, which are brought about and maintained by agricultural activities. This suggests that the agricultural system at Tumam has been in its present form for a long period of time and is presently undergoing a period of unprecedented change.

Notes

1. This section of the chapter also draws on material provided by Stephane McCoy and the late Chris Tokomeyeh.
2. It is common in Papua New Guinea to use the term "garden" for a field or cultivated plot of any size.
3. Numerous other restrictions should be observed by men and women from the time of the burn to the time of the first yam harvest. They apply to sexual relations and diet and times of eating. Excretion and menstruation can also limit access to garden sites. Most of these restrictions are necessary because the yams, which are thought to possess spirits, are at their best mischievous and at their worst delinquent. They demand respect and mollycoddling, and are extremely sensitive to female sexuality. Men should not engage in sexual intercourse between planting yams and harvesting them, and they should eat before entering a garden and not eat while they are within the garden, although most families eat immediately outside the garden at the end of a period of garden work. If they wish to defecate they must go some distance from the garden, and then return home and not re-enter the garden until the next day. They may urinate some distance away and then return to the garden. Menstruating women should not enter the garden at any time, nor the houses in which yams are stored. Men, women, and children never step over yam tubers lying on the ground nor over a yam vine.
4. Margaret Quin, an agronomist who worked on Sepik yams in the 1980s, argued that many named varieties were in fact genetically almost identical and that it was soil characteristics, including stoniness, fertility, soil fauna, and the occurrence of pathogens, that influenced tuber characteristics, which in turn determined the naming of the so-called variety (Quin undated). This explains why many men can sometimes not name a variety growing in a garden by examining the vine alone. They assert that yams can change from one named variety to another in the ground between planting and harvest.
5. However, *Pometia* leaves may have other functions too. A sample of *Pometia* leaves analysed for chemical composition showed 0.72 per cent nitrogen (dry air basis), whereas soil samples from 28 sites averaged only 0.2 per cent nitrogen with a range of 0.14–0.28 per cent. Enyi (1972) found leaf area and vine weight were associated with nitrogen availability, which caused increased tuber yields. When the *Pometia* leaves are placed in the ground they are dry and do not begin to decompose immediately. But from about one month after planting to about three months, the period during which the vine is growing and the leaves developing, the *Pometia* leaves may be supplying nitrogen and other minerals to the developing plant at a critical period of growth. Urat gardeners are also aware of the relationship between vigorous leaf and vine growth and larger tubers, but they do not relate the use of *Pometia* leaves to the production of a healthy vine. The geographical extent of this practice is restricted to Urat speakers, two southernmost Kombio villages, and Yambes village.

REFERENCES

Allen, B. J., T. Nen, R. M. Bourke, R. L. Hide, D. Fritsch, R. Grau, P. Hobsbawn, and S. Lyon. 1996. *Agricultural Systems of Papua New Guinea, Working Paper 15, Central Province*. Canberra: Australian National University.

Enyi, B. A. C. 1972. "The effects of seed size and spacing on growth and yield of lesser yam (*Dioscorea esculenta*)", *Journal of Agricultural Science*, No. 78, pp. 215–225.

Hanson, L. W., B. J. Allen, R. M. Bourke, and T. J. McCarthy. 2001. *Papua New Guinea Rural Development Handbook*. Canberra: Australian National University.

Lea, D. A. M. 1964. "Abelam land and sustenance." PhD thesis, Australian National University, Canberra.

McCoy, S. 2000. "The effects of shifting cultivation on plant diversity of tropical secondary forests: A comparative study of two regions with different population sizes in East Sepik Province, Papua New Guinea." Canberra, unpublished manuscript.

Novotny, V., Y. Basset, S. E. Miller, P. Drozd, and L. Cizek. 2002. "Hot specialization of leaf-chewing insects in a New Guinea rainforest", *Journal of Animal Ecology*, No. 71, pp. 400–412.

Umezaki, M., T. Yamauchi, and R. Ohtsuka. 1999. "Diet among the Huli in Papua New Guinea Highlands when they were influenced by the extended rainy period", *Ecology of Food and Nutrition*, No. 37, pp. 409–427.

Umezaki, M., M. Kuchikura, T. Yamauchi, and R. Ohtsuka. 2000. "Impact of population pressure on food production: An analysis of land-use change and subsistence pattern in the Tari basin in Papua New Guinea Highlands", *Human Ecology*, No. 28, pp. 259–381.

Yamauchi, T., M. Umezaki, and R. Ohtsuka. 2001. "Physical activity and subsistence pattern of the Huli, a Papua New Guinea Highland population", *American Journal of Physical Anthropology*, No. 114, pp. 258–268.

11

Peru

Miguel Pinedo-Vasquez, Pilar Paredes del Aguila, Roberto Romero, Michelle Rios, and Mario Pinedo-Panduro

Introduction

A remarkable adaptive diversity characterizes smallholder farming in Peruvian Amazonia, where the dynamism of the great river is even more marked than in the lower reaches described in Chapter 3. The resultant agrobiodiversity and other forms of biological diversity are the main resources upon which smallholder farmers, here known as *ribereños*, depend. Since the mid-1990s PLEC has been engaged in demonstration activities in villages located in the Sector Muyuy floodplain to identify, test, and promote production technologies that are both biodiversity friendly and economically rewarding (Figure 11.1). Over the years PLEC-Peru has found that demonstration methods are effective tools for recording agrodiversity and evaluating agrobiodiversity and other forms of biological diversity that are produced, managed, and conserved by *ribereños*. Through complex agrodiversity practices *ribereños* use the highly dynamic Muyuy environments to produce a great diversity of crops while creating habitats for endangered and overexploited species of fish, river turtles, plants, and other wildlife.

The *ribereño* approach of "producing to conserve and conserving to produce" allows them to conserve a great diversity of varieties and species of crops in their fields, house gardens, fallows, and forests. In addition, agrodiversity practices enable the small farmers to maintain a broad resource base that helps them obtain both food and cash income in difficult times when

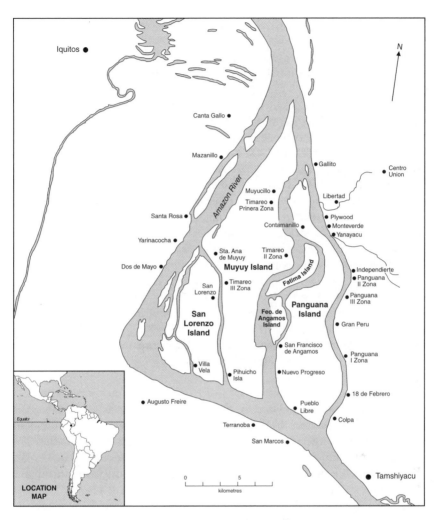

Figure 11.1 Muyuy in 1999

government agricultural loans and other services are withdrawn. The social and economic values of *ribereño* agrodiversity are emphasized in this chapter. PLEC-Peru believes that the demonstration approach is a critical concept for understanding how biodiversity can be conserved, managed, and produced in a sustainable way. Meaningful attempts at biodiversity conservation must begin at the interface between the ecological and social processes and incorporate locally developed knowledge and agrodiversity practices.

Evolution of the cluster and its work

After the cluster in Brazil was established (Chapter 3) it was proposed, in 1995, to form an additional group in Peru, where Pinedo-Vasquez and Pinedo-Panduro (1998), together with others, had already been working for several years. Work began in 1995–1996 but, because of supposed competition with another GEF proposal in Peru, government sponsorship was not obtained, and from 1998 work in Peru has been supported only from UNU funds and local sources. PLEC-Peru has maintained a small interdisciplinary team composed of three Peruvian researchers, three field assistants, six expert farmers, and two students from the local university in Iquitos (Universidad Nacional de la Amazonia Peruana, UNAP). Although the team trained an average of nine graduate and undergraduate students per year, only two were incorporated into the team. Three professors from UNAP and two from the Instituto de Investigaciones de la Amazonia Peruana (IIAP, Research Institute of Peruvian Amazonia) provided technical advice and access to laboratories and libraries. During the years of the project the team worked in partnership with IIAP and its director was one of the team's main advisers. In addition, a working relationship was maintained with leaders of the regional farmers' union (Federacion de Campesinos y Nativos de Loreto). From the outset a relationship was developed with a local NGO, the Centro del Hombre, Ambiente y Conocimiento de Recursos Amazonicos (CHACRA).

The nature and composition of the PLEC-Peru team has played a key role in the implementation and monitoring of demonstration activities. Villagers have appreciated the inclusion of expert farmers. With their help, PLEC attracted large participant groups to demonstration activities. The selection and training of field assistants from the villages also played a key role in advancing the exchange of technologies and germplasm during and after demonstration activities. The participation of local researchers with roots in rural communities also helped in negotiations and the establishment of partnerships with selected expert farmers, as well as with local authorities and others working in rural development and conservation programmes in the floodplains of Peruvian Amazonia.

Although the PLEC-Peru team has few core members, other researchers, farmers, leaders, and local experts participated in the processes of designing, planning, and carrying out demonstration activities. The participation of researchers from local research institutions provided valuable information on the activities of other institutions working in floodplain villages. This helped the PLEC team identify factors that promote successful demonstration activities and active participation of smallholders. Similarly, the close interaction with village and union leaders helped the team develop friendly and trusting relationships with villagers within and outside PLEC sites in Muyuy.[1]

The Muyuy floodplain

The area is immediately upstream from Iquitos, where the Amazon flood-plain has a width of more than 20 km and a very dynamic geomorphology. The area of the floodplain known as Sector Muyuy is approximately 292 km^2, of which approximately 223 km^2 is land and 69 km^2 is river during the season when river levels are at about an annual midpoint. Muyuy is one of the most densely populated rural floodplain regions in Amazonia, with about 67 people per square kilometre. *Ribereños* are the largest population group. Over the last few years the population has grown slowly, from approximately 3,560 in 1995 to 3,810 in 2002. Although eight villages changed their locations due to lateral erosion of the river, the population remained distributed in 38 villages during the period. The age and gender composition of the Sector Muyuy population is roughly similar to that of other Amazonian regions. The population is remarkably young and constantly moving between the villages and the city of Iquitos. Each family has relatives in the city and the majority of them maintain a house in the shanty towns of Iquitos. The *ribereños* of Muyuy and neighbouring communities are typically engaged in multiple production activities.

Muyuy is an area dominated by a yearly flood cycle during which river levels rise and fall over nine metres on average. When river levels are at their lowest annual level the land area increases by about 30 per cent; when the river is at its highest level virtually all land disappears. Due to its location within a highly dynamic floodplain, Muyuy has a diversity of environments exposed to flooding of varying intensities and frequencies, riverbank erosion, and deposition due to lateral migration and other powerful fluvio-dynamic processes. The exact timing and height of floods vary from year to year.

In 1999 there was a flood of exceptional, though not unprecedented, height associated with the La Niña event (Pinedo-Vasquez 2000). There were some important changes in the river channels, eroding away islands and levees, and all levees were under water for at least 45 days. Along 90 km of river channel, 468 ha of new silt bars were created. Silt and sand, more of the former than the latter, were deposited on fields and in fallows. However, the majority of farmers interviewed did not perceive the high flood as a catastrophic event. The flood brought benefits such as an abundance of fish, a decline in the population of fieldmice and other pests, and the deposition of fertile new sediments in their fields. Farmers reported that they tend to lose their agricultural crops more to pests than to floods. Although most bananas, plantains, papayas, and other semi-perennial plants were lost, most of these had been harvested before the floods came and seeds and other planting materials had been stored in houses or elsewhere. Some germ-plasm buried beneath mulch was uncovered to germinate after the flood was over.

The flood regime is not the only agent of change and instability in Muyuy; there are multiple social processes and events that shape the social and nat-ural landscapes. Socio-economic factors are also constantly altering the availability of resources and the value of what is produced. Historically, Muyuy has been the site of timber extraction and commercial cultivation of sugarcane, rice, jute and other products, and livestock. Political change and globalization have long played important roles in the lives of Muyuy resi-dents by creating periods of boom and bust that profoundly changed impor-tant resources of the region. At the beginning of the twentieth century there was a firewood boom to fuel steamboats on the river. During the First World War a turtle-egg boom provided a substitute for olive oil on the world market. Small estates (*fundos*) were established and then collapsed in the 1940s and 1950s. The 1950s and 1960s saw a timber boom, supplying the international demand for high-grade wood. In the 1970s oil exploration gave rise to a short-lived boom. Agricultural loans for farmers were intro-duced in the 1980s, only to be abolished in the 1990s under the Fujimori regime. Also in the 1990s, the national agrarian bank (the main source of rural loans) was closed down, the minimum price guarantees for cash crops such as rice were abolished, and the government rural extension agency closed down. In order to endure and prosper in this environment, the Muyuy residents developed technologies and strategies for managing and maintaining high levels of biodiversity, widening the resource base on which they depend.

Agrodiversity at Muyuy

The diversity of landscape elements such as water bodies, land forms, set-tlements, natural forest, agricultural fields, fallows, and forest gardens pro-duces a great diversity of habitats, making Muyuy one of the floodplain regions with the highest beta diversity (β) in Amazonia. Such landscape heterogeneity offers farmers many potential agro-environments. Farmers identify and select agro-environments by practising horizontal and vertical zonation. Based on landscape and land-use surveys conducted in 1995 and 2001, the four main land forms – high levee, low levee, silt bar, and sand bar – offer several environments to *ribereños* for production of crops (Table 11.1).

Table 11.1 Agro-environments used by *ribereños* in the four main land forms of the Muyuy floodplain

Land forms	Average number of agro-environments
High levee	34
Low levee	17
Sand bar	7
Silt bar	3

Note: Average numbers were estimated using data collected in three land surveys (1995, 1999, and 2001) in 38 villages.

High levees and low levees offer more agro-environments than silt and sand bars. While high levees are exposed only to unusually high floods and low levees, being inland, are not exposed to strong river currents, silt and sand bars are very unstable and are affected by both floods and river currents. Each one of the land forms is characterized by micro-topographic variations that offer different conditions for production and management. In addition to relief and other horizontal variations, the landscape of Muyuy presents important vertical variation that facilitates the formation of different agro-environments. Different degrees of canopy opening provide a series of light gradients for the growth of shade-tolerant and shade-intolerant species. Vertical layering of vegetation produces a variety of agro-environments in the canopy and subcanopy and suppresses layers of the forests. Vertical zonation helps *ribereños* choose and manage light gradients that are suitable for agroforestry and agriculture fields.

The degree to which agro-environments are used for production and management of resources varies during the aquatic (*creciente*) and terrestrial (*merma*) phases. In the highly dynamic landscape the number of agro-environments in each land form is constantly changing. After floods, farmers expect changes in the area and soil of sand and silt bars and are ready to change the species and varieties of crops planted. Every year the team observed that some areas of sand bars became silt bars or vice versa after floods.

Changes in land forms and agro-environments enhance rather than limit agrodiversity. Household surveys found that *ribereños* use a great diversity of technologies for the production, management, and conservation of resources (Table 11.2). Using complex technologies, they maintain large numbers of species and varieties of annual plants as well as habitats for wildlife and fish. For instance, the *tablone* system (cluster system) allows farmers to plant beans in beaches to create a habitat for fish during the flood season. Similarly, the *ladera* system (edge system) helps farmers reduce damage to corn and other crops by rodents such as capybaras, by planting sugarcane at the margin of fields made in low and high levees. On

Table 11.2 Average number of management systems and techniques used by *ribereños* to farm in the four main land forms

Land form	Number of systems	Number of techniques
High levees	32	53
Low levees	17	36
Sand bars	8	18
Silt bars	5	12

Table 11.3 Average number of land-use stages maintained by *ribereños* to farm the four main land forms

Land-use stage	High levees	Low levees	Sand bars	Silt bars
Fields	9	5	3	2
Fallows	18	13	1	1
House gardens	4	2	0	0
Forests	7	11	0	0

the relatively stable levees farmers practise a greater number of production and management systems and techniques than on the unstable silt and sand bars.

The combination of production and management practices allows farmers to build and maintain different kinds, sizes, and ages of fields, fallows, house gardens, and forests (Table 11.3). Each surveyed household, for example, maintains a field or fallow for trapping rodents and land birds. Similarly, managing forest for multiple uses, including fishing, explains why *ribereños* maintain more different kinds of forest in low rather than in high levees. In contrast, more kinds of fallows are managed in high than in low levees, because farmers need the areas for making fields or planting agroforestry species that are less resistant to floods. *Ribereños* also make more kinds of house gardens in high than low levee areas. The two kinds of house gardens managed on low levees produce habitats for fish and help farmers to catch fish during the flood season. The multifunctionality of farmers' technologies has helped to conserve biodiversity because of, not in spite of, the dynamism.

Biodiversity in the landholdings of *ribereños*

Ribereño landholdings contain an immense diversity of species, ecosystems, landscapes, and environments. The large number of species and varieties of crops allows them to keep farming the four main land forms (Figure 11.2). The varieties of beans, rice, water-melon, and other annual crops are par-

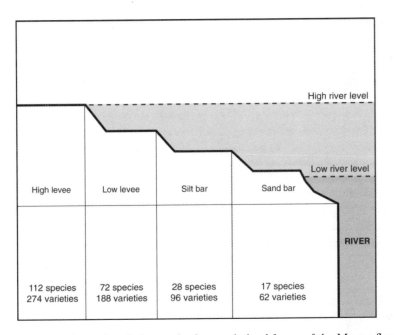

High river level

Low river level

High levee	Low levee	Silt bar	Sand bar

RIVER

| 112 species | 72 species | 28 species | 17 species |
| 274 varieties | 188 varieties | 96 varieties | 62 varieties |

Figure 11.2 Species and varieties on the four main land forms of the Muyuy flood-plain

ticularly adapted to the flood pulse. Some of the varieties locally known as *dos mesinos* (two months) are planted on the lowest parts of silt and sand bars. Most varieties of annual crops planted on silt and sand bars can withstand floods and remain under water for at least two weeks. Crops that remain alive under water attract fish and river turtles, making it easy to fish and farm.

The general pattern observed in Muyuy and reflected in the biodiversity inventory data is that smallholders tend to maintain or in some cases increase levels of biodiversity in all land-use stages. Plant species that produce valuable forest products are planted and incorporated in fields, fallows, forests, and house gardens. It is common to find seedlings of timber and forest fruit species growing in fields. The range of Shannon index values ($H' = 0.91$ to 1.87) show that *ribereños* maintain biodiversity-rich fields in the very dynamic floodplain (Table 11.4). In most cases *ribereños* have purposely planted fewer crops in their fields in order to encourage the natural regeneration of valuable shrubs and trees. Such strategies explain why it is common to find fallow areas where the density of juveniles of timber and other valuable tree species is very high.

Management of fallows for multiple uses, including habitats for rodents, land birds, and fish, enables *ribereños* to obtain many products for their

Table 11.4 Species richness and Shannon index of fields made on levees by 11 households

Area sampled (ha)	Number of individuals	Species richness	Shannon index
175	323	8	1.10
849	7,104	13	1.10
162	115	8	0.91
3,535	606	13	1.87
192	236	8	1.26
612	773	7	1.06
207	357	9	1.62
354	835	11	1.73
1,848	166	10	1.33
800	1,364	12	1.66
319	180	12	1.29

Note: Average size of each field was 0.5 ha.

Table 11.5 Species richness and estimated Shannon index for six managed fallows

Area sampled (m²)	Number of individuals	Species richness	Shannon index
900	114	25	2.80
900	363	38	2.35
342	55	10	1.99
900	259	36	2.45
900	369	72	3.68
900	158	22	1.79

consumption and the market. Each household maintains fallow areas under different intensities of management (Table 11.5). Differences in the range of Shannon index values (H′ = 1.79 to 3.68) among fallows demonstrate that biodiversity levels vary considerably with the intensity and frequency of the interventions. Interviewed farmers corroborated the estimated Shannon index values by mentioning that fallow vegetation where no management operations are conducted tend to be dominated by *cetico* (*Cecropia membraneaceae*). Farmers control the establishment and dominance of *cetico* by managing the spatial arrangement of valuable species to allow them to compete with this fast-growing species. The application of such management strategies varies not only among households but also among villages. Some farmers maintain more biodiverse fallows than those in other villages. These farmers are locally known to be *purmeros* (fallow users) due to the amount of fallow products that they consume and sell.

The majority of forest areas that are part of the landholdings of *ribereños* are the results of successive management operations that began at the field stage and continued into the fallow and forest stages. Inventories of a sam-

Table 11.6 Species richness and estimated Shannon index in nine managed forests

Area sampled (m²)	Number of individuals	Species richness	Shannon index
900	501	81	2.50
900	182	82	2.43
900	258	74	3.60
900	252	96	3.09
900	402	74	1.77
900	352	82	3.71
900	417	88	3.98
900	361	93	2.48
900	272	78	1.29

ple of nine plots of multiple-age managed forest (each 900 m² in size) show that these forests have high levels of species richness (Table 11.6). The mean average number of plant species per hectare estimated in the nine plots is greater (83) than the number found in forests that were reported as unmanaged (52). The range of variation in the Shannon index (H' = 1.77 to 3.98) is similar in pattern to that estimated for managed fallows. The differences in species richness and Shannon index values among forests reflect the histories of management and resource extraction practised by their owners.

Field observation and interviews suggest that some *ribereños* are more dedicated to enriching their forest with timber species, while others are more interested in fruit and medicinal species. Despite the abundance of commercially valuable plant species, inventory data show that *ribereños* also maintain small numbers of individuals of some non-commercial species. Among these are pioneer species such as *Cecropia membraneaceae* that play an important role in attracting game animals and fish during floods. *Ribereños* constantly keep removing individuals of *Cecropia* and other fast-growing species to make light available for the regeneration of more valuable species. By removing adult individuals and encouraging the establishment and growth of seedlings and juveniles, farmers maintain forests where the density of individuals is correlated with the number of species (Figure 11.3).

House gardens are also very important reservoirs of biodiversity, with many species and varieties of herbs, vines, shrubs, grasses, and trees. There is more variation in the number of individuals and species planted in house gardens than in fallows and forests (Figure 11.4). Variation in species and density of individuals reflects different uses of house gardens. While some are used more for ornamentation and shade, others serve as nurseries and for experimenting with the cultivation of forest or exotic species. In most cases house gardens provide fruits, medicinal plants, and other resources for

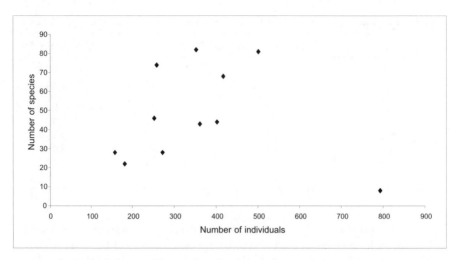

Figure 11.3 Comparison of species richness and number of individuals in 10 managed forests (average area 0.9 ha)
Note: All trees greater than or equal to 5 cm DBH were inventoried.

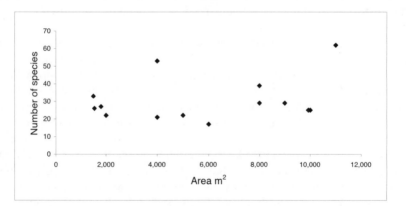

Figure 11.4 Comparison of area and species richness for 13 house gardens

consumption and the market. The kind of uses and the intensity of management reflect variation in species richness among house gardens (Table 11.7).

The biodiversity surveys discussed here demonstrate the great diversity of resources produced, managed, and protected by *ribereños* in their landholdings.

Table 11.7 Species richness and estimated Shannon index in 14 house gardens

Area sampled (m²)	Number of individuals	Species richness	Shannon index
9,928	401	25	2.15
1,176	1,584	62	3.19
8,000	568	29	2.44
1,800	135	27	2.88
8,000	765	39	2.03
2,000	259	22	2.40
1,500	303	33	2.25
1,539	109	26	2.24
4,000	480	21	1.86
6,000	161	17	2.31
9,000	210	29	2.37
5,000	696	22	2.01
10,000	353	25	1.75
4,000	337	53	3.24

Demonstration activities

Peruvian Amazonia government agencies play at most a very marginal role in rural development and conservation programmes, and in Muyuy, as in much of rural Amazonia, they are conducted by NGOs. Although PLEC-Peru did not function as an NGO, the residents of Muyuy at first perceived the team as one. Despite the team explaining that PLEC activities differed substantively from other "training courses", most farmers, particularly the leaders, initially did not identify PLEC's efforts as different.

After speaking with farmers about demonstration activities and how the team was interested in promoting local techniques, it emerged that the majority of them wanted to see results before they decided to incorporate any demonstrated techniques in their own repertoires. The expert farmers were involved in designing, planning, and implementing the demonstration activities, and they used their fields to demonstrate their management techniques and show concrete examples of the results. Gradually most farmers discovered that PLEC activities were different. Experimental and training centres were not used, but rather the fields, house gardens, fallows, and forests of expert and successful farmers.

Most farmers valued training courses as opportunities to socialize rather than to learn production techniques. Consequently, PLEC-Peru promoted demonstration activities as part of village or intervillage meetings (*reuniones*) and incorporated some social activities during the first year of the project. Expert farmers told the team that most farmers learn new techniques while working in *mingas* and by participating in *visitas a la familia*.

Mingas are shared labour groups organized by members of households to help each other with agricultural activities, and *visitas* are typically gatherings of families or close friends. In both the informal and more formal meetings, expert farmers are the leading figures and the ones who invite participants to demonstration sites. For the Peruvian team, demonstration activities provided an opportunity for identifying and critically analysing the processes and methods by which information is transferred and shared among *ribereño* farmers.

Over the five years, PLEC-Peru held an average of 12 *reuniones*, 60 *mingas*, and 25 *visitas* per year (Table 11.8). The largest number of participants were involved in *mingas* and the smallest in *visitas*. The increased participation of farmers in *mingas* is now greatly helping expert farmers to promote biodiversity-friendly and economically rewarding resource-use systems within and outside the Muyuy floodplain.

Although PLEC-Peru identified a large number of successful production and management systems and techniques (Table 11.2), only a few of these have been promoted in demonstration activities (Table 11.9). The main reason for this is because the expert farmers who are using them are still not willing to demonstrate them as part of PLEC activities. Expert farmers are demonstrating nine systems for producing and managing resources on higher levees (Table 11.9), four systems for planting crops on low levees, three systems to cultivate annual crops on sand bars, and two systems for planting rice and other crops on silt bars.

Most farmers who participated in demonstration activities have begun testing the techniques they learned from the expert farmers and observed at demonstration sites. They do not copy the demonstrated techniques, but combine these ideas with their own and create new techniques after a long process of experimentation. Exchange of knowledge and experiences among farmers is most successful in an informal environment. This makes it difficult to monitor the flow of initiatives. PLEC-Peru has overcome this problem by maintaining a team with a strong rural background and experience of working with *ribereños*; the team spends time in the field, conducting field observations, following farmers in their daily activities, and

Table 11.8 Average number of demonstration activities and participants from 1995 to February 2002

Demonstration activities	Average activities per year	Total number of participants	Average participants per activity
Reuniones	12	360	30
Mingas	60	1,140	19
Visitas	25	225	9

Table 11.9 Production and management systems demonstrated by expert farmers over five years

List of systems	Description
High levees	
Vuelito	Production of vegetables, spices, and medicinal herbs under shade
Bajada	Management of trees and vines that are tolerant to high humidity
Ladera	Production of annual or semi-annual crops at the edge of fields
Shunto	Production of spices and vegetables using ashes
Quiruma	Production of medicinal herbs and spices around tree stems
Retama	Production of beans, corn, and banana using leguminous trees
Estacas	A system to produce beans using poles of a *Gynerium* species
Ensombrado	A system to produce annual and semi-annual crops under trees
Huactapeo	A system for the management of seedlings of trees in fields and fallows
Low levees	
Encañdo	A system for controlling rain-water in fields
Enposado	A system that helps to maintain high humidity for rice production
Enpurmado	A system of leaving weeds to control infestation of insects on corn
Sogal	A system for managing selected vines in fallows and forests
Sand bars	
Tablone	A system for planting beans, peanuts, and water-melon in blocks
Hilera	A system for planting water-melon at the edge of sand bars
Tacarpeo	A system for planting cassava with squash in the highest part of sand bars
Silt bars	
Voleo	A system for planting pre-germinated rice in the lowest part of silt bars
Regado	A system for planting rice in the highest part of silt bars

engaging in informal conversations with farmers. Daily observations are recorded and a database record kept for each household whose members participated in demonstration activities. While the strategy used by the team is helping to document the expert farmer-to-farmer exchange, recording the flow of knowledge is still the most difficult and complex problem faced in the application of PLEC methods.

Conclusions and recommendations

Ribereños in Muyuy do not separate conservation from production, as is done by experts engaged in the promotion of conventional development and conservation programmes. The dynamic nature of the floodplain with a high local turnover of habitats and species creates ecological conditions for practising resource-use systems where conservation and production are united. Like their counterparts in Brazil (Chapter 3), residents of Muyuy "produce to conserve and conserve to produce" as part of a long tradition of making their livelihoods in a rich but highly risky environment characterized by extreme natural and social dynamism. Agrodiversity has allowed *ribereños* to profit economically while enhancing the conservation of floodplain biodiversity.

Ribereño production and management systems and conservation practices are valuable technological resources that can help to reduce the current rates of biodiversity loss while enhancing income sources for the rural poor. The authors offer the following recommendations for promoting and integrating small-farmer technologies into rural development and conservation programmes.

The transfer of technologies in *ribereño* societies is mainly through existing formal and informal channels rather than through training courses or other urban-style forms of training. PLEC's demonstration approach provides the framework for using the existing forms of farmer interaction. It is recommended that demonstration activities be more frequently employed in rural development programmes, using existing forms of social gathering.

The promotion of farmers' technologies is greatly facilitated when it is conducted by farmers. The inclusion of expert farmers as team members of rural extension programmes dedicated to train farmers is recommended, although it is important to identify and select the right individuals to do this training. It was found that in rural communities, the leaders or more outspoken members are often less qualified to promote successful and innovative farmer technologies. However, there are individuals who are well known by other members of the communities as good farmers with particular techniques for the production, management, and conservation of resources.

It is important to use the fields, fallows, forests, and house gardens of expert farmers as demonstration sites. *Ribereños* are generally very pragmatic, and they like to see results and not to hear about results of particular production systems or techniques tested under unfamiliar conditions. In addition, farmers tend to value the promoted technology more when they see how successful the expert farmer is. Those promoting the integration of farmer technologies and conservation initiatives in development and conservation programmes should be clear in how they aim to satisfy the farmers' agenda and not merely the priorities of the outside institutions. In many cases farmers have refused to participate in demonstration activities when it was not clear how they would benefit.

There are many programmes for inventorying biodiversity and uses of biodiversity in the Peruvian Amazonia. PLEC-Peru recommends that, as part of these programmes, some efforts should go to inventories of production and management systems as well as conservation initiatives used by farmers.

PLEC-Peru's experiences have resulted in several strategies useful in a wider social context than just that of Muyuy. The team helps rural community leaders summarize the results of demonstration activities and present them to government officials. The documents are used in discussion with government representatives for promotion of new demonstration activities. Visits to demonstration sites and demonstration sessions with expert farmers are organized for people working in development and conservation, and for politicians. The team produces manuals, posters, and pamphlets that illustrate the production technologies and conservation practices promoted.

Members of PLEC-Peru are also advising the government on the design of new rural development and conservation policies. While *ribereños* were the main target group in PLEC-Peru work, there are important impacts of the project on the way politicians, NGOs, researchers, and students think about rural development and conservation. The following are some of the most relevant impacts of the results of PLEC-Peru work.

- There has been interest expressed by local university officials in introducing PLEC ideas into a new curriculum for training agronomists, biologists, foresters, and sociologists. This development indicates a substantive change of view among university officials.
- All of the 34 students who were trained and advised by PLEC-Peru have graduated and are currently working in key positions in NGOs and government institutions. They are facilitating the incorporation of PLEC methodology and thus changing the rural development and conservation programmes of NGOs and government agencies.
- The demonstration sites of PLEC-Peru and the experienced expert farmers have been used by NGOs and government conservation officials as examples of the sustainable use of biodiversity. Two of the most influential elected local politicians are helping the team frame a proposal for implementing demonstration activities as part of rural extension.

Publications

In total, PLEC-Peru has published 18 articles and has submitted 13 others for peer-reviewed publication. Three books are in preparation. The team has also published nine chapters in books, and 16 are in press. Locally, 26 pamphlets have been published, and eight others are in preparation.

Note

1. Work began seriously with a set of meetings in 1996–1997. Preliminary organization was done by team members Mario Pinedo and Jose Barletti, in close collaboration with organized rural teachers of the floodplain upstream from Iquitos and with the rural workers of the Catholic Church. Three inter-community meetings were held, each lasting three days. The first meeting involved a total of 78 farmers from 25 hamlets and communities. The second engaged 83 *ribereños* from 46 communities. The third involved 65 farmers from 34 communities. The PLEC team helped to carry out the meetings and provided transportation and food for all farmer participants.

REFERENCES

Pinedo-Vasquez, M. 2000. "Changes in the natural and social landscapes produced by the 1999 high flood near Iquitos, Amazonia", *PLEC News and Views*, No. 15, pp. 31–37.

Pinedo-Vasquez, M. and M. Pinedo-Panduro. 1998. "From forests to fields: Incorporating smallholder knowledge in the *camu-camu* programme in Peru", *PLEC News and Views*, No. 10, pp. 17–26.

12

Mexico

*Octavio Castelán-Ortega, Carlos González Esquivel,
Carlos Arriaga Jordán, and Cristina Chávez Mejia*

History of PLEC work in Mexico

Centro de Investigación en Ciencias Agropecuarias (CICA) joined the
PLEC project in July 1997 with funding for 1997–1998. Further work was
carried out during separate periods as funding became available from 1999
to December 2001. The Universidad Autónoma del Estado de Mexico provided complementary funds during the three project stages. Two NGOs,
AMEXTRA (Asociación Mexicana para la Transformación Rural y
Urbana) and GIRA (Grupo Interdisciplinario de Tecnologia Rural Apro-
priada) joined the project in 1999. Initial activities were documentation of
local resources and their use and management, knowledge of agrodiversity,
conservation of indigenous varieties of maize through simple techniques
for seed selection, and the characterization of local and introduced plants
in home gardens.

The main objective of the project was to develop participatory sustainable models for the conservation and enrichment of local biodiversity
within current agricultural systems and to improve livelihoods of
campesinos through the rescue of the traditional Mesoamerican *milpa*, the
system of growing maize intercropped with vegetables. Demonstration
activities included on-farm trials conducted by farmers.

Site selection

Three villages, in two highland regions of central Mexico, were chosen as project sites (Figure 12.1). CICA and AMEXTRA were working in the Mazahua region in the western part of the state of Mexico in the communities of San Pablo Tlalchichilpa (San Pablo) and Mayorazgo in the municipality of San Felipe del Progreso and in San Marcos de la Loma (San Marcos) in the municipality of Villa Victoria. The Mazahua people are the second largest indigenous group in the state and also one of the poorest in the country. The AMEXTRA team expanded the activities to Yebucivi, the neighbouring Mazahua village, in the municipality of Almoloya de Juárez.

In San Pablo CICA has been working on agrodiversity management since 1996. A very close and successful relationship has developed with the community. In Mayorazgo the relationship with the families was less fluent than in San Pablo and the *campesinos* were less disposed to participate in projects, making monitoring work more difficult.

The municipality of San Felipe del Progreso is located in the northern part of the state of Mexico and lies between 19°28′ and 19°47′07″ north and 99°52′02″ and 100°16′26″ west. The climate is temperate subhumid with an average annual temperature of 10.3°C and annual rainfall of more than 800 mm. The CICA team rented a house in San Pablo with a *solar* of one hectare divided into three plots where several project activities were undertaken with the active participation of *campesinos*. It served as the main site for demonstration activities and workshops over the duration of the project. Inhabitants of the neighbouring villages of San Francisco Tlalchichilpa and San Juan Coajomulco expressed their interest and enthusiasm in project activities, so they were invited to participate and attended some of the workshops organized in San Pablo. In the state of Michoacán, Casas Blancas, in the municipality of Salvador Escalante, is the village where GIRA has worked and which became the centre of PLEC project activities. The region is in the highlands of the Pátzcuaro area of Michoacán, 420 km northwest of Mexico City, and is home to the Purepecha indigenous people. The project activities were expanded in the neighbouring village of Santa Isabel.

Method for characterization of farming systems

For the first stage of the project a formal survey was carried out, complemented by participatory methods including direct interviews, use of key informants and expert farmers, workshops, and field-days with farmers. Some farmers were selected and monitored for the duration of the project.

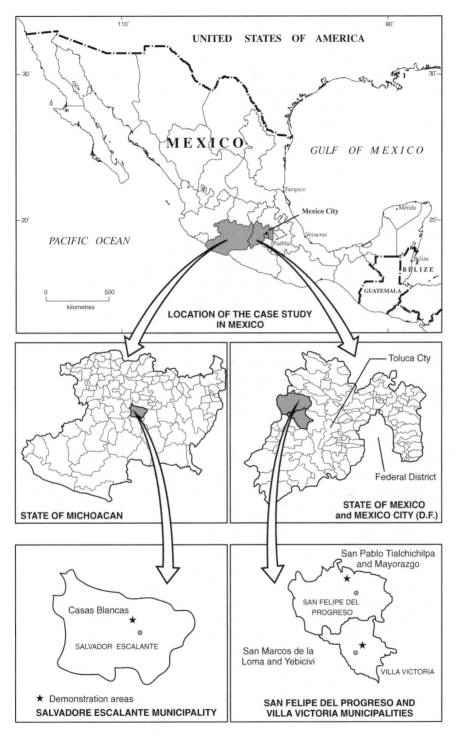

Figure 12.1 Central Mexico, showing demonstration sites

Later the use of expert farmers and on-farm trials was a key part of the work, because it permitted evaluation of the relationship between maize production and soil type, the temporal use of *solares*, and recording of the different plant species found in them. A literature review of *campesino* farming systems and biodiversity preservation and enhancement in Mexico and other developing countries was also carried out. Twenty-nine *campesino* families took part in the early part of the project, with 20 from San Pablo and nine from Mayorazgo.

In the continuing studies the use and management of plant species, the variation between land types and use by different farmers, and intercropping practices were monitored. Twenty-five farms (13 in San Pablo Tlalchichilpa and 12 in Mayorazgo) were visited at least once each month to record all the activities undertaken throughout the year. Open and semi-structured interviews were held, as well as participant observation of agricultural activities. Group discussions and workshops were also held. Monitored farms in San Pablo were selected to represent a range of sizes and farming practices. In Mayorazgo, where participation was more difficult, monitored farms were those participating in the study of the *campesino solar*. A similar approach was used in San Marcos and Casas Blancas. Work in the second stage of the project was concentrated on the rescue of the traditional *milpa* in all sites.

The role of livestock in the livelihoods of Mazahua *campesino* households was also evaluated in the villages of San Pablo in the sector of La Era and in Mayorazgo. Livestock are a very important aspect of the daily life and a major source of savings (Arriaga-Jordán *et al.* 1997). An inventory of animal resources per household was made. Ninety-five households were interviewed in the sector of La Era, representing 69 per cent of the households in the community. In Mayorazgo, 47 households or 10 per cent of the community were interviewed. After the initial census, 25 households were visited every eight weeks and open interviews were conducted. Changes in animal inventories were recorded, as well as any transactions in cash or in kind, with opportunity costs or values ascribed to the animals or their products and by-products (like manure) when contributions were in kind.

Given the scarcity of forage, some forage crops were promoted for cultivation in the fallow and for improving soil fertility by GIRA in Casas Blancas. Crops included faba beans (*Vicia faba*), peas (*Pisum sativum*), and rye grass. AMEXTRA carried out several on-farm trials to evaluate maize-faba bean intercropping and faba monocropping. A workshop was organized to plan the establishment of traditional *milpa* demonstration sites. Landrace seeds of faba beans were provided to 75 farmers, and 10 fields were selected as demonstration sites and monitored by the project's staff throughout the production cycle.

The landscape

Historic information on the north-western area of the state of Mexico and the Mazahua people goes back to pre-Columbian times. Information on San Pablo Tlalchichilpa and Mayorazgo from the early 1930s was based mainly on accounts of the older members of the community. The village of San Pablo Tlalchichilpa originally comprised a cluster of houses built around the Catholic church. By the 1960s, with the growth of the population, settlement of the north part was initiated on what was considered common land that mostly had not been assigned to anybody. These were forested areas and open grasslands (*llanos*) which were used for grazing animals.

San Pablo at present is comprised of four sectors. The settlement began in what is now known as the sector of La Era. *Era* means "threshing ground" in Spanish, and the sector takes its name from the *era* built by one of the first *campesinos* for threshing the oats and wheat that were commonly sown at that time. Early settlement was arbitrary and not planned. It consisted of felling the forest, building houses, and opening land for cultivation and roads. Families settled and established the number and size of their plots according to the labour they had available.

The two main land types are *monte* (forest) and *ejido*. The *monte* refers mainly to the forested area and the open grasslands (*llanos*) in the northern part of the village. This area has been used mainly for extractive purposes and grazing. It provides a number of products, some of which have now disappeared, such as wild grassland mushrooms (*hongos de los llanos*). Other products, although still available, have deteriorated severely, such as trees that provide firewood and wild plants and animals. Both the *monte* and the *ejido* are not associated with a strong sense of belonging or ownership by the inhabitants of La Era, since they are common areas for the four sectors.

The *ejido* land type is located in what was the cultivated land of the hacienda that formerly owned the area. The hacienda was expropriated after the land reform following the Mexican revolution of 1910–1917. Until 1992 the land was socially tenured. The majority of inhabitants of all sectors got access to plots where now maize cultivation predominates. *Ejidatarios* (*campesinos* with rights to *ejido* land) could hold their *ejido* land in usufruct since it was national property, but could not sell or rent their plots. However, they could bequeath the land to one of their children, usually the elder son. The endowment of *ejido* land was intended to satisfy the needs of a family. It varied in size in different parts of the country, partly in relation to the productive potential of the land but mostly in relation to population pressure, with smaller endowments in central and southern Mexico and larger endowments in northern Mexico. Current tenure is discussed below.

In terms of current cropping patterns, diversity has a direct relationship with the period that the plots have been opened to cultivation. In older plots more work has been invested to improve the quality of the fields, through the restoration of eroded land or the incorporation of soil amendments like "white sand" and organic matter such as manure and plant residues (Chávez-Mejía, Nava Bernal, and Arriaga Jordán 1998). The older plots are usually those adjacent to the houses. Diversity usually decreases with increasing distance of the fields from the house, although this is not the only determining factor. The diversity of the distant fields is also related to the soil types, since *campesinos* clearly identify the areas where it is not possible to grow certain crops. One farmer, for example, stated that "beans will not grow anywhere in the *ejido*". Similarly, *campesinos* identify areas most suitable for particular crops, as two other farmers stated that "in Tabache and Bombaro, faba beans grow well".

Some crops, like wheat and the "purple" and "strawy" barley, were grown before the settlement of La Era, earlier than 1960. By the 1970s these crops had been displaced by maize, in part due to its promotion by government support programmes which gave soft credits for maize cultivation. Another reason for substituting maize is that the grain from the barley, which was used for human consumption, is very hard for grinding. The most recently introduced crops in the community are oats (*Avena sativa*) and common vetch (*Vicia sativa*). Oats were introduced in the 1970s as forage for draught animals, and the demand for them has increased.

Table 12.1 shows how the land is classified by *campesinos* in La Era in San Pablo Tlalchichilpa. The designated names were given by the older farmers, and although some names refer to particular characteristics of the place and there have been changes over time, the original names tend to continue in use.

The presence of a crop in a particular field has a direct relationship with the soil type. Tabache, Bombaro, Barranca grande, Ishi, and Bonlloquiñi have durapan (*tepetate*) and clay soils in different proportions as well as stony areas that do not allow a great diversity of crops to be grown. These soils can only be worked until the rains are well established. Teneria, El Calvario, La Era, Ta peji, Tehi peji, N'dora, and Ranyo have predominantly *polvilla* (silt) soils which are of better quality and improved by the addition of "white sand" and manure. Soil improvement is facilitated in fields near the houses, as the proximity allows greater attention to management. Another aspect determining the location of crops relates to the steepness of the slopes, and possible soil loss through runoff. Soils in Bondabashe and Dolores stages are predominantly hard durapan *tepetates* and, although open due to deforestation, are not used for cropping.

In the current study five land-use stages were identified (Zarin, Guo, and Enu-Kwesi 1999; Brookfield, Stocking, and Brookfield 1999).

Table 12.1 Land-use stages and their use in San Pablo Tlalchichilpa

Land-use stage	Meaning	Use
*Tabache**	Large plain land (*llano*)	Grazing, maize and oat cropping
*Bombaro**	Black dove	Maize, oat, and wheat cropping, and forest
Teneria	Tannery	Grazing, maize, oat, and wheat cropping
Barranca grande	Large gulley	Oat and wheat cropping, and forest
*Ishi**	The apple	Forest and oat and maize cropping
*Bonlloquiñi**	The opuntia cactus (*nopal*)	Opuntia cacti, oat and maize cropping
*Ranyo**	The ranch	Maize cropping
*N'dora**	The peach	Maize cropping
*Ta peji**	Large *tejocote* (crab apple tree)	Maize cropping and forest
*Tehi peji**	Small *tejocote*	Maize cropping
El Calvario		Maize and oat cropping, and forest
La Era	The threshing ground	Central part of the sector, and *solar*
*Bondabashe**	Plenty of "broom" shrubs	Uncultivated plots and firewood collection
Dolores		Uncultivated plots and firewood collection

*Mazahua names written phonetically in Spanish.

- *Milpa.* Usually a field planted with maize in monoculture or associated with other crops, but nowadays also used to refer to other cultivated areas. It may be the field of the *solar*, or other fields which are separate from the house.
- *Solar.* The house buildings and yard, animal pens, and the surrounding field.
- *Monte* (forest). The forested areas of common land from where diverse products and benefits are obtained (firewood, medicinal and ornamental plants, forest soil and "white sand", and wild mushrooms).
- *Llano* (open grassland). Common land that retains some original vegetation, which is used for grazing.
- *Besanas* (field edges) and *orillas* (edges). *Besanas* and edges of roads and footpaths often include a livestock or poultry component.

The milpa *system*

The *milpa* system, in which several landraces of maize are grown in association with a variety of beans and squash types and species, was the basis for the development of pre-Hispanic cultures. It has continued to be a most important agricultural system for *campesinos* in Mexico and Central America into modern times (Ortega-Paczka 1999). Besides indigenous species, *campesinos* readily introduced temperate species into their cropping patterns and this has enabled them to overcome some of the limitations of farming at high altitudes and low temperatures. Among these were the crops brought by the Spaniards, including wheat, barley, and oats, food legumes like the faba bean, lentils (*Lens esculentum*), and peas, and forage legumes such as vetch and alfalfa (*Medicago sativa*). Species were also adopted from other lands. Potatoes (*Solanum tuberosum*) were introduced from South America during the seventeenth century and became the staple crop for communities located above 2,800 m, beyond which maize does not grow.

Over time the *campesinos* have developed local landraces of these temperate crops. The shorter-cycle frost-resistant cereals like wheat and barley complemented or substituted for maize. Farmers plant wheat in years when rains are late and the risk of early frosts damaging a late-sown maize crop is very high, as in 1998 when the El Niño weather pattern disrupted rains in Mexico. Faba beans substituted the common bean (*Phaseolus vulgaris*) in the *milpa* system in the highlands long ago, and elderly people regard faba beans as a traditional component of their *milpas*.

The main advantages of the *milpa* are high production of diverse food crops from small areas, greater availability and variety of food and better nutritional status of the household members, improved soil fertility, increased cash income through the sale of surplus food, and preservation and enhancement of biodiversity. These advantages have particular relevance in the face of diminishing prices for crops brought about by the North American Free Trade Agreement (NAFTA) and increasing costs of inputs for the maize crop now mostly grown as a monoculture in the highlands.

According to the *campesinos*, changes in management over time have been minimal and are due mostly to the availability of labour. Migration of the young members of the community to the cities has resulted in a decrease in the traditional multiple cropping that requires several people at sowing times. Another change has to do with the loss of some useful local plant species due mostly to the increased use of herbicides. Some farmers expressed an interest in recovering them. *Chivitos* (*Calandrinia micrantha*) and turnips (*nabo* or *Brassica campestris*) are local edible plants that are valued because of their taste but are now limited due to herbicide use. People used to collect them from their *milpa*, but now they are found only in fields located in the mountains and a long walk is necessary to get them. Some women collect seeds of *nabo* to sow in their *solar*.

The campesino solar

A characteristic of *campesino* culture and agriculture is the existence of an area with high diversity of animal and vegetable species located next to the family house. The *solar familiar campesino*, a type of home garden, is a place of enjoyment, work, and experimentation and a source of goods. Studies indicate the historic importance of the *solares*. González-Jácome (1985), cited by Herrera (1994), reports a pre-Hispanic origin in central Mexico for managed home gardens, and a number of terms in the Nahua language designate different kinds of home gardens. They were a place for intensive work, with irrigation and high productivity. The early gardens were mainly used for the production of cocoa. They were modified with the arrival of the Spaniards, who introduced new plant species, domestic animals, and tools.

From previous work (Chávez Mejía, Nava Bernal, and Arriaga Jordán 1998), it was found that the people from the study villages do not utilize the word *solar* to refer to the land where their house is settled. Each component is recognized separately as *casa* (house, *inguma* in Mazahua), garden or *huerto* (orchard), *patio* (yard), *milpa* (the adjacent arable field or *juama* in Mazahua), and the borders (*cerca*). *Campesinos* call the *huerto* all the area where fruit trees, medicinal plants, vegetables, and ornamental and condiment plants are grown. The *cerca* (or *conguare* in Mazahua) is often a live fence of maguey (*guaru* or agave cactus).

The *solares* were studied at 23 of the 25 monitored farms (Table 12.2). The arrangement of the *solar* components is not homogeneous and the area allocated to each component by the family is very variable. While the largest *solar* has an area of 4,255 m², the smallest is only 90 m² including the house. The *milpa* is the largest component, with areas ranging from 25 m² to 0.42 ha.

The *campesinos* have three categories of plants. The vegetation of the *solar* includes the trees, medicinal, ornamental, ritual, and food plants grown along with the crops of the *solar milpa*. *Vegetación ruderal* is the spontaneous vegetation from non-agricultural land (different from wild plants found in natural areas) found on edges of roads, fields, footpaths, and the borders of *solares*. *Vegetación arvense* is the associated vegetation or weeds in crops.

There is a specific way of naming the different plant species found in the *solar*. During the study, the colloquial expressions were used: *quelites* (*tzana* in Mazahua) for the edible local plants; *cultivos* ("crops") for maize, pumpkin, beans, and faba beans; ornamentals are *flores* (*dana* in Mazahua); those with no recognized use are *hierbas*; medicinal species are *medicina*; those for fuel are *leña*; and shrub species and fruit trees are *árboles*. Recognizing the distinction was important in order to gain an understanding of how and why people manage and use their resources as they do, and even to be able

Table 12.2 Area for each component of the monitored *solares* in Mayorazgo and San Pablo Tlalchichilpa

Component	Mean area	Area (m²)																						
		1	2	3	4	5	6	7	8	9	10	11	12	13	14	15	16	17	18	19	20	21	22	23
Solar total area	801.3	250	258	1,000	250	250	1,000	750	90	1,000	421	257	4,220	500	500	174	101	4,255	1,000	1,000	250	500	183	250
Milpa	672.0	100	150	600	150	200	750	500	–	582	250	147	4,200	456	456	150	25	4,000	670	750	100	348	100	100
House	71.4	88	60	250	50	25	188	150	12	300	60	60	40	16	16	12	12	64	20	40	60	19	12	88
Garden	29.3	20	20	20	20	9	25	25	60	10	28	2	60	2	2	4	10	160	50	6	10	70	40	20
Animal pens	11.7	9	6	9	16	4	25	25	2	64	31	14	–	2	8	2	2	–	9	4	2	12	4	9
Orchard	17.1	–	–	15	9	–	–	4	–	2	–	2	4	–	–	–	–	5	–	196	–	–	–	–
Patio	43.3	30	20	100	100	10	16	16	15	38	50	28	28	16	16	4	50	25	250	2	76	50	25	30
Washing area and water storage	2.6	2	6	5	2	2	5	1	4	2	4	2	2	2	2	2	3	1	2	2	1	2	–	–
Family shrine	2.0	–	–	–	–	–	–	–	–	–	–	–	–	–	–	–	–	–	–	–	2	–	–	–

to talk in the "same language". One day a *campesino* was carrying a bunch of different species and the researcher asked, "What do you need those plants for?" He replied, "They are not plants, they are '*hierbas*' (herbs) and they are for my animals."

There were 246 useful plant species identified in the areas studied (*solar*, weeds, and spontaneous vegetation) which were grouped in 10 uses. The greatest variety of useful plants were found in the solar, where use as medicinals and ornamentals was most frequent, and people gave more care (like watering) to those plants. Maize, squash, beans, faba beans, wheat, medicinal plants, condiments, building materials, and firewood are used throughout the year. Fruit, oat forage, other forage, and ornamental plants are used seasonally.

Family structure and tenure

Twenty-five families participated in a household survey in the two villages of Mayorazgo and La Era de San Pablo. Household size ranged from one to 11 members, and five households had only two members. Most households had four to six members. The types of families were nuclear or extended. Seventeen families regarded themselves as nuclear and five as extended. Three households were headed by single women; two women in Mayorazgo were widows, and one husband from La Era had emigrated to the USA.

The family type and the age of its members determine the availability of labour for agricultural activities. Young members of the family are important sources of labour. From six years of age children help with different household activities, such as fetching firewood, looking after animals (e.g. small sheep flocks), cleaning the house, and fetching water. The elderly also help, mainly by looking after the sheep when they are taken out to graze, or looking after the poultry.

With smaller land resources, monitored households in Mayorazgo relied more on off-farm work or remittances and only three households depended entirely on agricultural production for their livelihoods. The situation in San Pablo was different, where eight of the 13 households relied on agricultural production for their livelihoods. This could explain in part the greater interest of the people of San Pablo in participating in projects related to agricultural production without expecting payment or handouts.

The majority of land in the villages is under *ejido*. In Mayorazgo 91 per cent of the land of surveyed households is *ejido*, whereas in San Pablo 59 per cent is *ejido*, 28 per cent privately owned, and 13 per cent under other forms of tenure. In the state of Mexico the original *ejido* endowment was around 5–6 ha per *ejidatario*; however, in 1994 the average arable landholding per farming family was 2.46 ha (INEGI 1994). According to the law the endowments were to remain undivided, although it became common practice for *ejidatarios* to give a part of the land to their sons (not only the elder son) as they got married and in more recent times sometimes also to daughters. This explains the very small size of farms in the study site. The average *ejido* holding in Mayorazgo was 1.33 ha, ranging from none to 2.75 ha. One household in San Pablo also had no *ejido* land, but the average holding was 1.59 ha and the largest holding was 4.28 ha.

Land is usually owned by men, and traditionally the *ejido* endowment was only given to men. According to the old agrarian law, on the death of the man his wife became automatically the holder of the *ejido* usufruct rights. However, in many instances this legal provision was not observed. Widows, or other women on their own without elder sons to take their husband's land endowment, were dispossessed of their land. In the past any *ejido* fields that were not cultivated could be taken back by the community and reassigned to others in need of land. Buying *ejido* land is a way of gaining access to land, although buying and selling was not allowed under the previous agrarian law. The new terms of the agrarian law have made land purchase legal and easier, albeit not more common. Land can also be obtained through inheritance.

Non-*ejido* land may be privately owned, rented, or land belonging to somebody else held in usufruct. Three of the 12 sampled households in Mayorazgo had privately owned land, compared with 11 of the 13 households sampled in San Pablo. In this municipality, as in other parts of the state where men migrate to the cities in search of income, it is customary for a relative who remains in the village (father, brother, father- or son-in-law) to look after the land in usufruct. Consequently, farm size may be larger than what is formally owned. The conditions of "leases" vary. In some cases there is a sharecropping arrangement whereby the farmer gives a portion of the harvest to the owner of the fields, but frequently land is used for free as long as it is understood that ownership of the land is retained by the deed holder. Only two farmers in the survey, both in San Pablo, held land in usufruct.

Landholdings of the monitored farms range from 0.25 ha to 7 ha. The mean holding in San Pablo is larger (2.7 ha) than in Mayorazgo (1.4 ha), due mainly to one large farm of 7 ha. This farm has 2 ha of *ejido* and 1 ha of owned land. Of the remainder, 2 ha was *ejido* held in usufruct belonging to a brother who had died and whose widow left the community, and the other 2 ha was rented.

Non-tillable land, the *monte* and the *llanos*, is common land. Use of common land is managed by the "communal land deputy" who is in charge of observing state and federal regulations relating to the use of forest land, as well as rules established by the community by agreement or common law use.

Agrodiversity assessment

Maize diversity

Farmers in San Pablo Tlachichilpa identified eight local varieties of maize, compared with four varieties in San Marcos and four in Casas Blancas. Varieties are selected for characteristics such as early or late maturing, resistance to drought, floods, or frosts, and suitability to different soil conditions.

The Mazahua have a local classification system of maize and soils and there is a relationship between them. Farmers have early-maturing maize types (pink, yellow, and blue) to insure against uncertain rainfall and soil conditions, and late-maturing maize types (white) for better soils and weather conditions. Pink maize is sown in sandy, red, and clay-sand soils, while late-maturing white maize is sown in clay-sand soil which they call "moisture soil". Moisture soils can be sown with high-yielding white maize, while red soils only allow the sowing of early-maturing maize due to their low water-holding capacity and lower nutrient status. Knowledge of both soil and rainfall determine what maize is going to be cultivated by taking into account how the rains come in that particular year. If the rains are good all kind of maizes can be sown; but if there is drought only the early-maturing maize types will be cultivated.

Social factors, in terms of family preferences, are also important determinants of what is cultivated. At least some land is sowed to the preferred maize types (pink or blue), often against the will of male household members who prefer to sow maize that gives better prices and yield (white or yellow). Other aspects that influence the diversity of maize grown in a certain year are off-farm work, availability of family labour, help exchange, payment in kind, experimentation, and methods for seed selection.

During a seed workshop, *campesinos* demonstrated that they take into account more than one characteristic in selecting seed. Some are interested in the size of the cob and others in the size of the grain. The market influences selection, since white and yellow maize get better prices. In 1997 in San Pablo the participating families sowed 48 per cent of their total farm area (20.05 ha) to white maize, 31 per cent to yellow maize, and of the remainder 11 per cent was sown to pink maize, 7 per cent to blue, and 3 per cent to "pinto" maize. The same tendency was observed in Mayorazgo, where out of a total of 16.76 ha, 27 per cent was for white maize, 43 per cent for yellow maize, 21 per cent for the pink, 6 per cent for blue, and 3 per cent for pinto maize.

While biophysical and socio-economic factors are very important in determining the diversity of the cropped landscape year by year, culture ultimately influences biodiversity management. People enjoy living surrounded by a diversity of maize, pumpkins, field beans, weeds, faba beans, flowers, ornamentals, and medicine plants, commenting: "Our ancestors did it and so do we, we like it very much."

Diversity of the solar

In San Pablo Tlachichilpa five *solares* of high and five of low biodiversity were selected and all the plant species within them were identified by their local and scientific names. The farmers gave their common names, some in Mazahua. Over a hundred species were found, with their main uses being for food, forage, medicine, and ornamental use (see Table 12.3). There were more than 35 species found in the *milpas* of high and low biodiversity, but *solares* with high biodiversity had more species in the gardens (36) and edges (30) than the low biodiversity ones (13 species in gardens and 17 in edges).

In San Marcos de la Loma 10 *solares* were sampled and 82 species were found, including cereal and other crops, fruit trees, shrubs, forages, weeds, and medicinal plants, as shown in Table 12.4. Results indicate that the most prevalent species are those used for medicinal purposes, followed by those used as food. Medicinal plants were regarded as a very important asset by farmers, who mentioned that keeping medicinal plants is a way of saving money because they buy fewer prescription drugs.

The comparative yields of both single crops in the traditional maize system and associated crops in the diversified *milpa* system are shown in Table 12.5. It can be seen that the *milpa* system for maize/bean association had positive results in both years of evaluation. Even though maize yields were lower, beans and some amaranth were harvested, which led to land equiva-

Table 12.3 Number of useful species in the *solares* of San Pablo Tlachichilpa

Use	Number of species		
	Garden	*Milpa*	Edges
Food	41	25	9
Live barrier	5	–	23
Fuel	8	1	23
Condiment	2	1	2
Building	3	–	9
Forage	4	47	18
Medicinal	23	14	52
Ornamental	81	2	17
Ritual	9	–	3
Shade	4	–	7
Utensils	–	–	1
Other	2	–	1
Two or more uses	26	18	42

Table 12.4 Use of species in the *solares* of San Marcos de la Loma

Use	Number of species	%
Medicinal	28	34.1
Food	20	24.3
Condiment	2	2.4
Fuel	4	4.8
Ornamental	12	14.6
Forage	12	14.6
Ritual	4	4.8
Two or more uses	5	6.0

Table 12.5 Comparative yields of traditional maize versus the *milpa* production systems in Casas Blancas (tonnes/ha)

	Monocrop maize		*Milpa* system	
	1999	2000	1999	2000
Maize (grain)	1.90	2.70	1.60	2.60
Maize straw	4.10	3.90	3.20	4.00
Beans (grain)	–	–	0.13	0.34
Bean straw	–	–	0.27	1.20
LER maize/beans	–	–	1.16	1.94
Amaranthus	0.83*	–	0.33**	–

*Estimated on a 60 m^2 *mogote*.
**Estimated on a farmers demonstration site (150 m^2).

lent ratios (LER) higher than one.[1] However, costs were higher, mainly due to an increase in labour and seed costs.

Forest diversity and management

In the forest area of San Pablo Tlachichilpa the plant species were identified in walks with participating farmers. Fifty-four useful species were identified. The main uses were for medicine (26), firewood (seven), ornament (four), and food (three). Within the *solar* and the forest 54 different plant species are used for medicine.

There were concerns expressed about the decrease in availability of plants for medicines, fuelwood, and building materials because of overexploitation. Another perceived problem in San Pablo is that the forest is community-owned and farmers are not willing to introduce management or conservation practices on their own, since other members of the community could simply take advantage of the work done.

In the community of Casas Blancas there is a trend towards definition of specific areas for agricultural and forest production. Pine-oak forest, reforested pine, maize crop, and fallow fields were observed. Farmers have managed natural forest areas for decades for firewood, building materials, and fencing, and some commercial exploitation. A high extraction limit was established by the authorities until about 10–15 years ago, when farmers started to ask for studies on the amount of wood that could be extracted because it was being extracted above the capacity of the forest to regenerate. Extraction permits were not granted after 1998, which led to illegal wood extraction. New studies which are now necessary to obtain official permission have not been made.

Diversity of forest species was not completely assessed. Assessments did show that there is a density of about 600 pines/ha, compared with 180 oaks/ha and 40 other leafy species/ha. Most common management practices are digging firebreaks along the forest (100 per cent of farmers), weeding (25 per cent), pruning (12.5 per cent), and pest control (12.5 per cent). More than 60 per cent of interviewed farmers do not invest money in these activities, since they use family labour or exchanged labour. Some hire temporary labour for two or three weeks.

Demonstration site activities

Restoration of traditional milpa

The demonstration site for the restoration of the *milpa* was organized in a similar way to on-farm trials so that farmers, who have largely abandoned the associated crops, had the opportunity to explore the potential of these cropping patterns under current economic and social conditions. In early 2001 a workshop was organized in San Pablo to provide seeds to farmers wishing to establish *milpa* demonstration plots. Seeds were provided to 24 farmers and all planted them. In San Marcos and Yebuciví 75 farmers attended the workshops and 10 demonstration plots were monitored. *Milpas* of associations of maize/faba, beans/peas, *ayocote*, or common bean/squash (*Curcubita pepa* and *C. ficifolia*) and *Amaranthus hypocondriacus* were established during the spring and summer cropping cycle. Farmers decided the intercropping pattern and planted according to their experience and the availability of resources such as land, labour, fertilizers, and other inputs. A *milpa* was also established with the participation of the owner in the *solar* at San Pablo rented by the CICA team. Monitoring and assessment of the associated crops in comparison with maize monoculture were undertaken with the active participation of farmers. However, due to the low numbers of field staff only 14 demonstration sites belonging to 13 farmers were monitored. All the *milpa* cultivation practices and the use of different inputs were recorded from planting to harvest.

At the end of the season an evaluation workshop was held with farmers from San Pablo and San Marcos, CICA, and AMEXTRA. Four farmer leaders from San Pablo and 30 from San Marcos participated in the workshop. The evaluation considered the criteria used by *campesinos* in deciding whether to grow associated crops. A database was constructed of cultivation practices, including labour requirements, type and amount of inputs, and costs of production for different *milpa* intercropping systems. In November yields obtained from *milpas* were evaluated by 12 farmers. For the first time in several years farmers had surplus crops to sell in local markets, something rarely experienced with maize monoculture.

More than 90 per cent of participating farmers recognized the importance and benefits of preserving and enhancing current biodiversity resources. The uptake rate of the traditional *milpa* was very high, and almost all participant farmers have continued with the *milpa* cultivation system and with the use of associated crops. Moreover, for the new growing cycle more farmers were going to put in the *milpa* cultivation system and also forage production. As mentioned by farmers, "before the PLEC project we only had maize and very few vegetables, now after the PLEC project we can also eat faba beans soup or beans or peas; our diet is more varied and rich".

Crop reintroduction

A drought- and frost-tolerant landrace of barley called *cebada morada* was reintroduced into the *milpa* system in San Pablo. It was planted by 11 farmers in 2001, and these farmers shared seeds with more farmers for the subsequent planting season. A demonstration site at Casas Blancas was planted with Tziwin beans and maize. The Tziwin beans are a highly resistant and adapted landrace that was reintroduced in this community through the PLEC project activities.

Farmers noted there was a scarcity of some local seeds. Following the last workshop, a seed exchange was arranged between San Pablo and Casa Blancas farmers for about four hectares of beans, faba beans, and maize cultivation. One of the main priorities for farmers was seed production, and it was considered even more important than crop production at least for the first year as a way to ensure production in future years.

Vegetable production

In the community of San Marcos de la Loma, 30 vegetable production demonstration sites were established and 10 sites were monitored. These were established beside the farmers' houses and the species sown were lettuce, tomato, squash, *huazontle* (*Chenopodium* spp.), cauliflower, spinach, amaranth, and coriander.

Forage production

In San Marcos de la Loma 10 sites were planted with oats and vetch for improved forage. Winter crops were also established in Casas Blancas in plots with residual moisture, in order to maintain some cover during the dry season and obtain food and forage. Forage production is a priority for farmers in this community, and during all the workshops they stressed the need to produce more and better-quality forage. Four farmers produced good-quality forages on land where no crops were produced in the past. Peas and rye grass gave the best results with the highest cover and average dry matter yields of between four and eight tonnes/ha. Rye grass was the crop that produced the most attractive returns, according to farmers, due to the higher labour requirement of peas. They also found that peas are more susceptible to damage by bad weather. Participating farmers recognized the usefulness of winter crops in providing forage during a critical stage for their animals.

Educational materials

Four leaflets on amaranth technologies and demonstration sites were published and distributed among non-participating farmers. Traditional practices for pest control were documented, and a leaflet containing this information is being prepared for dissemination in the participating communities and to non-participating farmers.

Evaluating demonstrations

Recovered or introduced species have had variable success. For example, in San Pablo and San Marcos faba beans, peas, and vetch gave good yields, whereas beans did not do very well. In contrast, farmers at Casas Blancas had better results with beans and amaranth, while faba beans and vetch performed poorly. Farmer evaluation led to assumptions on the most appropriate types of soils for these crops. Crops were also evaluated in terms of crop arrangement. Thus, on more fertile soils it is possible to sow grains and legumes in the same row (although this practice increases labour use), whereas sandy or less fertile soils require grains and legumes to be arranged in separate rows or groups of rows within the same plot.

Generally farmers recognized an improvement of soil conditions with the use of associated grain and legume crops. Fertilizer requirements were less, although there was also a reduction in overall maize yield. Pesticide applications were not possible in these areas, and manual weeding increased labour. Participants asserted that the areas which can be sown under associated crops are rather small. An optimum size of 0.25 ha per farmer under associated crops worked well.

In the initial stages of *milpa* establishment there is higher dependence on external inputs, since many farms still do not have their own bean or amaranth seed. They still depend on NGOs or other farmers to obtain seed. However, agrochemical use in the *milpa* is low compared to conventional maize monoculture.

The MESMIS framework for sustainability evaluation of *campesino* systems (Masera, Astier, and López-Ridaura 1999) was applied to the results obtained from intercropping systems.[2] Optimum values were determined for each indicator and then represented in a sustainability assessment map (Clayton and Radcliffe 1996).

As observed in Table 12.6 and Figure 12.2, the environmental and socio-

Table 12.6 Sustainability evaluation of traditional maize and *milpa* systems in Casas Blancas expressed as a percentage of optimum (100%)

Indicator	Traditional maize	*Milpa* system
External input independence	58	46
Number of adopting farmers	80	20
Cost/benefit	40	100
Food sufficiency	50	100
Maize grain yield	100	84
Number of cultivated species	33	100

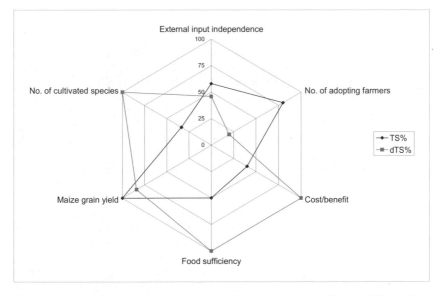

Figure 12.2 Sustainability assessment map (SAM) for the traditional (TS) and the diversified *milpa* (dTS) systems in Casas Blancas, Michoacán

economic indicators improve with diversification. Even though maize grain yield decreases, there is an important yield of beans which eliminated the need for purchasing this food. At present external input dependence is higher in the *milpa* system, mainly due to the introduction of beans and amaranth seed. The benefit/cost relationship is increased due to higher overall yields (LER) and better prices for beans compared to maize, and farmers' diet is improved. The *milpa* system is practised by 25 per cent of farmers in the community, which is considered high for the size of the PLEC project in Mexico, and it is envisaged that the numbers will increase over the coming years.

Notes

1. Land equivalent ratio (LER) is the ratio of the area under sole cropping to the area under intercropping needed to give equal amounts of yield at the same management level. It is the sum of the fractions of the intercropped yields divided by the sole-crop yields.
2. MESMIS (Metodología de Evaluación de Sistemas de Manejo Incorporando Indicadores de Sustentabilidad) is a multidisciplinary and multi-institutional effort to evaluate natural resource management systems incorporating sustainability indicators. The aims are to develop an evaluation framework to assess the sustainability of alternative natural resource management systems; apply the framework to case studies in Mexico; generate and disseminate materials to facilitate the application of the framework; contribute to the discourse on sustainability; and conduct training on the use of the framework.

REFERENCES

Arriaga Jordán, C. M., J. G. González Díaz, C. E. González Esquivel, E. G. Nava Bernal, and L. G. Velázquez Beltrán. 1997. "Caracterización de los sistemas de producción campesinos en dos zonas del Municipio de San Felipe del Progreso, México: Estrategias contrastantes", in G. Rivera Herrejón, A. Arellano Hernández, L. González Díaz, and C. Arriaga Jordán, (eds) *Investigación para el Desarrollo Rural: Diez Años de Experiencias del CIC*. Coordinación General de Investigación y Estudios de Posgrado. Toluca, Mexico: Universidad Autónoma del Estado de México, pp. 171–197.

Brookfield, H., M. Stocking, and M. Brookfield. 1999. "Guidelines on agrodiversity assessment in demonstration site areas", *PLEC News and Views*, No. 13, pp. 17–31.

Chávez Mejía, C., G. Nava Bernal, and C. Arriaga Jordán. 1998. *Agrodiversity Management and Sustainable Agriculture in the Hill Slopes of the Highlands of Central Mexico. Final Report.* [*Manejo de la Agrodiversidad y Agricultura Campesina Sostenible en Laderas del Altiplano Central de México. Primera Etapa.*] Informe Académico Final para el Proyecto "Pueblos, Manejo de Tierras y Cambio Ambiental (UNU/PLEC)". Centro de Investigación en Ciencias Agropecuarias. Coordinación General de Investigación y Estudios de Posgrado. Mexico: Universidad Autónoma del Estado de México.

Clayton, A. M. H. and N. J. Radcliffe. 1996. *Sustainability: A Systems Approach*. London: Earthscan.

Herrera, C. N. D. 1994. *Los Huertos Familiares Mayas en el Oriente de Yucatán. Etnoflora Yucatense*. Fascículo 9. Mérida, Mexico: Universidad Autónoma de Yucatán.

INEGI (Instituto Nacional de Estadística, Geografía e Informática). 1994. *México: Resultados Definitivos*. VII Censo Agrícola-Ganadero. Tomos I–III. Mexico: Instituto Nacional de Estadística, Geografía e Informática.

Masera, O., M. Astier, and S. López-Ridaura. 1999. *Sustentabilidad y Manejo de Recursos Naturales. El Marco de Evaluación MESMIS*. Mexico: MundiPrensa, GIRA-UNAM.

Ortega-Paczka, R. 1999. "Genetic erosion in México", in *Proceedings of the Technical Meeting on the Methodology of the FAO World Information and Early Warning System on Plant Genetic Resources*. Prague: FAO, pp. 69–75.

Zarin, D. J., H. Guo, and L. Enu-Kwesi. 1999. "Methods for the assessment of plant species diversity in complex agricultural landscapes: guidelines for data collection and analysis from the PLEC biodiversity advisory group (BAG)", *PLEC News and Views*, No. 13, pp. 3–16.

13

Jamaica

Elizabeth Thomas-Hope and Balfour Spence[1]

History of the cluster

Scientists of the Department of Geography and Geology at the University of the West Indies (UWI) have been the core members of the Jamaica PLEC team since 1998. While the early intention was to develop a Caribbean interdisciplinary team of Jamaican scientists in association with scientists from Barbados and the Dominican Republic, this proved difficult and it was decided that to achieve a more manageable and productive project the work should focus on Jamaica alone for the development of demonstration activities. The initial focus, between 1996 and 1998, was on comparisons in the patterns of traditional farming practices, and it was intended to compare agriculture in different environments. After selection of the Rio Grande Valley (Figure 13.1), more concentrated work first examined the extent and rate of erosion and soil loss, biological diversity loss and the nature of biodiversity change, land-use changes, land tenure, farming systems and the relationships between them, farming practices, technologies and conservation practices, the ancillary economic activities, household social structures and gender roles in farming, and demographic change and migration and their implications for farming.

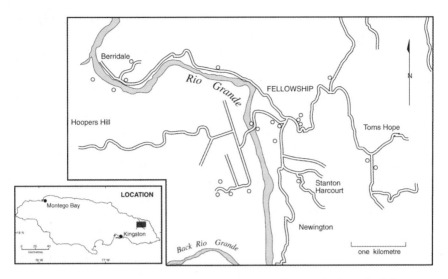

Figure 13.1 Location of the demonstration site in the Rio Grande Valley

The demonstration site

In 1998 the Rio Grande Valley was selected as the demonstration site as it is rich in biodiversity, relatively remote, dominated by small-scale farming, and is well integrated into national and global markets. On the basis of the preliminary studies before 1998, three potential focus sites had been selected – in the upper, middle, and lower sections representing the different agro-ecosystems within the valley – but because of the small size of the PLEC team the project eventually centred only on the Fellowship area in the lower section of the valley. The composition of the scientific team changed significantly. Although there had always been a number of scientists associated with PLEC, there has only been a very small group actually implementing the activities at the demonstration site. Student participation is short term, though some students have subsequently remained in contact with the project as associated scientists. However, an important aspect of the pattern of participation is that an attrition in the team of PLEC scientists has taken place while the numbers of farmers participating has increased significantly.

Characterization of the demonstration site

A team of four PLEC scientists and six field assistants carried out the initial characterization of the demonstration site in late 1998. Using participatory methods, the team documented the characteristics and diversity of small-farming systems, in particular:

- the demographic and socio-economic characteristics of the farm households
- the organizational and management structures of the farms
- the biodiversity of the farms.

The data collection at farm household level involved systematic sampling. The main access road into each farming community was used as a transect. Beginning with the first household on both sides of the road, every fifth household was chosen as a possible unit for selection. Where the household was not a farm household, the next in sequence was substituted. A total of 45 farm households were selected, representing 20 per cent of the total number of households in the demonstration site. The household members were interviewed and biological characteristics of the farm plots recorded with the assistance of the farmers.

On individual farms, five transects were taken on each plot surveyed. Four of these transects followed the cardinal compass directions from the edge of the plot, while the fifth was taken in an upslope direction following the border of the plot. Assessment of agrodiversity was conducted, covering most aspects of the biophysical diversity, cropping systems, and land management practices. In farmers' fields, observed field types and land-use stages were identified and recorded following the methodology of Zarin, Guo, and Enu-Kwesi (1999). In all cases farmer input and information were solicited to promote the participatory exchange of information between scientists and the farmers.

For the assessment of biodiversity in each land-use stage, plots were selected on each farm. Four 5×5 m quadrats were pegged and these were further divided into numbered 1×1 m quadrats. Using random tables, four of the 1×1 m quadrats were chosen from each large quadrat for recording plant species with local and scientific name where possible, abundance, and use. Quadrat sampling was done in a north-west direction for each farm. For the edge, the perimeter of the farm was measured to determine the interval for quadrat sampling using a 1×1 m quadrat. Additional information on the sample area, namely location, elevation, slopes, and aspect, was also collected.

Crop type, cropping systems, and other land management practices assessed management systems. Crop dominance, planting material, land preparation practices, labour inputs, income-earning function, and the farmers' market orientation were recorded. Land management was assessed using questionnaires recording farm layout and practices such as agrochemical use, soil conservation, and hazard impact and management response. Information on the demographic composition of the farming households included the age and sex of members, educational levels achieved, occupation and income-generating activities, gender roles, and the functional relationships of the household members in farm organization and management.

An important additional aspect affecting project work

After the conclusion of landscape characterization, the full characterization of the demonstration site still required an understanding of the social dynamics of the communities. The issues, which needed to be researched and recorded qualitatively, were the characteristics and explanations of inter- and intra-community conflict and trust, and factors conditioning acceptance of persons as leaders and effective transmitters of knowledge within or on behalf of the community.

Among rural communities in Jamaica, including those of the demonstration site, there exist strong networks based on family and kinship groups. Church affiliation is also the basis of networks of friends and supporters in times of difficulty. Associations, such as the Burial Scheme Society and other informal "fraternities" and "partner" groupings, provide various levels of assistance, especially in times of grief or other personal distress. However, social capital, taken as the set of resources inherent in patterned or structured social relations within the context of farm management and practice, was surprisingly low.

On matters relating to farm management and crop selection, there seemed to be no communication between farmers. For example, the Jamaica Agricultural Society is an association of farmers that meets to discuss common problems in relation to agriculture. The topics of discussion are usually those relating to problems faced by the government and its agencies, factors that are controlled externally such as the price of seeds and agrochemicals, the problems of the fluctuating market for major crops, and poor road access, rather than crop management.

The Banana Export Company (BECO), which is the sole channel for exporting bananas, presses farmers to produce the crop as a monoculture, with clean weeding and intensive use of fertilizers and agrochemicals for pest control. The company itself sells and distributes the agrochemicals. The farmers complained that the price of agrochemicals was high and that, despite their best efforts, the level of rejection of their bananas for export left them perpetually impoverished. Nevertheless, many farmers felt that they had no option but to keep producing for BECO since there were virtually no other market opportunities. Those farmers who have rejected the traditional system of diversified farm plots and complied with the requirements of BECO are held up by the extension officers of the Rural Agricultural Development Agency as models of good practice.

There had been no support for or acknowledgement of agrobiodiversity as a model of good practice until the arrival of the PLEC team. Yet some farmers had persisted in intercropping bananas with a wide variety of other plants, ranging from timber and fruit trees to a ground cover of condiments and medicinal plants. The rationale was explained to other farmers at a demonstration site field-day – it was based on the economic advantages of having alternative cash crops to supplement variable income from bananas, as well as increasing the range of crops available for household consumption. Farmers who practised intercropping were also aware of the ecological benefits in providing shade, ground cover, and some measure of pest control.

Activities associated with the research of postgraduate students studying environmental management at UWI helped to develop PLEC's relationships with farmers. Students conducted fieldwork exercises with farmers' participation. In addition, six postgraduate students conducted their project research and lived for weeks at a time in the demonstration site area. These contacts greatly boosted the confidence of the farmers and deepened the relationship between them and the PLEC scientists in the sharing of knowledge. The themes of study undertaken were agrobiodiversity conservation techniques and technologies used by farmers, agricultural chemical use, food security, and farmer responses to flooding and landslide hazards.

Altogether, the interactions brought about the gradual building of trust between the PLEC researchers and members of the communities and, with this, the farmers became increasingly open in the views and attitudes that were disclosed. This made it possible for the researchers to gain an understanding of the nature of the social dynamics of the communities and the areas of cooperation or conflict between individuals and groups. These factors were particularly significant where they affected the pattern of farmer interaction and the strategies necessary to ensure the success of the PLEC activities (Thomas-Hope and Spence 2002).

Description of the demonstration site

The demonstration site is located in the lower Rio Grande Valley within the easterly parish of Portland (see Figure 13.1). The site covers an area of 10.36 square kilometres with a population of 1,023 people distributed among the five communities of Fellowship, Toms Hope, Berridale, Golden Vale, and Coopers Hill. The population density is 99 persons per square kilometre, which in the context of rural Jamaica is fairly low. However, owing to the predominantly steep terrain, physiographic density is relatively high with fairly intensive cultivation of land.

The Rio Grande watershed consists of steep, hilly terrain, with 75 per cent of the area having elevations exceeding 1,500 metres and over 50 per cent of the area having slopes exceeding 20 degrees. At the demonstration site, elevations generally exceed 600 metres and slopes range from less than 10 degrees in Toms Hope to over 30 degrees in Coopers Hill (Morrison 2001).

The geology of the demonstration site is comprised primarily of Cretaceous sedimentary rocks with subordinate volcanic and volcaniclastic deposits. These deposits are sporadically interrupted by white and yellow limestone outcrops, especially in Fellowship, Coopers Hill, and Berridale. The permeability of the rocks is low, which, along with their high swelling potential, makes them susceptible to landslides. Low permeability also contributes to high runoff potential, which increases the possibility of flooding. Much of the Rio Grande, which drains the area, is bordered by moderately permeable alluvial deposits (Mines and Geology Division 2000). Clay and stony loams dominate the soils of the demonstration site. These soils are for the most part moderately well drained and sometimes consist of deeply weathered conglomerate tuffs of acid shale. Conglomerates on steep slopes contribute to slope instability during periods of moderate to high rainfall.

There is a prolonged wet season. The area receives an annual average rainfall ranging from 3,810 mm to over 5,080 mm. The temperatures range between 23°C and 26°C. The humidity varies with elevation, but for the study area it is estimated to be more than 60 per cent, with a high of 85 per cent in the morning (NRCD 1987). High frequency and intensity of rainfall in conjunction with geology, slopes, and anthropogenic activities are major factors contributing to the high vulnerability of the area to flood and landslide hazards.

Land use

Forestry is the dominant land use in the Rio Grande Valley, with 19,657 ha covered by forest. Cultivated crops for both export and local markets cover 2,072 ha. A further 944 ha are covered by pasture and 638 ha in settlements (Ferguson 1998). Within the demonstration site area, the dominant agricultural land-use stages are house gardens and orchard, consisting primarily of banana monoculture and agroforestry. The settlements are concentrated on lower lands close to the main river and its tributaries, while the farms are located on the steep slopes and are susceptible to erosion resulting from landslides (Thomas-Hope, Spence, and Semple 1999).

Population characteristics

The demonstration site farmer population showed ageing trends, although there were a number of active younger farmers. The modal age of the sample population was 43 years, with the majority of the farmers being male. It is important to note that while the substantive farmer is male, there are significant female contributions to the farming process, particularly in the areas of field maintenance, planting, and marketing. A significant number (more than 60 per cent) had been involved in farming for 25 years and over, and have been involved from childhood. For most farmers traditional export crops were the main income generators, although over 40 per cent indicated that farming was supplemented by other income-generating activities such as shop keeping, rafting – a tourism activity – and work outside of the valley. Remittances from relatives abroad or working outside the study area were also an important source of income for some older farmers. Farm income is difficult to assess as farmers rarely keep a record of inputs, costs, and expenditures. In addition, expenditure and income vary from month to month depending on the stage of crop development.

Generally farm households have one or two plots, which are planted with root crops such as yams, *dasheen* (*Colocasia esculenta*), and sweet potato as well as traditional export crops such as banana, coffee, and sometimes plantain, some of which is consumed by the households. Most of the income-generating farming activity is concentrated on the second plot, while the first, commonly dubbed the house plot, supports a variety of food and medicinal plants for household consumption.

Agricultural surplus is normally sold in local markets in the case of food crops, or overseas markets in the case of banana and coffee. Overseas marketing is normally organized by commodity associations and tends to be the preferred option by farmers because of the relative ease of market access. Although the farmer and members of his households input their own labour, over 64 per cent of farmers interviewed hired additional help.

Constraints

Resource degradation at the demonstration site takes the form of physical resource erosion as well as the erosion of human resources. Physical resource degradation results mainly from floods and landslides. The impermeable nature of the underlying geology in conjunction with frequent and intense rainfall and banana monoculture on steep slopes has resulted in recurrent flood and landslides events. These are major agents of soil loss, and while there are no specific estimates from the demonstration site, soil loss from similar environments in Jamaica is estimated to be between 99 and 124 tonnes per hectare per year. Loss of topsoil at this magnitude has serious implications for livelihoods and incomes as it impacts on crop production. Where there have been landslides the eroded material is redistributed within the catchment.

Loss of human resources is primarily due to outmigration of young potential farmers as well as the ageing of the farm population. The entire Rio Grande Valley is a major feeder for cruise-ship labour demand and more recently for an overseas hotel labour programme. These options are extremely attractive to young people given the vagaries and uncertainties associated with small-scale farming. In addition, as the average age of farmers increases and older farmers die the community loses valuable knowledge and skills, most of which relate to the sustainable management of agrobiodiversity.

Agrodiversity at the demonstration site

The biophysical description of the Rio Grande Valley emphasizes diversity as a characteristic feature of the watershed, and PLEC work at the demonstration site has supported the legacy of agricultural diversity. Small farmers have been found to cultivate and maintain a wide variety of crops and other plants to meet their food, nutrition, cultural, and economic needs. Agrodiversity assessments attempted to capture most aspects of the biophysical, crop, and land management diversity to understand the dynamics of these farming systems better. The current land-use stages and field types were identified. The farm management regimes were also assessed, particularly in terms of crop and associated cropping systems and land management practices. This analysis focused on the cultivated, wild, and semi-domesticated plant species found on the farms in order to highlight local trends in:

- the dynamics of agrobiodiversity, land and crop management decisions, and tenurial arrangements and their impacts on diversity
- environmental and socio-economic impacts of change on diversity
- models of tree and field-crop combinations found on small farms.

Land-use stages and field types

Within the sampled farm units there were five dominant land-use stages (Table 13.1). The agroforest, house garden, and edge land-use stages were the most commonly observed within the demonstration area, constituting over 80 per cent of the total sample units. House gardens were multi-storeyed configurations of food trees such as breadfruit (*Artocarpus altilis*), an array of fruits including bananas for local consumption, root crops such as *dasheen*, herbs, and medicinal plants. Agroforests were banana dominant, since the Rio Grande Valley is one of the leading areas for the production of export bananas in Jamaica. Although the monopoly BECO discourages the intercropping of bananas with other crops except coffee, and encourages the removal of undergrowth, all expert farmers maintained a diverse system of interplanting.

While the configuration of edges varied among expert farmers, edges were extensively used for the production of grass as fodder for farm animals as well as the maintenance of medicinal plants. This was because the location was free from pesticides and herbicides used in banana production. Although species on the edges had personal value for farmers, most did not have significant market value and were therefore less vulnerable to praedial theft than other land-use stages. Edges therefore function as protective barriers for more valuable crops.

Within each land-use stage, the field types varied as farm management reflected a complex mix of different types of cultivated and non-cultivated crops, trees, and shrubs promoted by each farmer. Field types within land-

Table 13.1 Land-use stages and field types in the Rio Grande Valley

Land-use stage	Field type	Frequency of incidence
House garden	Spontaneous growth of grasses (*Commelina diffusa*, *Panicum maximum*), shrubs (*Gliricidia* spp.), and ornamental plants (*Croton* spp.)	1
	Multistoreyed mixture of staple crops: banana, dasheen (*Colocasia esculenta*), coco (*Xanthosoma sagittifolium*), breadfruit (*Artocarpus altilis*) with herbs and medicinal plants (*Aloe vera*), fruit trees (e.g. *Mangifera indica*), and ornamental plants (*Croton* spp.)	5
Shrub-dominated fallow	Multistoreyed mixture of abandoned staple crops (banana, *dasheen*, *coco*, breadfruit) with herbs and medicinal plants and fruit trees	1
Orchard (banana plantation)	Banana (*Musa sapientum*) fields with little or no intercropping of other crops and undergrowth of shrubs	3
Agroforest	Mixed crop of banana between which *dasheen* and *coco* are intercropped and other food crops (yams, maize, pumpkin) and fruit trees (e.g. *Ananas comosus* – pineapples) are planted randomly	1
	Banana-dominant farm intercropped with *dasheen*	1
	Dormant banana plantation and actively farmed vegetable ground	1
	Banana (*M. sapientum*) and plantain (*M. paradisiaca*) dominant field	1
	Mixture of banana plantation and vegetable farming	1
	Mixed array of bananas, *dasheen*, *coco*, and a number of fruit trees	1
	Mixture of food crops e.g. *dasheen*, banana, and plantain	1
	Timber intercropped with coffee and bananas	1
Edge	Grassy verge around agroforest with a mixture of grasses, ornamental plants, and fruit trees	3
	Grassy verge and mixture of shrubs (e.g. *Sida acuta* – broomweed) and medicinal plants (e.g. *Aloe vera*)	5
	Grassy verge around agroforest with a mixture of grasses, ornamental plants, and fruit trees and food crops (*M. sapientum, coco*)	4
	Grassy verge mixed with a number of wild-growing herbs and shrubs (*Gliricidia* spp., *Weldelia trilobata*), food crops (*coco*), and fruit trees (e.g. *Syzgium malaccense* and *Cocus nucifera*)	1
	Spontaneous growth of grasses (*Commelina diffusa*, *Panicum maximum*), shrubs (*Gliricidia* spp.), and ornamental plants (*Croton* spp.)	2
	Verge around farmhouse dominated by shrubs e.g. *Gliricidia* spp., *Weldelia trilobata*, and *Boerhavia cocinea*	2

use stages ranged from one to eight, with the agroforest and edge land-use stages showing the highest variations in field types (Table 13.1). A total of 235 different species of plants were identified on the farms in the study area. These plants included roots and tubers, vegetables, legumes, cereals, fruits, condiments, ornamental and medicinal plants, and timber trees. Approximately 70 per cent of the plants were used. Uses included food, building material, erosion and flood control, mulch, medicine, spices, stimulants, and fencing material.

Assessments also showed that field types on some farms changed frequently, primarily as a function of the farmer's crop and land management decisions. For example, one farm was initially characterized to have three dominant land-uses stages with six field types. This farm occupied flat lands on the floodplains of a river where the farmer intercropped plots of banana, coffee, and coconuts with a variety of vegetables, including pumpkin, cucumber, cabbage, pak choi, and peppers. This farmer indicated to researchers that his decision to farm this mix of crops was based primarily on the availability of markets, access to technical assistance, and the availability of the lands and their proximity to water sources. Subsequent visits with this farmer showed that changes in market availability and other socioeconomic pressures led to a change in his cropping system. He had converted his vegetable plot to banana monoculture. This case also highlighted the dynamic nature of the farmer activities at the demonstration site, and hence the need for long-term monitoring as a means of accurately capturing the diversity and the impact of change.

Species occurrence and abundance varied according to land-use stages and field types. Agroforests and house garden land-use stages displayed the highest diversity of crop, fruit trees, shrubs, and other valuable plants as the species richness index reflects (Table 13.2). The agroforest, edge, and house gardens also showed a higher abundance index than the orchard. Margalef index values for the dominant land-use stages ranged from 20 to 58, while those of the banana orchards were as low as six. Where other plants were intercropped within banana fields (generating the agroforest or house garden land-use stage) the abundance index increased dramatically, sometimes by as much as a factor of three. Another land-use stage showing high

Table 13.2 Species richness of land-use stages of sampled farms

Land-use stage	Incidence of the land-use stage	Average species richness
Agroforest	9	26
House garden	6	27
Edge	20	16
Fallow	1	26
Orchard	3	12

species diversity was the fallow, which is an area that is not actively managed due to its susceptibility to flooding.

The higher diversity of crops and trees common to the agroforest, house garden, and edge land-use stages can be attributed to the intensive management practices employed by farmers as physical and economic coping mechanisms. These strategies diversify agricultural production and improve market access which in turn assists in fulfilling the food and cash requirements of the farmer and his household. Management practices allow for variations in cropping types and patterns from farm to farm, further increasing overall agrobiodiversity at the site. These practices and approaches to crop production, land management, and livelihood security formed the basis of the "good practice" models of the farmers and used for demonstration by expert farmers in the later stages of project work.

The field-type data also support the observation that variation in diversity is a function of farmer management. The sample area showed species richness that ranged from seven to 59, with the observed variations following the trends in the land-use stages discussed above. The agroforest land-use stage showed the highest variation in field types, with over nine identified. Field-type species richness within this land-use stage ranged from 13 to 59. On farms where there was an emphasis on a mixture of banana, root crops, vegetables, and fruit and lumber trees there was greater organizational diversity and the species richness index was above 25. The field type showing the highest species richness (59) was found on a farm divided into several subplots in which a number of crops were planted for sale to the local market. This farm also showed the highest level of species abundance within the agroforest and edge field types. This farmer's management practices reflect the relationship between market orientation and the occurrence of diversity, as he sells all his produce locally. In contrast, farmers targeting export markets receive technical support from BECO that promotes a reduction in diversity. For example, a farmer producing for the export market will clear his banana plot to reduce "wastage" of nutrients through uptake by other plants and to reduce the incidence of diseases. This reduction in diversity is reflected in the uniformity of the field type observed in the banana plantation/orchard land-use stage. It had the lowest species richness values, ranging from seven to 19, with an average of 12. Most farms had species richness of 20 and above.

The field types of the house garden land-use stage showed less variation within the field types. Edges also had a significant contribution to make to diversity, as in many instances the edge contained crops, fruit trees, and medicinal plants not commonly grown in the main farming area.

Crops and cropping systems

Diversity within the demonstration site can also be examined at the level of the crops and crop management systems. Bananas dominate land-use stages and field types of the demonstration site. Within the sampled farms, over 75 per cent of the farmers indicated that they cultivated a second major crop alongside the main income-generating crop, and 61 per cent planted a third income-generating crop. These included plantain, coconut, coffee, yam, and *dasheen*. Some farmers also plant vegetables such as tomato and legumes. Plantain and yam are commonly associated as dominant and secondary crops, whereas other individuals were recorded cultivating coconut and melon, yam and pineapple, *calaloo* (leafy green) and cucumber, pak choi and pumpkin, and pineapples and sweet potato.

Thirteen different types of vegetables were observed on the sampled farms. These included cabbage, cucumber, pumpkin, tomato, cauliflower, okra, and *calaloo*. Legumes are both cultivated and consumed widely, but farmers grow limited varieties, mainly kidney beans, string beans, *gungo* peas (pigeon pea, *Cajanus cajan*), cowpeas (*Vigna unguiculata*), and broad bean.

Non-cultivated species commonly thrive within all land-use stages except orchards (see Table 13.3), and this is associated with an increase in diversity. This diversity is directly a reflection of the farmer's methods of weed or wild plant control and crop and plant choice. The occurrence of medicinal and ornamental plants varied between field types, and was found to be more prevalent in the edge land-use stage. Despite socio-economic, cultural, and political pressures, agrodiversity is flourishing within the Rio Grande Valley demonstration site, from which other farmers can learn more sustainable farm management practices.

Demonstration site activities

Community meetings

Following the completion of work on landscape and social characterization, and some initial work with farmers, two community meetings were organized to inform the wider farming community of the nature, objectives, and activities of the PLEC project. In each case farmers responded by raising a number of related issues of concern to them, and discussion ensued. The first community meeting was held in Fellowship in the main community in the demonstration site in August 2000. This meeting sought to introduce the "demonstration activity" phase of PLEC, to communicate the concept of agrobiodiversity. The benefits to be gained from this approach, to both the community and the environment, were emphasized.

This was followed by a meeting in Toms Hope in September 2000, at which the common problems and strategies for coping with the problems raised by the farmers brought the focus of PLEC on to substantive issues of concern within the wider context of agrodiversity and biodiversity. This

Table 13.3 Common plants cultivated or promoted in the land-use stages

Land-use stage	Crops	Trees	Medicinal and other useful plants
Agroforest	Banana Plantain *Dasheen* Sweet potato Yam Peas/legumes Vegetables Pineapple	Growing or fence stake Ackee Coconut Mango Apples Coffee Citrus	Mint (varying species) Bird pepper Aloe vera Susumber
House garden	Banana Plantain *Dasheen* Sweet potato Yam Peas/legumes Vegetables Pineapple	Growing or fence stake Ackee Coconut Mango Apples Coffee Citrus Sour sop Sweet sop *Guinep*	Ornamental plants Mint (varying species) Bird pepper Aloe vera Susumber
Edge	Yam Banana Plantain	Nutmeg Apple Mangoes Citrus	Grasses Mints Growstake Hogmeat Aloe vera
Orchard	Banana	Apple	Within the orchard very few aggressive wild-growing plants found: hogmeat, marigold, Guinea grass
Shrub-dominated fallow	*Dasheen* Coco	Coconut Yam	Bachelor button Mongoose weed Milk weed Watergrass Rat ears Cowfoot Marigold Guinea grass

meeting was instrumental in the planning of the field-based demonstration activities to be implemented on the plots of expert farmers. These field-days, by common agreement termed "work experience days", became the primary means of knowledge sharing, thus serving as a forum for the sharing of experiences and the transfer of knowledge on sustainable agrobiodiversity practices from farmer to farmer and between farmer and researchers.

Selection of the expert farmers

Issues that were a source of conflict in the communities were important in guiding the selection of expert farmers. Political differences provided one important area of disharmony and suspicion between groups. A majority in each local community supported one or other of the two major political parties. Though hostility was not expressed most of the time, negative feelings were sufficiently strong that farmers from certain communities would not go to some other communities for meetings. For that reason the initial community meetings were held in different locations. It was essential that expert farmers be selected from communities on both sides of this political divide, even if this meant some compromise in terms of the range in diversity of farming systems that would be represented.

Additional tensions concerned the acceptability of some persons to teach or otherwise disseminate information. For example, one outstanding farmer was a returned migrant from the UK, having lived there for more than 30 years. A highly progressive farmer, he demonstrated potential leadership qualities and seemed willing to share his skills and ideas with other farmers. He engaged in organic farming and had introduced a number of non-traditional plants and livestock that had greatly increased the agricultural diversity on his land. He specialized in growing exotic fruit for the hotel industry, and sought out marketing outlets and organized the process himself. In addition he kept geese, produced honey, and was a member of the national beekeepers' association. Despite all this, and the fact that he had been born and grew up in the area and had retained his family connections there, he was widely resented. His wife was a foreigner and well educated, and the farmer had become more sophisticated in his approach to farming, and in his social and business contacts and livelihood generally. These factors had combined to create a significant barrier to his acceptance in the community. It soon became evident that he would not be able to demonstrate anything effectively to other farmers. Although he has remained loosely connected with PLEC activities and was invariably the one who loaned his drinks cooler and went into town to purchase the food required for the meetings, it became clear that he could not be included as an expert farmer.

There was a general suspicion of leaders who emerged within the community. People were ready to accept leadership from outside the community – and the further away, the better. Those from outside were assumed to be genuinely more knowledgeable, and were seen to provide a means of generating social capital that could have other benefits. Networks established with persons "outside" were therefore valued, and those established "inside" were seen as being of little use except for social support. The propensity for seeking "assistance" from outside explains why the PLEC team was accepted, even though it did not give the kind of assistance that farmers had come to expect from outside organizations.

The first expert farmers were all distinguished by their mixed-farming practices, including the diverse combinations and configurations of plants on their farms (Table 13.4). They represented the various communities in terms of political affiliation and it seemed that they would all be effective communicators. The eldest farmer was highly respected by other farmers and is the local representative to the Jamaica Agricultural Society. It was also intended that the expert farmers would reflect the gender balance of farmers in the community. However, none of the early collaborating female farmers could be selected on the basis of the above criteria. It was only at a later stage, after community meetings and work experience days, that more female farmers became involved and suitable female representation became possible.

The size of farms of expert farmers ranged from 2.2 to 4.9 ha, and each farm was comprised of either two or three plots. The farmers selected the plots for the demonstrations. The dominant crop was the main income-generating crop on the farm. In the agroforest land-use stage (Plot 1 in Table 13.4), banana was the dominant crop on two farms. There was a possible connection with the level of education, reflecting a dependence of those with least education on the export crop promoted by the agricultural agency and no alternative or additional livelihood options. The younger and more educated farmers, who had alternative income-earning strategies, depended on non-traditional crops. Only two farmers grew income-generating crops on their house gardens (Plot 2 in Table 13.4). The other three farmers grew various plants for household consumption, including fruit trees in single stands, bushes for tea, spices, plants for medicinal use, and ornamental plants.

All the expert farmers used agrochemicals. The cost was high in relation to the profits. This was particularly true of export bananas. The main chemical fertilizer used on all the expert farmers' plots was sulphate. Second in terms of usage was potash. At least two, and in some cases four, different types of chemical fertilizers were regularly used. Farmer 2, the vegetable farmer, used 60 bags, and each bag contained 45.4 kg.[2] Methods of pest control included chemical pesticides as well as mixed cropping and the removal of pests by hand. The farmers indicated that things had changed from the past. They had all adopted "modern" techniques in their farming practices, and all felt that agrochemical use was essential for successful food production.

Farmer-to-farmer training

The transfer of knowledge between farmers took place in meetings and on the work experience days when they and other collaborating farmers met on the farm of one of the expert farmers. In all cases the plots that repre-

Table 13.4 Characteristics of the first five expert farmers

Farmer	Age	Education	Household size	Years farming	Other income	No. of family overseas	Farm size (ha)	No. of plots	Main income-generating crop Plot 1 Agroforest	Plot 2 House garden	Hired labour	Market	Agrochemical usage (45.4 kg bags)
1	39	Primary	7	24	No	0	4.1	3	Banana	None	Yes	Local	25
2	43	Secondary	5	20	No	0	4.9	2	Pak choi	Banana	Yes	Local	60
3	32	Vocational training	4	3	Yes	1	4.5	2	*Calaloo*	Breadfruit	Yes	Local	13
4	60	Primary	3	45	No	1	2.2	2	Banana	None	No	Export	14
5	38	Vocational training	3	15	Yes	1	2.4	2	Plantain	None	Yes	Local	2

sented the agroforestry land-use stage of the farms, together with the edges, were used for demonstration purposes. Part of the success of these activities was due to the level of discussion of common problems and strategies that occurred. A range of topics relating to agrodiversity and the conservation of biodiversity within the context of farmer livelihoods and land management were raised by farmers and discussed with reference to their own experience and knowledge. The topics included:

- models of tree and crop combinations that could be used in the edges, with specific attention to the possibilities of introducing ackee[3] plants and the species of ackee most suited the soil and climatic conditions of the valley
- models of fallowing
- the aspects of traditional agricultural practices that should be retained, particularly in relation to biodiversity versus monoculture
- the benefits and problems involved in high levels of agrochemical use
- the role of beans and peas as nitrogen-fixing agents and the implications for the application of nitrogen fertilizers
- the role of plant diversity in pest management and experiences of this
- the changing knowledge levels and usage of local plants for medicinal purposes in the community, and the value of conservation of such plants
- strategies for harvesting and marketing specific fruit crops out of season
- the nature and benefits and problems involved in non-organic farming
- the problems involved in obtaining and retaining a regular market for locally cultivated produce
- the problems of crop losses, from floods primarily but also landslides, and the best types of plants that should be used in the management of flood- and landslide-prone farm plots.

Activities on the work experience days sought to facilitate farmer-to-farmer training, using plots with different cropping and management systems as well as plots on slopes of different steepness. In each case the hosting farmer demonstrated the nature of the system used, and discussed the advantages of cultivating the crops selected and their value for market and household use as well as for land management. The measures used by the farmers to reduce erosion and mitigate the effects of flooding were also demonstrated and discussed.

Two of the themes that had been a topic of the meetings were the introduction of legumes into orchard and agroforestry plots and the introduction of the ackee tree, for which there would be good markets. The ackee could be planted as corridors of agroforestry. The farmers further suggested the introduction of the june plum tree (*Spondias dulcis*), since it grows well in the area and its fruit produces a good juice. Farmers were unaware of value of intercropping with peas and beans for nitrogen fixing, and became very interested and enthusiastic about the indirect benefits of producing additional cash or subsistence crops in addition to reducing the volume and cost of nitrogen-based fertilizers.

There were some hindrances to accessing sufficient ackee seedlings in the desired time frame and, with the greater enthusiasm for intercropping of peas and beans, farmers requested to begin with the legumes. The PLEC researchers provided the seeds. This activity, however, had to be postponed because of severe flooding and the results from the experimental plots were not monitored by the end of 2001. Heavy rain, floods, and landslides have interrupted the demonstration activities each year. The 1998 and 2001 flooding in the area, much wider than the demonstration site, constituted a national disaster. These events interrupted activities for several weeks at a time.

The establishment of experimental fields on the plots of the expert farmers was one of the principal ways for farmers to evaluate the benefits of adapting their existing systems to incorporate the new features for improved production and diversification. They could assess the cost-effectiveness and environmental benefits that may be derived through future efforts to reduce the volume of agrochemical fertilizers and pesticides currently used.

The lack of easily accessed markets was one of the main complaints voiced by farmers. Innovative and cooperative marketing approaches and seeking niche markets for products are essential if different crops are to be grown. Markets for crops fluctuated significantly from one year to another. Banana export was controlled by BECO and had declined in recent years, and the domestic market for crops such as pepper and plantain was unpredictable. The market and cash sales were the prime motivating force in decisions concerning the selection of crop combinations. This was particularly the case among the younger farmers, who were more adept at accessing markets than were the older farmers.

Social benefits of the PLEC approach

Despite the social networks that existed in the communities, they had generated little social capital in the context of agricultural knowledge and management strategies. The PLEC team found a local culture of conservatism among farmers whereby it was felt that one ought not to walk on to other farmers' plots or ask questions about other farmers' activities. What farmers planted and what techniques they employed were their business and no one else's. This had largely prevented the sharing of ideas and hindered the development of any openness about new market opportunities or strategies for dealing with common problems faced by farmers.

The PLEC demonstration activities, in particular the work experience days, gradually broke down these barriers for the farmers who participated.

The increase in the sharing of information and knowledge, and the eagerness to host work experience days, were remarkable. They were highly enjoyable days, as lunch and drinks were provided and the atmosphere became convivial. Tasting of fruit, and giving and receiving plant clippings and roots for planting, contributed to the spirit of sharing that became characteristic of these field-days.

Some farmers who had not previously communicated with each other concerning farming strategies, especially in relation to the various challenges they faced, are now discussing these issues. Specialized management issues are raised and shared. The PLEC activities have increased awareness of the importance of agricultural biodiversity among the farmers and their families. This has increased the confidence of those already engaged in increasing diversity, which has helped them to take a firmer stand in relation to the monocropping and heavy use of agrochemicals promoted by the banana export company. There has also been evidence of enhanced morale, interest, and enthusiasm among farmers in a situation where small farming is regarded as marginal in terms of both economic return and social status.

For the PLEC scientists, important findings from the demonstration site activities are being disseminated to policy-makers. These include the importance of addressing agricultural and biodiversity issues in ways that are cognizant of the social dynamics of the community. It is important that farmers be facilitated in the process of building networks that increase social capital in the community. Demonstration site activities constitute a highly dynamic process. The selection of expert farmers, and the increased number of farmers participating in work experience days, are processes that are ongoing as changes occur in the communities.

Other research at the demonstration site

The establishment of a PLEC demonstration site and the subsequent activities at the site have spawned a plethora of collateral analyses, mostly by postgraduate students, that have not been directly funded by the PLEC. The objectives of these researches and their findings are presented below.

Agrobiodiversity responses to flood and landslide hazards

In light of the vulnerability of the demonstration site to flood and landslide hazards and the dearth of extension interventions to help farmers mitigate the impacts of these destructive events, a study was undertaken to investigate farmers' management of biodiversity to reduce physical and economic resource losses from natural hazards. Results of the study suggest that, along with biological management and organizational factors, natural hazards influenced the biodiversity of plots at the demonstration site. The influences on agrobiodiversity relate to the type of natural hazard and the severity of impact, and affect the extent to which a plot can be replanted. Replanted plots tend to have less diversity than fallow or permanently abandoned plots, since vegetation regenerates by succession. Flood impacts, including waterlogging, were experienced on 56 per cent of farms at the site, while landslide impacts were felt on 28 per cent. Only 16 per cent of farms did not experience hazard impacts. Floods destroyed crops and land and caused waterlogging. These impacts were experienced by 52 per cent of farms on the site, while 18 per cent experienced crop loss as a direct effect of landslides and 18 per cent had crops destroyed by debris deposits from both floods and landslides.

Some hazard impacts resulted in the direct loss of topsoil from plots, leading to a reduction in available space for cultivation and, in some cases, loss of planting material. This occurs with riverine flooding and erosional landslides. In contrast, plots affected by slide deposits, sheet floods, and waterlogging were better able to accommodate replanting efforts, thereby promoting higher levels of agrobiodiversity. Indications are, however, that replanting of crops such as banana monoculture following a hazard impact reduces the area of non-cultivated plant species, thus reducing overall biodiversity. Banana monoculture orchards were the most severely affected crop, reflecting not only the dominance of banana production at the demonstration site, but also the biological properties of banana which make it vulnerable to waterlogging and bruising.

Overall, floods and/or landslides have impacted on 88 per cent of the sampled plots. Of these, over 27 per cent sustained damage to more than three-quarters of the area and about 30 per cent sustained damage to less than a quarter. A significant relationship was observed between field type and the proportion of the plot affected by hazards. Field types involving monoculture banana were found to be most severely impacted. Spatial location of field types relative to slope and drainage significantly affect the type of impact. With the more vulnerable plots it is more likely the farmers will employ biodiversity management strategies to mitigate impact; areas that are highly vulnerable to flooding are either planted with water-tolerant crops such as *dasheen* or left in fallow. Sixty-six per cent of farmers cultivating steep slopes employed plants to control soil erosion.

Farmers use a variety of cultivated and non-cultivated species to mitigate the impact of floods and landslides. Species used include banana, coconut, fruit trees, grass, growsick, lumber, sugarcane, wild cane, and pineapples. Bamboo and lumber were the most commonly used species. Interestingly, farmers' knowledge and awareness of the utility of certain species for hazard mitigation did not always correspond with their actual use of these species. In most cases knowledge of utility exceeded actual use primarily because growing a specific plant is largely dependent on its income-generating capacity and other characteristics may make it unattractive to farmers. The use of bamboo and grass in binding soil and reducing soil erosion was well known, but their use was not widespread as they lack economic value. Farmers were also aware that the matted roots of bamboo stifle the growth of cultivated crops.

Agrochemical use and agrodiversity among small-scale farmers

The research sought to establish the types of fertilizers and pesticides used, factors influencing their use, and the types of crops and plants present on farms. Through these assessments the study hoped to gather information on variations in agrochemical use as farm and crop types change, and the interrelationships between agrochemical use and agrobiodiversity.

Eighty-two per cent of the farmers in the valley used an agrochemical, and more than 80 per cent thought agrochemical application was a key part of crop production. A total of seven fertilizers and 20 pesticides were used by farmers within the demonstration site. Within the agroforest and house garden land-use stages there were less chemical inputs compared with the orchard/plantation land-use stage. Sixty-six per cent of the agrochemical use was in the export cropping system. These farms produced banana and coffee, which both require substantial inputs of agrochemicals to meet market standards. The orchard/plantation land-use stage employed more than one and up to five types of fertilizers, which include ammonia, sulphate, phosphate, and a range of mixtures. Eight pesticides were used. Fertilizers were also used on yam, plantain, vegetables, peppers, and *dasheen*. Pesticide use on farms has short-term impacts on the agrobiodiversity of the farm. Fortunately, many of the species removed are resilient and will regenerate.

Agrobiodiversity and food security among farming households

A study was conducted to assess the interrelationships between the level of agrobiodiversity on small farms and the food security of farm households. Generally there was a high level of food security, although incidences of short-term food shortage were found and 42 per cent of farm households reported experiencing food shortage during the past year. The shortage was seasonal and transitory for segments of the site population. Strong community ties and a culture of sharing contribute to the assurance of adequate food for all households. Most households use a number of coping strategies, including seeking off-farm employment, borrowing money from friends and relatives, getting remittances from relatives overseas, using credit, eating with friends or relatives, changing food preparation patterns (one-pot meals), reducing consumption (one meal a day), and changing the diet to more accessible foods.

There was only a weak relationship between agrobiodiversity on cultivated plots and food security of the household. Even though cultivating a larger variety of crops gives some households greater access to food, they were not necessarily more food secure than households that grew fewer crops but purchased what they need. Export farmers are least likely to be food insecure because a large proportion of the local diet is imported (milk, cheese, butter, wheat flour, rice, and cod fish) and export farmers are more able to purchase these products. In contrast, income from the sale of farm produce in the domestic market does not always cover household expenditure. Household income and not the level of agrobiodiversity is more critical to food security.

Conclusion

PLEC activities have brought about a process of change, with the overarching achievement being the acceptance, by expert and collaborating farmers, of a new paradigm for the dissemination of knowledge. The farmers came to recognize that they themselves had valuable knowledge of agricultural and environmental management. The knowledge flow occurred between farmers and scientists in a two-way direction, but it has also occurred between farmers. Another important outcome was the development of collaborative experimentation on the farms of the expert farmers, with farmers discussing strategies and results of the experiments. The specifics of the relationships and the process are unique to each group and are different from one community to another. There is no template or fixed model for the successful transfer of knowledge at a demonstration site, except that both agricultural practices and social relations must be considered in facilitating the process of agrodiversity knowledge transfer. The way in which the process unfolds is always tentative. The researchers must therefore be led by the specific dynamics of each demonstration site in which they may work. PLEC activity included meetings with agencies involved in community development and agricultural projects, and the PLEC student members have moved on to posts in national and international agencies where they will be in positions of influence.

A number of measures have been taken to ensure the continuation of PLEC outcomes beyond 2002. These include establishing a framework for the continued exchange of ideas and transfer of good farming practices between expert farmers and other community members. The project activities have facilitated a breakdown of interpersonal suspicions and enabled a level of openness that will allow farmers to continue the process of information transfer. The success of this process will require some intervention by PLEC scientists, as a holistic approach is required involving all stakeholders at the site. PLEC has sought to engage local stakeholders such as the Rural Agricultural Development Agency and national policy-makers, particularly within the Ministry of Agriculture and Lands but also at the

Office of Disaster Preparedness and Emergency Management, and local NGOs. While demonstration activities have been conducted, monitoring and evaluation of outcomes will need to be ongoing.

Notes

1. The authors wish to acknowledge the large contribution of Karyll Johnston to the Jamaica-PLEC work.
2. There was a high level of awareness on the part of the expert farmers of the dangers of improper handling of the agrochemicals. Only one used a broadcasting method of applying chemical fertilizers to the crops; the others used a "ringing" method. Protective gear used by the farmers included gloves, respirators, and masks. Unused agrochemicals were either buried or burned.
3. Ackee is the national fruit of Jamaica. Its name is derived from the West African *akye fufo*. The tree is not endemic to the West Indies but was introduced from West Africa during the eighteenth century. A member of the *Sapindaceae*, ackee is a relative of the litchi and longan. The fruit itself is not edible. It is the fleshy arils around the seeds that are edible, and they must be collected only after the fruit has opened naturally. The remainder of the fruit, including the seeds, is poisonous.

REFERENCES

Ferguson, H. 1998. *The Effective Allocation of Watershed Resources Using GIS Technology: The Case of the Rio Grande Watershed*. Kingston, Jamaica: University of Technology.

Mines and Geology Division. 2000. *Landslide Susceptibility Map of the Rio Grande Valley, Portland*. Kingston, Jamaica: Mines and Geology Division, Ministry of Mining and Energy.

Morrison, E. 2001. "Agrobiodiversity responses to flood and landslide hazards in the Rio Grande watershed, Jamaica", unpublished MSc dissertation, UWI Mona, Kingston, Jamaica.

NRCD. 1987. *Jamaica: Country Environmental Profile*. Kingston, Jamaica: Natural Resources Conservation Department.

Thomas-Hope, E., B. Spence, and H. Semple. 1999. "Biodiversity within the small farming systems of the Rio Grande watershed, Jamaica", paper presented at the Seminario Internacional Sobre Agridiversidad Campesina, Toluca, Mexico.

Thomas-Hope, E. and B. Spence. 2002. "Promoting agrobiodiversity under difficulties: The Jamaica-PLEC experience", *PLEC News and Views*, No. 19, pp. 17–24.

Zarin, D. J., H. Guo, and L. Enu-Kwesi. 1999. "Method for the assessment of plant species diversity in complex agricultural landscapes: Guidelines for data collection and analysis from the PLEC biodiversity advisory group (BAG)", *PLEC News and Views*, No. 13, pp. 3–16.

14

Thailand

Kanok Rerkasem[1]

Introduction

Thailand was one of the countries in which PLEC began work in 1992, and
from 1993 to 1997 it formed part of a joint "Montane Mainland South-east
Asia" cluster with China (Chapter 9). Unfortunately, Thailand is among a
small number of countries that have not ratified the 1992 Convention on
Biological Diversity, thus ruling it out of eligibility for GEF support. Support came from the United Nations University and national sources, in particular the Thailand Research Fund. By 2002 the cluster had achieved a
coup attained by no other when its principal demonstration site at Pah Poo
Chom became a national pilot village for a government programme entitled "Farmers' Field School for Sustainable Highland Development and
Environmental Conservation".

Evolution of work

Work in Thailand evolved out of a 20-year period of work on traditional
shifting cultivation among the minority groups of the northern uplands,
with its strong focus on finding viable systems to replace the cultivation of
opium and ease concern over deforestation (Kunstadter and Chapman
1978; McKinnon and Vienne 1989; Anderson 1993). It grew also out of the
work of the South-east Asian Universities' Agroecosystem Network, which
had been inspired by Conway (1986).

Initially the team selected four villages, Pah Poo Chom (Hmong Njua) in Chiang Mai province, Mae Salap (Akha, or Hani in China), and Mae Rid Pagae and Tee Cha (Karen) in Mae Hong Son province, covering a wide range of historical and present production systems and land use. From 1999 onwards, with limited resources, the team concentrated only on Pah Poo Chom and Tee Cha. The former is easily accessible, but Tee Cha is high on a divide close to the Myanmar border, and during most of the wet season is inaccessible by road. It therefore remained mainly a research site, and most demonstration work was done in Pah Poo Chom. PLEC survey methodology was applied in both locations, in place of earlier work using Conway's agroecosystem approach. The team consists of scientists from Chiang Mai University, extension and development workers from the Department of Public Welfare and the Royal Forest Department, and some NGOs, principally CARE/Thailand.

The Hmong of Pah Poo Chom are former opium growers who traditionally practise pioneer shifting cultivation. Unlike the Karen, who practise rotational shifting cultivation around permanent settlements, the Hmong shifting cultivation involved clearing mature forests for intensive opium production until soil fertility was completely exhausted. Then they moved to the next forest area to open new fields. The community has successfully changed from its traditional system to intensive vegetable and fruit production. In contrast, Tee Cha is a Karen community with dominant subsistence production of upland rice in a rotational shifting cultivation system, which continues. Mae Salap and Mae Rid Pagae fall in between the two extreme communities described above, with partial commercialization with cash crops (Figure 14.1).

Pah Poo Chom

Pah Poo Chom is a Hmong Njua (green/blue Hmong) village. It is located at 920 m in a small watershed of the Huai Mae Chaem, which drains ultimately into the Chiang Mai Valley. The village administration falls under the Keud Chang subdistrict of Mae Taeng in Chiang Mai province. The thoroughgoing changes that have taken place in Pah Poo Chom since 1960 are set out in detail by Thong-ngam *et al.* (2002).

The modern history of Pah Poo Chom began in the early 1960s when some 10 Hmong households voluntarily moved into the area which had been designated as Nikhom (government resettlement scheme) in the districts of Chiang Dao and Mae Taeng (Van Roy 1971). During 1960–1969, a period in which some Hmong and other insurgents were fighting the government, many settlers fled to join relatives or find other alternative sites for settlement. This was a difficult time when the majority of villagers suf-

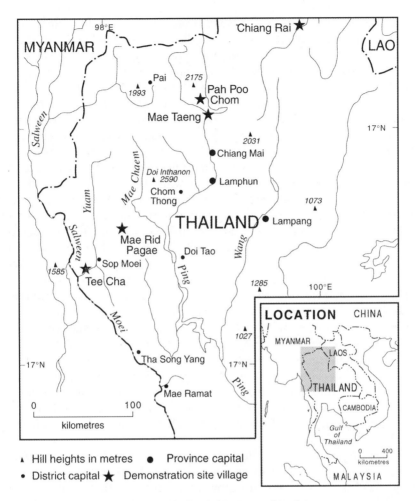

Figure 14.1 Thailand demonstration sites

fered from severe poverty and food shortage. Social and economic conditions in the village were difficult, with a high population of opium addicts and little opportunity for employment. The village was then located on a bare ridge at a low altitude of about 900 m, and this was uncomfortable for the Hmong who had previously lived at a high altitude, 1,300–1,500 m (Walker 1975). According to Cooper (1984) the village was, in this period, on the brink of collapse due to unfavourable social and economic conditions.

Matters improved rapidly after 1970, and the population had grown to 343 persons in 57 households by 2000. At present the village is formally registered as a cluster of a nearby lowland village, Ban Ton Kham. External development support from the Royal Thai Government and international agencies started early after village establishment. By the late 1990s the village was regarded as one of the more prosperous hill-tribe villages with intensive land use, permanent housing, and improvement of living conditions. With the recent establishment of the Tambon Administrative Organization according to government policy on decentralization, small financial support can be accessed. As Pah Poo Chom is being processed to obtain official status, an increase in government funding for village development is expected.

The land form of the site is residual hills, with weathered granite and shale as parent materials. The soil is acid, with pH of 5.0–5.3. The texture is mainly sandy loam with good internal drainage. The soil is fairly deep (more than 1.5 m) in the major agricultural area in the lower fields with gentle slopes (10–25 per cent), due to erosional deposits from the steeper upper fields, where the soil depth is only 20–30 cm (Rerkasem and Guo 1995). Cabbage is the dominant cash crop with sprinkler irrigation. With increasing areas planted to litchi, cabbage production is being pushed to the upper fields by extending irrigation. Using local innovation and traditional knowledge of land husbandry, the vegetable farmers manage the land with massive regeneration of *Mimosa invisa* ground cover in the wet season, escaping the heavy rains of June–August to plant the first cabbage at the end of September to early October. The dominant land-use patterns are monoculture of cabbage or a simple mixture of litchi as a canopy crop with vegetables or traditional crops grown underneath. Two crops of cabbage are grown with irrigation during the cooler months of the year. Marketing is by pick-up truck, of which more than 15 were owned in the village by 2002.

At field-type level, the production systems are more diverse. Many farmers are managing patches of varying size and shape within and between major land uses, as "edges" for growing a variety of traditional crops and local vegetables formerly grown in swidden fields for household consumption. This type of field can be seen with scattered patches of forest trees and other useful species between major agricultural fields and in the riparian area (Korsamphan, Thong-ngam, and Rerkasem 2001). There is high proportion of forests on steep slopes and hilltops, with community management for conservation and local use.

PLEC activity at Pah Poo Chom: Local expert farmers

The selection and participation of local expert farmers are crucial to ensure the success of a PLEC demonstration. Expert farmers were selected on the basis of their innovative management skills and knowledge. They are from mixed social and economic backgrounds. In Pah Poo Chom one of the local experts was elected as village headman in 2000, while others are older women from poor households with no cabbage fields or litchi. Initial contact and assistance from village leaders provided the entry point for demonstration activity in the village.

Selection of expert farmers began with field assessment at the preparatory phase of demonstration site work. Farmers were invited to participate in the village ecosystem appraisal, identification and assessment of land-use stages and field types, field inventory, and assessment of biodiversity and agrodiversity management. Distinct farmers' management and innovation observed during the assessment identified experts who were doing something different from the others. With discussion and consultation, field owners agreed to establish demonstration plots for field measurement and monitoring. There are a total of 10 plots for demonstration: seven for edge management and three for agrodiversity management of intensive cropping. Selection of local experts was an interactive and iterative process from site preparation to demonstration. The number of local experts increased from four to 10 as demonstration activity progressed. Female participation was maintained throughout the project cycle, with the number of women expert farmers increasing from three to five.

Expert farmers work with the PLEC team to conduct field experiments, assist in data collection and plot monitoring, and share their views on the interpretation of field results. Knowledge gained is used for farmers' exchanges in and between the villages, field training, and other government programmes. Village workshops were arranged to support farmer-to-farmer exchange. This method was found to be very effective, with the help at the beginning of a PLEC member as facilitator. PLEC helped the local experts to prepare field results and present their demonstration plots to other farmers from inside and outside the village, in particular during farmers' field-school sessions in 2001. Some local experts in Pah Poo Chom have been chosen as local trainers in a government programme for rural development.

Formation and value of the farmers' association

Before PLEC work began there was an informal village organization for forest protection and water management for sprinkler irrigation, but its mandate and function were not clear to the community. As a result, internal conflicts arose and increased over time, due to forest clearing for farming and inadequate water supply for dry-season irrigation, for cabbage in particular. Introduction of an idea for community land-use planning was successful. With relevant data and information, such as land use, landholdings, crops and cropping practices, and other biophysical and agricultural information, the method helped to bring the community to work together and sort out the problems. Along with PLEC demonstrations, many people have seen the examples of "best practices" from local experts and have had the opportunity to discuss them openly.

The example of Saophang Saetao, who manages agroforest edges up a small watershed on the western side of the village, clearly illustrates "best practice" for alternative biodiversity-rich systems. This kind of field demonstration also helps to raise discussion in group meetings on values and knowledge of traditional (Hmong) management and conservation. Many young people in the village have actually lost these values and traditions. They have never practised any form of shifting cultivation and have negligible knowledge about the systems.

With confidence gained through the learning process, people decided to set up a farmers' association for forest protection and biodiversity conservation, now formally organized as the Village Committee for Forest Protection and Biodiversity Conservation. The PLEC team provided technical training to the members of the committee on land-use planning, field mapping, and monitoring and evaluation of land use and change. With the implementation of a national policy and cabinet decision on land use in the mountains in early 2000, villagers from Pah Poo Chom were able to submit their village land occupation plan to the local authority for a land-use permit. The committee is currently working with the Tambon Administrative Organization to coordinate land-use planning and conservation at a subdistrict level, with possible expansion of the village association to an inter-village network. The development of the village committee in this direction has attracted the local Royal Forest Office to coordinate villagers for the government reforestation and forest protection programme in the near future. This means that the reforestation budget will be another funding source for village development. Plans to sustain this PLEC activity are now under way.

Value of PLEC activity to the farmers and their families

PLEC works with six local experts on the production and management of complex and diverse systems, ranging from mixtures of swidden crops to annuals mixed with perennials to form a complex structure of multiple canopy layers for agroforestry systems. The activity aims to demonstrate the value of the systems for household food security, stable income, and maintenance and enhancement of biodiversity through *in situ* conservation.

Production of former swidden crops, annual and perennial legumes and non-leguminous crops, vegetables, spices, herbs, and many other plants is one of the major functions of women in the households. They grow the crops in small plots in or between the major production fields, creating the edge field type. The production from edges is mainly related to cooking and food preparation for the family.[2] Supply from edges is ideally made possible all year round if adequate local germplasm is available to provide suitable crops for different seasons. The products may also be used for bartering with neighbouring households or selling to external markets for supplementary cash income. In the local market near the village, growers sell fresh chilli at B50–60/kg, fresh pods of local yardlong bean at B12/kg, a bunch of boiling waxy corn cobs at B10/bunch (five or six cobs), and fresh fruit of Hmong cucumber at B5–10/kg.[3] Supplementary income is used to purchase food flavourings such as soy sauce, fish sauce, monosodium glutamate, and salt for cooking.

As men are not involved in feeding the family, their perceptions of crop diversification are very different from those of the women. Men have a strong bias toward specialized production of cabbage or litchi in monoculture or with a few simple mixtures of cash crops. For them, this provides the major source of income for the family and the opportunity for high capital investment in years with favourable cabbage prices and good yields, when they can buy such things as a new pick-up vehicle. Unfortunately, the strategy does not work very well. The probability of a "good year" for cabbage is very low indeed – usually when the price is exceptionally high, output turns out to be very low. Furthermore, cabbage prices fluctuate, for example from B2–3/kg to B5–15/kg in a matter of a few days. Only a few people have been lucky in the past.

Saophang Saetao, who is more than 65 years old, is an outstanding expert farmer. He had a higher income and greater crop diversification with his agroforest edges than from either cabbage or litchi. Annual income from Saophang's agroforest edge varies between B40,000 and B60,000, as compared with B15,000–35,000 for the cabbage growers. With his skill, Saophang is able to make and sell a musical instrument, locally referred to as *can* (a kind of traditional pipe), at B3,500–4,000 each. The pipe is made from a special bamboo species (*zong qeng* in Hmong) of fairly small size and with a hard stem. He also maintains a large number of medicinal herbs, wild trees for vegetables, and wild fruits for his household.

The idea of crop diversification promoted from PLEC demonstrations now provides an alternative agricultural strategy for income generation and food security, with more resilience to external forces such as variable market prices.

Management diversity in relation to land and biodiversity in Pah Poo Chom demonstration site

Use of natural vegetation as ground cover

Mixtures of annuals, perennial grasses, and some introduced legume species, including *Ageratum conyzoides*, *Brachiaria ramosa*, *Chromolaena odorata, Chrysopogon aciculatus, Eupatorium adenophorum, Mimosa invisa, Pennisetum purpureum, P. pedicellatum, Panicum repens, Paspalum* spp., and others are used as ground cover and green manure during fallow periods in the wet season.

Management of weeds for soil improvement

This is now very common in Pah Poo Chom. Since the introduction of mimosa (*Mimosa invisa*) from an adjacent lowland village for fencing to protect a vegetable garden from farm animals, rapid dispersal of the weed was fairly troublesome at the beginning of its introduction. A few farmers began to observe the positive contribution of *M. invisa* residue on the following maize crop. At that time, soils in Pah Poo Chom were exhausted due to intensive use of land for permanent agriculture. Soils under mimosa plants after clearing and burning have improved physical properties (increased porosity) and fertility. The weed has become an important part of farm management, and farmers occasionally sow seeds to increase its density with uniform distribution. Some even buy the seeds from their neighbours. Management of mimosa is simple. Slashing will easily kill the vines of mature mimosa. Plant residues are left for about four to six weeks before the first-season cabbage is planted in September. Burning residues on the soil surface helps to clean the fields before seedbed preparation using hand tools. Soils are then turned over to cover ashes and plant residues provide organic matter to the soils. The amount of nitrogen fixed by mimosa as live mulch or green manure in the maize crop was estimated at about 47 kgN/ha, giving a total amount of nitrogen with corn trash of 67 kgN/ha (Rerkasem, Yoneyama, and Rerkasem 1992).

Management of edges for soil, water, and biodiversity conservation

This is observed as
- *Vitiveria zizanioides* or *Leucaena leucocephala/Cajanus cajan* strips, trashlines of crop residues, and weeds (e.g. *Chromolaena odorata*) on contour strips for soil conservation
- maintaing natural agroforestry edges between agricultural fields for water conservation and conservation of swidden crop species or wild fruits and other perennials or forest trees
- narrow strip of wild banana or bamboo as an edge for field marking.

External development agencies and extension workers introduced the idea of vegetative strips. However, the maintenance of the strips was poor and they deteriorated on a long-term basis. A few areas of vegetative strips can be seen in the village. It remains unclear whether the strips are necessary to prevent soil erosion as farmers are managing the land with minimum disturbance.

Use of physical barriers such as dead logs, tree stumps, and big rocks to protect soil on sloping fields

Farmers often leave these in the fields across the slope. With intensive cultivation, tree stumps will possibly be removed or burned. Coppicing is uncommon, as the Hmong seldom maintain big trees in agricultural fields. Big trees are left for spiritual reasons or personal preference.

Row planting across the slope

This is adopted in the dry season for the convenience of crop irrigation by movable sprinklers, and helps to prevent soil erosion. Row planting along the slope was said to prevent landslides in the wet season. Excessive rain is drained out. The amount of erosion depends on the percentage of groundcover.

Minimum tillage

The traditional Hmong method of planting opium is using hand tools for land preparation. A few farmers use tractors to plough their lands in the low-lying fields where slopes are gentle.

Unclean weeding

This is traditional practice with annual crops and vegetables. Farmers leave useful species naturally emerged in the fields for their household consumption and the method helps to increase the percentage of ground cover between crop rows.

Fallow management in the wet season

Fallowing is somewhat uncommon for Hmong farmers in general. Some farmers in Pah Poo Chom start their first-season cabbage fairly late, in the middle of October to early November. Only small patches are opened up for the cabbage nurseries. The major land preparation is delayed until the end of the wet season and most cropping is finished before the beginning of the next wet season, except those fields planted to hot-season crops such as glutinous corn and soyabean. With intensive cropping practices, the field has adequate time for mimosa growth to accumulate significant biomass before slashing. Soil erosion in this system is fairly low, varying from 1.05 to 4.93 tonnes per hectare per year. The extent of erosion depends on the timing of land preparation, unpredictable rain at the end of the season, and cropping intensity.

Incorporation of crop and weed residues

This is also a common practice of hill farmers. In the case of fruit trees, branches pruned off to open up the tree canopy will be left underneath the trees. Weeds would be slashed down and the trash left to cover the ground.

Using shade-resistant bush species like coffee to improve and sustain bench terraces

This is farmers' innovation after the introduction of bench terraces by some development projects. A litchi grower in the village was observed to practise interplanting of coffee under the mature litchi along the edge of a terrace that would become a bench terrace in the long term. Contrasting habits of annuals and perennials differentiate the environmental space, providing a superior intercropping system.

Sustainable harvest of minor forest products

Harvesting has been agreed for the extraction of bamboo shoots in utility forests in the village. In the past, the bamboo forests almost collapsed due to uncontrolled harvesting to meet external demand for wood and young shoots. Currently shoot harvesting is not permitted in order to improve natural regeneration. Young shoots may be collected for a canning factory as long as an adequate number of shoots per tree are left behind for regeneration. Destructive harvesting of bamboo worms is also not permitted.

Intercropping and strip planting of swidden crops and Hmong vegetables

This is widely practised in the cabbage fields to meet household needs and to some extent conserve genetic resources of the local varieties. This may be seen as another edge type, but the practice is much simpler than in the edges found in separate patches of swidden crops. Hmong leaf mustard (*Brassica junceae*) is the common species found in this type of edge. A one-row strip of the leaf mustard is directly seeded along the border of cabbage fields, with staggered planting for successive harvesting.

Staggered planting and rotating crops between different fields with traditional and local crop species

These are cropping strategies to reduce pest and disease problems and use fertilizer residue from the previous crops. Cabbage is never planted immediately after harvesting in the same plot. There is a break to reduce pest and disease problems. The first-season cabbage requires minimum spraying as compared to the second crop in the dry season. Fertilizer residue from the first-season cabbage may be carried over to the following glutinous corn in the next season on the same piece of land. Farmers never apply any fertilizer to the glutinous corn.

Spot application of chemical fertilizers

Fertilizers are applied to individual hills of cabbage and other cash crops, such as Chinese cabbage, potato, carrots, other vegetables, and soyabean. This practice not only saves large amounts of fertilizer but it increases fertilizer use efficiency. For cabbage, only a small amount of a complete fertilizer such as 15-15-15 NPK is applied to individual hills one or two weeks after transplanting, when seedlings fully recover from the transplanting shock. Another top-dressing application may be required before head formation. Vegetables are normally harvested about 50–60 days after transplanting.

Branch pruning, girdling, and cincturing

These practices, undertaken to induce flowering and fruit set in commercial fruit trees, especially the litchi in Pah Poo Chom, are being tested by growers. It is generally believed that litchi need a period of vegetative dormancy in the cool season to flower successfully at the beginning of the hot dry season. The dormancy is normally induced by biophysical stresses, such as moisture or temperature. Artificially induced techniques such as controlling irrigation and fertilizers, growth regulators, root pruning, branch girdling, or cincturing may work. An in-depth interview with key growers in the villages and other Hmong villages in Chiang Mai province cannot confirm whether the methods of branch girdling or cincturing work. Nevertheless, this practice indicates a flow of local innovation among the focus group.

Growing living fences in home gardens

This practice is adopted to protect animals and prevent soil erosion. The practice is, however, limited to a few farmers who have taken reasonable care of their home gardens. The reasons for undeveloped home gardens in Pah Poo Chom are as yet unknown.

Effects of management on biodiversity

Among other ethnic groups in northern Thailand, the Hmong are known to grow a diversity of non-rice staple crops, legumes, local vegetables, herbs, medicinal plants, and some perennials in association with both upland rice and opium in their traditional shifting cultivation (Anderson 1993; Sutthi 1989, 1990, 1996). After the shift from traditional agricultural systems to permanent agriculture, the conservation of traditional crop species and many landraces became more difficult due to the introduction of alternatives from external sources (Sutthi 1990). However, the role of traditional crops remains for daily meals for the family, as local food habits have remained unchanged. In the case of Pah Poo Chom where cabbage is the dominant crop for cash income, women in the households have to find ways to produce traditional crops for cooking and other needs. Some grow local spices and herbs in a few containers in front of the house, while others grow them in home gardens and other field types, including the cabbage fields.

From the agrodiversity field assessment and monitoring plots, 52 species of traditional crops, not including fruit trees and herbaceous shrubs, were identified in the village. In a survey of 23 households using a semi-formal

Table 14.1 The extent of traditional crops grown by women in Pah Poo Chom

	Number of respondents (n = 23)				
	0	1–5	6–10	11–15	Total
Species grown	7	23	14	8	52
Percentage	13.5	44.2	26.9	15.4	100

questionnaire conducted to follow up the estimate, only eight species were grown by the majority of respondents (Table 14.1). In contrast, seven species or 13.5 per cent of the total number of traditional crops were not grown at all. Fortunately, they still remain in the expert farmers' plots.

Traditional crops are found in edges within and between the major production fields for crops such as cabbage, carrots, canning beans, and upland rice. Examples of the diversity of species and varieties of traditional crops, ranging from annual crops to various kinds of vegetables, herbs, edible vines and other perennials, a few wild and domesticated fruit trees, and spontaneous wild species, are shown in Table 14.2.

About 10 women are managing the complex mixture of edges at the moment. Five of them have joined PLEC demonstrations as expert farmers to promote enriched edge systems as potential areas for *in situ* conservation. In comparison to other traditional crop growers, the local experts grow the highest number of species, ranging from 17 to 40 species, with staggered planting of different crops throughout the growing seasons. The species richness of traditional crops in managed edges is higher, more abundant, and of even distribution compared to upland rice plots (Tables 14.3 and 14.4).

Agroforest edges: A model of production diversification and conservation objectives

Agroforest edges are common in Pah Poo Chom, but the field type can be easily missed in field assessment. The edges are production fields – they are "village property" assigned to adjoining landowners to care for natural vegetation cover to conserve the underground water supply for domestic use in the dry season. In general, the responsible households look after the edges with minimum management, except Saophang who is managing his agroforest edge with production and conservation objectives (Korsamphan, Thong-ngam, and Rerkasem 2001).

As expected, the managed edges of the expert farmer show higher values of abundance and diversity indices in comparison to the minimally managed edges of non-experts (Table 14.5). Through a continual process of species enrichment, the agroforest edge managed by the local expert has

Table 14.2 Plant species and their numbers in an edge containing a mixture of local plants and wild vegetables

Plant name	Plant count (numbers/sample)
Domesticated species	
Hmong glutinous corn (*Zea mays* L.)	300
Shallot (*Allium ascalonicum* L.)	1,150
Hmong leaf mustard (*Brassica juncea* L. [Czern and Coss])	250
Pumpkins (*Cucurbita moschata* [Duch. ex Laus] Duch. ex Poir)	4
Coriander (*Cariandrum sativum* L.)	5
Sweet potato (*Ipomoea batatas* (L.) Lamk.)	3
Litchi seedlings (*Litchi chinensis* L.)	1
Semi-domesticated species	
Wild bitter gourd (*Momordica* sp.)	20
Susumber (*Solanum torvum* Sw.)	1
Wild herbaceous species naturally emerged	
Lum phasi (*Crasscepphalum crepidiodes* [benth.] S. Moore)	. 1
Amaranth for pig feed (*Amaranthus viridis* L.)	1
Edible fern (*Asytasiella neesiana* Lindau.)	11
Tong sard for food or sweet wrapping (*Phrynium capitatum* Willd.)	9 (hills)
Wild banana (*Musa acuminata* Colla.)	22 (hills)
Kong (*Zingiberaceae*) edible fruit, leaves used for rice barn and fibre for rope	5 (hills)
Total (15 species)	1,783

Note: Plant counts were taken from a sample size of 5×10 m across the edge at the end of the growing season of swidden crops in February 2000. A few species remained to be harvested for seeds.

Table 14.3 A comparison between plots of expert farmers and other growers

Category of growers	Number of samples	Species	
		Number	Range
Expert farmer	5	29	17–40
Typical growers[1]	14	16	8–25
Strip planting[2]	9	6	4–8

Notes
1. Typical growers represent women who are growing traditional crops in any field types, including edges.
2. These are growers who planted their traditional crops in a narrow strip in the cabbage field or other vegetable plots. The strip may be a single row of leaf mustard or pumpkin along the boundary.

Table 14.4 Species abundance, richness, and derived Shannon index of managed edges of expert farmers compared to traditional upland rice plots

Systems of cultivation	Area (rai)[1]	Plot size (m × m)	Abundance (plants/rai)	Species richness	Shannon index
Managed edges of local experts	(2.16)		(57,419)	(18.7)	(2.00)
Farmer 1	2.00	30 × 30	1,073	15	2.39
Farmer 2	2.00	10 × 10	205,024[2]	20	2.31
Farmer 3	0.14	10 × 10	5,446	17	2.26
Farmer 4	4.50	10 × 10	18,136	23	1.02
Upland rice plots	(1.5)		(1,967/18,400)[3]	(14.5)	(0.65)
Plot 1	2.00	40 × 40	256/14,400	22	1.01
Plot 2	2.00	10 × 10	5,824/25,600	15	0.96
Plot 3	1.00	10 × 10	1,620/14,400	10	0.59
Plot 4	2.00	40 × 40	168/19,200	11	0.07

Notes
1. One rai is equivalent to 1,600 m^2 or 0.16 ha. Measurements were taken (November 2000) to coincide with the time when formerly harvest of upland rice overlapped with the beginning of the opium season and diverse traditional crops grown in association with the crops could be seen in edges with good residual soil moisture.
2. The high abundance value in Farmer 2's plot was due to high numbers of three species, brassica seedlings, glutinous corn, and shallot, recorded at 160,000, 25,600, and 16,000 plants/rai respectively.
3. Figures are given for the abundance of traditional crops/upland rice.

Table 14.5 Biodiversity assessment of agroforest edges

Responsible person for management	Total individuals	Species richness	Shannon index	Margalef index
PLEC expert farmer Saophang	717	114	2.77	17.19
Non-experts (average)	315	38	2.35	6.39
– Juk Saehang	332	33	2.29	5.51
– Jointly managed by Chao and Chang Seng	315	18	1.54	2.96
– Unidentified person	300	62	3.24	10.69

114 species with a total of 717 individuals in the sample plots. Most of the tree species can be used for firewood, and other species are more specifically used as food, construction material, and for making tools (Table 14.6). There are herbs and spices for medicinal and other household uses. The economic benefits and source of income gained from diversified products have been discussed above.

Saophang's agroforest edge is located in a riparian area of a small water-

Table 14.6 Use of tree species in an agroforest edge managed by the expert farmer in Pah Poo Chom

Use	Number of species	Other uses				
		Herbs and spices	Construction	Farm tools	Firewood	Other
Food	25	1	6	6	14	4
Herbs/spices	16		3	1	5	2
Construction	24			8	20	1
Farm tools	18				14	2
Firewood	78					4

shed of a tributary of the Mae Taman. The management of the agroforest edge provides an ecological service, as the watershed is a headwater for dry-season irrigation. The area protected is 56.5 ha used for intensive production of vegetables and litchi orchards by eight households that formed into a small water-user group to manage and maintain the headwater and irrigation system.

Apart from the conservation value of agroforest edges, the agrodiversity management of the agroforest edges by Saophang also illustrates the positive economic and ecological values of agroforest edges beyond the field type. It links the economic incentive of the managing farmer to the headwater conservation objective of the water-users' group. The demonstration has had significant implications for the larger-scale management of village headwaters, where the intensity of conflicts and disputes had been increasing in the community and between Pah Poo Chom and other villages downstream.

Community-based land-use planning for maintenance and enrichment of biodiversity

From November 2001 to January 2002, a short series of field workshops was arranged for the village committee to discuss and share different views about future village development. These workshops were based on experiences and lessons from PLEC demonstration activities over the previous three years, with emphasis on agrodiversity, and maintenance and enrichment of biodiversity in the context of land use in the village. The idea was to find ways in which PLEC demonstration of agrodiversity management with the focus on biodiversity maintenance and enrichment would go beyond the field level of local experts. A village meeting involved other members of the village. There was also a need for negotiation with a few landholders whose plots are located in the boundary of the protected area to limit further expansion or to return the land to natural forest wherever appropriate. Members of Tambon Administrative Organization, local development agencies from the district and subdistrict, and foresters were invited to discuss and share the results of the community workshops at the end of the series. A draft of the village plan for land use, forest protection, and biodiversity conservation was presented. While the Tambon Administrative Organization took up the plan for further development action, foresters took an interest in working with villagers on reforestation and rehabilitation of degraded forests in the village.

One of the major results was consensus on a revision of village land use to encourage the maintenance and enrichment of biodiversity and prevent further encroachment into the headwater area for the production of cash crops. The most critical area is the headwater forest above the upper part of the village. Water from the headwater area is used for dry-season crops by most farming households in the village. At the end, it was decided to revise the demarcation of the headwater boundary to incorporate a larger area (Figures 14.2 and 14.3). The revised headwater boundary overlaps many

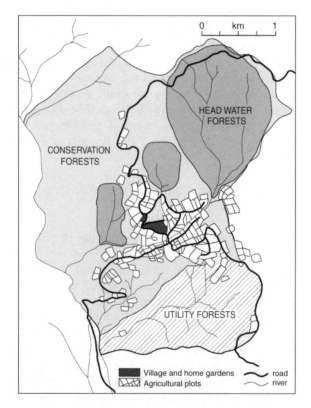

Figure 14.2 Pah Poo Chom land use in 1999

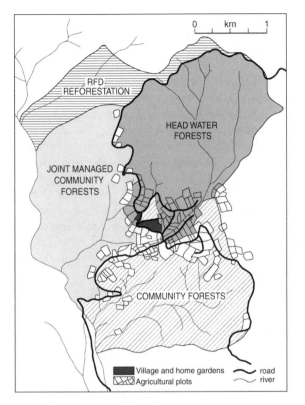

Figure 14.3 Planned land use at Pah Poo Chom as by community agreement in 2002

parcels of land already allocated in the early 1970s to households for wet-rice cultivation.[4] This does not mean that the landholders will have to give up their production for the purpose of conservation. The intention is to conserve natural biodiversity in the existing agroforest edges, with a dominance of wild banana and other wild species for local use.

Tee Cha

Tee Cha is a Pwo Karen village in Sop Moei, a border district of Mae Hong Son province. It is situated in a mountainous area, at an altitude of about 700 m, in the lower part of the Salween River basin. Karen is the largest population group along the Myanmar border in this area. Cross-border migration was normal between the Karen communities in the past, but this movement is now under government control with migration camps located near the village along the border. The village was said to have been established more than 200 years ago. In modern times it has had very little development assistance from external agencies, including the national government. Only unpaved roads were built by logging concessions in the teak forests in the past. The branch road from the valley up to Tee Cha takes at least 40 minutes to travel in good weather, but in the wet season, if it is passable, it can take three or four hours to reach the village. In recent years an international NGO (CARE/Thailand) has given some assistance to local communities on land-use planning and natural resource conservation. The area is being planned for a future national park, and community empowerment has been one of the issues addressed by the NGO to strengthen local communities and their traditional institutions.

The village has a total population of 148 persons in 41 households. The economy is geared to household consumption and subsistence, with production of upland rice and swidden crops. Some farmers may grow local chilli for the external market, but the area is limited and competes directly with traditional shifting cultivation of upland rice. Near the village are some wet-rice fields that are used to grow vegetables in winter, and there is also some cultivation of sugarcane from which villagers make a tasty muscovado-type sugar. It is sold in leaf-wrapped blocks down the neighbouring valley as far as the town of Mae Sariang.[5] Farmers may earn additional income from selling minor forest products, but the market is unreliable and there is a risk of being accused of breaking forestry laws and regulations. The household income ranges between B5,000 and B10,000 per year. Livestock, cattle in particular, are the major income source in some years. Rich households may own an elephant, valued at >B200,000 per animal, but with logging activity now almost ceased there is little income from elephants.

Traditionally, the Karen in Tee Cha could afford to grow upland rice in shifting cultivation, with a long fallow rotation of up to 15 or 20 years. With long fallow management, the community could produce adequate upland rice for its own consumption throughout the year. Productive regeneration of the long fallow is the key to sustainability of this type of shifting cultivation, and its agrodiversity management has been reported elsewhere (e.g. Rerkasem 2001; Sabhasri 1978; Zinke, Sabhasri, and Kunstadter 1978). At present the Karen in Tee Cha still maintain the traditional practice of collectively clearing a large fallow forest for production of one season of upland rice, but with increasing pressures on land the number of fallow fields has to be reduced. There are now only six pieces of fallow fields for rotation. This is very short compared with the cycle of 15–20 years in the past. Despite the fact that a large area in the village remains under forest cover, the clearing of forests is prohibited, with agreements both within and between the villages for communal use or conservation. Expansion of wet rice is another option for food security, but physical limitations (steep slopes and limited water supply) are severe constraints.

Productivity depends on the managed use of a local tree species for fallow enrichment, locally known as *letha* or *pada* (*Macaranga denticulata*). It is a prolific seed-producing species with massive production of biomass, and it associates with 20 arbuscular mycorrhizal fungi (Yimyam, Lodkaew, and Rerkasem 2001; Yimyam, Rerkasem, and Rerkasem 2003; Youpensuk and Lumyong 2001; Youpensuk *et al.* 2003). Experimental work has confirmed the value of mycorrhiza to the tree. The major soil type in Tee Cha is clay loam and highly acid, with pH between 4.2 and 5.5. PLEC is working with the local farmers to gain a better understanding of the contribution and agrodiversity management of *M. denticulata* to overcome the degradation of shifting cultivation and enhance the natural process of forest regeneration.

Yimyam, Lodkaew, and Rerkasem (2001) conducted a number of measurements in dense and sparse stands of *M. denticulata*, and in upland rice fields derived from such stands. *M. denticulata* establishes spontaneously in a rice field, and by the time the rice is harvested it has attained a height of up to two metres. Over the six years of fallow regeneration, the number of individuals per hectare falls from 66,000 to 4,200 in a dense area and 32,700 to 1,000 in a sparse area. Other species become more numerous than *M. denticulata* in a sparse area. In a dense area the amount of dry matter rises to over 42 t/ha, with all principal nutrients higher than in the biomass of a sparse area. In the subsequent rice crop, grain yield and straw weight are both much higher in the plots that carried dense *M. denticulata*, with grain yield of 3.04 t/ha, which is far higher than the regional average. This good result is obtained only if the fallow runs to the full six years; a plot cleared after three years showed only poor results.

Work with farmers in Tee Cha has involved three households engaged in field experimentation on management of *M. denticulata* and the effects on upland rice. They work with PLEC to collect data and monitor their upland rice fields. A few women also assisted the PLEC-Thailand team to carry out field surveys to assess the existing agrodiversity management and conservation practices of traditional crops in their shifting cultivation fields. Work continues, and Tee Cha is a now major site for research on "Agrodiversity for *in situ* Conservation of Thailand's Native Rice Germplasm", a new project supported by the McKnight Foundation for the next five years, beginning in 2002.

Research and the future of PLEC work

PLEC research has produced some significant results that have been reported widely in Thailand and internationally. PLEC organized a joint workshop with the Thailand Research Fund for national and international participants on regeneration ecology and management for degraded land-scapes and forest ecosystems during February 2001. Two of the PLEC papers presented in this workshop (Yimyam, Lodkaew, and Rerkasem 2001; Youpensuk and Lumyong 2001) have been accepted for international publication (Yimyam, Rerkasem, and Rerkasem 2003; Youpensuk *et al.* 2003). PLEC arranged annual review meetings each year with partner insti-tutions to inform partners about the project progress. In 2001 the meeting was jointly organized with the Thailand Research Fund for a wider audi-ence, to include researchers and undergraduate and graduate students from Chiang Mai and Mae Jo Universities, research institutes of the Department of Agriculture, and others. PLEC members have attended numerous national and international meetings and conferences, organized both by PLEC and by non-PLEC institutions, to share the experience and lessons learned from the demonstration sites.

There were many informal training and village meetings for farmers and the farmers' association. Village forums at least once a year were organized for groups interested in the demonstration activities. A field-day was held at the end of the project to involve other nearby villages and members of local administrative organizations. PLEC is actively involved in formal training conducted by the Department of Public Welfare in the form of farmers' field-schools, where expert farmers have opportunities to present their demonstration plots and management techniques or innovative prac-tices.

The sustainability of PLEC work in Thailand has already been estab-lished with the adoption of Pah Poo Chom as a village model for a national programme. This is particularly important. The farmers' field-school pro-gramme aims to demonstrate successful development and local capacity to maintain and manage the rich biodiversity on marginal uplands. The pro-gramme is devoted to farmer-to-farmer extension of local ideas and inno-vations. This gives an opportunity for the extension of the PLEC model beyond the demonstration site.[6]

The likelihood of success will depend on technical and financial support from the responsible agency, the Department of Public Welfare. More extension and development workers will have to learn from PLEC experi-ences for future multiplication and replication of PLEC work in other areas with more ethnic diversity under different conditions. Training in the PLEC approach and methodology for field assessment of agrodiversity or biodi-versity and other related subjects is essential to build up the technical capacity of the responsible institution to sustain PLEC work in the context of the national programme. Without the training element, the programme is likely to fall back to a conventional approach with little participation of the people, poor understanding of the village ecosystems, and ignorance of the local knowledge and indigenous values of the people.

Notes

1. The author gratefully acknowledges contributions from Charal Thong-ngam, Prasong Kaewpha, and Songsak Thepsarn of the Highland Agriculture and Social Development Programme, Department of Public Welfare, and of Thamanoon Areetham of the Chiang Mau Hill-tribe Welfare Provincial Office, Department of Public Welfare. Narit Yimyam and Chawalit Korsamphan of the Highland Development Research and Training Centre, Faculty of Agriculture, Chiang Mai University, contributed substantially to the research.

2. Many production fields have "edges" containing different abundance and diversity of traditional crop and vegetable species, and sometimes including other useful plants which emerge naturally or are transferred from natural habitats. These edges may be easily observed in the major production fields (cabbage or litchi orchards), and are refered to as edges for traditional crops from former shifting cultivation. With elimination of traditional shifting cultivation and opium growing, women in the households continue to conserve the diversity of traditional non-opium crops for food, vegetables, and other necessities. Edges appear in the landscape with the simple structure of a single row with only one to three species of swidden crops in or around the boundary of cabbage fields.

   Five women, 65 years old or more, joined PLEC as local experts to demonstrate management of biodiversity-rich edges. They grow a complex mixture with staggered planting of up to 40 different species of traditional crops, vegetables, spices, herbs, and perennials. Some edges appear in areas considered as "not suitable" for crop cultivation, e.g., narrow banks between the fields, or rock outcrops. Others occur in agricultural fields, with a small plot or narrow strip along the edges of the fields. The size of the edges varies from 2 × 10 m to 30 × 30 m. In surplus years, the edge growers may sell their products to local markets nearby. Edges may start at the onset of wet season in late April to early May with traditional crops from the former upland rice in shifting cultivation, including sorghum, chilli, cowpeas, gourds, loofahs, taro, pumpkins, Hmong cucumbers, yams, and sweet potatoes. If residual soil moisture is adequate for the following cool-dry season, the growing season of edges may be extended to include many traditional vegetables and annual and perennial crops formerly grown in association with opium. These may include a wide variety of Hmong green mustards, many kinds of eggplant, lemon grass, glutinous corn, corianders, chayote, shallots, onion, ginger, banana, papaya, and others. There are at least 75 species of crops, useful annual and perennial species, and newly introduced crops or fruit trees in the edges. The whole production system of edges varies considerably, and some edges may support the household for as long as eight to 10 months in a year.

   One woman expert has found a special market for traditional vegetables and wild herbs in Chiang Mai city, especially where the Hmong people move to sell their traditional weaving and other products for tourists. Edges also serve as *in situ* conservation of diverse genetic resources to improve productivity of the commercial systems. All varieties of Hmong glutinous corn, for example, are being continuously conserved in the edges for home consumption. As the crop is becoming popular in the lowland markets, Pah Poo Chom farmers can readily grow glutinous corn after main-season cabbage for cash. The price of a bundle (five or six ears) is up to B10–15.

3. In July 2002, 40.7 Thailand baht equals one US dollar; 0.5 million baht therefore equals US$12,281.

4. This was the contribution of an aid project. The sandy soils would not hold water, so the pond fields were abandoned. Nonetheless, the idea of irrigation was later taken up again in other ways, using the sprinkler system.

5. The simple technology used is quite unlike the Indian method of preparing refined sugar (*kendi*). In all essentials it is a scaled-down version of that used formerly to manufacture muscovado sugar in the West Indies. Its origin at Tee Cha has not been researched.

6. At the local level in Pah Poo Chom, the village committee is expected to continue PLEC work with local administration and government agencies. Technical monitoring and evaluation of this activity will be valuable to strengthen the capacity of the village committee and relevant local organizations.

REFERENCES

Anderson, E. F. 1993. *Plants and People of the Golden Triangle: Ethnobotany of the Hilltribes of Northern Thailand.* Bangkok: Silkworm Books.

Conway, G. R. 1986. *Agroecosystem Research and Development.* Bangkok: Winrock International.

Cooper, R. G. 1984. *Resource Scarcity and the Hmong Response: A Study of Resettlement and Economy in Northern Thailand.* Singapore: Singapore University Press.

Korsamphan, C., C. Thong-ngam, and K. Rerkasem. 2001. "Biodiversity management and utilization of forest edges in a Hmong community", in *CMUPNlab Working Papers 1: Report of a Workshop on Regeneration Ecology and Management for Degraded Landscapes and Forest Ecosystems.* Chiang Mai: Chiang Mai University, pp. 95–110.

Kunstadter, P. and E. C. Chapman. 1978. "Problems of shifting cultivation and economic development in northern Thailand", in P. Kunstadter, E. C. Chapman, and S. Sabhasri (eds) *Farmers in the Forests: Economic Development and Marginal Agriculture in Northern Thailand.* Honolulu: University Press of Hawaii for East-West Center, pp. 3–23.

McKinnon, J. and B. Vienne. 1989. *Hill Tribes Today: Problems in Change.* Bangkok: White-Lotus/Orstom.

Rerkasem, K. 2001. "Farmers' management of fallow succession in northern Thailand", paper prepared to an international symposium on Managing Biodiversity in Agricultural Ecosystems, organized by the United Nations University, Secretariat of the Convention of Biological Diversity, and International Plant Genetic Resources Institute, 8–10 November 2001, Montreal, Canada.

Rerkasem, K. and H. Guo. 1995. "Report on a workshop on agroecosystems and biodiversity in montane mainland southeast Asia", *PLEC News and Views*, No. 5, pp. 5–10.

Rerkasem, B., T. Yoneyama, and K. Rerkasem. 1992. "Spineless mimosa (*Mimosa invisa*), a potential livemulch for corn", Agricultural Systems Programme working paper.

Sabhasri, S. 1978. "Effects of forest fallow cultivation on forest production and soil", in P. Kunstadter, E. C. Chapman, and S. Sabhasri (eds) *Farmers in the Forests: Economic Development and Marginal Agriculture in Northern Thailand.* Honolulu: University Press of Hawaii for East-West Center, pp. 160–184.

Sutthi, C. 1989. "Highland agriculture: From better to worse", in J. McKinnon and B. Vienne (eds) *Hill Tribes Today: Problems in Change.* Bangkok: White-Lotus/Orstom, pp. 107–142.

Sutthi, C. 1990. "Mountain and upland agriculture and genetic resources in Thailand", in K. W. Riley, N. Mateo, G. C. Hawtin, and R. Yadav (eds) *Mountain Agriculture and Crop Genetic Resources.* New Delhi: IBH Publishing, pp. 201–216.

Sutthi, C. 1996. *Traditional Slash and Burn Agriculture on the Highlands: Indigenous Technical Knowledge*. Chiang Mai: Tribal Research Institute (Technical Report 00-39-12). In Thai.

Thong-ngam, C., T. Areetham, P. Kaewpha, S. Thepsarn, N. Yimyam, C. Korsamphan, and K. Rerkasem. 2002. "Scaling-up PLEC demonstration site for national pilot programme: A case example of a Hmong Njua village in northern Thailand", *PLEC News and Views*, No. 19, pp. 7–16.

Van Roy, E. 1971. *Economic Systems of Northern Thailand*. Ithaca: Cornell University Press.

Walker, A. R. 1975. "Two blue Meo communities in north Thailand", in A. R. Walker (ed.) *Farmers in the Hills: Ethnographic Notes on the Upland Peoples of North Thailand*. Pulau Pinang: Penerbit Universiti Sains Malaysia, pp. 73–79.

Yimyam, N., K. Lodkaew, and K. Rerkasem. 2001. "Nutrient cycling through *Macaranga denticulata* in rotational shifting cultivation", in *CMUPNlab Working Papers 1: Report of a Workshop on Regeneration Ecology and Management for Degraded Landscapes and Forest Ecosystems*. Chiang Mai: Chiang Mai University, pp. 81–94.

Yimyam, N., K. Rerkasem, and B. Rerkasem. 2002. "Pada (*Macaranga denticulata* (Bl.) Muell. Arg.), a fallow enriching species in shifting cultivation", *Agroforestry Systems*, Vol. 57, No. 2, pp. 79–86.

Youpensuk, S. and S. Lumyong. 2001. "Endomycorrhizas in *Macaranga denticulata* on the highlands in Mae Hong Son province", in *CMUPNlab Working Papers 1: Report of a Workshop on Regeneration Ecology and Management for Degraded Landscapes and Forest Ecosystems*. Chiang Mai: Chiang Mai University, pp. 182–185.

Youpensuk, S., S. Lumyong, N. Yimyam, and B. Dell. 2003. "Biodiversity of arbuscular mycorrhizal fungi from rhizosphere of *Macaranga denticulata* (*Eupharbiaceae*) on the highland rotational shifting cultivation area in Thailand", *Australian Journal of Botany* (in press).

Zinke, P. J., S. Sabhasri, and P. Kunstadter. 1978. "Soil fertility aspects of the Lua' forest fallow system of shifting cultivation", in P. Kunstadter, E. C. Chapman, and S. Sabhasri (eds) *Farmers in the Forests: Economic Development and Marginal Agriculture in Northern Thailand*. Honolulu: University Press of Hawaii for East-West Center, pp. 134–159.

15

Findings from the PLEC project

Harold Brookfield, Helen Parsons, and Muriel Brookfield

In the Foreword to this book, Miguel Pinedo-Vasquez faces the issue of translating the hard-won achievements of the PLEC teams, and of the expert farmers, into long-term programmes with durable benefits. This is indeed a major challenge: to build on what has been achieved instead of seeing it – as so often happens – perish when the external support and stimulus are withdrawn. As is appropriate for the project's new scientific coordinator, Miguel looks at the larger measures that can be taken to main-stream PLEC initiatives. The editors have worked through a varied set of country chapters, with the aim of extracting what has emerged over the years from the level at which the project's clusters have worked. This leads to some ideas on what might be useful in the future.

Lessons from the scientists

First, one very striking conclusion is that while PLEC was conceived in Tokyo, Canberra, New York, and Norwich, it very quickly became truly a "country-driven" project in the hands of local groups of scientists who enthusiastically embraced its objectives and made them their own. In doing so, different groups interpreted the PLEC approach in different ways. Some saw it as a very "close-to-the-ground" form of extension, with the expert farmers interpreting and extending the work of scientists and technicians. In this approach, a fairly clear status distinction remained between the scientists and the farmers. Others overcame such "class" problems to communication, patiently explored what the best farmers were doing, and accepted all sorts of resistance from the farmer experts in order to allow them effectively to take charge. In this shift, they also moved away from seeing farmers and their systems in terms of categories, and found value in seeking the exceptions rather than the rule.

The varying experience of the scientists reflected more than their own predilections. It was easier to get a handle on diversity and complexity among some farmer societies than among others. There is a world of difference between working with politically active Brazilian *caboclos*, suspicious Papua New Guinea villagers unwilling to trust anyone at all, or Chinese farmers with their long and recent experience of top-down commandism. Once PLEC scientists started to work among the farmers, rather than merely studying them, lecturing them, or instructing them, they became very sensitive to these nuances. One consequence is the diversity of PLEC. It was inevitable that the project should build on local variation rather than seeking to impose a standardized blueprint or project protocol. The latter would, quite simply, never have worked.

In the post-project period, most of the scientists remain in touch with the farmers among whom they worked and, as several of them report in the country chapters, they themselves have been changed by the PLEC experience. Some of them have been able to influence their colleagues and institutions in new ways of thinking. All have got to know farmers as people, sharing problems and the results of experimental work with them. The longer they spend working with farmers, the more they learn, and now that enduring personal relations have been established this learning is unlikely to cease with the formal end of the first phase of the project.

Lessons from the farmers

Most of what the editors know about the expert farmers comes through the words of the scientists. The editors have encountered a few of these farmers in the field, but only briefly. There is no obvious way to distinguish expert farmers from ordinary farmers. They are not members of an élite; few of them had leadership roles before they were involved in PLEC demonstration activities; only a minority are confident public speakers. What does distinguish them is their pride in their skills and achievements, a pride reinforced by recognition first from the scientists and later by their fellows. One group to whom Brookfield talked described themselves as the innovators, the ones who took the risks and showed others what could be done.

The demonstration methodology has contributed greatly to the self-respect of the farming people, and, to the extent that PLEC has been only a demonstration project, the expert farmers are the heart and core of the whole enterprise. They are the ones who blend new with traditional knowledge to devise ways of coping successfully with specific problems of production and conservation. They are the ones who, encouraged by PLEC, demonstrate these ways to others, and are therefore the main agents of farmer-driven development. To observers, including one or two of those who have reviewed the project, this may seem an inexpensive way in which to achieve conservationist rural development, but there is a large cost underlying this achievement. The replicability of the PLEC model relies critically on selecting the right expert farmers and, as several of the chapters have demonstrated, this is no easy or simple task. It is not a job that local agricultural agents can do without retraining in the methods described in this book, and in Brookfield *et al.* (2002). Future proposals, as described by Miguel in the Foreword, include substantial input into such training.

There is a continued need for scientific guidance and participation. PLEC has shown what might be possible, but it is not now a question of just removing the scientists from the scene and allowing the extension agents and farmers simply to work together. As Kanok Rerkasem wrote in Chapter 14, there is real danger that any programme without a scientific component is "likely to fall back to a conventional approach with little participation of the people, poor understanding of the village ecosystems, and ignorance of the local knowledge and indigenous values of the people".

The larger contribution of PLEC

One of the final evaluators of the project has remarked that not only was PLEC "more than the sum of its clusters", but that it was designed to "jumpstart global change", developing methodology to meet worldwide problems of declining biodiversity in landscapes and also the feared impact of land degradation. While PLEC did not set out to be so ambitious, it is agreed that the aim was to seek findings that would be applicable across a wide range of environments. This is why, although ready to accept substantial variation in demonstration site method in relation to local social conditions and perceived problems, the coordinators and advisory groups put great effort into obtaining something much closer to standardization in the recording of biodiversity at landscape and farm levels, and of management practices. Every cluster varied its biodiversity sampling methods in relation to conditions in its own area, but within the sample areas determined all tried to use a standard approach. Their conclusions, if not the numerical indices they obtained, do therefore have some comparability.

PLEC intended to test if biodiversity could actually be enhanced by management, rather than necessarily be reduced under human use. The country chapters in this book show that the project got some very positive findings. The outstanding example is at sites on the Amazon floodplain in Brazil and Peru, where there is specific management to increase biodiversity while producing commodities from the fallow and succeeding forest stages. Elsewhere there is strong indication that biodiversity enhancement is possible (if not always achieved by the majority) by particular types of management in environments as diverse as those of West Africa, on Mount Meru in Tanzania, in Thailand, and on the forest edge in south-western China. Although still to be confirmed by further analysis of the data, this is an important result, and one made possible by the rigorous data collection and analysis methods set up by PLEC's internal advisers.

Enhancing biodiversity through management has political as well as scientific value. In a recent paper, Pinedo-Vasquez *et al.* (2003), the members of PLEC's final scientific and technical advisory team (STAT), call attention to the power of numbers when quantitative results were presented to other scientists, technicians, politicians, and officials at formal meetings in 2000 and 2001. Many in the audiences realized for the first time that conservation is not simply a matter of protecting wild biodiversity from damaging interference, but is also a matter of diversifying habitat through skilful farm and fallow management. The notions of patch ecology and the advantages of intermediate levels of disturbance for biodiversity, fairly new in ecology, have for a long time been deeply embedded in farmers' knowledge and practice. Farmers manipulate this knowledge for both subsistence and profit.

It is much the same with soil management. Many studies around the world in the past 50 years have shown that, while new clearance or more intensive farming on sensitive or fragile land does commonly lead to degradation, a great many traditional and adaptive farming systems contain practices that help sustain or restore fertility, and check or manage erosion. With greater or lesser success in different clusters, PLEC sought to place emphasis on the soil and water management practices used by the farmers, and some of the country chapters demonstrate the detail of recording that was produced.

Once again, it is the expert farmers whose land tends to be best managed, sometimes by adopting control measures proposed to them by extensionists and soil-conservation projects, sometimes through their own adaptations. Good soil and water management does not readily lead to the immediate enjoyment of increased production and profit; it is an investment in the longer term. Therefore it is more readily neglected by a majority of farmers, for whom the attainment of short-term goals is of paramount importance. Nonetheless, a range of good practices does exist, and is continually developed by the adaptive and experimental farmers that PLEC sought.

A dimension for the future

PLEC's remit was to study biodiversity in relation to agricultural and related practices, and this was abundantly achieved. Most of the clusters also put considerable emphasis on assisting farmers to enhance the value of their production by activities which either conserve biodiversity or reduce pressure on biodiverse areas. The country chapters present some striking results. It became clear that diversification of production was itself an important strategy. Often this took place within a wider diversification of opportunities. The PLEC teams saw many consequences in terms of marketing, and the changing genderization of farm work.

In some areas there was already substantial reliance on incomes obtained from non-farm work. For example, at Muyuy in Peru most farmers also live and work in nearby Iquitos for some part of most years, and earn incomes by providing services as well as produce to urban dwellers. Elsewhere, off-farm incomes are important in the Tanzania sites close to the city of Arusha, allowing some farmers the means to invest on their farms. Farmers at Pah Poo Chom (Thailand) who have pick-up trucks market their own produce in Chiang Mai and even beyond, and can earn other income by use of these vehicles. In northern Ghana and on the Fouta Djallon in Guinée, some PLEC initiatives have been specifically directed to developing local sources of income generation so as to provide year-round work and reduce the need for migration to the cities and elsewhere.

Whether close to cities or far away, all the groups studied by PLEC remain fundamentally agrarian, and the developmental aspect of the project has concentrated on making agrarian work more remunerative. Concurrently, there is a growing literature about "de-agrarianization" of rural societies, for example in Africa (Bryceson 1996) and in south-east Asia (Rigg 2001). For the people studied by PLEC this has not yet happened, though the project noted, for example, that the men of Jachie, a short bus ride from the city of Kumasi in Ghana, now largely work in the city; a high proportion of farm work is therefore done by their wives. Yet these same wives have formed one of the most active and fast-growing farmers' associations in the whole of PLEC. They are not giving up interest in farming. Diversification of income sources to include off-farm employment, rural or urban, is a well-established phenomenon in many rural areas of the developing countries, and there is no doubt that it is growing and spreading rapidly. In future work it will be important to pay closer attention to diversification of opportunity. It is important to the people, and it will undoubtedly have a growing impact on farming practices.

Conclusion

This latter aspect emerges only here and there in the country chapters of this book, and it is clear that the improvement of agricultural production and of farm-based incomes is still seen everywhere as a worthwhile goal. It is also apparent that protection of complexity and diversity are valuable resources for farmers seeking to defend their livelihoods. Farmers either already understand, or quickly accept, that farming technologies which sustain both the productivity of the soil and the diversity of biota are strongly conducive to the satisfaction of their primary purpose. In a globalizing world, this is a very encouraging finding. But for the future it may become important to take more specific account of the comparative value placed by the young on other means of gaining a living. It will also be important to be sensitive to the effect of wider horizons and education on attitudes toward conservation. On prima facie grounds these could be positive as well as negative.

The recognition of smallholder farmers' dynamism has been a strong feature of PLEC. What the project has most signally learned from farmers around the world is that nothing in their pool of knowledge, technology, and skills has remained static in at least the last century. If they continue old practices, they do so mainly for new reasons. If they drop old practices, this is because new considerations arise that make old ways burdensome or seemingly ineffective. Farmers are adaptable people, and none more so than those outstanding men and women whom PLEC calls expert farmers. They are the people from whom the project has mainly learned.

REFERENCES

Brookfield, H., C. Padoch, H. Parsons, and M. Stocking (eds). 2002. *Cultivating Biodiversity: Understanding, Analysing and Using Agricultural Diversity*. London, ITDG Publications.

Bryceson, D. F. 1996. "De-agrarianization and rural employment in sub-Saharan Africa: A sectoral perspective", *World Development*, No. 24, pp. 97–111.

Pinedo-Vasquez, M., K. Coffey, L. Enu-Kwesi, and E. Gyasi. 2003. "Synthesizing and evaluating PLEC work on biodiversity", *PLEC News and Views*, NS No. 1, pp. 3–8.

Rigg, J. 2001. *More than the Soil: Rural Change in Southeast Asia*. Harlow: Pearson Education.

Bibliography

This bibliography provides detail of references used in constructing the chapters of this book other than those cited in the text and detailed at the end of each chapter. Some of these are published sources, but most are (or were at the time of preparing this book) in the "grey literature" category. They are listed to present the very considerable volume of work done by members of PLEC.

Chapter 3

McGrath, D. 1997. "Ituqui: A traditional lake fishery on the lower Amazon *várzea*", *PLEC News and Views*, No. 8, pp. 23–32.

McGrath, D. and M. Crosso. 1998. "Restoration of a floodplain lake habitat: A PLEC demonstration project", *PLEC News and Views*, No. 11, pp. 10–17.

Padoch, C., M. Ayres, M. Pinedo, and A. Henderson (eds). 1998. *Varzea: Diversity, Conservation and Development*. Advances in Economic Botany 13. New York: New York Botanical Garden Press.

Pinedo-Vasquez, M. 1996. "Local experts and local leaders: Lessons from Amazonia", *PLEC News and Views*, No. 6, pp. 30–32.

Pinedo-Vasquez, M. and F. Rabelo. 1999. "Sustainable management of an Amazonian forest for timber production: A myth or a reality?", *PLEC News and Views*, No. 12, pp. 20–28.

Winkler-Prins, A. M. G. A. and D. McGrath. 2000. "Smallholder agriculture along the lower Amazon floodplain, Brazil", *PLEC News and Views*, No. 16, pp. 34–42.

Zarin, D., V. F. G. Pereira, H. Raffles, F. Rabelo, M. Pinedo-Vasquez, and R. G. Congalton. 2001. "Landscape change in tidal floodplains near the mouth of the Amazon River", *Forest Ecology and Management*, Vol. 154, No. 3, pp. 383–393.

Chapter 4

Anonymous. 2002. "Findings on the management and organization of agrodiversity in central Ghana." Unpublished manuscript.

Ardayfio-Schandorf, E. 1994. "Women as farmers in Ghana", *PLEC News and Views*, No. 2, pp. 19–21.

Ardayfio-Schandorf, E. and M. Awumbila. 2000. "Gender and agrodiversity in southern Ghana: Preliminary findings", *PLEC News and Views*, No. 15, pp. 23–26.

Asante, F. 2000. "Adaptation of farmers to climate change: A case study of selected farming communities in the forest-savanna transitional zone of southern Ghana." M.Phil. thesis, Graduate School and Department of Geography and Resource Development, University of Ghana, Legon.

Asante, F. 2002. "Experimental and monitoring programmes of sites in Northern Ghana." Unpublished manuscript.

Buabeng, S. K. 2001. "Social analysis of demonstration site populations in central Ghana." Unpublished manuscript.

Buabeng, S. K. 2002. "Integration of scientific with community information on resources (the relation of community information to scientific information on resource assessment in central Ghana)." Unpublished manuscript.

Dittoh, S. 2001. "Integration of scientific and community information on resources: The northern Ghana case." Unpublished manuscript.

Dittoh, S., G. Kranjac-Berisavljevic', B. Yakubu, and B. Z. Gandaa. 2002. "Social analysis of demonstration site populations: The case of Bongnayili-Dugu-Song, and Nyorugu-Binguri-Gonre, northern Ghana." Unpublished manuscript.

Dittoh, S. and B. Yakubu. 2002. "Management and organization of agrobiodiversity at PLEC demonstration sites in northern Ghana." Unpublished manuscript.

Enu-Kwesi, L., D. Amirou, V. V. Vordzogbe, and D. Daouda. 2002. "Comparative management of savanna woodland in Ghana and Guinea." Unpublished manuscript.

Gyasi, E. A. 1993. "Environmental endangerment in the forest-savanna zone of southern Ghana", *PLEC News and Views*, No. 1, pp. 14–15.

Gyasi, E. A. 1996. "WAPLEC activities in 1995 and early 1996, including a workshop in northern Ghana", *PLEC News and Views*, No. 6, pp. 2–3.

Gyasi, E. A. 1996. "Land holding and its relationship with biophysical status: Case study of tenancy and non-tenancy farming in Ghana", *PLEC News and Views*, No. 7, pp. 21–25.

Gyasi, E. A. 1998. "PLEC experiences with participatory approach to biophysical resources management in Ghana", *PLEC News and Views*, No. 10, pp. 27–31.

Gyasi, E. A. 1999. "Claim that tenant-farmers do not conserve land resources: Counter evidence from a PLEC demonstration site in Ghana", *PLEC News and Views*, No. 12, pp. 10–14.

Gyasi, E. A. 2000. "Demonstrating the value of agrodiversity. Report of a show of traditional foods based on vanishing biotic species, hosted by southern Ghana association of PLEC farmers, at Sekesua, Upper Manya Krobo, Ghana, 5 November 1999." Unpublished manuscript.

Gyasi, E. A. 2001. "Development of demonstration sites in Ghana", *PLEC News and Views*, No. 18, pp. 20–28.

Gyasi, E. A. 2002. "Summary report of PLEC work with special reference to history, demonstration site development/activities and achievements in Ghana with special reference to the south." Unpublished manuscript.

Gyasi, E. A. 2002. "How systems of resource access and distribution relate to use of land (with special reference to biodiversity and biophysical status) in southern Ghana." Unpublished manuscript.

Gyasi, E. A., G. T. Agyepong, E. Ardayfio-Schandorf, L. Enu-Kwesi, J. S. Nabila, and E. Owusu-Bennoah. 1994. "Environmental endangerment in the forest-savanna zone of southern Ghana." Unpublished manuscript.

Gyasi, E. A. with F. Asante and Y. A. Gyasi. 2002. "Integrated final report of PLEC work in Ghana, August 1992–February 2002." Unpublished manuscript.

Gyasi, E. A. and L. Enu-Kwesi. 1996. "Collaborative Agroecosystems Management Project (CAMP): A proposed community-based initiative in Ghana, by WAPLEC in collaboration with the chief and people of Gyamfiase", *PLEC News and Views*, No. 6, pp. 11–13.

Gyasi, E. A. and L. Enu-Kwesi. 2000. "Promotion and monitoring of home gardens, plant nurseries and on-farm conservation of trees." Unpublished manuscript.

Kranjac-Berisavljevic', G. 2001. "Biodiversity and agrodiversity inventory (with review of causes of land degradatioin) in northern Ghana." Unpublished manuscript.

Kranjac-Berisavljevic', G. and B. Z. Gandaa. 2002. "Sustaining diversity of yams in northern Ghana", *PLEC News and Views*, No. 20, pp. 36–43.

Laing, E. 1999. "Attributes required of the new expert", *PLEC News and Views*, No. 14, p. 8.

Nabila, J. S., S. Agyei-Mensah, F. Asante, and E. A. Gyasi. 2002. "Social analysis of PLEC demonstration site populations in southern Ghana." Unpublished manuscript.

Ofori-Sarpong, E. 2000. "The effect of climate change and biota in the southern ecotone zone in Ghana." Unpublished manuscript.

Owusu-Bennoah, E. and L. Enu-Kwesi. 2000. "Soil conservation practices to control soil and biodiversity losses in farming." Unpublished manuscript.

PLEC Farmers of Gyamfiase-Adenya. 1998. "Reports from farmers on demonstration sites in Ghana", *PLEC News and Views*, No. 11, pp. 23–25.

Tanzubil, B., J. S. Dittoh, and G. Kranjac-Berisavljevic'. 2002. "*In situ* conservation of indigenous rice varieties at Bawku Manga in the Sudan savanna zone of Ghana." Unpublished manuscript.

Chapter 5

Barry, A. K. 2001. *Rapport de l'atelier national de WAPLEC du 26 au 27 septembre 2001: Agro-biodiversité et développement rural durable.* Conakry: WAPLEC-Guinée.

Barry, A. K., S. Fofana, A. Diallo, and I. Boiro. 1998. *Rapport final: Système de production et changement de l'environnement du secteur de Kollagui-Pita*. Conakry: WAPLEC-Guinée.

Chapter 6

Busingye, P., J. K. Tumuhairwe, and E. N. Nsubuga. 1999. "Factors influencing farmers' decisions to use mulch and trenches in the banana plantations in Mwizi, Mbarara district", in *Proceedings of the 17th Conference of the Soil Science Society of East Africa*, p. 267. Kampala, Uganda.

Kaihura, F., R. Kiome, M. Stocking, A. Tengberg, and J. Tumuhairwe. 1999. "Agrodiversity highlights in East Africa", *PLEC News and Views*, No. 14, pp. 25–32.

Nkwiine, C., J. K. Tumuhairwe, and J. Y. K. Zake. 1999. "Farmer selection of biophysical diversity for agricultural land uses in dissected highland plateaus of Mbarara, Uganda", in *Proceedings of the 17th Conference of the Soil Science Society of East Africa*, p. 304. Kampala, Uganda.

Nsubuga, E. N. B., J. K. Tumuhairwe, and F. Kahembwe. 1999. "Socio-economic factors influencing adoption of soil and water conservation strategies in southwestern Uganda", in *Proceedings of the 17th Conference of the Soil Science Society of East Africa*, p. 312. Kampala, Uganda.

Tumuhairwe, J. K. and C. Nkwiine. 2000. *Agrodiversity (Including Management Regimes) and Biodiversity Potential of Bushwere Demonstration Site in Mbarara*. Technical Report No. 4. Mbarara, Uganda: PLEC-Uganda.

Tumuhairwe, J. K. and C. Nkwiine. 2000. "Mid-term report on training programmes", Report 5 (submitted together with progress report of February). Mbarara, Uganda: PLEC-Uganda.

Tumuhairwe, J. K. and C. Nkwiine. 2001. *Plant Biodiversity and Agrodiversity Database of Bushwere Demonstration Site in Mbarara*. Technical report. Mbarara, Uganda: PLEC-Uganda.

Tumuhairwe, J. K. and C. Nkwiine. 2001. *Relating Community Information to Scientific Information on Resource Evaluation and Utilization*. Technical Report No. 6. Mbarara, Uganda: PLEC-Uganda.

Tumuhairwe, J. K. and C. Nkwiine. 2001. *Indigenous Knowledge and Farmer Experiments on Handling and Storage of Valuable Agrobiodiversity in Bushwere Demonstration Site, Uganda*. Technical Report No. 7. Mbarara, Uganda: PLEC-Uganda.

Tumuhairwe, J. K., C. Nkwiine, G. Eilu, C. Gumisiriza, and F. Tumuhairwe. 2001. "Agrobiodiversity potential of smallholder farms in a dissected highland plateau of western Uganda", paper prepared for the East Africa PLEC annual general meeting, Arusha, Tanzania, 26–28 November.

Tumuhairwe, J. K., C. Nkwiine, G. Eilu, and J. Obua. 2001. "The impact of traditional farming on plants species diversity in agricultural landscape of south-western Uganda." Unpublished manuscript.

Tumuhairwe, J. K., C. Nkwiine, and J. Kawongolo. 2001. "Developing policy and technical recommendations: Agrobiodiversity conservation – The PLEC-Uganda experience", paper prepared for the East Africa PLEC annual general meeting, Arusha, Tanzania, 26–28 November.

Tumuhairwe, J. K., C. Nkwiine, and J. Kawongolo. 2002. *Final Report of the GEF Phase of UNU/PLEC Project by Uganda Cluster*. Mbarara, Uganda: PLEC-Uganda.

Tumuhairwe, J. K., C. Nkwiine, and E. Nsubuga. 2001. "Using farmer-led exhibitions of agrobiodiversity to reach policy makers and other farmers: Experiences of PLEC-Uganda", *PLEC News and Views*, No. 18, pp. 29–33.

Chapter 7

Kang'ara, J. N., E. H. Ngoroi, J. M. Muturi, S. A. Amboga, F. K. Ngugi, and I. Mwangi. 2001. "The role of livestock in soil fertility, biodiversity, land use, cultural and welfare change in Nduuri Embu, Kenya", paper presented at the East Africa PLEC annual general meeting, Arusha, Tanzania, 26–28 November.

Kang'ara, J. N., E. H. Ngoroi, J. M. and C. M. Rimui. 2002. *Kenya Sub-cluster Final Report*.

Kaburu, K., E. H. Ngoroi, J. N. Kang'ara, S. Amboga, I. Mwangi, and C. M. Rimui. 2001. "The vegetables and fruit biodiversity and seasonal distribution trend in Nduuri", paper presented at the East Africa PLEC annual general meeting, Arusha, Tanzania, 26–28 November.

Mangale, N., J. N. Mwangi, J. M. Miriti, J. N. Chui, W. Gikonyo, and J. M. Njoroge. 1999. *Participatory Appraisal on People, Land Use, Management and Environmental Changes in Lari Division, Central Kenya*. Embu, Kenya: PLEC-Kenya.

Ngoroi, E. H., J. N. Kang'ara, B. O. Okoba, and C. R. Mugo. 2001. "An investigation into botanical knowledge gap between age groups in the Nduuri community of Embu, Kenya", paper presented at the East Africa PLEC annual general meeting, Arusha, Tanzania, 26–28 November.

Ngoroi, E. H., B. O. Okoba, and C. M. Rimui. 2001. *Agrodiversity in the Smallholder Farms of Nduuri, Embu, Kenya*. Embu, Kenya: PLEC-Kenya.

Ngoroi, E. H., B. O. Okoba, C. M. Rimui, and J. N. Kang'ara. 2001. "Effect of the fig tree (*Ficus sycamorus*) on the soil and yield of coffee, Nduuri, Embu, Kenya", paper presented at the East Africa PLEC annual general meeting, Arusha, Tanzania, 26–28 November.

Rimui, C. M., E. H. Ngoroi, J. N. Kang'ara, and B. O. Okoba. 2001. *Household Diversity of the Nduuri Community, Embu, Kenya*. Unpublished manuscript, Embu, Kenya: PLEC-Kenya.

Chapter 8

Anonymous. 1999. *Socio-Economic Characteristics of Selected Households in Arumeru District, Arusha Region, Tanzania. Report of Baseline Survey in Arumeru District*. Mwanza: PLEC-Tanzania.

Kaihura, F. B. S. and E. Kahembe. 2000. *Experimental and Monitoring Work in PLEC Demonstration Sites of Olgilai/Ng'iresi and Kiserian Villages, Arumeru District, Tanzania*. Mwanza: PLEC-Tanzania.

Kaihura, F. B. S., D. M. Rugangira, and P. Sululu. 2001. "PLEC-Tanzania technical and policy recommendations for sustainable agrodiversity management (with modifications from meeting participants)", paper presented at the East Africa PLEC annual general meeting, Arusha, Tanzania, 26–28 November.

Kaihura, F. B. S., M. A. Stocking, and N. Murnaghan. 2001. "Agrodiversity as a means of sustaining small-scale dryland farming systems in Tanzania", in M. A. Stocking and N. Murnaghan (eds) *Handbook for the Field Assessment of Land Degradation*. London: Earthscan.

Mbago, F. M. Undated. *The Impacts of Population Pressure and Resource Availability on Agrodiversity: A Pilot Study in Ng'iresi Village, Tanzania*. Mwanza: PLEC-Tanzania.

Mbago, F. M. 1999. *Agrobiodiversity Assessment in Olgilai/Ng'iresi and Kiserian Demonstration Sites, Arumeru District, Tanzania*. Mwanza: PLEC-Tanzania.

Mwasumbi, L. B. and F. M. Mbago. 1999. *Agrobiodiversity Assessment of the Arumeru Area, Arusha Region, Tanzania*. Mwanza: PLEC-Tanzania.

Chapter 9

Chen, A., Y. Fu, H. Guo, and Z. Dao. 2001. "Farm-system change induced by socio-economic development at the village level", *Acta Botanica Yunnanica Supplement*, Vol. XIII, pp. 50–58.

Cui, J., Y. Fu, H. Guo, and A. Chen. 2000. "Household agrobiodiversity assessment of tropical home gardens: The case of Daka, Xishuangbanna", *Acta Botanica Yunnanica Supplement*, Vol. XII, pp. 81–90.

Cui, J., Y. Fu, H. Guo, and A. Chen. 2001. "Household agrobiodiversity assessment of tropical fuelwood: The case of Daka, Xishuangbanna", *Acta Botanica Yunnanica Supplement*, Vol. XIII, pp. 84–92.

Dao, Z. and H. Guo. 1999. "Diversity and sustainable use of *Ericaceae* in Gaoligongshan", *Acta Botanaica Yunnanica Supplement*, Vol. XI, pp. 24–34.

Dao, Z. and H. Guo. 1999. "Endemic plants of *Ericaceae* in Gaoligongshan", *Acta Botanaica Yunnanica Supplement*, Vol. XI, pp. 16–23.

Dao, Z., W. Chen, and H. Guo. 2000. "Household agrobiodiversity assessment of home gardens: Hanlong, Baihualing village, Gaoligongshan", *Acta Botanica Yunnanica Supplement*, Vol. XII, pp. 102–112.

Dao, Z., H. Guo, and W. Chen. 2000. "Community forest agrobiodiversity assessment of Hanlong, Baihualing village, Gaoligongshan", *Acta Botanica Yunnanica Supplement*, Vol. XII, pp. 74–80.

Dao, Z., H. Guo, and J. Duan. 2001. "Household-based agrobiodiversity assessment (HH-ABA) of paddy fields of Gaoligongshan region: A case from Hanlong village, Baihualing, Baoshan, west Yunnan", *Acta Botanica Yunnanica Supplement*, Vol. XIII, pp. 128–133.

Dao, Z., H. Guo, and D. Jingang. 2001. "Gaoligongshan household-based agrobiodiversity assessment of agroforestry systems: A case from Hanlong of Baihualing administrative village, Baoshan, west Yunnan", *Acta Botanica Yunnanica Supplement*, Vol. XIII, pp. 134–139.

Du, X.-F. and J. Cui. 2001. "Study of the relationship of indigenous medicine and agrobiodiversity in Daka, Xishuangbanna, Yunnan", *Acta Botanica Yunnanica Supplement*, Vol. XIII, pp. 164–170.

Fu, Y. and A. Chen. 1999. "Diversity of upland rice, and of wild vegetables in Baka, Xishuangbanna, Yunnan", *PLEC News and Views*, No. 12, pp. 15–19. Reprinted in H. Brookfield, C. Padoch, H. Parsons, and M. Stocking (eds). 2002. *Cultivating Biodiversity: Understanding, Analysing and Using Agricultural Diversity*. London: ITDG Publications, pp. 194–199.

Fu, Y., A. Chen, and J. Cui. 1999. "Relationship between agro-landscapes and crop conservation, Daka, Xishuangbanna", *Plant Resources and Environment*, Vol. 8, No. 1, pp. 28–32.

Fu, Y., A. Chen, J. Cui, and H. Guo. 2000. "Agrobiodiversity assessment of tropical landscape: The case of Daka and Baka villages, Xishuangbanna", *Acta Botanica Yunnanica Supplement*, Vol. XII, pp. 52–66.

Fu, Y., A. Chen, J. Cui, and H. Guo. 2000. "Assessment of tropical plant resources degradation in different land-use stages: The case of Daka and Baka villages, Xishuangbanna", *Acta Botanica Yunnanica Supplement*, Vol. XII, pp. 67–73.

Fu, Y., A. Chen, J. Cui, and H. Guo. 2000. "Household agrobiodiversity assessment of tropical rubber plantations and upland rice fields", *Acta Botanica Yunnanica Supplement*, Vol. XII, pp. 91–101.

Fu, Y., A. Chen, J. Cui, and Z. Liu. 1999. "Ecological issues in agro-landscapes, Baka, Xishuangbanna", *Rural Ecology and Environment*, Vol. 15, pp. 26–29.

Fu, Y., A. Chen, J. Cui, and F. Shi. 1998. "Investigation on land-use change and species richness in the Hani agroecosystem in the past ten years, Daka, Xishuangbanna", in H. Jiang and X. Ou (eds) *Biodiversity Conservation and Sustainable Development in Biosphere.* Kunming: Yunnan University Press, pp. 169–173.

Fu, Y., A. Chen, H. Guo, and J. Cui. 2001. "Agro-landscape change in Daka, Xishuangbanna", *Journal of Ecology*, Vol. 20, pp. 28–31.

Fu, Y., A. Chen, Z. Liu, and J. Cui. 2000. "Plant diversity and usable plants in tropical fallows", *Journal of Ecology*, Vol. 19, pp. 1–6.

Fu, Y., H. Guo, A. Chen, and J. Cui. 2002. "Surveying household-level diversity in wet-rice fields at Daka, Yunnan", in H. Brookfield, C. Padoch, H. Parsons, and M. Stocking (eds) *Cultivating Biodiversity: Understanding, Analysing and Using Agricultural Diversity*. London: ITDG Publications, pp. 207–212.

Fu, Y., J. Cui, and A. Chen. 2001. "Plant diversity of community forest and holy hill forest: A case from Daka, Xishuangbanna, southern Yunnan", *Acta Botanica Yunnanica Supplement*, Vol. XIII, pp. 93–100.

Fu, Y., J. Cui, and H. Guo. 2001. "Agrobiodiversity assessment of a three-year-old fallow field in Daka, Xishuangbanna, Yunnan", *Acta Botanica Yunnanica Supplement*, Vol. XIII, pp. 75–83.

Guo, H., Z. Dao, and H. Brookfield. 1996. "Agrodiversity and biodiversity on the ground and among the people: Methodology from Yunnan", *PLEC News and Views*, No. 16, pp. 28–33.

Guo, H., H. Li, and Z. Dao. 2000. "Dynamism of social-economy and biodiversity interaction: A case from Gaoligongshan", *Acta Botanica Yunnanica Supplement*, Vol. XII, pp. 42–51.

Guo, H., C. Padoch, Y. Fu, Z. Dao, and K. Coffey. 2000. "Household agrobiodiversity assessment (HH-ABA)", *PLEC News and Views*, No. 16, pp. 28–33. Reprinted in H. Brookfield, C. Padoch, H. Parsons, and M. Stocking (eds). 2002. *Cultivating Biodiversity: Understanding, Analysing and Using Agricultural Diversity*. London: ITDG Publications, pp. 70–77.

Li, H., C. Long, Z. Dao, and others. 1999. "A study on Aroids in Gaoligongshan mountains", *Acta Botanica Yunnanica Supplement*, Vol. XI, pp. 44–54.

Li, J., Z. Dao, and H. Guo. 2001. "Interaction of socio-economy and biodiversity change: A case from Baihualing, Baoshan, west Yunnan", *Acta Botanica Yunnanica Supplement*, Vol. XIII, pp. 171–177.

Li, J., H. Guo, and Z. Dao. 2001. "Dynamism of traditional knowledge and practice on the management of *Quercus* fuel forest at Shabadi, Tengchong county", *Acta Botanica Yunnanica Supplement*, Vol. XIII, pp. 150–156.

Li, Z. and Y. Rui. 2001. "Report on cultivating butterfly in Baka, Xishuangbanna", *Acta Botanica Yunnanica Supplement*, Vol. XIII, pp. 157–163.

Yin, L., H. Guo, and Z. Dao. 2001. "The impacts of different managements on the biodiversity of a community forest", *Acta Botanica Yunnanica Supplement*, Vol. XIII, pp. 140–149.

Zeng, R., Z. Li, and J. Huang. 2000. "Investigation on fuelwood status, Baka, Xishaunbanna", *Acta Botanica Yunnanica Supplement*, Vol. XII, pp. 123–128.

Zeng, Y., H. Guo, S. Yin, and A. Chen. 2001. "Causes and dynamics of the changing of agroforestry practices at Baka (Xishuangbanna)", *Acta Botanica Yunnanica Supplement*, Vol. XIII, pp. 101–112.

Chapter 10

Quin, F. M. Undated. *East Sepik Rural Development Project: Report on Yam Research (Dioscorea spp.) 1981–84*. Wewak: East Sepik Rural Development Project, Agricultural Research Sub-Project.

Chapter 11

Padoch, C. and W. de Jong. 1992. "Diversity, variation, and change in *ribereño* agriculture", in K. Redford and C. Padoch (eds) *Conservation of Neotropical Forests*. New York: Columbia University Press, pp. 158–174.

Paredes, P. 1999. *Como integrar y producir flores en huertas de acuerdo a la experta productora Juana Nuñez*. Boletin técnico 3. Iquitos, Peru: Instituto de Investigaciones de la Amazonia Peruana.

Paredes, P. 2001. "Aprovechamiento de cuerpos de agua en áreas inundables", *Folhia Amazonica*, Vol. 34. Manaus, Brazil: Instituto Nacional de Pesquisas Amazonicas.

Paredes, P., M. Pinedo, R. Romero, and M. Rios. 2001. "Extracción de recursos en un sistema natural de la palmera Aguaje (*Mauritia flexuosa*)", *Acta Amazonica*, Vol. 23. Iquitos, Peru: Instituto de Investigaciones de la Amazonia Peruana.

Pinedo-Vasquez, M. 2001. "PLEC's demonstration and training activities in a dynamic political landscape", *PLEC News and Views*, No. 18, pp. 15–19.

Pinedo-Vasquez, M. and J. Barletti. 2000. *Parámetros historicos que definen los sistemas productivos y de manejo que usan las poblaciones ribereñas de la zona Muyuy, Iquitos*. Revista de Estudios Sociales 8. Lima, Peru: Universidad Catolica.

Pinedo-Vasquez, M., J. Barletti, and M. Del Castillo. 2002. "A tradition of change: The dynamic relationship between biodiversity and society in sector Muyuy, Peru", *Environmental Science and Policy*, Vol. 5, pp. 43–53.

Pinedo-Vasquez, M., J. Layne, M. Pinedo, and J. Barletti. 2001. "Métodos etnobotánicos para predecir el sexo y facilitar el cultivo del aguaje (*Mauritia flexuosa*) en sistemas agroforestales", in M. Hiraoka (ed.) *Pautas Sobre Desarrollo Sustentable en la Amazonia*. Quito, Ecuador: Ayala Ediciones.

Pinedo-Vasquez, M. and C. Padoch. 2002. "Ribereños y la actividad maderera: Técnicas de manejo y biodiversidad", in S. Flores-Paitan and R. Kalliola (eds) *Amazonia: Orientaciones para el desarrollo sostenible*. Lima, Peru: Tarea Asociacion Grafica Educativa, pp. 75–87.

Pinedo-Vasquez, M., D. Zarin, and P. Jipp. 1992. "Community forest and lake reserves in the Peruvian Amazon: A local alternative for sustainable use of tropical forests", in D. Nepstad and S. Schwartzman (eds) *Non-timber Products from Tropical Forests*. Advances in Economic Botany, Vol. 9, pp. 79–86.

Romero, R. and M. Rios. 2000. "Cultivo de tuberosas (papas) en suelos inundables", *Boletin Informativo del Instituto Nacional de Investigaciones Agrarias*, Vol. 14.

Chapter 12

Arriaga-Jordán, C. and L. Velázquez-Beltrán. 1999. "Economics of draught animal ownership in smallholder *campesino* (peasant) hillslope agricultural production systems in the state of Mexico", *Draught Animal News*, Vol. 31, pp. 12–15.

Chávez Mejia, C., G. Nava Bernal, and C. Arriaga Jordán. 1998. "Elements of biodiversity in the homegardens in the highlands of central Mexico", *PLEC News and Views*, No. 11, pp. 18–19.

Chávez Mejía, C., G. Nava Bernal, C. Arriaga Jordán, and L. González Díaz. 1997. *Agrodiversidad en el altiplano central de México: Un proyecto piloto sobre maíz en la agricultura campesina. Informe Académico Final para el Proyecto "Pueblos, Manejo de Tierras y Cambio Ambiental (UNU/PLEC)."* Centro de Investigación en Ciencias Agropecuarias. Coordinación General de Investigación y Estudios de Posgrado. Mexico: Universidad Autónoma del Estado de México.

González, D. J. G., C. M. Arriaga Jordán, and V. E. Sánchez. 1996. "The role of cattle and sheep in *campesino* (peasant) production systems in the highlands of central Mexico", in J. B. Dent, M. J. McGregor, and A. R. Sibbald (eds) *Livestock Farming Systems: Research, Development Socio-Economics and the Land Manager*. Proceedings of the Third International Symposium on Livestock Farming Systems. EAAP Publication No. 79. Wageningen: Wageningen Pers, pp. 103–108.

González-Esquivel, C. E., L. G. Velázquez-Beltrán, C. M. Arriaga Jordán, and E. Sánchez-Vera. 1995. "Comparación de aves (*Gallus gallus*) tipo criollo con aves de líneas comerciales bajo condiciones de traspatio en sistemas de producción campesinos del Altiplano Mexicano", *Ciencia Ergo Sum*, Vol. 2, No. 2, pp. 239–246.

Chapter 14

Brookfield, H., M. Stocking, and M. Brookfield. 1999. "Guidelines on agrodiversity assessment in demonstration site areas", *PLEC News and Views*, No. 13, pp. 17–31.

Khruasan, D. 2000. "Management, conservation and utilization of plants: A village case of Pah Poo Chom, Mae Taeng district, Chiang Mai province", master's thesis, Department of Biology, Faculty of Sciences, Chiang Mai University.

Rerkasem, K. 1996. "Population pressure and agrodiversity in marginal areas of northern Thailand", in J. I. Uitto and A. Ono (eds) *Population, Land Management, and Environmental Change. UNU Global Environmental Forum IV.* Tokyo: United Nations University Press, pp. 55–66.

Rerkasem, K. 1998. "Shifting cultivation in Thailand: Land-use changes in the context of national development", in E. C. Chapman, B. Bouahom, and P. K. Hansen (eds) *Upland Farming Systems in the Lao PDR – Problems and Opportunities for Livestock.* Canberra: Australian Centre for International Agricultural Research, ACIAR Proceedings No. 87, pp. 54–63.

Rerkasem, K. 2001. "Upland land use in Greater Mekong", paper prepared for a workshop on Social Challenges for the Greater Mekong: Cambodia, China, Lao PDR, Myanmar, Thailand, and Vietnam, 28–29 November, Social Research Institute, Chiang Mai University.

Rerkasem, K. 2001. "Vegetation management by forest farmers in montane mainland Southeast Asia", in *CMUPNlab Working Papers 1: Report of TRF/UNU-PLEC Workshop on Regeneration Ecology and Management for Degraded Landscapes and Forest Ecosystems.* Chiang Mai: Chiang Mai University, pp. 53–80.

Rerkasem, K. and B. Rerkasem. 1994. "Shifting cultivation in Thailand: Its current situation and dynamics in the context of highland development", *IIED Forestry and Land Use Series*, No. 4.

Rerkasem, K., C. Thong-ngam, C. Korsamphan, N. Yimyam, and B. Rerkasem. 2002. "Intensification and diversification of land use: Examples from highlands of northern Thailand", in H. Brookfield, C. Paddoch, H. Parsons, and M. Stocking (eds) *Cultivating Biodiversity: Understanding, Analysing and Using Agricultural Diversity.* London: ITDG Publications, pp. 220–232.

Rerkasem, K., N. Yimyam, C. Korsamphan, C. Thong-ngam, and B. Rerkasem. 2002. "Agrodiversity lessons in mountain land management", *Mountain Research and Development*, Vol. 22, No. 1, pp. 4–9.

Rerkasem, K., N. Yimyam, C. Korsamphan, C. Thong-ngam, and S. Thepsarn. 2001. "Agrodiversity management of ethnic minorities on highlands", in *CMUPNlab Working Paper 2: Report of Annual Review.* Chiang Mai: Chiang Mai University, pp. 226–250 (in Thai).

Thepsarn, S. 1998. "Information on Ban Pha Pu Chom village", in *Community Based Natural Resource Management Experiences in Upland and Highland Areas*, proceedings of international workshop. Chiang Mai: Thai-German Highland Development Programme.

Thepsarn, S. 2001. "Results of farmers' field school session in Pah Poo Chom, 8–11 April 2001", report submitted to Hill-Tribe Welfare Division, Department of Public Welfare, Ministry of Labour and Social Welfare, Thailand (in Thai).

Thepsarn, S., D. Khruasan, and C. Trisonthi. 2001. "Ethnobotanical survey of community forests of the Pwo Karen", paper prepared for TRF/UNU-PLEC workshop on Regeneration Ecology and Management for Degraded Landscapes and Forest Ecosystems. Chiang Mai: Chiang Mai University.

Thong-ngam, C. 2001. "Results of farmers' field school session in Pah Poo Chom, 21–24 August 2001", report submitted to Hill-Tribe Welfare Division, Department of Public Welfare, Ministry of Labour and Social Welfare, Thailand (in Thai).

Contributors

Dr Bryant J. Allen, Department of Human Geography, RSPAS, Australian National University, Canberra ACT 0200, Australia.

Dr Carlos Arriaga Jordan is Coordinador General de Investigación, Universidad Autónoma del Estado de México (UAEM), Instituto Literario No. 100, Col. Centro, 5000 Toluca, Mexico. He was the original head of the PLEC-Mexico cluster.

William Asante, Department of Geography and Resource Development, University of Ghana, PO Box 59, Legon, Ghana.

M. Abdoul Karim Barry, Centre d'études et de Recherche en Environnement, Université de Conakry, BP 3817, Conakry, Guinée.

Professor Ibrahima Boiro is Director of the Centre d'études et de Recherche en Environnement, Université de Conakry, BP 3817, Conakry, Guinée.

He was head of the PLEC-Guinée cluster.

Professor Harold Brookfield, formerly principal scientific coordinator of the PLEC project, is in the Department of Anthropology, RSPAS, Australian National University, Canberra, ACT 0200, Australia.

Muriel Brookfield, visitor at the Department of Anthropology, RSPAS, Australian National University, Canberra, ACT 0200, Australia, was formerly editor of *PLEC News and Views*.

Dr Octavio Castelan-Ortega, Centro de Investigación Agropecuarias (CICA) Universidad Autónoma del Estado de México (UAEM), Instituto Literario No. 100, Col. Centro, 5000 Toluca, Mexico, latterly heads of the PLEC-Mexican cluster.

Cristina Chavez Mejia, Centro de Investigación en Ciencias

Agropecuarias (CICA), Universidad Autónoma del Estado de México (UAEM), Toluca, Mexico.

Chen Aiguo, Xishuangbanna Tropical Botanical Garden, Chinese Academy of Sciences, No. 50 Xuefu Road, Kunming, Yunnan 650223, China.

Associate Professor Dao Zhiling is in the Kunming Institute of Botany, Chinese Academy of Sciences, Heilongtan, Kunming, Yunnan 650204, China. He has been head of the PLEC-China cluster since 2001.

Dr Amirou Diallo, Centre d'études et de Recherche en Environnement, Université de Conakry, BP 3817, Conakry, Guinée.

Dr J. Saa Dittoh, Department of Agricultural Economics and Extension, University of Development Studies, PO Box 1350, Tamale, Ghana.

Fu Yongneng, Xishuangbanna Tropical Botanical Garden, Chinese Academy of Sciences, Menglun, Mengla County, Xishuangbanna, Yunnan 666303, China.

Carlos Gonzalez Esquivel, Centro de Investigación en Ciencias Agropecuarias (CICA), Universidad Autonoma del Estado de México (UAEM), Instituto Literario No. 100, Col. Centro, 5000 Toluca, Mexico.

Professor Guo Huijun, Xishuangbanna Tropical Botanic Garden, Chinese Academy of Sciences, Menglun, Mengla County, Xishuangbanna, Yunnan 666303, China. Professor Guo was head of the PLEC-China cluster until 2001.

Professor Edwin A. Gyasi, Department of Geography and Resource Development, PO Box 59, University of Ghana, Legon, Accra, Ghana. Professor Gyasi is head of the PLEC-Ghana cluster, and has been coordinating leader of West Africa PLEC.

Kajuju Kaburu, RRC Embu, PO Box 27, Embu, Kenya.

Edina Kahembe, Field Officer, District Agriculture and Livestock Development Office, Arumeru, Arusha, Tanzania.

Fidelis Kaihura, Senior Agricultural Research Officer, Agricultural Research and Development Institute Ukiriguru, PO Box 1433, Mwanza, Tanzania. Mr Kaihura is head of PLEC-Tanzania.

Edward Kaitaba (the late), formerly of Mlingano Aagricultural Research Station, Tanga, Tanzania.

John N. N. Kang'ara, Kenya Agricultural Research Institute (KARI), RRC Embu, PO Box 27, Embu, Kenya. Mr Kang'ara has been head of PLEC-Kenya since 2000.

Gordana Kranjac-Berisavljevic', Department of Agricultural Mechanization and Irrigation Technology, Faculty of Agriculture, University for Development Studies, PO Box TL 1882, Tamale, Ghana.

Dr David G. McGrath, Geography and Cultural Ecology, NAEA/UFPa, Campus Profissional Guama, Universidade Federal do Para, CEP 66075-900, Belém, Para, Brazil.

Charles Ngilorit, Field Officer, District Agriculture and Livestock Development Office, Arumeru, Arusha, Tanzania.

Ezekiel H. Ngoroi, RRC Embu, PO Box 27, Embu, Kenya.

Dr William Oduro, Institute of Renewable Natural Resources, Kwame Nkrumah University of Science and Technology, Kumasi, Ghana.

Barrak O. Okoba, RRC Embu, PO Box 27, Embu, Kenya.

Pilar Paredes del Aguila, Facultad de Biologia, Universidad Nacional de la Amazonia Peruana, Iquitos, Peru.

Helen Parsons, PLEC Project, Department of Anthropology, RSPAS, Australian National University, Canberra ACT 0200, Australia.

Dr Mario Pinedo-Panduro, Instituto de Investigaciones de la Amazonia Peruana (IIAP), Casilla Postal 471, Iquitos, Peru.

Dr Miguel Pinedo-Vasquez, Center for Environmental Research and Conservation, Columbia University MC 5557, 1200 Amsterdam Avenue, New York NY 10027-6902, USA. Dr Pinedo-Vasquez has been head of PLEC-Peru and convenor of the scientific and technical advisory team, and, since 2002, is scientific coordinator of the PLEC project.

Dr Kanok Rerkasem, Multiple Cropping Centre, Faculty of Agriculture, Chiang Mai University, Chiang Mai 50200, Thailand. Dr Rerkasem is head of PLEC-Thailand.

Charles M. Rimui, RRC Embu, PO Box 27, Embu, Kenya.

Michelle Rios, Instituto de Investigaciones de la Amazonia Peruana, Iquitos, Peru.

Roberto Romero, Facultad de Agronomia, Universidad Nacional de la Amazonia Peruana, Iquitos, Peru.

John Sowei, Social and Environmental Studies Division, National Research Institute, PO Box 5854, Boroko NCD, Papua New Guinea. Mr Sowei is head of PLEC-Papua New Guinea.

Balfour Spence, Environmental Management Unit, Department of Geography and Geology, University of the West Indies, Mona Campus, Mona, Kingston 7, Jamaica.

Professor Dr Elizabeth Thomas-Hope, Department of Geography and Geology, University of the West Indies, Mona, Kingston 7, Jamaica. Professor Thomas-Hope is head of PLEC-Jamaica.

Professor Dr Tereza Ximenes-Ponte, Nucleo de Altos Estudos Amazonicos, Campus Profissional Guama, Universidade Federal do Para, CEP 66075-900 Belém, Para, Brazil. Professor Ximenes-Ponte is head of PLEC-Brazil.

Index

Catalogue Request

Name: _____

Address: _____

Tel: _____

Fax: _____

E-mail: _____

To receive a catalogue of UNU Press publications kindly photocopy this form and send or fax it back to us with your details. You can also e-mail us this information. Please put "Mailing List" in the subject line.

United Nations
University Press

53-70, Jingumae 5-chome
Shibuya-ku, Tokyo 150-8925, Japan
Tel: +81-3-3499-2811 Fax: +81-3-3406-7345
E-mail: sales@hq.unu.edu http://www.unu.edu